BARACK OBAMA

BARACK OBAMA

Political Frontiers and Racial Agency

Ama Mazama, Temple University

Molefi Kete Asante, Temple University

Editors

Los Angeles | London | New Delhi
Singapore | Washington DC

Los Angeles | London | New Delhi
Singapore | Washington DC

FOR INFORMATION:

CQ Press
An Imprint of SAGE Publications, Inc.
2455 Teller Road
Thousand Oaks, California 91320
E-mail: order@sagepub.com

SAGE Publications Ltd.
1 Oliver's Yard
55 City Road
London, EC1Y 1SP
United Kingdom

SAGE Publications India Pvt. Ltd.
B 1/I 1 Mohan Cooperative Industrial Area
Mathura Road, New Delhi 110 044
India

SAGE Publications Asia-Pacific Pte. Ltd.
33 Pekin Street #02-01
Far East Square
Singapore 048763

Acquisitions Editor: Charisse Kiino
Production Editor: Elizabeth Kline
Copy Editor: Sarah Duffy
Typesetter: C&M Digitals (P) Ltd.
Proofreader: Inge Lockwood
Cover Designer: Malcolm McGaughy
Marketing Manager: Christopher O' Brien

Printed in the United States of America

Library of Congress Cataloging-in-Publication Data

Barack Obama: political frontiers and racial agency/
Ama Mazama [and] Molefi Kete Asante, editors.

p. cm.
Includes bibliographical references and index.

ISBN 978-1-4522-1670-6 (alk. paper)

1. Obama, Barack—Influence. 2. United States—Politics and government—2009- 3. Presidents—United States—Election—2008. 4. Political campaigns—United States—Case studies. 5. United States—Race relations—Political aspects—History—21st century. 6. Race relations in mass media. 7. United States—Politics and government—Historiography. I. Mazama, Ama, 1961- II. Asante, Molefi K., 1942-

E908.3.B37 2012
973.932092—dc23   2011037980

This book is printed on acid-free paper.

11 12 13 14 15 10 9 8 7 6 5 4 3 2 1

CONTENTS

PREFACE

There have been few transformative American political events to rival the presidential election of Barack Obama in 2008. Numerous articles have been written attempting to characterize the meaning of Obama's election in light of the racial politics in American society. In fact, the articles on this subject have come not only from the United States but also from Europe, Africa, South America, and Asia. Thus, when we discussed what was missing in the discourse on the Barack Obama phenomenon, we found that there was no accessible interdisciplinary collection of serious studies of the transformative event that gave the nation this president.

The presidency is the epitome of the American political hierarchy. It carries with it the specific executive powers dictated by the Constitution and the iconic power of office that makes the post one of the most effective bully pulpits in the world. The speech, gestures, and official statements of the president of the United States are significant historical and political actions. Implications of the president's words reverberate throughout the American political system. Therefore, no office in the world is as powerful an instrument of political, economic, and cultural policy as that of the president of the United States. The fact that President Obama sits atop the pyramid of power in the United States is a remarkable social feat for the people of the nation. As professors who teach various courses that deal with the meaning of class, race, images, language, and power, we wanted to choose articles for this volume that represented different aspects of Obama's political playing field.

We organized this collection with three purposes in mind: to provide the reader with a collection of articles from more than one discipline, to reveal the wide spectrum of thinking on the meaning of Obama's campaign and election, and to demonstrate that the historiography of the Obama era has already produced a considerable social science corpus. It was important for us to keep in mind the fact that this book would be read by some students who had limited understanding of politics and by others who would be more advanced students seeking to master their own approaches to political, social, or cultural analysis.

Beyond these typical administrative and editorial concerns, however, is the advancement of democracy by encouraging a full analytical discourse around the subject of presidential politics. Who can say that we have not seen a revolution in the political campaign process and the role of the president over the past century? Of course, campaigning for the office has undergone radical changes since the legendary appearance of George Washington in his military uniform. One could quite easily paint a picture of the nation's history by looking at the various campaign styles, pressures, activities, and communication instruments. Abraham Lincoln used large posters and trains, John F. Kennedy used television and airplanes, and Barack Obama used social media. There is no way to predict what future presidential candidates will use in their efforts to reach the masses of this country. What we do know, at this time, is that Obama's campaign and election introduced not only sophisticated social media technology, but also a new form of thinking about the kind of person who could run for this highest office.

Social scientists are fond of making discoveries related to human relationships, and they have had a festival of information from which to explore human emotions, social relations, and psychological attitudes when it comes to the election of a person who has an African ancestor. To what degree does the election of a black man, although with Irish ancestors as well, show that the American nation has turned a corner in its race relations? Is the election of Obama an anomaly in the march of American political history, or is it the beginning of a much fuller democratic electorate? While we would be the first to say these and other questions are clearly without definitive answers, the authors of the articles presented in this book have demonstrated that the Obama phenomenon has attracted reflective and analytical works that assist us in making sense of this particular political transformation.

ACKNOWLEDGMENTS

There are some individuals who are always eager to support the highest intellectual contributions to the academy, and for them we are eternally grateful. We first discussed the idea for this book with Rolf Janke, a vice president for reference at Sage Publications, who encouraged us but knew quickly that this project belonged with CQ Press. Since we had done two encyclopedias with Rolf, he knew that we were serious about completing this project in a timely fashion, and he communicated that to Charisse Kiino, who was extraordinary in her review and recommendations for the project. Consequently, we must acknowledge Charisse for her diligence, commitment to excellence, and ability to see the value of an interdisciplinary work of this magnitude. Of course, we also acknowledge our spouses and our children, without whose love, devotion, and loyalty we would have been unable to complete this project.

Ama Mazama
Molefi Kete Asante
June 2011

ABOUT THE EDITORS

Ama Mazama is an associate professor in the Department of African American studies at Temple University. She graduated with a Ph.D. from La Sorbonne in Paris with the highest distinction. She is the managing associate editor of the *Journal of Black Studies,* considered the premier journal in its field. Dr. Mazama's publications include thirty books and more than seventy articles and chapters in books, and she is currently completing two additional books, *Black and Homeschooled* and *The Dilemma of Black Studies.* She has received the top awards in the field of Africana Studies, including three Cheikh Anta Diop Awards for scholarship (1998, 2000, and 2010) from the Diopian Institute. In addition, in 2007 the National Council of Black Studies awarded Dr. Mazama its highest award for scholarship, the Ana Julia Cooper and C. L. R. James Award.

Molefi Kete Asante is a professor in the Department of African American studies at Temple University. He holds a Ph.D. from the University of California, Los Angeles. He is the founding editor of the *Journal of Black Studies* and the creator of the first doctoral program in Africana Studies in an American university. A principal mentor to graduate students, Dr. Asante has directed more than 140 dissertations and is the author of seventy books. He is currently completing *The African American People: A Global History* and is author of *As I Run Toward Africa.* He holds honorary positions at Zhejiang University and the University of South Africa.

INTRODUCTION:
THE BARACK OBAMA
PHENOMENON: POLITICS, SYMBOL,
AND REALITY

Ama Mazama

In anticipation of the election of Barack Obama, in 2007 I (Ama Mazama) edited the first special issue of the *Journal of Black Studies* on the campaign. It appears to have been the first-ever journal issue dealing with the Obama phenomenon. This intellectual interest in Obama's presidential campaign would be followed by numerous issues on the campaign and the election of the first African American president. Indeed, I wrote at the time, "Given Obama's apparent and rapid success in positioning himself as a viable and credible candidate for the presidency of the United States, the editors of the journal feel that Obama's quest for the White House provides scholars with a unique opportunity and lens to examine or reexamine race, arguably the most significant category in American society" (*Journal of Black Studies*, Vol. 38, No. 1, p. 3). Not only was my prediction correct, but during the campaign and after the election of Obama the salience of race has dug itself more deeply into the American psyche.

While, like others, I argued that the phenomenon of many whites supporting a visibly black man for the presidency created the energy that would generate scores of critical and theoretical studies in political science, sociology, and African American studies, we (Ama Mazama and Molefi Kete Asante) believe that the arguments surrounding Obama's persona during the campaign and the first few years of his presidency have created a unique set of works that must be organized, categorized, and presented as a comprehensive creative response to the phenomenon. The first years of the Obama presidency have been full of legislative, political, commercial, and military actions. Yet these activities and the Obama phenomenon were anticipated by outstanding researchers prior to his election. Not everything could be anticipated, however, and certain actions have occurred during the first years of the Obama administration that have made some of the earlier articles on his life, campaign, and challenges extremely important.

When an American Navy Seal team stormed Osama Bin Laden's compound in Abbottabad, Pakistan, and killed the Al Qaida leader on April 29, 2011, most analysts considered it the most significant action in America's struggle against terror. President Obama received credit for making "a gutsy call" to send the special team into the million-dollar compound. However, just a few weeks earlier he had been battered by demands from wealthy builder Donald Trump to produce his birth certificate. Soon after Obama produced the birth certificate, Trump, the would-be Republican candidate for the presidency, asked the president to reveal his education credentials. This request went nowhere, and a week later Obama launched the raid on Osama Bin Laden's stronghold. The president's ratings shot up among Americans, and he rode a crest of popular goodwill. The fact that Osama Bin Laden, the most-wanted enemy of the United States, was cornered during the third year of his presidency meant that Obama had finally found an iconic image for his first term in office. The BP oil spill in the Gulf of Mexico had loomed large earlier in his administration, but the killing of Osama Bin Laden soon became the legend of Obama's success.

We have examined many articles and journals in an effort to see what the state of the research is on the Obama phenomenon. The result of our work is contained in this volume, which we believe will be exceedingly valuable to political scientists, sociologists, and communicationists.

Therefore, we have culled the material for this book from hundreds of journals articles written about the Obama political phenomenon. The field of political discourse has been enriched by the enormously textured pieces inspired by the Obama era. Our intention was to capture the uniqueness of the Obama candidacy, election, and presidency as a record of social science and critical research, thereby marking the era as a reference on the important transformation brought about by a transitional leader. We are sure that at some future time scholars will announce that the Obama era was a period of great political change in American society, when the political landscape shifted from one age to another. It will be possible to speak of a before- and after-Obama era because certain assumptions, made prior to Obama's election, will not be able to be made after his presidency.

Clearly, with the election of Obama American society attained a position that was the envy of modern heterogeneous societies such as France and Brazil. In some senses one might say that the American election of Obama is confirmation of the domination of the bourgeois class as the confluence of racial, ethnic, sexual, and worker communities grouped together to elect its first real president. Others had aspired to be the standard bearer of the bourgeois class, but with the rise of Senator Obama, that coveted prize was taken away from all others and placed squarely in his hands.

The writers of the essays in this book appear to understand the importance of two aspects of this situation: the historical and the confluence. The historical refers to the chronological structure that finds us arriving at the election of the first African-descended person to the presidency. The confluence refers to the fact that, at a certain moment in the historical record, the political, technological, social, economic, and religious dimensions of Obama's campaign reached a convergence. What was created by Obama's bid for the presidency of the United States was certainly an unusual political climate. Arguably, one might have also been intrigued by the early reticence of some visible leaders in the African American community to endorse Obama. Again, in a society in which politics (and just about everything else) is so highly epidermatized and in which black people have consistently experienced political disenfranchisement, such reluctance seems abnormal. However, this cautious attitude toward Obama was based on a questioning of his "blackness," with some contending that, given his background, he might not be black enough (i.e., not in tune with the African American experience) and therefore might not be capable of speaking on behalf of African Americans or of displaying race loyalty. White voters wondered if Obama would be white enough, because of his white heritage, to speak for the white community. Thus, social science and humanities scholars who wanted to understand the nature of Obama's appeal waded into the treacherous waters of interpretation.

See How Barack Obama Ran: The Campaign for the Presidency

How did the most legislatively active state senator in Illinois rise to the presidency? He was active in sponsoring social welfare legislation, using cosponsorships, and demonstrating from the very beginning of his career that he had the ability to be politically proactive and willing and able to compromise for the sake of effective governance. David J. Andersen and Jane Junn's "Deracializing Obama: White Voters and the 2004 Illinois U.S. Senate Race" provides an important examination of how white voters saw Barack Obama during his first and only U.S. Senate race as he moved up from being a state senator. Using findings from survey data from a probability of white voters conducted during the election, they tested four distinctive framings of Obama by altering the degree and content of his racialization to demonstrate the effect of the degree of blackness on white voters. Thomas Edge's "Southern Strategy 2.0: Conservatives, White Voters, and the Election of Barack Obama" seeks to determine whether race helped shape the way white voters responded to Obama. In fact, Edge suggests that Republicans tried to shape the political discourse by questioning Obama's "Americanness." Seeing some of this talk about Obama's racial identity as overt racism, Edge points out that the real issue for many whites was whether or not Obama was willing to lead the country as a white person would lead it. Yet at the same time, they used his image as a sign that racism was dead. Meanwhile, Phillip S. Howard's "Turning Out the Center: Racial Politics and African Agency in the Obama Era" establishes Obama's ambiguity about race as one of the tactics that were used in the campaign. Indeed, the contradictions noted by Edge were present in the thinking of many black voters who wondered what it would mean that an African American would occupy the White House while the nation had yet to eradicate anti-black racism. Thus, Howard searches for the political and moral limits to African agency within dominant white institutions.

Research has shown that Democrats usually benefit from higher voter turnout, and in the case of the 2008 presidential election Democrats were able to substantially increase the number of liberal voters by registering more African Americans and Latinos. A combination of voter groups— including liberal and moderate whites, liberal blacks, and liberal Latinos— won the election for Obama. Nevertheless, in "An Immigrant's Dream and the Audacity of Hope: The 2004 Convention Addresses of Barack Obama and Arnold Schwarzenegger" Babak Elahi and Grant Cos show that the political convention is the place where politicians make their case for American symbolism. No two politicians did this any better than Arnold Schwarzenegger and Barack Obama in their respective 2004 conventions. The iconic nature of the American narrative that they told suggests that each attempted—and with some success—to tie their own immigrant dreams to the major American myth. Moreover, Obama would later prove that social media would assist him in creating and maintaining the iconic image necessary to fascinate the American public.

The Iconic Obama: Controlling the Identity of a President

Bart Schultz's "Obama's Political Philosophy: Pragmatism, Politics, and the University of Chicago" takes on the image of Barack Obama as a pragmatist from the Chicago School. In fact, he argues that the form of philosophical pragmatism that he sees in Obama comes out of a reform tradition and follows the paths of John Dewey, Jane Addams, Saul Alinsky, Abner Mikva, David Greenstone, Richard Rorty, Danielle Allen, and Cass Sunstein. Schultz believes that Obama appropriated this tradition and used it effectively in defining his own iconic image. On the other hand, in "Barack Obama and the Politics of Blackness," the late Ronald Walters deals precisely with the challenge presented by Obama's white American mother and Kenyan father, his upbringing in Hawaii, and his universal rhetoric to some African Americans. Walters suggests a useful distinction between physical, cultural, and political blackness and argues that it is mainly on the political front that Obama's blackness is perceived as problematic by many African Americans. While black voters saw Obama as African American, they were willing to distinguish between the biological and the political fact of his blackness. Christopher J. Metzler's "Barack Obama's Faustian Bargain and the Fight for America's Racial Soul" uses a critical race theory approach to expose the uses of race and racism in the United States. Indeed, Metzler's argument is that the term *postracial* is meaningless as a critique. He explains that whites do not necessarily want a black president, but rather a president who happens to be black.

Taken together, this section of the book demonstrates how whites and blacks are able to use the political icon for self-representation. Was Obama a black nationalist, an integrationist, a secret white slumming in the black neighborhoods, a radical, or simply a politician trying to be everyperson? Indeed, as these authors contend, the political narrative interrogates the idea of race as a driving force in racialist thinking and racist behavior. As Obama actually did, we are capable of producing self-presentation and construction of identity that works because of the social network.

The Lessons of the Obama Presidential Election

Does Barack Obama's election go a long way toward fulfilling the promise of one nation? This has been one of the most hotly contested topics during the first years of his presidency. Indeed, his success reflects retrospective changes, a shift toward tolerance on the part of whites, and the advent of viral technology. The question the authors in this section ask is, "Will these retrospective changes benefit future African American candidates?" Of course, there will be no way to answer that question until the nation is presented with another viable African American presidential candidate.

Radhika Parameswaran's "Facing Barack Hussein Obama: Race, Globalization, and Transnational America" challenges the reader to question why race has not received enough attention in the discourse on globalization. Therefore, the article examines the implication of Obama's successful presidential candidacy and how it expanded and reduced the meanings of blackness in relation to transnational America. In an exciting turn on the lessons of the election Parameswaran demonstrates the potential of stretching blackness from the American hegemonic base to a broader discussion of race in a global context. In effect, hope is an alternative reading of the American presidency, which some saw as lacking in hope during the previous eight years. Dewey Clayton's "The Audacity of Hope" chronicles the origin of Obama's rise to power and his appeal to whites who saw him as a figure who transcended race. Yet almost 30 percent of white voters claimed that they could not vote for a black presidential candidate. There is no question that latent racial attitudes and racial beliefs underscored the negative attitudes that some whites had about Obama. Of course, while that left 70 percent who would have voted for a black candidate, in actuality he received less than 50 percent of the white vote. Although Obama's campaign and election generated intense enthusiasm that allowed some whites to overcome their latent concerns about race, we must recognize that race still plays a role in our politics. Keeping up the discourse on white voters and Obama, in "Obama and the White Vote" Todd Donovan argues that Obama increased the white share of the presidential vote in those places with a lower percentage of black voters, demonstrating that race remains a factor in elections.

The Limits of Governance in Obama's Administration

Jerry Harris and Carl Davidson's "Obama: The New Contours of Power" claims that the election of Barack Obama demonstrates a shift in the political landscape in the United States. They believe that the election was a victory for progressive coalitions and suggest that we could learn a lot about the future of American politics by ferreting out the causes for the broad-based alliance that put Obama in the White House. Molefi Kete Asante's "Barack Obama and the Dilemma of Power: An Africological Observation" expresses the provocative idea that the election may not have mattered very much. Asante argues that the president would always be confronted with a set of issues created by the structure of the American political economy and international relations that would largely tie the hands of any person who put himself or herself forward to run the country. Among the issues would be the staggering national deficit, the bankrupt educational system, and other problems that would challenge any president. Furthermore, Asante asserts, as other scholars have noted, that the tremendous pressure that white Americans would undoubtedly place on a president insisting on a liberal and progressive agenda would create an irresolvable dilemma of power. Various interest groups, union leaders, civil rights constituencies, teachers, and environmentalists would bathe in the afterglow of the election as one of the most significant progressive political actions in America's history. However, as others have cautioned, the election of the most progressive president in decades did not necessarily mean that the nation accepted the victory without strong opposition. Shawn Michelle Smith's article, "Obama's Whiteness," seeks to contrast the iconic value between Obama and George W. Bush: smart versus stupid, eloquent versus inarticulate, flexible versus rigid, modest versus arrogant, an African

American with a white mother cosmopolitan type versus a white Texas cowboy, subtle and complex versus simplistic and reductive, confident in reason and science versus a faith-based science and foreign policy based on gut feelings. Smith reveals the potential for a collective American image. Charlton D. McIlwain's "Perceptions of Leadership and the Challenge of Obama's Blackness" undertakes a survey and content analysis of newspaper coverage during the first three months of Obama's candidacy in order to reveal how Obama's race was consistently and frequently mentioned in the context of discussions about his leadership capabilities. In "Barack Obama and the Politics of Race: The Myth of Postracism in America," Martell Teasley and David Ikard claim that regardless of the enthusiasm about the campaign, there was an ideological disconnect between the desire and reality in American society. In fact, the authors argue that the symbolic capital of hope can be exposed with its pitfalls of postracial thinking simply because Obama's campaign did not mean that Americans had conquered racism. Willie J. Harrell Jr.'s "The Reality of American Life Has Strayed From Its Myths: Barack Obama's *The Audacity of Hope* and the Discourse of the American Reclamation Jeremiad" seeks to convey Obama's America as a new vision of what is possible if people work toward a common goal. The fact that political discourse was used to restore America's democratic mission and potential is considered one of Obama's greatest achievements.

Part I

SEE HOW BARACK OBAMA RAN: THE CAMPAIGN FOR THE PRESIDENCY

Since George Washington peers were first convinced to elect him president, the feat of running for the presidency has become one of the most entrenched of American institutions. Yet it was clear even prior to the election season of 2008 that Barack Obama, U.S. senator from Illinois, was laying the groundwork for a different type of campaign. In effect, the "We are the United States of America" speech at the 2004 Democratic National Convention put Obama on a direct course toward the Democratic nomination four years later. The fact that it would be a unique campaign was dictated by the candidate's personal history as well as the circumstances of his candidacy. Planting the philosophical and social seeds that he would harvest during the 2008 campaign, the young senator spoke passionately about his vision of a united America.

There were two especially significant elements to the 2008 presidential campaign narrative. First, Obama would become the first African American candidate to run for the highest office in the nation as the head of a major party's ticket. Second, the context of his campaign would be impacted by new social media technology to an extent not seen before in a national election. Given these two dimensions of the campaign narrative, it appeared at the outset, to many scholars, that Obama was on the road to a historic rendezvous with destiny.

Keeping close to the personal narrative and the innovations in communication, scholars in this section show considerable interest in examining the complexities of Obama's campaign. As a state senator Obama set himself on an ambitious route to the U.S. Senate and then to the presidency. Given his personal narrative as the son of a Kenyan man and a white American woman, Obama's trajectory might well have been improbable at any other time in American history. This realization did not escape the candidate, and he used it to further weave himself into the fabric of the American imagination. In effect, he was the improbable candidate, but this improbability could not have happened anywhere except the United States. "Would white Americans vote for Obama without deracializing" him became one of the questions that intrigued researchers. Furthermore, what would a deracialized Obama look like for the politics of African agency?

The scholars in Part One engage the issues of the personal narrative of race, voter mobilization, and social media in Obama's march toward the presidency. Readers may discover in the 2008 campaign some strategies that will likely become prevalent during future presidential campaigns. Clearly, social media, the Internet in general, and mobile devices are here to stay and will probably impact the nature of political organizing, marketing, and communicating in the foreseeable future.

1

DERACIALIZING OBAMA: WHITE VOTERS AND THE 2004 ILLINOIS U.S. SENATE RACE

David J. Andersen

Rutgers, The State University of New Jersey, New Brunswick

Jane Junn

University of Southern California, Los Angeles

The election of Barack Obama as the 44th President of the United States put to rest the notion that American voters—still comprised primarily of Whites—would not vote for a Black man. However, before election night on November 2008 there was little consensus on the dynamics of electoral choice among White voters faced with a major party candidate who was not also White. Improbable as Obama's journey to the White House may have seemed before the 2008 Democratic Party primaries, it was his victory in the 2004 U.S. Senate Illinois race that was perhaps more surprising and unique. Obama's easy win over Alan Keyes, the Republican introduced to Illinois voters only months before the general election, highlighted a novel election scenario, ultimately featuring two Black candidates competing for a Senate seat in a primarily White state, a first in the United States. The unique circumstances of that contest provide a window to examine how White voters react when presented with a Black candidate (in this case two), an occurrence that, though still rare, is becoming less unusual. As Black candidates compete increasingly in White dominated constituencies, the roles that racial perceptions exert on the White electorate become critical factors to electoral success. If Obama's success presages the entrance of more Black candidacies in heterogeneous electorates, more must be understood about how White voters evaluate those candidates based on their race.

Source: American Politics Research, May 2010; vol. 38, 3: pp. 443-470, first published on October 3, 2009.

Racial Attitudes and Elections

Beginning in the late 1970s, Black candidates have increasingly run for political office at all levels of government. Starting on the local level, particularly with mayors, but expanding to U.S. House districts, Black candidates have become more common, particularly in minority–majority districts (Hajnal, 2006). Similarly, minority candidates have entered in larger numbers into state- and national-level campaigns, raising the frequency of Black candidates campaigning in majority White electorates. Minority candidates, who 30 years ago were confined mainly to districts in which they represented the majority of the population, now compete to win in racially heterogeneous electorates.

Even as the frequency of candidacy rises, the dynamics of the relationship between the race of the candidate and electoral success, however, is less well understood. With few cases to examine, and little data drawn from those contests, it is difficult to pinpoint if the race of the candidate plays a significant role in the campaign, yet there are reasons to suppose that it might. In a scenario where a Black candidate campaigns in a White dominated district, White voters, some who may have never been presented with a minority candidate, must simultaneously reconcile covert racial beliefs with perceptions of that non-White candidate. There are reasons to believe that this may influence candidate evaluations.

Race clearly remains a potent factor in political campaigns in other ways. Political issues, such as welfare (Peffley, Hurwitz, & Sniderman, 1997) and crime (Gilens, 1996; Mendelberg, 1997; Valentino, 1999), remain racially coded. Other issues, such as government spending, have also been linked to race in campaigns as an even more subtle invocation of the role of race (Valentino, Hutchings, & White, 2002). Candidates, unwittingly or not, are able to stoke the fires of racial attitudes by invoking concerns about these issues. Voters who are spurred to consider such issues, especially in the context of Blacks in America, are often pushed to favor particular political ideals and candidates. The infamous Willie Horton ads of the 1984 election are perhaps the most well discussed example of the role that racial politics still exerts (Mendelberg, 1997). More recent examples include attempts to appeal to Whites whose votes remain influenced by racial attitudes. Those beliefs can also be primed by attacking Black candidates themselves, as seen in the 2004 Tennessee Senate Race between Harold Ford and Bob Corker, where an ad against Ford depicted a White woman imploring Ford to "Call Me."

Also, previous research using quasi-experimental methods and survey data has directly explored the influence of perceived candidate race on White voters, finding that it does exert an influence. There are three traditional approaches: (a) present a single candidate to evaluate, and vary that candidate by race (Colleau et al., 1990; Reeves, 1997; Terkildsen, 1993); (b) present two candidates, one White male and one non-White male, varying the non-White male (McDermott, 1998; C. K. Sigelman, Sigelman, Walkosz, & Nitz, 1995; L. Sigelman & Sigelman, 1982;); and (c) gather survey data from an actual election involving a Black candidate (Citrin, Green, & Sears, 1990). Each method has unique strengths and weaknesses, adding to our knowledge in this area, but also demonstrating the difficulties in studying the dynamics of the race of the candidate race and electoral behavior.

Presenting a single candidate for respondents to evaluate allows for control over all aspects of evaluation and permits easy analysis of how respondents' evaluations of candidates can vary simply due to the race of the candidate. In a strictly controlled environment, respondents are presented with information regarding a political candidate, including their issue stances, party loyalty, previous experience, and biographical information, all that one would expect a voter to use in evaluating a candidate. The only variation in what respondents receive is the candidate's picture. Some respondents receive a picture of a White candidate, whereas others receive a picture of a Black candidate. Any differences reported between group evaluations of the candidates must be a result of the photos provided, as they represent the only variance in stimuli. Although the tight controls on this design provide clear causal attribution to the manipulated variable, the difficulty with this tight experimental design is the demonstrated phenomenon of self-monitoring by respondents when faced with questions about Black candidates (Colleau et al., 1990; Terkildsen, 1993).

The pressure to present socially acceptable answers often leads respondents to overcompensate in their answers to mask potentially biased answers. Whites are aware that they may hold socially unacceptable racial biases and, when asked questions relating to Blacks, tend to increase their ratings in order to compensate for any biases that they think they may hold. Colleau et al. even discovered in their 1990 article that African American candidates were rated higher than White candidates, holding all else equal, a finding that stood apart from what they anticipated. While one could hope this would be a sign of changing race evaluations in society, it is also possibly, and perhaps more plausibly, the result of self-monitoring by subjects. As Mendelberg (2001) argues, self-monitoring occurs when respondents become aware of race as a salient factor and overcompensate their evaluations to prevent the appearance of a racial bias. This often results in higher ratings than would otherwise occur, even under race-neutral situations (Mendelberg, 2001).

Terkildsen (1993) also discovered evidence of self-monitoring among Whites when presented with Black candidates in a similar experiment, additionally finding that self-monitoring is more pronounced when respondents view candidates with darker skin compared with those with light skin. However, Terkildsen presents contradictory evidence to Colleau et al. (1990) finding that Whites evaluate White candidates more favorably, though reporting only marginally higher likelihood of voting for them. This introduces an additional difficulty with single-candidate designs. Evaluations made of candidates, displayed alone without an election opponent, are evaluated essentially in a vacuum. Real-world vote choices and real candidate evaluations are not made in a vacuum, but always in comparison with another candidate, weakening the generalizability of these results. Respondents evaluating a single candidate are always able to inflate their evaluations in the absence of another option.

One way to counter this difficulty is to provide an alternative choice for respondents to "vote" for or evaluate in surveys, typically a traditional White male. By gathering data about two candidates, and registering how evaluations and vote support for the varied candidate change based on their assigned race, it is easier to capture some of the disparities between reporting positive evaluations for a minority candidate in theory and ultimately supporting them when given an alternative. Having two candidates to explore provides an avenue to test whether reported sentiment actually translates into true vote support as well.

L. Sigelman and Sigelman (1982), when evaluating sexism, racism, and ageism in voting behavior, discovered that ageism had a more pronounced affect on decreasing voter support for a nontraditional candidate, but ultimately showed that when given the choice between a White male and not–White male candidate, respondents tend to defer to the White male candidate (C. K. Sigelman et al., 1995; L. Sigelman & Sigelman, 1982). Respondents across all demographic characteristics registered stronger support for candidates who were similar to themselves across race, gender, and age, but still displayed the tendency to defer to White male candidates when asked to vote (L. Sigelman & Sigelman, 1982). Presented with either a middle-aged White male, White female, Black male, Black female, or older male candidate, the two Black candidates in these studies fare the worst of all the possible options, other than the older White male candidate, in registering vote support against a middle-aged White male candidate. With all else held equal, it still appears as though race plays a role in evaluations of candidates.

In a follow-up design, C. K. Sigelman et al. (1995) discover that Black candidates are generally perceived as being more compassionate toward disadvantaged groups, but also as less competent than their White counterparts. This is not matched by voters reporting that they would switch their vote away from Black candidates though, an interesting finding that is explained as a balancing of the positive aspect of compassion toward disadvantaged groups with the negatives of lower competence scores. As an experiment, it is still questionable whether some of the responses indicating a willingness to vote for a nontraditional candidate, even as they receive lower competency evaluations, would actually transition to votes in the poll. The tendency to report favorably for Black candidates may continue when respondents realize that their votes are for an experiment, and not for true political office. This is a standard difficulty with experimental designs, generalizing laboratory results onto real-world politics.

Candidates who occur only on paper in an experimental setting simply do not have the depth of actual candidates. Real-world candidates are not static images, but live, moving figures that emerge throughout a campaign. They are portrayed in various ways by their own campaign, their rivals, as well as the media. Voters do not simply review facts and create summary judgments but develop an impression of candidates as the campaigns run, updating their opinions as they learn new information (Lodge, McGraw, & Stroh, 1989). Experimental designs presenting fictional and static candidates for quick review cannot match onto the conditions of a real election environment.

A third option for examining the role of race in elections has been to use actual elections that involve a Black candidate. This is typically done by gathering exit poll data or looking at public opinion surveys conducted during the campaign (Citrin et al., 1990). The benefit of this method is that it permits an analysis of actual conditions, comparing how respondents evaluate real candidates, and then ultimately how that translates into vote support in the election. This positive correspondence to the real world is tempered by the lack of control over the election, and a loss of causal attribution that can be made regarding the significance of race.

Citrin et al. (1990) analyze the 1982 gubernatorial race in California, involving Tom Bradley, an African American Democrat, and George Deukmejian, a White Republican, using other campaigns involving two White candidates as controls, by using two polls assessing voters' political opinions and their vote decisions.[1] They find that, even when controlling for other factors such as partisanship, ideology, and demographic variables, racial attitudes are significant predictors of the vote choice. Although the intuitive answer is that this is a result solely of Bradley's race, the lack of experimental controls reduces the conclusiveness of these findings.

Candidate race clearly seems to play a role in voter evaluations, as suggested by these methods, but it is difficult to pinpoint how this happens. Each of the three designs discussed above points toward the presence of an influence but is necessarily limited by the confines of a research method. Another option for research would be to conduct a hybrid of the above designs, taking the strengths of each and incorporating an experimental research design within a suitable real-world election. An even better scenario would be one in which voters are presented with a Black candidate without opposing a White male candidate. This critical control is necessary due to the findings of

L. Sigelman and Sigelman (1982) that respondents, while altering their evaluations of candidates to reflect personal similarities, still defer to White male candidates when asked to vote. An ideal election would pose a real-world scenario where voters are asked to choose between two Black candidates, forcing them to evaluate candidates and make vote decisions without having the ability to defer to the typical White male option. The major obstacle to such a design has been finding an appropriate race to study. Fortunately, in 2004 a nearly ideal situation occurred in the unique Illinois U.S. Senate election.

An Unusual Race: The 2004 U.S. Senate Election in Illinois

Incumbent Republican Senator Peter Fitzgerald decided in 2003 not to run for reelection and the lead candidate to replace him in the office, Democrat Carol Moseley Braun, also declined to run, leading to 15 candidates entering into the Democratic and Republican primaries. Barack Obama entered the final month of the 2004 race for the Democratic Party nomination trailing in the polls. Obama's main opponent for the nomination was Blair Hull, a wealthy Chicago businessman. Hull enjoyed support from prominent African American elected officials as well as the Chicago Democratic Party organization, and had a strong lead over Obama in the polls. Shortly before the primary election, a scandal involving allegations that Hull had abused his ex-wife surfaced in the press and forced Hull to withdraw from the race. Obama defeated his remaining opponent for the nomination, Dan Hynes, the son of an influential Chicago politician, with just more than 50% of the vote. Obama entered the race for the U.S. Senate seat in the general election against Jack Ryan, a retired millionaire investment banker turned schoolteacher and the nominee of the Republican Party. In a set of events oddly parallel to the Hull scandal, Ryan withdrew his candidacy following allegations of sexual impropriety involving his ex-wife, actress Jeri Ryan. In disarray, the Illinois Republican Party chose Alan Keyes, a conservative African American commentator and a perennial candidate for political office (though typically from his home state of Maryland), to run against Obama in the general election. Although Keyes had never lived in Illinois, he established a residence in the state several weeks prior to the announcement of his candidacy as the Republican Party nominee. The presence of two Black candidates as nominees from the two major parties for a U.S. Senate seat was a first, presenting a unique opportunity to conduct an experiment within the context of an actual election. The presence of Barack Obama, a little known State Senator, added to the strength of this scenario, as voters had much to learn about the candidate, aiding the effectiveness of experimental manipulations as voters update their relatively small store of information (Lodge, Stroh, & Wahlke, 1989).

Racializing and Deracializing Obama: Data and Methods

During October and November of 2004, a random probability sample of 567 people in Illinois provided responses to the survey we describe below.[2] Data were collected from 420 Whites and 108 Blacks, the latter of whom were oversampled in an effort to increase the number of observations among African Americans.[3] The oversample of African Americans facilitates analysis between racial categories, completed in other work,[4] though we concentrate our analysis here on the perceptions and attitudes among White voters only, disaggregating them by partisan affiliation and analyzing separately the views of Democrats and Republicans. Before proceeding with the analysis, we describe the experimental manipulations embedded in the survey, our dependent variables, our restrictions on the samples analyzed and our hypotheses about how these stimuli systematically influence Illinois voters. Our experimental design assesses the role that race plays on respondent trait evaluations of a United States Senate candidate, requiring a few explanations.[5]

Our use of race takes advantage of recent advances in studies of race in America that view race as a continuum, rather than a dichotomous variable. Black candidates for office portray themselves, and are portrayed by their opponents, in varying degrees of "Blackness." In minority–majority districts, African American candidates may be able to successful use ties to the community to mobilize Black voters, but this strategy may be less successful when used in majority-White electoral districts where Black candidates may feel pressed to deracialize or "Whiten" their image. This is an important step forward, akin to Terkildsen's use of light-skinned and dark-skinned Black candidates in her study, reflecting that race is not simply an "on or off" cue, but occurs in varying degrees based on the presentation of the candidate.

Coinciding with this is the growing literature on racial attitudes and implicit versus explicit racial priming (Huber & Lapinski, 2008; Mendelberg, 2008; White, 2007). According to Mendelberg's (2001) influential book, implicit messages are more powerful because they convey racial stereotypes without signaling to respondents the need to self-monitor in order to appear consistent with the widely accepted norm of equality. Explicit racial priming, on the other hand, is too blatant in its presentation of stereotypes (particularly those most capable of discerning a racial cue), and causes subjects to recognize the negative stereotype. This recognition dampens the expression of negative racial attitudes and renders explicit racial primes less effective in moving racial attitudes.

Much of the controversy in this area has revolved around the extent to which implicit primes are more effective at evoking negative racial attitudes among Whites. Competing studies marshal evidence, the bulk of it generated from experimental studies, to support or refute the theory of implicit racial priming as a model of political communication. Despite the disagreement among scholars in this field, there is a growing consensus that the treatment of racial primes in dichotomous terms—as either fully implicit, where stereotypes work by subconscious cues, or entirely explicit, where the negative stereotypes are blatant—should be refined instead to exist on a continuum (Mendelberg, 2008, p. 118).

There were two experimental manipulations embedded in the Illinois study. Both were delivered to random halves of the survey population (see Table 1).[6] In the first manipulation, half the sample received the following text (see Figure 1):

Table 1   Descriptive Statistics for White Likely Voters by Manipulation

Variable	Most Whitened Treatment	Slightly Whitened Treatment	Slightly Blackened Treatment	Most Blackened Treatment	Significance
Party ID	3.84 (2.24)	3.91 (2.19)	4.16 (2.19)	4.19 (2.13)	.706
Strength of party ID	2.04 (0.91)	1.89 (1.08)	1.96 (0.96)	1.86 (1.04)	.678
Female	0.43 (0.50)	0.54 (0.50)	0.47 (0.50)	0.39 (0.49)	.298
Income	11.18 (3.91)	10.92 (3.88)	11.38 (3.02)	11.19 (3.57)	.905
Church attendance	2.95 (1.78)	3.41 (1.81)	3.59 (1.59)	3.63 (1.76)	.066
Interest	2.16 (0.96)	2.08 (0.79)	2.10 (0.96)	2.05 (0.85)	.893
Age	4.10 (1.64)	3.92 (1.79)	4.31 (1.82)	4.01 (1.66)	.564
Education	2.65 (1.09)	2.97 (0.99)	2.64 (1.07)	2.70 (0.89)	.183
Racial resentment	2.70 (0.73)	2.80 (0.64)	2.77 (0.74)	2.62 (0.63)	.416
n	82	72	70	84	

Note: The table reports means with standard deviations in parenthesis and one-way analysis of variance significance.

Figure 1   Obama Portrayed as a Black Candidate

Barack Obama is running for the U.S. Senate. He was a community organizer on Chicago's south side and was the first Black president of the Harvard Law Review. If elected, he would be only the 5th Black Senator in U.S. history.

A headshot photograph of the candidate accompanied the text. This stimulus was designed to highlight the racial identity of Barack Obama as Black in a number of ways. He is described as an organizer on the south side of Chicago—a location known to residents of Illinois as a predominantly African American area of the city. In addition, Obama's position as a Black man both at Harvard and potentially in the U.S. Senate is highlighted. There is no emphasis on his political experience, and his educational background at Harvard Law School is mentioned.

In contrast, the second half of the sample received a different stimulus that attempted to deracialize Obama, emphasizing his qualifications instead. Respondents who received this prime were shown a photograph of the Illinois State House with the accompanying text: "Barack Obama is running for the U.S. Senate. He is currently an Illinois State Senator. He is a graduate of Harvard Law School, and on the faculty of the University of Chicago Law School" (see Figure 2). This description and picture of the Illinois capitol building was intended to deemphasize Obama's race and highlight his educational, professional, and political background. Instead of focusing on how Obama could empathize with Whites, this context discusses Obama in race-neutral terms.

Figure 2   Race Neutral Portrayal of Obama

A second manipulation occurred a short time later in the survey and was again administered to random halves of the respondent population. In this second manipulation, half of the sample received a photograph of Obama and African Americans. The photograph was accompanied by the following text: "Barack Obama is an Illinois State Senator and a former community organizer. He and his wife Michelle, a native of Chicago's south side, have two children" (see Figure 3). Again, Obama's connection to Chicago's south side and his experience as a community organizer are highlighted here. This stimulus was constructed to convey Obama's relationship to other African Americans, thereby emphasizing his identity as a Black man.

Alternatively, the second half of the sample viewed the following text:

> Barack Obama gave the keynote address to the 2004 Democratic National Convention where he presented a positive theme of national unity by citing the diversity of his own heritage. He said we have shared values, values that aren't Black or White or Hispanic—values that are American and Democratic.

This text was accompanied by a photograph of Obama with White people (see Figure 4). This stimulus was designed to prime the idea that Obama transcends traditional racial categories, thereby deemphasizing his Blackness. In so doing, we hypothesized that White voters would feel a stronger connection to Obama. In contrast to the frame using the Illinois state house that did not

Figure 3   Obama Portrayed With Blacks

Figure 4   Obama Portrayed With Whites

implicate race, this stimulus explicitly invokes Obama's multiracial status and highlights his call for racial unity.

Taken together, respondents in the Illinois survey could have received one of four combinations of the two manipulations. These combinations are detailed in Table 2. The quarter of the sample that received the most deracialized treatment are those who received a combination of Figure 2, the photograph of the Illinois State House, and the language of transcending race accompanied by a picture of Obama with Whites in Figure 4. In contrast is the quarter of the sample viewing the most racialized treatments. This set of stimuli explicitly frames Obama as a Black man with ties to the African American community, combining Figure 1, the photograph of Obama's face, and the picture of Obama with African Americans (Figure 3). This set of stimuli emphasizes the connection Obama has to Blacks by invoking his role as a community activist on Chicago's south side.

In between these more clearly deracialized (Whitened) and racialized (Blackened) frames are two more mixed treatments. The first, which we identify as "mixed deracialized," pairs Figure 1 with Figure 4, and leans toward deracializing Obama because of the strong message about transcending race, and by picturing White people in the photograph. The other mixed treatment we term "mixed racialized" combining Figure 2 and Figure 3. We reasoned that the effect of combination of the photograph of the Illinois State House and the picture of Obama with African Americans

Table 2   Combinations of Experimental Manipulations

	Manipulation 1: Obama as Black (Figure 1: Headshot)	Manipulation 1: Obama Deracialized (Figure 2: Illinois State House)
Manipulation 2: Obama as Black (Figure 3: With African Americans)	1. Most Blackened: Black and seen with Blacks	2. Slightly Blackened: Deracialized but seen with Blacks
Manipulation 2: Obama beyond race (Figure 4: With Whites)	3. Slightly Whitened: Black but seen with Whites	4. Most Whitened: Deracialized and seen with Whites

would have a stronger influence than the other mixed treatment set because Figure 3 implicates race and political activism while picturing Obama with African Americans.

The treatments were designed to reflect realistic and potential campaign portrayals of Obama during the election and the combination of the two embedded manipulations represents gradations of racializing Obama to run along a continuum of more racialized to deracialized. A manipulation check on the random distribution of subjects into these conditions reveals only a single significant difference between the groupings, with the subjects in the "slightly Blackened" treatment reporting lower church attendance than subjects in the other groups. In all other ways measured, the groups appear similar (Table 1).[7]

We focus our analysis on how White voters evaluated qualities of Barack Obama. It is unlikely that these visual treatments would have the power to move survey respondents into changing their vote choice because they were in the middle of a real election, and because the information provided in the slides was consistent with existing campaign messages. However, like most campaign ads, our expectation is that the treatments would systematically alter how respondents evaluated the candidate as they updated their summary judgments of that candidate's traits (Lodge, McGraw, & Stroh, 1989; Lodge, Steenbergen, & Brau, 1995).

Voters typically evaluate candidates along four trait dimensions, as pioneered by Kinder and refined by Funk: their abilities, their leadership qualities, their empathy, and their integrity (Funk, 1999; Kinder, 1983). We rely on the ability and empathy traits because they are well supported as sources of candidate evaluations in contests such as the Keyes–Obama race. Research on Senate races has indicated that, unlike Presidential races, the major traits voters look for in Senators are their competence, integrity, and empathy, but not including their leadership (Miller, 1990, see also Abramowitz, 1980; Weisberg & Rusk, 1970). Thus, we retain the ability measures and include empathy measures, while ignoring leadership trait scores for these Senate candidates.[8]

In the survey, and after the second experimental manipulation, respondents were asked, "Thinking of Barack Obama, how much do you agree or disagree with the following statements?" They were given a scale from 1 to 7 with these response categories: 1 = *strongly disagree*, 2 = *disagree*, 3 = *slightly disagree*, 4 = *neutral*, 5 = *slightly agree*, 6 = *agree*, and 7 = *strongly agree*. Respondents were asked to select a response for five qualities: "He would make a good U.S. Senator," "He has qualities that I look for in an elected official," "He seems qualified for office," "He would probably understand my concerns," and "He reminds me of people I know." We combined the first three items into one overall scale, taking the average responses for the statements and identifying the characteristic as ability. We combined the last two items to create a second scale to correspond to candidate empathy.[9]

Before running our analysis, we made three crucial restrictions on our sample. First, we restrict the analysis to Whites only. The core of our question pertains to how Whites will react to Black candidates, necessitating a Whites-only sample. Second, we limit our analysis to likely voters. Although the behavior of unlikely voters is interesting, our primary interest is to identify what impact our racialized portrayals have on people who will cast a vote for a candidate in the Senate race, and not just hold a general opinion of the candidate. The latter question, although also valuable, remains pertinent throughout an elected official's tenure in office, once elected, while the unique situation offered in an election is how those who are likely to vote are affected by candidate portrayal. Thus, we reserve studying nonvoters for a later time while focusing on the group uniquely relevant to the presence of an election.

We defined likely voters as those who reported voting in the previous presidential election and report that they intended to vote in 2004. Finally, we disaggregate the sample of White likely voters by partisanship, analyzing self-declared Democrats and Republicans and the relationship between experimental treatments and evaluations of Obama (Table 3).[10]

Our rationale for disaggregating by party identification is based in the partisan nature of the treatments used in the experiment. The information about Barack Obama clearly indicated that he was the Democratic candidate, as respondents were likely aware from previous campaign material they had encountered. The single largest predictor of the vote choice and candidate evaluations remains partisanship, as clearly indicated by the partisan differences in the overall candidate evaluations and likelihood of voting for Obama. Considering this, we do not expect that the impact of our racialized stimuli on candidate evaluations is in a straight linear fashion, but rather, we suspect that it is moderated by party identification. We hypothesize that Republicans will

Table 3   Descriptive Statistics for White Likely Voters by Party Identification

Variable	White Democrats	White Republicans	Significance	White Partisans Combined
Party ID	1.85 (0.77)	6.20 (0.78)	.000	4.02 (2.31)
Strong ID	2.15 (0.77)	2.20 (0.78)	.647	2.18 (0.77)
Female	0.45 (0.50)	0.45 (0.50)	.986	0.45 (0.50)
Income	10.95 (3.85)	11.56 (3.47)	.183	11.25 (3.67)
Church attendance	2.87 (1.65)	3.91 (1.72)	.000	3.39 (1.76)
Interest	2.09 (0.93)	2.05 (0.86)	.725	2.07 (0.90)
Age	3.97 (1.68)	4.13 (1.76)	.469	4.05 (1.72)
Education	2.66 (1.05)	2.82 (1.01)	.198	2.74 (1.03)
Racial resentment	2.57 (0.70)	2.81 (0.68)	.007	2.69 (0.70)
Obama's ability	5.67 (1.65)	4.38 (1.58)	.000	5.03 (1.74)
Obama's empathy	5.08 (1.63)	3.86 (1.39)	.000	4.47 (1.63)
n	130	129		259

Note: The table reports means with standard deviations in parentheses and one-way analysis of variance significance.

react differently to campaign ads about a Democratic candidate than respondents who call themselves Democrats. An alternative way to observe any differences is the inclusion of interaction terms into an inferential model, but we chose here to split the sample by partisan identification and report separate results (for similar use of separated samples, see Lupia, Levine, Menning, & Sin, 2007, as well as the response to that, Bartels, 2007).

Results

Our first analysis uses one-way analysis of variance (ANOVA) to examine how respondents evaluated Obama's perceived ability as a senator and his empathy toward themselves and people like them depending on which set of manipulations they viewed.

Among Republicans, we find no significant differences between the results in respondents' evaluations of Obama's ability or his empathy in response to the stimuli they received. For both traits, the ratings peak at their poles, with Republicans rating Obama highest when he is portrayed at his "Whitest" and his "Blackest," with the mixed scenarios receiving slightly lower scores. These results are not statistically distinguishable from each other however, providing no strong indications that White Republican respondents responded to or were affected by the primes. Interestingly, the highest ratings, for both traits, come from the most racialized scenario, where Obama is portrayed as a Black candidate representing Blacks, a surprising result, especially for the empathy trait. The lack of statistical differences between the representation of Obama in the least racialized terms and the most strongly racialized portrayal could indicate that White Republicans view any Democratic candidate as similarly unlikely to represent their interests. Alternatively, for White Republicans, race may not be as relevant a factor in assessing candidate empathy compared with White Democrats. Some support for the former is found in the finding that, even at their highest ratings, Republicans never equal the height of even the lowest Democratic ratings of Obama on either trait. Assessing the latter assumption will require additional controls and follows later.

White Democratic respondents do show a clear and significant trend in responding to the manipulations, decreasing their evaluations of Obama's ability as a senator and his empathy toward them and people like them as the portrayal was "Blacker." Democrats viewing the most Whitened portrayal of Obama scored him highest, averaging 6.15 in ability (out of 7) and 5.53 in empathy (also out of 7). As Obama was portrayed more strongly racialized, White Democrats ratings dropped by similar amounts for both traits. For his ability, Obama's average score fell to 5.96 in the slightly Whitened portrayal, then 5.48 in the slightly Blackened, and bottoming at 4.90 in the most Blackened, a total decrease of 1.25 between the extremes in racialization (Table 4). On a 7-point scale, that translates to an 18% drop in his average evaluation between the extreme frames.

The empathy scores reflect similar results. Obama starts at a peak of 5.53 in the most Whitened portrayal, decreasing to 5.34 in the slightly Whitened and then dropping further to 4.93 in the slightly Blackened portrayal (Table 5). His evaluations again reach their lowest score, 4.32, in the most racialized portrayal, sliding 1.21 points from the most deracialized frame. This marks a 17% reduction in his average empathy trait evaluation, attributable simply to the racial portrayal provided.

According to these results, racialized portrayals of Obama do have a demonstrable impact, but only on White voters who identify as Democrats.

Table 4 Analysis of Variance of Obama's Ability by Treatment

Treatment Condition	White Democrats		White Republicans	
	n	Mean (SD)	n	Mean (SD)
Most Whitened	41	6.15 (0.98)	36	4.63 (1.54)
Slightly Whitened	30	5.96 (0.95)	31	4.07 (1.75)
Slightly Blackened	31	5.48 (1.86)	33	4.10 (1.68)
Most Blackened	28	4.90 (2.36)	29	4.69 (1.24)
Total	130	5.65 (1.67)	129	4.38 (1.58)
F-statistic	3.896		1.435	
Significance	.011		.236	

Table 5   Analysis of Variance of Obama's Empathy by Treatment

	White Democrats		White Republicans	
Treatment Condition	n	Mean (SD)	n	Mean (SD)
Most Whitened	41	5.53 (1.18)	36	3.78 (1.23)
Slightly Whitened	30	5.34 (1.14)	31	3.53 (1.58)
Slightly Blackened	31	4.93 (1.82)	33	3.92 (1.34)
Most Blackened	28	4.32 (2.14)	29	4.24 (1.36)
Total	130	5.08 (1.63)	129	3.86 (1.39)
F-statistic	3.575		1.389	
Significance	.016		.249	

There is a clear linear decrease on Democratic evaluations of Obama as the portrayals we present depict him more as a Black candidate representing African American constituents. This is a rather surprising finding, indicating that the "Party of Civil Rights" may not be as tolerant and race-neutral as is portrayed in campaign and party advertisements. Even in the context of a real-world election campaign where respondents have likely already formed impressions of the candidate, our experimental manipulation of the portrayals of Barack Obama as a candidate shifted his evaluations by nearly 20%, a sizeable amount by nearly any standard.

The lack of significant findings for White Republican voters is also remarkable, as they seem to be free of the influence of race that moves evaluations among White Democratic voters. This could be because Republicans have less of a response to race than Democrats, or because their evaluations were so much lower to begin with that there was little room for further decrease. However, Obama's ability ratings never dropped below neutral and his empathy ratings remained only slightly negative with that group, leaving great room for further decrease. It appears that White Illinois Republicans simply did not report negative evaluations of Obama, regardless of his racial portrayal in the various treatments. A potential confound to that interpretation would be that Republican respondents could be consistently higher self-monitors than Democratic respondents, an interpretation that would explain the high markings at the extremes, rather than the center, as Republicans responded quicker to racialized stimuli (Mendelberg, 2001, see also Berinsky, 2002; Huber & Lapinski, 2006). Disentangling the non-finding for Republicans requires additional measures, which we do not have fully at our disposal in this effort.

The ANOVA analysis provides interesting results, but simple bivariate ANOVAs do not provide the insight of multivariate techniques, leading us to also run ordinary least squares (OLS) regressions to see which particular factors affect respondent evaluations of a Black candidate most. We retain our separated sample for this analysis and add in a series of control variables as well. Our OLS model (Table 6) controls for sex, income, church attendance (used as a proxy for religiosity), age, education, and racial resentment[11] (see Table 7 for correlations and reliability of indexed variables), as well as dummies for our racialization manipulations, similar to the models used by other research in this area (McDermott, 1998; Terkildsen, 1993). The omitted variable for the treatment dummies is for the "most Blackened" category, as we assume that a Black candidate would start the campaign perceived as a Black candidate and would need to work harder to deracialize his or her image. All the variables are put on a 1-point scale, permitting direct comparison of their standardized coefficients.

A couple of similarities are apparent in both the ability and empathy models. Both explain greater variance in Democratic responses than Republican and also have more significant predictors for the models estimated among White Democratic voters. The only predictor that is constant in all four regressions is sex, with women consistently rating Obama's traits higher than men, whether Republican or Democratic. The only other variables to prove significant in at least three of the four equations are the racial resentment and two of the treatment variables, a testament to the role that race plays in evaluating Black candidates.

For Republican respondents, strength of political party identification has a strong negative association with ability ratings, as does racial resentment. Surprisingly, the largest negative predictor for evaluations of Obama among White Republicans is church attendance. This could be attributable to the strong emphasis on religious values, particularly the anti-abortion stance taken by Alan Keyes during the campaign. The only significant positive predictor for Republicans on ability scores is sex, with women rating Obama's ability much higher than men. The three treatment dummies all have negative coefficients, indicating that Republican respondents rated Obama's ability lower on the deracialized treatments, though only one, the slightly Whitened condition, is significant.

The results of the model estimated for White Democrats is very different from that of Republican voters in Illinois. Strength of party identification is not a significant predictor, nor is church attendance, but income and education are, with both poorer and higher educated Democrats rating Obama's ability higher, as do women. Racial resentment is a strong predictor of Democratic evaluations of Obama and is the strongest predictor outside of the treatment variables. All of the treatment variables are positive, a reversal of what is found for Republicans, and the latter two, the slightly Whitened and most Whitened

Table 6 Ordinary Least Squares Regression Tables

	Dependent Variables			
	Obama's Ability		Obama's Empathy	
Independent Variable	White Democrats	White Republicans	White Democrats	White Republicans
Strength of Party ID	0.076 (0.840)	−0.188** (−2.257)	0.186** (2.124)	−0.100 (−1.129)
Female	0.147* (1.767)	0.242*** (2.622)	0.276*** (3.422)	0.265*** (2.709)
Income	−0.179** (−2.125)	0.142 (1.557)	−0.217*** (−2.643)	0.015 (0.153)
Church attendance	−0.091 (−1.105)	−0.249*** (−2.871)	−0.056 (−0.700)	−0.212** (−2.306)
Age	0.034 (0.360)	0.001 (0.014)	0.019 (0.208)	0.114 (1.104)
Education	0.201** (1.971)	0.135 (1.265)	0.160 (1.613)	0.059 (0.518)
Racial resentment	−0.275*** (−3.143)	−0.155* (−1.653)	−0.262*** (−3.078)	−0.057 (−0.569)
Slightly Blackened	0.129 (1.283)	−0.171 (−1.580)	0.157 (1.608)	−0.153 (−1.332)
Slightly Whitened	0.237** (2.268)	−0.232** (−2.180)	0.205** (2.024)	−0.272** (−2.405)
Most Whitened	0.320*** (3.058)	−0.081 (−0.774)	0.294*** (2.894)	−0.204* (−1.830)
n	127	128	127	128
Adjusted R^2	.212	.182	.257	.081
Standard error	0.244	0.238	0.235	0.222

Note: Coefficients are standardized ordinary least squares regression values; t scores are in parentheses.
*$p < .10$. **$p < .05$. ***$p < .01$.

Table 7 Correlations and Reliability of Indexed Variables

| | Racial Resentment; $\alpha = .762$ | | | | |
	Q1	Q2	Q3	Q4	Q5
Q1	—	—	—	—	—
Q2	.260***	—	—	—	—
Q3	.238***	.619***	—	—	—
Q4	.199***	.552***	.524***	—	—
Q5	.323***	.406***	.401***	.419***	—

| | Obama's Ability; $\alpha = .965$ | | |
	Q1	Q2	Q3
Q1	—	—	—
Q2	.934***	—	—
Q3	.895***	.877***	—

| | Obama's Empathy; $\alpha = .855$ | |
	Q1	Q2
Q1	—	—
Q2	.750***	—

conditions, are both significant and strongly positive. The most deracialized treatment is the strongest predictor for more positive ratings for Obama.

The empathy ratings follow similar patterns. Racial resentment drops out as a significant predictor of White Republican voters' ratings of Obama's empathy, but church attendance remains a strong negative predictor and being female remains a strong positive. The only other significant predictors are the two deracialized treatment variables, but both are negative, indicating that Republicans found Obama as less empathetic with their condition when he was presented as a race neutral candidate with race neutral concerns. This is an unusual finding that White Republican voters evaluate a Black candidate portrayed as closely identified with African Americans as more empathetic than in the deracialized conditions.

For White Democratic voters, an identical pattern of predictors holds for Obama's empathy ratings as for his ability ratings, with the addition of partisan strength as an added positive predictor and the loss of education as a significant predictor. Women still rate Obama much higher than do men, whereas income is still negative and racial resentment has a strong negative coefficient. The three treatment variables are again all positive, with the two Whitened conditions being significant and increasing in strength. Democrats felt Obama empathized with them much more strongly when he was Whitened than when he was portrayed as a Black candidate.

Discussion

Our results from this unique data collection during the heat of the 2004 Illinois U.S. Senate election add to the growing literature on the significance of racial attitudes in evaluations of African American candidates running for political office. As unusual as the election environment in this case was—two Black candidates running for the U.S. Senate, both nominated by the two major parties, and in a state where the electorate remains overwhelmingly White—the findings have relevance to studying the dynamics of race and candidate evaluations in other settings. Experimentally manipulating the visual images and portrayals of then-candidate Barack Obama from treatments deemphasizing his race and connection to the African American community to primes at the opposite end of the spectrum highlighting those traits had an immediate impact on evaluations of Obama among White Democratic voters in Illinois. The more deracialized the treatment, the more positive White Democrats were about Obama in their assessment of both his ability and empathy. To the extent that voting dynamics among White Democrats in Illinois follow similar patterns among White Democrats in other states, our findings suggest Obama's race remained a potent and easily manipulated factor in how he was evaluated during the 2008 Presidential election as well.

The story for White Republican Illinois voters is quite different. There were no statistically significant differences in evaluations of Obama's empathy or ability among the four treatment groups. We have two potential explanations for this result, neither suggesting that Republican voters do not have racial attitudes. First, it is simply possible that the race of a candidate from the opposing party—and variation of the candidate's portrayal from deracialized to racialized—has less influence on candidate evaluations than the fact that the candidate is a Democrat. As expected, average scores on the evaluations of Obama's ability and empathy were systematically and substantially lower among White Republican voters than for White Democrats across all of the different treatments. This suggests that none of the forms of priming provided in the stimuli could strongly influence the evaluations of White Republican voters. Barring considerations of race, Republicans simply did not like the Democrat.

An alternative interpretation of the results for White Republican voters could be that they became aware of the manipulations whereas White Democrats did not. It is possible that Republicans were, as a group, higher self-monitors than Democrats, becoming explicitly aware of the primes that remained implicit to Democrats. As those primes became explicit in the most racialized portrayal, Republicans may have begun monitoring their responses, masking further changes along the expected path. Reversal of the trends notable in lesser levels of the manipulation that are found in the most extreme racialized manipulation could provide evidence for this. However, without additional data, such a conclusion is tenuous. To date, no research exists suggesting that Republicans are higher self-monitors than Democrats on matters of race, but it is possible that people identifying as members of the "Party of Civil Rights" consider themselves more immune to racism than do members of the "Party of Lincoln" leading them to lower levels of self-monitoring. More research in this area would be an interesting addition to the field.

The implications of these findings are significant. Our findings suggest that the portrayal of candidates' race does affect how they are evaluated, and that this is particularly strong, in this scenario, on White Democratic voters evaluating a Black Democratic candidate. We have no leverage to discuss whether White Democratic voters would respond similarly to a Black Republican candidate, or if White Republican voters would suddenly have a response to that candidate. What we can predict is that racialized portrayals do matter and Black candidates running for political office in predominantly White districts would be advised to take this into account. Race, unsurprisingly, still plays a role in the American electorate.

Of course, these are findings from one experimental manipulation taken among one sample of voters during one election in the state of Illinois. Larger generalizations about racial attitudes, White voting behavior in the face of minority candidates, and the impact of short-term communications await additional studies and creative research designs. But with a sitting African American president and the prospect of more frequent elections including minority candidates on the ballot for statewide and national elections, the time is ripe for scholars to carefully examine the wide range of questions implicated in the dynamics of race and voting in the United States.

Appendix A
Variables Used and Descriptive Statistics by Groups

Variable Name	Variable Label and Type	Description
Party Identification	7-point scale	1 = Strong Democrat 4 = Independent 7 = Strong Republican
Strength of Party ID	4-point scale	0 = Independent 3 = Strong partisan
Female	Sex (dummy)	1 = Female
Income ($)	17-point scale	0 = Less than 5,000 17 = 175,000 or more
Church attendance	6-point scale	1 = Never 6 = More than once a week

(Continued)

(Continued)

Variable Name	Variable Label and Type	Description
Age (years)	7-point scale	1 = *18-24* 2 = *25-34* 3 = *35-44* 4 = *45-54* 5 = *55-64* 6 = *65-74* 7 = *75 or older*
Education	4-point scale	1 = *Less than high school* 2 = *High school graduate* 3 = *Some college* 4 = *College graduate or higher*
Racial resentment	5-point scale	1 = *Low racial resentment* 5 = *High racial resentment*
Most Blackened	Racialized treatment (dummy)	1 = *Received Obama headshot and the "Obama with Blacks" treatment*
Slightly Blackened	Slightly Blackened treatment (dummy)	1 = *Received Illinois State House picture and the "Obama with Blacks" treatment*
Slightly Whitened	Slightly Whitened treatment (dummy)	1 = *Received Obama headshot and the "Obama with Whites" treatment*
Most Whitened	Whitened treatment (dummy)	1 = *Received Illinois State House picture and the "Obama with Whites" treatment*
Obama's ability	Obama's ability as a senator (7-point scale)	1 = *No ability* 7 = *Great deal of ability*
Obama's empathy	Obama's empathy for respondent (7-point scale)	1 = *No empathy* 7 = *Great deal of empathy*

Appendix B

Components of and Reliability Scales for Indexed Variables

Racial Resentment (Reversed)	Average Score of Five 5-Point Questions
Q1:	It is easy to understand the anger of Black people in America
Q2:	Blacks are getting too demanding in their push for equal rights
Q3:	Over the past few years Blacks have gotten more economically than they deserve

Racial Resentment (Reversed)	Average Score of Five 5-Point Questions
Q4:	Blacks should not push themselves where they are not wanted
Q5:	Discrimination against Blacks is no longer a problem in the United States
1	*Strongly disagree*
2	*Disagree*
3	*Neither agree nor disagree*
4	*Agree*
5	*Strongly agree*
Obama's Ability	Average Score of Three 7-Point Questions
Q1:	He would make a good U.S. Senator
Q2:	He has qualities that I look for in an elected official
Q3:	He seems qualified for office
1	*Strongly disagree*
4	*Neutral*
7	*Strongly agree*
Obama's Empathy	Average Score of Three 7-Point Questions
Q1:	He would probably understand my concerns
Q2:	He reminds me of people I know
1	*Strongly disagree*
4	*Neutral*
7	*Strongly agree*

Declaration of Conflicting Interest

The authors declared that they had no conflicts of interests with respect to their authorship or the publication of this article.

Financial Disclosure/Funding

The authors declared that they received no financial support for their research and/or authorship of this article.

Notes

1. One of the key reasons they chose this race to analyze was specifically because race did not become a salient issue, yet appeared to exert a subtle force on the election results. This research design, focusing on race as an implicit factor, relates to our own focus, described later.
2. Knowledge Networks of Palo Alto, California, was contracted to collect the data. The surveys are delivered via the Internet, allowing respondents to complete the questionnaire themselves, and also to view the visual primes used for the embedded experiments. Panel participants are not limited to only those with Internet

access. Knowledge Networks provides Internet access as part of the incentive for respondents to participate. The survey population is a random probability sample of residents of the state of Illinois.

3. Samples of Latinos, Hispanics, and other racial minorities are too small to analyze and are not included here. According to U.S. Census data from 2004, the state of Illinois was 67% White, 15% Black, 14% Hispanic, and 4% other at the time of the election.

4. See Harris-Lacewell and Junn (2007) for further analysis of the full data collected.

5. Keyes is omitted from this analysis, as the experimental design varied the religious presentation of Keyes, rather than his racial presentation. Keyes, a Catholic, ran as a religious conservative, attempting to focus on his broader Christian beliefs over his specific denomination. Results of the Keyes manipulation will be presented elsewhere.

6. A descriptive analysis of the four subgroups appears in Table 5.

7. Results of this manipulation check appear in Table 5.

8. The survey contained no questions relating to candidate integrity, so that trait is omitted from our analysis.

9. Information about the creation of and the reliability of the scales can be found in Appendixes A and B.

10. We coded respondents who declared being a strong partisan, leaned toward a party, or tended to vote for a party as a member of that party. We exclude the 31 respondents who declared being pure independents from this analysis purely because the small sample size restricts the conclusions we can draw from the results we find. Descriptive statistics of the partisans in the sample can be found in Table 6.

11. Details on the questions used and reliability scores for our racial resentment scale can be found in the appendixes (see also Table 7).

References

Abramowitz, A. I. (1980). A comparison of voting for U.S. senator and representative in 1978. *American Political Science Review, 74*, 633-640.

Bartels, L. (2007). Homer gets a warm hug: A note on ignorance and extenuation. *Perspectives on Politics, 5*, 785-790.

Berinsky, A. J. (2002). Political context and the survey response: The dynamics of racial policy opinion. *Journal of Politics, 64*, 567-584.

Citrin, J., Green, D. P., & Sears, D. O. (1990). White reactions to Black candidates: When does race matter? *Public Opinion Quarterly, 54*, 74-96.

Colleau, S. M., Glynn, K., Lybrand, S., Merelman, R. M., Mohan, P., & Wall, J. E. (1990). Symbolic racism in candidate evaluation: An experiment. *Political Behavior, 12*, 385-402.

Funk, C. L. (1999). Bringing the candidate into models of candidate evaluation. *Journal of Politics, 61*, 700-720.

Gilens, M. (1996). "Race Coding" and White opposition to welfare. *American Political Science Review, 90*, 593-604.

Hajnal, Z. (2006). *Changing White attitudes towards Black political leadership.* New York: Cambridge University Press.

Harris-Lacewell, M., & Junn, J. (2007). Old friends and new alliances: How the 2004 Illinois senate race complicates the study of race and religion. *Journal of Black Studies, 38,* 30-50.

Huber, G. A., & Lapinski, J. (2006). The "Race Card" revisited: Assessing racial priming in policy contests. *American Journal of Political Science, 48,* 375-401.

Huber, G. A., & Lapinski, J. (2008). Testing the implicit-explicit model of racialized political communication. *Perspectives on Politics, 6,* 125-134.

Kinder, D. R. (1983). *Presidential traits: Pilot study report to the 1984 NES Planning Committee and NES Board.* Ann Arbor: University of Michigan, Center for Political Studies.

Lodge, M., McGraw, K. M., & Stroh, P. (1989). An impression-driven model of candidate evaluation. *American Political Science Review, 83,* 399-419.

Lodge, M., Steenbergen, M. R., & Brau, S. (1995). The responsive voter: Campaign information and the dynamics of candidate evaluation. *American Political Science Review, 89,* 309-326.

Lodge, M., Stroh, P., & Wahlke, J. (1990). Black-box models of candidate evaluation. *Political Behavior, 12,* 5-18.

Lupia, A., Levine, A. S., Menning, J. O., & Sin, G. (2007). Were Bush tax cut supporters "simply ignorant"? A second look at Conservatives and Liberals in "Homer Gets a Tax Cut." *Perspectives on Politics, 5,* 773-784.

McDermott, M. L. (1998). Race and gender cues in low-information elections. *Political Research Quarterly, 51,* 895-918.

Mendelberg, T. (1997). Executing Hortons: Racial crime in the 1988 presidential campaign. *Public Opinion Quarterly, 61,* 134-157.

Mendelberg, T. (2001). *The race card: Campaign strategy, implicit messages, and the norm of equality.* Princeton, NJ: Princeton University Press.

Mendelberg, T. (2008). Racial priming revived. *Perspectives on Politics, 6,* 109-123.

Miller, A. H. (1990). Public judgments of Senate and House candidates. *Legislative Studies Quarterly, 15,* 525-542.

Peffley, M., Hurwitz, J., & Sniderman, P. M. (1997). Racial stereotypes and Whites' political views of Blacks in the context of welfare and crime. *American Journal of Political Science, 41,* 30-60.

Reeves, K. (1997). *Voting hopes or fears? White voters, Black candidates, and racial politics in America.* New York: Oxford University Press.

Sigelman, C. K., Sigelman, L., Walkosz, B. J., & Nitz, M. (1995). Black candidates, White voters: Understanding racial bias in political perceptions. *American Journal of Political Science, 39,* 243-265.

Sigelman, L., & Sigelman, C. K. (1982). Sexism, racism, and ageism in voting behavior: An experimental analysis. *Social Psychology Quarterly, 45,* 263-269.

Terkildsen, N. (1993). When White voters evaluate Black candidates: The processing implications of candidate skin color, prejudice, and self-monitoring. *American Journal of Political Science, 37,* 1032-1053.

Valentino, N. A. (1999). Crime news and the priming of racial attitudes during evaluations of the president. *Public Opinion Quarterly, 63*, 293-320.

Valentino, N. A., Hutchings, V. L., & White, I. K. (2002). Cues that matter: How political ads prime racial attitudes during campaigns. *American Political Science Review, 96*, 75-90.

Weisberg, H. F., & Rusk, J. G. (1970). Dimensions of candidate evaluation. *American Political Science Review, 64*, 1167-1185.

White, I. (2007). When race matters and when it doesn't: Racial group differences in response to racial cues. *American Political Science Review, 101*, 339-351.

2

SOUTHERN STRATEGY 2.0: CONSERVATIVES, WHITE VOTERS, AND THE ELECTION OF BARACK OBAMA

Thomas Edge

Northwestern University

S ince the beginning of his bid for the presidency, Barack Obama's campaign has come to represent different things for different people. Certainly, the reactions to his victory on November 4, 2008, point to the deep emotional connection of many African Americans with this campaign. Within hours of his triumph, YouTube clips of spontaneous parades and celebrations demonstrated an outpouring of joy—from the Apollo Theater and the White House to the streets of Itta Bena, Mississippi. Interracial groups broke out into renditions of "The Star-Spangled Banner" and danced in the streets and aboard subway trains. Such reactions seemed more in keeping with a *19th-century* presidential election, when cannon salutes and torchlight parades marked the victory of a campaign. The cynicism of political life faded, for a fleeting moment, behind the historic nature of the events at hand.

The reactions of African Americans in particular reflected an outpouring of joy that has no real parallel in recent American history. What is fascinating about this trend, however, is that it came in response to a candidate who did so much to *avoid* discussing race as an aspect of his campaign. Asked by Gwen Ifill (2009) during the primary season whether a "blowup about race" was "inevitable" for his campaign, Obama responded,

> It would have been naïve for me to think that I could run and end up with quasi-front-runner status in a presidential election, as potentially the first African American president, and that race wouldn't come up. . . . But, ultimately, I don't think it's useful. I think we've got to talk about it. I think

Source: Journal of Black Studies, January 2010; vol. 40, 3: pp. 426-444.

we've got to process it. But we've got to remind ourselves that what we have in common is far more important than what's different. (p. 61)

Throughout the campaign and even in the aftermath of Election Day, however, it became apparent that whether Obama liked it or not, racial meanings were being ascribed to his campaign from across the political spectrum, sometimes with dangerous implications for future racial dialogues in this country.

The point of this article is not to downplay the significance of the election for the nation at large or for any particular group of Americans. Rather, it is concerned with some of the specific uses of the election of Barack Obama for conservative purposes. In the hours and days following the election, two types of opinions emerged that cast Obama's presidency in somewhat troubling tones. On one hand, some commentators saw this election as representative of an important change in the *White* electorate. On the other, Obama's compelling personal narrative—son of an African immigrant, worked his way through the Ivy Leagues, community organizer—and rapid political rise were set forth as prima facie evidence of the lack of racism in the United States. In combination, these themes were used to argue that America has moved beyond the racial paradigms set forth by the civil rights movement and consequently has moved beyond the need for the remedies set forth by that movement.

All of this plays into the rise of the Southern Strategy 2.0. There are three essential parts to this phenomenon. All three points utilize Obama's individual success that depended at least in part upon the advances of the civil rights movement to undermine calls for structural change. First, according to the arguments, a nation that has the ability to elect a Black president is completely free of racism. Second, attempts to continue the remedies enacted after the civil rights movement will only result in more racial discord, demagoguery, and racism against *White Americans*. Third, these tactics are used side-by-side with the veiled racism and coded language of the *original* Southern Strategy. Thus, Obama is simultaneously held up as an example of how far the nation has come in race relations and used as a racial bogeyman: a Muslim terrorist, a Black radical who befriends other anti-American activists, a noncitizen trying to usurp power. Aspects of these strategies have been used in the past to attack liberal racial policies, but never has there been a specific political event like the Obama election that resonated with so many people and had such transformative potential. Conservatives have been quick to attribute their own racial meanings to the election. But at a moment of national crisis when President Obama seeks to use the power of the federal government toward progressive political ends, these forces use his success as an argument *against* the intervention of the government in the social problems of the nation.

The White Electorate and Obama

To make this case that America has entered a "postracial" age, the media need to demonstrate that there is a lack of racism on the part of the White public at large. After all, they argue, in the absence of overt forms of racism, why are the old remedies necessary? Pundits of all political stripes have been quick to point to the role of White voters in the Obama election as a sign of significant change in the country's racial outlook. Frank Rich (2008b), a consistently liberal editorialist for the *New York Times*, struck such a tone in the days after the election.

> The most conspicuous clichés to fall, of course, were the twin suppositions that a decisive number of [White] Americans wouldn't vote for a [Black] presidential candidate—and that they were lying to pollsters about their rampant racism. But the polls were accurate. There was no "Bradley effect." A higher percentage of [White] men voted for Obama than any Democrat since Jimmy Carter, Bill Clinton included. (p. WK9)

Asked about the Bradley effect the day after the election, Jon A. Krosnick of Stanford University told the *Times*, "There's no point in continuing that discussion anymore" (Zernike & Sussman, 2008). Before the election took place, contributors at themonkeycage.org, a Web site organized by a small group of political scientists, questioned whether there would be a Bradley effect; afterward, they pointed out that Obama's popular vote tally was in line with most projections (Sides, 2008).

The problem with so many of the articles written along these same lines is that they rest on a certain assumption: Since Obama won the election, race could not have been a significant factor for the White electorate. What is lacking is any attempt to place his numbers into any context, beyond a superficial comparison with prior Democratic candidates. A deeper analysis of Obama's poll numbers, however, indicates that very little changed in terms of White voting habits in this election cycle.

Pundits have been quick to point to Obama's showing among White voters—roughly 43%—as indicative of his success at drawing Whites into his campaign. Most notably, they point out that this matched the success of Bill Clinton in 1996, equaling him for the high watermark among Democratic presidential contenders since 1976 ("National Exit Polls Table," 2008; Todd & Gawiser, 2009, p. 29). (The 1976 election, of course, is a bit of an anomaly in the post-1964 landscape, thanks to the influence of the Watergate scandal.) On the surface, it does seem impressive that Obama reproduced the polling numbers of Clinton, a White Southerner. Taking it a step further, one can argue that Obama benefited from the success of a full generation of African American elected officials, particularly congressional representatives in majority-White districts who "[won] the confidence of [Whites] that they could represent both [White] and Black interests" (Clayton, 2003, p. 355).

Again, though, the raw numbers do not tell the whole story. First, Clinton managed to get these numbers *in spite of* the woes of the Democratic Party in the mid-1990s. During the congressional elections of 1996, the Democrats received a slight bump in the House of Representatives, from 198 to 206 seats, leaving the Republicans with a 22-seat majority. In the Senate, however, Republicans added slightly to an existing lead, coming away from the elections with a 10-seat majority. In contrast, Obama rode to the White House on a wave of frustration with the Republican Party—a wave that also delivered the Democrats 60 seats in the Senate (including 2 independents voting with the Democratic majority and Arlen Specter's defection in April 2009) and 257 in the House. Both margins were substantially greater than those enjoyed by the Republicans after the 1996 elections. Both indicate a widespread disenchantment with the Republican Party as a whole. Yet Obama's numbers with White voters did not improve upon Clinton's polling in 1996.

This does not even take into account the other dynamic that Clinton faced in 1996: a strong third-party candidate in H. Ross Perot. Granted, Perot was much stronger in 1992, when he polled roughly 19% of the popular vote. Still, approximately 10% of the electorate voted for independent candidates in 1996, compared to about 1.5% in 2008. Perot's candidacy attracted disenchanted voters from both parties and a significant number of independents, which would have negatively affected Clinton's standing among White voters and kept his numbers artificially low. (White voters were much more likely than Blacks and Hispanics to vote for independent candidates in 1996.) It is telling, however, that Perot's weakest area of support came from the South, the most heavily conservative area of the nation, because of his lack of emphasis on issues important to social conservatives. This supports the idea that he appealed to moderates in both parties, thus taking at least some voters away from Clinton (Stone & Rapoport, 2001, p. 53). Consequently, Clinton's 43% among White voters cannot be directly compared with that of Obama in 2008.

But how did Obama compare to more recent Democratic nominees Al Gore and John Kerry? Again, for all the talk of dramatic gains, the numbers do not support such a conclusion. Al Gore polled 42% among White voters in 2000, while John Kerry reached 41% of Whites in 2004. Obama did improve slightly on these numbers, but his 1% to 2% improvement hardly qualifies as a revolution in White voting patterns. Regionally, Obama secured 30% of the Southern White vote, compared to 31% for Gore (another Southern candidate) and 29% for Kerry—in other words, he split the difference between the two White nominees. In the Northeast, a traditional Democratic stronghold, Obama received 52% of the White vote, equaling Gore's 2000 numbers and improving upon Kerry's showing by 2 points.

Obama *did* show modest gains in the Midwest and West, where he polled 47% and 49%, respectively. This may have helped turn Ohio, Indiana, Colorado, and New Mexico into Democratic wins in 2008. In all four regions, however, the gaps between Obama's overall vote totals and his *White* vote totals are significant: 7 points apiece in the Northeast and Midwest, 8 points in the West, and 15 points in the South. Moreover, the wide gaps between Obama's performance with other racial groups and that of White voters deserve attention. Nationally, he received 95% of the Black vote, 67% of the Latinos, and 62% of Asian Americans. Why, then, is there a *19-point gap* between the lowest of these and his White vote total? In light of the circumstances—the absence of strong third-party candidates, a well-run campaign by Obama, tactical missteps by the McCain-Palin ticket, a severe recession, and historically low approval ratings for the incumbent Republican president—why did the White vote trail that of every other racial group by such a significant margin?

As previously mentioned, the press was more obsessed with the possibility of the Bradley effect affecting Obama's performance, rather than a substantive breakdown of the actual results. The Bradley effect is the belief that White voters are reluctant to share their true feelings on a Black candidate with pollsters, thus artificially inflating a Black candidate's numbers and leading to surprising results on Election Day. This focus, however, was misguided. It pointed to the accuracy of the polling but did not take into account the impact of race on the decisions that people already reached *before* they were polled. Polls indicating that Obama would receive approximately 53% of the popular vote did not tell us, with any degree of accuracy, the role that racism played in the minds of some voters to support his opponent. If anything, it can be argued that a Bradley effect was much more likely to affect polling that asked people whether race affected their choice in the election, with people reluctant to admit the truth of the matter (CNN, 2008).

None of this is meant to dampen the enthusiasm of the moment or to make light of President Obama's showing in the general election. It is intended to show how quick the media have been to use this election as a litmus test for White racism, without any real degree of analysis. Nobody is asking why, in light of circumstances highly favorable to a Democratic landslide, Obama's margin of victory as a percentage of the popular vote was actually *less than* Clinton's margin over Bob Dole in 1996? Why did Obama poll 66% of the youth vote nationally but 54% of the White youth vote? Why were there such tremendous gaps between his White vote and that of every other racial group? The pundits have been too quick to insist that since Obama won the election, race had no impact on the vote. With nearly *one fifth* of the electorate admitting that race played some factor in their decision (CNN, 2008), however, racism should be taken into account as one of many factors that led to Obama's gap with White voters.

All this obscures the degree to which the *Republican Party* has become the true marker of identity politics in contemporary America. Ninety percent of John McCain's vote total came from White voters, compared to 61% for Obama (Todd & Gawiser, 2009, p. 29). McCain's campaign thus reveals the degree to which the Republican Party has become a party of older White voters, largely in the South and in a handful of scarcely populated interior states (Wyoming, Montana, the Dakotas, Oklahoma, etc.). The lack of outreach to people of color over the last few decades has finally begun to affect Republicans at the polls, where they are increasingly seen as clinging to a narrowing White constituency. Even when Republicans attempted to run Black candidates for office, such as Michael Steele and Alan Keyes, the party's history of race-baiting outweighed any current attempts to reach African American voters (Blumenthal, 2008, pp. 127-134). Thus, the tremendous impact of race on the contemporary two-party system is belied by the silence of the pundits on this very issue.

Just as startling as the lack of analysis of the figures is the lack of historical context offered. The role of race in forming the current incarnations of the major political parties has been well documented, particularly with the influx of White Southern Democrats after the passage of the 1965 Voting Rights Act (Carter, 2000). Even a fleeting overview of the past 40 years of party politics demonstrates a strong link between the Republican Party and appeals to racism: Nixon's Southern Strategy, Reagan's "states' rights" speech in Philadelphia (Mississippi) and invocation of the "welfare queens," the Willie Horton ad, Jesse Helms's campaigns against Harvey Gantt, Karl Rove's smear campaign against John McCain in the 2000 South Carolina primary, the suppression of voting rights in the 2000 and 2004 presidential elections, and Bob Corker's "Playboy ad" against Harold Ford Jr. in 2006. With race playing such a crucial role in the development of the Republican Party since 1965, it seems highly unlikely that it would suddenly cease to have an impact in a campaign against the first African American to secure the nomination of a major political party. In essence, pundits would have us believe that race had an impact on every *White* Democratic nominee from 1968 to 2004 but not the campaign of Barack Obama.

Conservatives and Race: Before and After Election Night

Such analyses of the racial basis for the modern party system, however, were rarely engaged during the campaign, even though race played such an important role in how Republicans *and* Democrats attacked Obama. During the primaries, an anonymous Clinton staffer sent a note to the *Drudge Report*, alerting it to a photo of Obama in traditional Somali garb and asking, "Wouldn't we be seeing this on the cover of every magazine if it were [Hillary Rodham Clinton]?" (FOX News, 2008). Geraldine Ferraro, the 1984 Democratic nominee for vice president and a Hillary Clinton adviser, essentially dubbed Obama the "affirmative action candidate," saying,

> If Obama was a [White] man, he would not be in this position. . . . And if he was a woman (of any color) he would not be in this position. He happens to be very lucky to be who he is. And the country is caught up in the concept. (Signorile, 2008; Younge, 2008)

Toward the end of the primary season, Clinton herself infamously pointed to Obama's waning support among "hard-working Americans, [White] Americans," prior to the Kentucky and West Virginia primaries (Conason, 2008).

Before Obama even clinched the nomination, Republicans picked up the same ideological threads that the Clinton campaign employed. Ann Coulter, speaking before the Young America's Foundation in February 2008, used much the same language as Geraldine Ferraro did a month later:

> Barack's really been kind of coasting on his record, since his first big accomplishment of being born half-[Black]. I keep hearing people say, "Oh, Obama could never be elected because he's half-[Black]. You know, 'cause we're just such a racist country." What are they talking about? He wouldn't be running for president if he weren't half-[Black]. (Media Matters, 2008a)

Following Obama's address on race in Philadelphia in March 2008, Patrick Buchanan (2008) invoked the specter of the Reverend Jeremiah Wright, Obama's former Chicago minister whose fiery oratory on American race relations and foreign policy unleashed a firestorm of controversy earlier in the primaries. Buchanan not only attacked Obama for "[taking] his wife and daughters" to a "church where hate had a home in the pulpit"; he also assailed Obama's defense of affirmative action, decrying continued Black accusations of racism as a "racket" in which "[White] men are passed over for jobs and promotions in business and government, and denied admission to colleges and universities to which their grades and merits entitle them, because of their gender and race."

Tellingly, conservative critics of Obama were only too happy to use the trope of the "affirmative action candidate" in various incarnations during the months leading up to the presidential election. In August 2008, Rush Limbaugh attributed Obama's nomination to the inability of the Democratic Party to "say 'no' to a [Black] man," while declaring that "affirmative action has reared its ugly head against [Democrats]" (History Commons, 2008; Metacafe, 2008). When Obama's running mate, Joe Biden, referred to the "transformative" potential of the election of the first Black president, Lisa

De Pasquale (2008) of the American Conservative Union and Conservative Political Action Committee wrote about the event under the heading "Affirmative Action Election." Right-wing political analyst and lawyer Phyllis Schlafly (2008) questioned his intellectual contributions as the "affirmative-action president" of the Harvard Law Review. And Michael Savage, following up on his depiction of the "affirmative action" primaries between Obama and Clinton, told an October 27, 2008, rally, "Obama claims to have been poor, but he, unlike me, benefited from affirmative action, while I suffered from affirmative action. . . . [We] have America's first affirmative action candidate about to become president" (Media Matters, 2008b).

Recently, Eric Boehlert (2009) has asserted that compared with their liberal counterparts, conservative bloggers have been less effective in taking advantage of the Internet as a tool for shaping opinion. While Boehlert offers an excellent critique of the shortcomings of the conservative blogosphere, or "rightroots," his work underscores the degree to which it supports the political mudslinging already being perpetrated by conservative radio and television personalities. Thus, its effectiveness is not necessarily creating new lines of conservative thinking. Rather, conservatives see it as a support system. As in the buildup to the Iraq War in 2003, conservative bloggers put forth the same stories about the Obamas that FOX News and Rush Limbaugh peddled from their platforms, thus giving greater exposure and a patina of acceptability to scurrilous rumors. They repeated accusations of Obama's associations with radicals and his questionable citizenship status, while occasionally passing along new stories that were even too radical for the mainstream conservative media. These accusations—questioning his sexual orientation, accusing him of changing his birth certificate, even attributing "violent terrorist bombings" in the 1980s to Obama—all served to foment the same racist and conservative elements that Sean Hannity and Michael Savage cultivated elsewhere (pp. 214-215). On a deeper level, they raised questions about Obama's "Americaness" and, by extension, his ability to represent the nation. In the final months of the campaign, these tendencies repeatedly arose at McCain-Palin campaign events, with their supporters calling Obama a terrorist, questioning his loyalty to the nation, and occasionally offering racial epithets at the mention of Obama's name (Rich, 2008a; Toplikar, 2008; Weiner, 2008).

The use of affirmative action and other racial markers as stigmatizing tools against the Obama campaign served as a forerunner to the swift about-face performed by conservatives in the immediate aftermath of the election. Often, the same voices who criticized Obama as unpatriotic or questioned his very citizenship were quick to use his election to demonstrate how far America had come in race relations. Suddenly, the "closet Muslim" that associated with "radicals" and threatened to undermine American security was appropriated by right-wing pundits to argue for an end to affirmative action policies and other forms of race-based redress. For conservatives, Obama's election signaled a long-awaited opportunity: a clear advance in race relations that the Right could use to attack the legal legacies and protections of the civil rights movement.

As one might expect, affirmative action was the first policy on the conservative chopping block. Days before the election, conservative blogger Adam Owenby's review (2008) of the presidential debates warned of the "danger" that Obama's foreign policies posed to the nation. After Obama's election, however, Owenby celebrated the milestone in American race relations:

> Apparently the use of racial preferences is no longer necessary to promote the success of those in the minority. With this election, we have achieved equality. Dr. King would be very proud. Affirmative action did provide many with opportunities that historically would have been forbidden. But, in this era, race should cease to be the issue deciding the fates of individuals. All of us, men and women, [Black] and [White], are free to compete on the merits of our hard work, intelligence, and determination.

Similarly, Rolfe McCollister (2008), publisher and CEO of BusinessReport .com, set aside his own ideological differences with Obama to celebrate the meaning of the moment—or, at the very least, the meaning that he *imposed upon* the moment. In light of Obama's election with "massive support from [White] voters," McCollister argued, "it's going to be hard to make the 'discrimination argument' against [Whites] with President Obama in the Oval Office." More insidious than this, however, was the manner in which he used this to attack the generation that continued the struggles of the 1960s, particularly activists like Jesse Jackson.

> The way I see it, Jackson is "out of business." And so are many others who have used the "R" word as a club to get leverage or concessions—or as an excuse for failure or lack of even trying. The club has been removed and the game has forever changed. There is now proof that minorities have the same opportunity as everyone else to get an education, work hard, compete and go as far as their dreams will take them—even to the White House.

Adding insult to injury, McCollister ended his epitaph for the civil rights movement with his own invocation of the African American spiritual: "We are all free at last!"

More prominent voices than Owenby and McCollister invoked the same types of arguments. Before the final votes were tallied on Election Night, former Reagan cabinet member William Bennett responded to a question from CNN's Anderson Cooper about the potential meaning of an Obama presidency. "Well, I'll tell you one thing it means, as a former Secretary of

Education: You don't take any excuses anymore from anybody who says, 'The deck is stacked, I can't do anything, there's so much in-built this and that.'" While another conservative commentator on the panel questioned whether Obama's election would solve America's racial problems, Bennett's analysis that night was part of a much broader conservative attack on the notion that racism still affects the opportunities available to minorities (Neiwert, 2008).

Bennett was one of the crucial members of the Right in terms of painting this election in a manner beneficial to conservatives. Ten days before the inauguration of Barack Obama, Bennett and John Cribb (2009) invoked Martin Luther King in calling Obama's election a "mountaintop moment" that allowed Americans to "put the politics of race behind us." There are several points from their analysis that need to be raised. First, they specifically invoked Obama's showing among White voters in the primaries against Hillary Clinton. Unfortunately, they were disingenuous in their approach. For them, the fact that Obama received higher White vote percentages in Virginia and Georgia than he did in New York indicated a sea change in race relations. They never noted, of course, that he was running against *the junior senator from New York State*, a fact that might have influenced the poll numbers. Second, the authors contrasted Obama's decision to run "as an American" with previous African American candidates who each chose to run "as a [Black] man." Aside from the gendered nature of this analysis that excluded Shirley Chisholm and Carol Moseley Braun, it created a false dichotomy, as if one cannot be both "Black" and "American." It also raised questions within conservative ranks about the status of politicos like Alan Keyes, who ran for president as a Republican in 1996 and 2000.

Third, they praised Obama's decision to separate himself from Jeremiah Wright as a signal that Obama "wanted to move beyond racial categorization and reference." This, of course, ignored an article that Bennett coauthored for the *National Review* in June 2008 that questioned Obama's relationship with Wright and criticized him for casting aside the reverend only "once he ceased being a political asset and turned into a political liability" (Bennett & Leibsohn, 2008). Finally, Bennett and Cribb (2009) used all these arguments, by way of King, Lincoln, and the Huxtable family of television's *The Cosby Show*, to illustrate "a new self-evident truth: that there is no ceiling to achievement in America based on race." Throughout these analyses, there was no attempt to provide context relating to the everyday lives, experiences, and standing of African Americans, as if the success of one Black politician outweighed the collective suffering of the masses.

Attacks on affirmative action, however, represented only one part of this attack on the civil rights movement. Take, for instance, the perspectives set forth in the *Wall Street Journal* by Abigail Thernstrom and Stephan Thernstrom (2008). Referring to Obama's showing among White voters, they wrote, "Racism is the Sherlock Holmes dog that did not bark in the night." They compared Obama's showing among White voters with that of Al Gore and John Kerry (without any context, of course) to illustrate that "[Black] candidates can win in multi-ethnic and even majority-[White] districts with color-blind voting." From their perspective, Obama's election demonstrated that "racial gerrymandering," as dictated by the 1965 Voting Rights Act to ensure proportional African American representation, is no longer needed. There are significant problems with this analysis, of course. For example, they are quick to cite Obama's success in states with small percentages of Black voters, like Iowa, Minnesota, and Wisconsin. They do *not* consider, however, Obama's showing in the states most directly affected by the scope of the Voting Rights Act: 11% of the White vote in Mississippi, 10% in Alabama, 14% in Louisiana, 23% in Georgia, 26% in Texas, and 26% in South Carolina (CNN, 2008). As David Bositis has pointed out, Obama's showings among White voters in Alabama, Mississippi, Louisiana, and Arkansas were actually *worse* than Kerry's in 2004 (Ifill, 2009, p. 244). Nor did Thernstrom and Thernstrom address any accusations in recent years of attempts to disenfranchise Black, Latino, and Native American voters from Florida to Ohio to New Mexico. Such an analysis might stand in the way of their assertions that "American voters have turned a racial corner. The law should follow in their footsteps."

Others hoped that Obama's election could be used to defuse serious examinations of American racism. Tunku Varadarajan (2009), the executive editor for opinions at *Forbes*, derided attorney general Eric Holder for his February 2009 speech that characterized the United States as a "nation of cowards" when it came to frank discussions of race relations. Varadarajan called on Obama to repudiate the "mistaken and misguided" comments of his top law enforcement official, while cloaking his critique in the aura of postracialism.

> Many of us had believed that the Age of Obama would bring us deliverance from the Al Sharptons and Jesse Jacksons and other racial actuaries, whose modus operandi—relentlessly, scurrilously—has been to distort the American public conversation, and to grow fat politically on [White] guilt (to use Shelby Steele's phrase). Now we have, as President Obama's attorney general, a man who plies the same corrosive accusations and pieties.

In Varadarajan's view (2009), Holder and Jeremiah Wright were of the same ideological ilk, and their mutual desires to promote open discourse on race and racism threatened to "sow unnecessary divisions" at a time of national economic crisis. Thus, for some, Obama's election did not just mean an end to policies seeking to promote opportunities across racial lines. Rather, it was such a transformative event that we no longer needed to even *discuss* race. More to the point, conservatives seemed unwilling to allow *Democrats* to dictate the terms of these racial dialogues, if they needed to take place. Republicans, for instance, did not criticize Secretary of State Condoleezza Rice in March 2008 when she offered her own version of Holder's 2009 comments:

> Africans and Europeans came here and founded this country together— Europeans by choice and Africans in chains. . . . That's not a pretty reality of our founding, and I think that particular birth defect makes it hard for us to confront it, hard for us to talk about it, and hard for us to realize that it has continuing relevance for who we are today. (Ifill, 2009, pp. 175-176)

Apparently, the real fear is not that Holder or Obama will discuss race relations openly or criticize the nation for its lack of engagement with such issues but that they might actually *act* upon these critiques.

By Obama's first summer as president, the *National Review* attempted a staggering logical jump, at once questioning Obama's racial authenticity while simultaneously accusing him of engaging in identity politics and placing too much emphasis on race. As Victor Davis Hanson (2009) wrote, Obama "piggy-backed onto the African American experience" in spite of his biracial background, his upbringing in the "somewhat more relaxed" environs of Hawaii, and his father's African birth and Muslim faith. From Hanson's point of view, Obama "lacked an African American pedigree" because he was "not a descendant of American slaves," as if the African American community has never included geographic diversity, multiracial members, or immigrants of various backgrounds. The author blasts "wealthy [White] liberals" for questioning the "authenticity" of a Clarence Thomas or Colin Powell. As a Caucasian professor of classical studies and a fellow at the Hoover Institution, Hanson apparently has no qualms about questioning Obama's racial standing.

Hanson (2009) cites conservative campaign rhetoric through the invocation of the Reverend Wright controversy and "[White] guilt" as a factor in Obama's victory, whose election offered "instant exemption from all prior racial guilt" to his White supporters. Much more distressing to Hanson, however, is the notion that Obama has actually engaged some racial issues since coming to power. Beginning with the Holder comments, Hanson draws a straight line through the nomination of judge Sonia Sotomayor as a Supreme Court justice to Obama's criticism of the White police officer who arrested Harvard professor Henry Louis Gates Jr. Interestingly, the author links Obama's racial views with his overseas statements that discussed American history from a critical perspective. The overall impression given by Hanson is that Obama represents a threat to the United States, between his lack of belief in "American exceptionalism" and his "polarizing lead" in "[emphasizing] racial identity to further his own advantage."

Hanson's article is instructive of the paradox facing Obama through the lens of conservative political thinking. It does not matter whether Obama has ever labeled himself "postracial." Hanson and other conservatives are only too happy to invoke the term, without offering a real definition of it, in speaking of the first African American president and the era he supposedly ushered into existence. In the Right's use of the word, positive references to one's racial identity, such as Sotomayor's "wise Latina" remark, are viewed as insidious and archaic. Criticisms of historical and contemporary racial issues, from the slave trade to racial profiling, are downright taboo. Conservatives see no positive way to discuss race in this "postracial" America—unless, of course, *conservatives* are discussing White victimization, criminality among people of color, and race-based notions of patriotism and American identity, all of which Hanson engaged in his article. Indeed, at least one member of the Right, Glenn Beck, has utilized such a vision of "postracialism" to actually label Obama a "racist" and to suggest he has a "deep-seated hatred for [White] people or the [White] culture" (Huff, 2009).

By the end of the summer of 2009, conservative rhetoric against Obama had become downright shrill. Blogger Knute Berger, for instance, pointed to the "creeping Nazi rhetoric against Obama," particularly as the health care debate became more heated (Berger, 2009). Berger indicated that radical viewpoints comparing Obama to Adolf Hitler "are being mainstreamed," logically contributing to hysteria over nonexistent "death panels." Even innocuous Obama strategies are greeted with a firestorm of controversy, like his plan to address students with a back-to-school speech on "personal responsibility" and working hard to achieve goals. The head of the Florida GOP, Jim Greer, assailed Obama for attempting to "indoctrinate" school children with his "socialist ideology" and "liberal propaganda" (Linkins, 2009). In the aftermath of Greer's tirade, conservative parents openly talked about keeping their children out of school or asking their schools not to show the speech (McKinley & Dillon, 2009). Conservative commentator Mark Steyn even "accused Mr. Obama of trying to create a cult of personality, comparing him to Saddam Hussein and Kim Jong-il, the North Korean leader." Apparently, the same voices that attacked any opposition to President Bush's policies as treasonous do not want to hear an African American president lecture children on the importance of personal responsibility.

Conclusion

Some writers have attempted to limit the potential meanings of Obama's election in terms of American race relations. Tim Wise, for example, was deeply troubled by what he dubbed "Racism 2.0": namely, the tendency of some White voters to embrace Obama *because* they see him as "postracial." Such constructs, Wise argued, draw a sharp distinction between African Americans like Obama and the masses of Blacks in the United States who did not have access to his education or professional opportunities. In essence, Racism 2.0 allows Whites to accept individual Blacks who are seen as "different" from the rest of their race, without challenging their racist assumptions about the Black community at large (Wise, 2009, 22-24). Yet Wise noted with alarm the swiftness with which the media at large sought to exonerate White America of racism based on the election. If Obama had lost, he wondered, would these same figures argue that it was proof of the continuation of American racism (p. 27)?

As much as certain media figures would like to believe otherwise, Barack Obama's victory on November 4, 2008, was much more about the building of a successful political coalition across several racial lines than it was about any significant change among White voters. Blacks, Latinos, Asians, young voters of all races—these groups formed the backbone of Obama's constituency. The question, then, as Chuck Todd and Sheldon Gawiser (2009) put it, is whether or not this is the beginning of a new realignment in American politics, one that has the potential to affect the party system for years to come. Todd and Gawiser refused to take the bait this soon after the election and with good reason: The last 15 years clearly demonstrated how quickly a "permanent majority" for either party can evaporate (p. 30).

The authors did point to some important trends, however, that could hold the key to future political alignments. Perhaps most important, the percentage of young White voters, as a share of the entire youth electorate, has dropped precipitously in the last two election cycles. When George W. Bush was elected to his first term, in 2000, Whites represented 74% of voters under the age of 30. Just 8 years later, Whites accounted for only 62% of this demographic, while Blacks composed 18% and Latinos 14%. Todd and Gawiser (2009, pp. 29-32) are quick to point out that the youth vote did not increase dramatically from 2004 to 2008 and that Obama drew more than three quarters of his vote total from people over 30 years of age. Still, Obama's strong showing among an increasingly diverse young demographic (66%) could be important in the years to come. Likewise, with Blacks and Latinos accounting for 38% of *new* voters in this election, the possibility of a coalition between these groups and young White voters could become the basis for a new Democratic coalition.

Such trends, however, will not make themselves apparent for years to come. What is already apparent is that Obama's election had a dramatic and immediate impact on *perceptions* of race relations in the United States, especially among African Americans. Polling numbers showed phenomenal increases in the number of Blacks who felt optimistic about race relations, based largely on the Obama election (CBS News, 2009; CNN, 2009). Such trends, of course, should be welcomed as opportunities to soothe a nation that has witnessed increased racial polarization over the last few decades, thanks to issues such as police brutality, immigration, resegregation of the public schools, and the like. If Obama's election gives hope to people of color that new doors of opportunity have been opened to them, then it has already paid dividends for the nation's psyche.

But the fact of the matter is that the election of Barack Obama to the highest office in the land does not actually resolve any of the problems that have plagued American race relations in recent years. Obama's election, in and of itself, did not bring a single new job to deindustrialized urban sectors or retain a talented young teacher in an inner-city school. His positive campaign did nothing to persuade police officers to value White and Black lives on the same plane, as evidenced by the January 2009 shooting of Oscar Grant in Oakland, California (Stannard & Bulwa, 2009, p. A1). If conservatives have their way, Barack Obama will not have the opportunity to actually use the expanded powers of the 21st-century presidency to tackle the most pressing issues facing many African Americans today. Rather, while continuing the demonization of poor Black communities as a whole, conservatives will continue to use his *individual* success to argue for the end of group politics. Without completely relinquishing the older, more brazen aspects of the *first* Southern Strategy, they will continue to use tranquilizing terms such as *postracial* and *color-blind* to lull America into a false sense that racism died in November of 2008. Their success or failure may well define the legacy of the current presidential administration and the hopes for future Democratic majorities.

Note

1. On sources: Given the impact of new media and technology on contemporary American politics, this article includes substantial attention to blogs and other online sources for opinion and news. Since these media are quickly outpacing newspapers and even nightly news broadcasts from the major networks, I believe it is crucial to incorporate them into my analysis of the recent election and its aftermath. Most of the statistics on the results of the 2008 election, as well as comparative figures for previous elections, came from exit polling conducted by CNN and the *New York Times*, respectively. Full results from both sources are available online.

References

Bennett, W., & Cribb, J. (2009, January 10). *A mountaintop moment: A new era of post-racial politics?* Retrieved March 10, 2009, from http://culture11.com/article/36359

Bennett, W., & Leibsohn, S. (2008, June 24). 10 concerns about Barack Obama. *National Review*. Retrieved March 10, 2009, from http://article.nationalreview.com/?q=MzQ4YTY4YjQyMzRjYjA5MGZlNDBiZTkwYmEyODg5NTc=&w=MA==

Berger, K. (2009, August 18). *Who's a Nazi now?* Retrieved September 4, 2009, from http://crosscut.com/2009/08/18/mossback/19169/

Blumenthal, S. (2008). *The strange death of Republican America: Chronicles of a collapsing party.* New York: Union Square Press.

Boehlert, E. (2009). *Bloggers on the bus: How the Internet changed politics and the press.* New York: Free Press.

Buchanan, P. (2008, March 27). *Why did Obama oppose Connerly on affirmative action?* Retrieved March 9, 2009, from http://www.vdare.com/buchanan/080327_obama.htm

Carter, D. T. (2000). *The politics of rage: George Wallace, the origins of the new conservatism, and the transformation of American politics.* Baton Rouge: Louisiana State University Press.

CBS News. (2009, April 27). *Poll: Blacks See Improved Race Relations.* Retrieved May 15, 2009, from http://www.cbsnews.com/stories/2009/04/27/opinion/polls/main4972532.shtml

Clayton, D. M. (2003). African American women and their quest for Congress. *Journal of Black Studies, 33,* 354-388.

CNN. (2008, November 17). *CNN election center 2008.* Retrieved May 14, 2009, from http://edition.cnn.com/ELECTION/2008/results/president

CNN. (2009, January 19). *Most Blacks say MLK's vision fulfilled, poll finds.* Retrieved May 15, 2009, from http://www.cnn.com/2009/POLITICS/01/19/king.poll

Conason, J. (2008, May 9). *Was Hillary channeling George Wallace?* Retrieved March 8, 2009, from http://www.salon.com/opinion/conason/2008/05/09/clinton_remarks/

De Pasquale, L. (2008, September 18). *Obama watch: Affirmative action election.* Retrieved March 9, 2009, from http://www.humanevents.com/article.php?id=28589

FOX News. (2008, February 25). *Kenya photo worth several sharp words from Clinton, Obama camps.* Retrieved March 8, 2009, from "http://www.foxnews.com/politics/elections/2008/02/25/photo-showing-obama-in-somali-garb-circulated-by-clinton-campaign-source/

Hanson, V. D. (2009, July 27). What happened to our postracial president? *National Review Online.* Retrieved July 27, 2009, from http://article.nationalreview.com?q=ZTRlNDM5YTIxMGUzMjdiM2I5MWFjZDAzZTM3Nzg5N2U=

History Commons. (2008). *Context of "September 22, 2008: Conservative radio host Limbaugh: Obama an Arab, not African-American."* Retrieved March 9, 2009, from http://www.historycommons.org/context.jsp?item=a092208obamaarab

Huff, R. (2009, July 29). Pundit Glenn Beck calls President Barack Obama a "racist," FOX News Channel execs downplay comments. *New York Daily News.* Retrieved July 30, 2009, from http://www.nydailynews.com/news/politics/2009/07/29/2009-07-29_fox_news_glenn_beck_president_barack_obama_is_racist_with_deepseated_hatred_of_w.html

Ifill, G. (2009) *The breakthrough: Politics and race in the age of Obama.* New York: Doubleday.

Linkins, J. (2009, September 2). *Jim Greer, Florida GOP chair, warns that Obama "Back to School" speech will foment socialism.* Retrieved September 4, 2009, from http://www.huffingtonpost.com/2009/09/02/jim-greer-florida-gop-cha_n_275287.html

McCollister, R. (2008, November 17). *Buck stops with Obama now*. Retrieved March 8, 2009, from https://www.businessreport.com/news/2008/nov/17/buck-stops-obama-now/

McKinley, J. C., Jr., , & Dillon, S. (2009, September 3). Some parents oppose Obama school speech. *New York Times*. Retrieved September 4, 2009, from http://www.nytimes.com/2009/09/04/us/04school.html

Media Matters. (2008a, February 8). *Coulter: Obama's "first big accomplishment" was "being born half-Black. . . . He wouldn't be running for president if he weren't half-Black."* Retrieved March 9, 2009, from http://mediamatters.org/research/200802080017

Media Matters. (2008b, October 28). *Savage on Obama: "America's first affirmative action candidate about to become president."* Retrieved May 14, 2009, from http://mediamatters.org/research/200810280016

Metacafe. (2008, August 22). *Limbaugh blames affirmative action for Obama's success*. Retrieved March 9, 2009, from http://www.metacafe.com/watch/1652458/limbaugh_blames_affirmative_action_for_obamas_success/

National exit polls table. (2008, November 5). *New York Times*. Retrieved March 3, 2009, from http://elections.nytimes.com/2008/results/president/national-exit-polls.html

Neiwert, D. (2008, November 5). *Bill Bennett: Obama's win means "You don't take excuses anymore" from minorities*. Retrieved March 8, 2009, from http://crooksandliars.com/david-neiwert/bill-bennett-obama-wins-means-no-mor

Owenby, A. (2008, November 7). *Affirmatively over: Obama election signals end of affirmative action in America*. Retrieved March 8, 2009, from http://aowenby.wordpress.com/2008/11/07/affirmatively-over-obama-election-signals-end-of-affirmative-action-in-america/

Rich, F. (2008a, October 11). The terrorist Barack Hussein Obama. *New York Times*. Retrieved May 15, 2009, from http://www.nytimes.com/2008/10/12/opinion/12rich.html

Rich, F. (2008b, November 9). It still felt good the morning after. *New York Times*, p. WK9.

Schlafly, P. (2008, October 28). *Big media pull out all stops to elect Obama*. Retrieved March 9, 2009, from http://www.creators.com/opinion/phyllis-schlafly/big-media-pull-out-all-stops-to-elect-obama.html

Sides, J. (2008, November 5). *Truths and myths about the 2008 election, part II*. Retrieved March 2, 2009, from http://www.themonkeycage.org/2008/11/truths_and_myths_about_the_200.html

Signorile, C. (2008, March 11). *Geraldine Ferraro calls Barack Obama the affirmative action candidate*. Retrieved March 8, 2009, from http://constitutionallyright.com/2008/03/11/geraldine-ferraro-calls-barack-obama-the-affirmative-action-candidate/

Stannard, M. B., & Bulwa, D. (2009, January 7). BART shooting captured on video. *San Francisco Chronicle*, p. A1.

Stone, W. J., & Rapoport, R. B. (2001). It's Perot stupid! The legacy of the 1992 Perot movement in the major-party system, 1994-2000. *PS: Political Science and Politics, 34*(1), 49-58.

Thernstrom, A., & Thernstrom, S. (2008, November 11). Racial gerrymandering is unnecessary. *Wall Street Journal*. Retrieved March 9, 2009, from http://online.wsj.com/article/SB122637373937516543.html

Todd, C., & Gawiser, S. (2009). *How Barack Obama won: A state-by-state guide to the historic 2008 election*. New York: Vintage Books.

Toplikar, M. (2008, October 22). Anger, fear, and racism follow Palin rally. *Las Vegas Sun*. Retrieved May 15, 2009, from http://www.lasvegassun.com/videos/2008/oct/22/983/

Varadarajan, T. (2009, February 23). America, a nation of cowards. *Forbes*. Retrieved March 9, 2009, from http://www.forbes.com/2009/02/22/obama-eric-holder-racism-america-cowards-opinions-columnists_attorney_general.html

Weiner, R. (2008, October 16). Racism at Palin rally: "Blacks will take over." *Huffington Post*. Retrieved May 15, 2009, from http://www.huffingtonpost.com/2008/10/16/racism-at-mccain-rally-bl_n_135303.html

Wise, T. (2009). *Between Barack and a hard place: Racism and White denial in the age of Obama*. San Francisco: City Lights Books.

Younge, G. (2008, March 20). Obama, Ferraro, Wright: "Postracial" meets racism. *The Nation*. Retrieved July 28, 2009, from http://www.thenation.com/doc/20080407/younge

Zernike, K., & Sussman, D. (2008, November 6). For pollsters, the racial effect that wasn't. *New York Times*, p. P8.

3

TURNING OUT THE CENTER: RACIAL POLITICS AND AFRICAN AGENCY IN THE OBAMA ERA

Philip S. S. Howard

University of Toronto

Since the time that it became evident that Barack Obama was a serious contender for the Democratic Party nomination, a number of intriguing questions have been raised with respect to the implications of his bid for president for African Americans, race, and the struggle against racism. For example, questions have been raised about whether Obama will be an African American president or a president who happens to be African American and what the difference might be between these two positions. Others have wondered whether the imperative for him to be a president for all Americans conflicts with the hope that he will be a president who promotes the interests of *African* Americans and whether his election will help or hinder the cause of racial equity and justice.

Fundamentally, these are questions that focus attention on the intricacies and contradictions of African American identity as well as on the ways that race organizes how power is distributed within racially stratified Eurocentric American society (and indeed other European and North American nations). Specifically, the Obama presidency prompts us to think more deeply about African agency and how it might be expressed in different contexts. Through the historical examples of the civil rights movements in the United States and decolonization movements the world over, we know a great deal about what African agency looks like when it challenges dominant institutions from the outside.[1] What we know less about is what African agency and a racially progressive politics might look like when they challenge dominant institutions (e.g., the U.S. government) from within. In other words, is African agency possible within dominant institutions? Can a racially progressive politics

Source: Journal of Black Studies, January 2010; vol. 40, 3: pp. 380-394.

be pursued from "the inside," or, in what seems like a contradiction, must African Americans who seek racial justice and equity be perpetually relegated to the margins? If African agency is possible from within dominant institutions, what does it look like from this location, and what strategies and arrangements might support its full realization?

This article endeavors to be a contribution to the ongoing conversation about race raised by the Obama presidency. I write as an African Canadian academic, and I am keenly aware that there are many of the fine details and day-to-day particulars of the Obama saga of which I may not be aware. Thus, although I engage the above questions in the context of the Obama presidency, my hope is that this article will be a contribution to a much broader conversation about African agency.

The African political concerns at the root of the above questions point us toward an Afrocentric discursive framework as the appropriate framework within which to contemplate these questions. The article therefore grapples with the questions in relation to Afrocentric understandings of agency and community, hoping to maintain a rigorous antiracist politics without undermining the agency of Africans who find themselves within dominant institutions.

African Agency in Dominant Centers of Power: Contours, Contradictions, and Constraints

In many ways, to examine the Obama presidency, its meaning, possibilities, and perils, is to revisit one of the unresolved questions of sociological inquiry—that of the relationship between agency and structure. In particular, with regard to race, it is to analyze "the dilemma of power in a racial politic" (Asante, 2007, p. 105).

Some have taken up this discussion from a fairly predictable liberal, postmodern, and intensely individualistic position, seeming to be largely concerned in their analyses about whether and to what extent Obama, regardless of his personal politics, might be able to transcend race and/or possibly be rid of any particular (ostensible) burden of responsibility to the African American community (see, e.g., Bai, 2008; Steele, 2008).[2] Yet for others of us, the tension between agency and structure is salient in a very different manner.

Afrocentric discourse has consistently asserted *African* agency—here understood as the right and duty of Africans to interpret the world on their own cultural terms (Asante, 1998, pp. 19-23, 1999, p. 108, 2002). Agency within Afrocentric discourse is intricately linked to the African notion of the interdependence of individual and community (to be further discussed later in this article) and therefore is less about the *individual's* possibility of race transcendence and much more about the individual's ability to assert one's *community* (racial/cultural) interests (Lundy, 2003, pp. 465-466) and to do so in opposition to symbolic and structural forces that attempt to dislocate the African individual from her or his community and, ultimately, from the possibility of true African liberation. Analytically, this Afrocentric understanding of agency also helps us to strike the delicate balance between assessing the centeredness of particular African individuals on the one hand with, on the other hand, the tendency to dismiss outright the agency and ability of Africans to make decisions in their own interest—particularly within complex and contradictory social situations (see, e.g., Lundy, 2003). As Asante (1999) has written,

> The Afrocentrists . . . believe strongly in the autonomy of the African's agency, even an autonomy that gives the African the right to choose or not to choose to ally at certain points. In analysis, this means that the Afrocentrist seeks any method to explicate the agency of Africans in any given situation. (p. 108)

President Obama is currently found in just such a complex and contradictory situation requiring an explication of African agency. This is because we might consider the Obama situation to be a question about the contradiction inherent in inhabiting, as Obama does, both a (or *the*) central office of power in the United States *as well as* an oppressed location by virtue of his racial positioning within the American racial hierarchy that places Blacks at or near the bottom. We are interested in the extent to which Obama (if he is so inclined) might resist the limits of mainstream, color-blind, racial discourse and the structures that surreptitiously dare him to suggest that racial injustice might indeed still be a reality in America and to be a president who acts in the interest of African Americans. So what might African agency look like from such a center of dominant power?

When we consider the African agency involved in the Obama presidency, we must first recognize that there are two levels, however interrelated, at which we can perform this analysis. Steele (2008) alludes to this when he distinguishes between looking to Obama to "*be* something" or "*do* something" (p. 133). The first level is the symbolic level. At this first level, we consider the agency involved simply in the fact that an African American has decided to enter the presidential race, has become the leader of one of the two major political parties in the United States and now occupies the office of president. This article does not focus on this level. However, suffice it to say that the symbolism is enormous. Obama's occupying the office of president speaks of possibility, persistence, and perseverance and of audacity and hope, as his writing (Obama, 2006) and campaign have underlined. In itself, the decision to enter this race in the first place, realizing how he is racially positioned in American society, is for Obama (as it was for the several other African Americans who have sought to be president) an act of African agency—a decision not to be marginal in the construction of the history of his time

(Asante, 2007, p. 106). Yet it must be admitted that the agency demonstrated here is largely symbolic. The African agency here flows from how Obama's body positions him—regardless of whether he has pursued the presidency out of a desire to make a difference for African Americans and advance the cause of racial justice or whether he has pursued it purely out of selfish, individualistic ambition. Furthermore, there are those who read the fact of the Obama presidency either as evidence that the United States has entered a postrace era or as confirmation of an already long-standing reality in which race does not matter (e.g., Bai, 2008). Hence, from an Afrocentric and antiracist perspective, the symbolism is ambiguous and limited (Bonilla-Silva, 2008). Thus, our analysis must go further. At the more substantive level of doing and not just being, the Afrocentrist must ask the Afrocentric question: "Now that he has gained the office, what will *this* African American president do to serve the agency and interests of African Americans and, more broadly, the cause of racial justice?" Quite simply, now that Obama is in office and lauded as the first *African American* president, the African American community may legitimately require him to "put up."

Yet we cannot lose sight of the fact that one of the longstanding contradictions of American democracy (and other "Western" democracies) is that serving the democratic rights of people of Color (in this case, African Americans) seems to be considered within dominant discourse to be at loggerheads with serving the rights of "all Americans," while, in actual fact, these projects should be seen as reinforcing each other. For example, addressing the injustices of the criminal justice system, education, housing, banking, and other institutions toward African Americans is regarded in dominant discourse as though it meant bowing to illegitimate demands of a special interest group for special privileges rather than as a necessary step in securing universal access to the lofty democratic rights and privileges about which the United States boasts. This, of course, simply highlights the way in which the citizenship of African Americans is compromised and African Americans are never quite "American." In other words, full de facto citizenship is not extended to African Americans, and Americanness is implicitly held to mean *White* Americanness. We see, then, that White dominance and privilege are embedded in the fabric of the society yet made to seem fair, normal, and unremarkable.

Given this state of affairs, there are always risks involved with doing the antiracist work of challenging Whiteness and systems of racial dominance (Dei, 2008, p. 69). Thus, intellectual honesty will not allow us to easily overlook or trivialize the fact that, president or not, Obama faces considerable risks if he is to speak out against and address racial injustice in America and thereby truly be a president for all Americans. In the U.S. political system, the office of president is structurally limited by a number of built-in checks and balances that limit the ability of the president to single-handedly see his policies through to realization.[3] Rather, the president must be able to build and maintain consensus. Furthermore, the historical function of the office in maintaining the status quo of White privilege and upholding White American interests (Asante, 2007, p. 115) also limits Obama's agency in this situation. The normalization of racial injustice makes challenging White dominance and privilege and pursuing racial justice appear as though it were fundamentally unfair. Obama's position and efficacy are therefore extremely precarious, as race very much has the potential to be a consensus breaker—even within his own party. Yet act Obama must if the symbolic meaning of his presidency is not to turn against African Americans and become a tool for the shirking of governmental and White racial responsibility (along with community-level responsibility and the responsibility of all people of Color) to recognize and oppose racial inequity.

One possible manner in which Obama might respond to this imperative while managing the risks flows from the argument that African Americans bear a disproportionate share of the consequences of broken systems such as education, health care, taxation, and criminal justice. Accordingly, so the argument goes, the fact that Obama seeks to reform these systems will serve African Americans in significant ways, and the fact that he has made these, as opposed to other priorities, his platform and agenda reveals his commitment to serving the African American community. However, the shortcomings of this kind of liberal argument are immediately evident to the critical antiracist. First, this argument clearly subordinates a race analysis to a class-based analysis and conflates the two, suggesting that if we address the injustices of an inequitable class system, racial inequity will take care of itself. It fails to recognize race as an axis of injustice that operates, at times, independently of class (as evidenced by the racial injustice experienced by middle- and upper-class African Americans despite their class status). Second, the argument does not problematize the fact that Blacks and other people of Color suffer so disproportionately within the American system, nor does it address the fact that uplift for all within this skewed system may raise the bar but is doomed to leave the racial hierarchy intact. Antiracists and critical race theorists have long insisted that within a fundamentally racially inequitable social arrangement, color-blind strategies cannot achieve racially just ends (Bonilla-Silva, 2003a, 2003b; Brown et al., 2003; Carr, 1997; Dei, 2006; Hamilton, 2009). Thus, paradoxically, this color-blind approach may well somewhat improve the lot of African Americans in general without ever challenging racial injustice. Clearly, such an outcome would be grossly unacceptable. Now, it may be that there is some way that race-conscious reforms could be quietly instituted without declaring them so—though I struggle to imagine how that would be possible. In either case, such a strategy would be dangerous in terms of its implications for racial discourse and its potential to reinforce the dominant fantasy that racism is no longer an important concern in American society.

It seems evident, then, that from an Afrocentric, antiracist perspective, it is insufficient for Obama to work through color-blind policies or even quietly use his office to do those things that he feels will serve African American interests. It is incumbent on Obama, in addition to whatever else he might do, to at some point actively contribute toward shifting the discourse around race and racism to undermine liberal race discourse and move it in the direction of a more critical discourse about race. The prevailing dominant understandings of race make this a necessity. At present, dominant liberal discourse deals with race and racism largely through denial, silences, and omissions (Dei, 1999, 2000, pp. 23-24; Razack, 2002, p. 3) and through color blindness and coded language (Kailin, 1999, p. 739; Lipman, 1997, p. 19; Morrison, 1992, p. 6), which undermine the salience of race and racism and suggest that racism in America is a phenomenon of the past. Against the background of the ambiguous symbolic meaning of his presidency, then, for Obama to remain silent about race or to attempt to be racially progressive on the down-low is to play directly into conservative arguments that declare that the real problem facing African Americans is not race and to strengthen discourses that blame those oppressed by racial injustice for their own plight. As an African American president, and given the failure of his White predecessors to do so as they ought to have, President Obama must seek out opportunities to reinsert the silenced histories and present realities of African Americans into the national conversation (Hamilton, 2009), and certainly into his rhetoric of change, while implementing policy that effectively redresses racial inequity.

Yet here again the risks are significant for Obama. In the poisoned context of the denial of racism and normalized White dominance, how does Obama, from his Black body, speak the realities of race and racism without immediately being dismissed and rejected by those who choose to be convinced by the prevailing discourse? Indeed, there has been much ado about his being the first "credible" Black candidate for president, and this dubious credential has largely been based on the distinctions made between him and previous Black candidates—such as Chisholm, Jackson, and Sharpton—who were more clearly associated with, and grounded in, the civil rights movement (see, e.g., Smith, 2007; also see Cose, 2007; Sharpton, 2008; Walters, 2007, pp. 15-16) and who are/were dismissed as consumed by racial politics, unable to be impartial, and lacking a vision for all Americans (see Alston, 2008). Indeed, it is this distance and his own ambiguity in the face of it that have allowed him to garner sufficient political support to become president, and conceivably it is the same distance and ambiguity that will be necessary for him to maintain enough political consensus to get anything done as president. These are the things that might be jeopardized by his speaking out, though I maintain that it is imperative that he does.

However, it is in this matter of moving the public discourse on race in a more critical direction that Obama's record as president/presidential candidate has not been stellar. Thus far in the unfolding story of the Obama presidency, we have seen few if any of the bold steps that African Americans might wish for Obama to take. Many of his public statements have been (deliberately) ambiguous—such as his comments about his vision for a Supreme Court justice (Murray, 2009), and his only substantial discussion of race and the plight of African Americans—the "More Perfect Union" speech in March 2008—did nothing to shake problematic understandings of race and racism in America. Indeed, it seems to me that the March 2008 speech in Philadelphia—in which he largely makes Blacks' concerns about racism to simply be holdovers from the past while he validates Whites' anxieties about unfairly paying the price for past injustices—could hardly have been more closely aligned with the popular liberal discourse on race (see Logan, 2008).

Yet we need to be cognizant of the fact that, at the time of this writing, he is not yet 4 months into at least a 4-year presidency, and given our discussion of risk above, it is clear that any intentions Obama might have to take some of the bold steps we hope to see will need to be carefully planned and timed. Certainly, strategy is necessary. Yet from an Afrocentric, antiracist position, we also have reason and right to ask where the boundaries might be between strategy and capitulation and between a politics of biding one's time and the mistake of waiting too late. We also have good reason to wonder whether Obama's race speech, if we take it to be delivered in a moment of expediency in order not to abort the bid for the presidency, has not limited or negated his potential to ever speak race more critically.

Turning the Inside Out: Supporting African Agency at the Center

It is futile at this point to speculate about whether Obama intends at some later date to make a clear, public stand that measures up to the standards of a more critical race analysis. It is even more futile to argue about what we think Obama's stance might really be amid his tendency to "cast issues in universal terms" (Walters, 2007, p. 22) that seem ambiguous or to guess whether, in his race speech, he has spoken his true position or just hidden some deeper, more critical politics that he ostensibly holds internally and intends to unveil at some future date.[4] These are matters that we cannot know in advance (despite our telling investments in believing one way or the other). However, a much more fruitful discussion would be one that considers how, as a broader

African community, we might collectively support and protect African agency at the center of dominant institutions.

This, for me, is a deeply important question—perhaps the most important question so far in the contemplation of the Obama presidency. I say this in light of Obama's personal and institutional track record. What we see of him now seems quite out of step with what we seem to know of him otherwise. Obama's trajectory and commitments have not been those of the typical liberal centrist or racial conservative (Walters, 2007, p. 22). Walters (2007) writes,

> [Obama] begins the cultural presentation with strong assets: He is of African descent, he married a Black woman, he belongs to a Black church, and he lives in a racially integrated community. This cultural context alone defines him as very different from the normative Black conservative and creates the expected access and level of association with the Black community that is the starting point for accountability for any Black politician. (p. 22)

There is not space to do so here, but without belaboring the point, in the present racial context, the above credentials are meaningful when considering a professional African American man from a multiracial family—at least they seem to be for Obama (1995, pp. 99-100). Furthermore, the events of Obama's life, at least in his own telling of them, seem to indicate that he held, at least at that time, quite a radical race analysis. The title and subtitle of his first book, *Dreams of My Father: A Story of Race and Inheritance* (1995), seem to declare his intention to make a personal statement about race, identity, and community. In it, he indicts those Blacks who seek to transcend race and the significance of being a part of the African American community, while he also indicts the privilege of normalized Whiteness (pp. 99-100). We also know that between his undergraduate degree and his entry into law school, Obama worked as a full-time community organizer in the primarily African American communities on the South Side of Chicago.

Also very salient is his relationship at Harvard with Derrick Bell, a foremost critical race scholar and one of the founders of critical race theory. Obama was a student of Bell and supporter of him in his public, yet controversial, protest against the university for its failure to hire African American women scholars to tenured positions (Hebel, 2007b). Likewise, his affiliation with Trinity United Church of Christ and its Black value system (Trinity United Church of Christ, n.d.) could hardly have been accidental or incidental and cannot be thought not to have shaped Obama's thinking—regardless of the fact that he has now distanced himself from that congregation.

Very importantly, on his election as the first Black editor of the *Harvard Law Review*, Obama clearly understood the ways that the symbolism of that "famous first"—perfectly analogous to his present situation—might be read and spoke up quickly to undermine it. He is reported to have said,

> The fact that I've been elected shows a lot of progress. . . .
>
> But it's important that stories like mine aren't used to say that everything is O.K. for blacks [*sic*]. You have to remember that for every one of me, there are hundreds or thousands of black students with at least equal talent who don't get a chance. (Butterfield, 1990)

Finally, Obama has been outspoken about his support of affirmative action based on race. He states that we cannot dismiss the significance of historical *and present* racism in creating inequity, which the society now has a responsibility to redress (Hebel, 2007a, 2007b). And as recently as in his 2006 book, Obama displays quite a critical and nuanced understanding of race and its operation in the United States (see, e.g., Obama, 2006, pp. 235-236, 242-244).

Thus, over time and until very recently, Obama had a clear critical race analysis and consciousness that appears to be quite inconsistent with his present rhetoric and avoidance. The point I am making here is that the mediating circumstance has been his bid for the presidency and the lack of popularity of such critical positions with a large portion of his voter base. In response to this push for the center, Obama has either abandoned his critical race politics in order to curry the favor of the dominant or been brainwashed, or he is treading carefully (timidly?) and strategically as he plans how he can use the office in a way that is consistent with the social and political positions he has taken in the past. Again, we cannot know which of these is true, but in any of these cases we are contemplating the threat that is posed to African agency as it moves to the center of dominant social institutions. If we know this, then rather than leave it to chance or fate, what might be done to protect and support African agency at the center? In the remaining portion of this article, I hope to gesture toward some possible starting points. In answering this question, I suggest that because we are considering African agency (which is group based), the Afrocentric understanding of the relationship between the community and the individual is salient.

Afrocentric discourse points out that "the concept of *individual* makes sense only within the concept of *community*" (Dei, 1994, p. 12, italics original) and that "the individual cannot be understood separate from other people" (Schiele, 1994, p. 154). This position does not suggest that there is no value to individuality, but it does argue that individuals realize their fullest purpose in the context of community. In other words, "the dichotomy is not between the *individual* and *community*, but between the *competitive individual* isolated from his or her community and the *cooperative individual* enriched by the community" (Dei, 1994, p. 12, italics original). If we thus unsettle the dichotomy between community and individual, then with regard to Obama and his position of power we also unsettle the dichotomy between inside and outside, margin and center. In other words, to whatever extent that Obama considers himself to be "rooted in the Black community" (Tapper & Hinman, 2007), he is not alone at the center, but he takes the rest of the community there with him, even as he is simultaneously at the margins (and the locations between these poles on this continuum) with other African Americans.

This has implications both for Obama and for the rest of the African American community if we want to realize the full potential of having an African American president. First, Obama may need to reconsider and reinforce his own rootedness. A study conducted by the author in which he investigated the relationships between Blacks and Whites who collaborate in racial equity work determined that, in the opinion of Black racial equity workers, one of the most important strategies for ensuring the success of the racial equity project is for them to nurture strong relationships with the Black community, which can support them as they navigate the contradictions of interracial collaborations for racial equity (Howard, 2009, pp. 330-335). In his present position, Obama may owe as much to the White and other non-Black voters who have placed him where he is as he does to his Black supporters, yet the findings of the above study suggest that the success of any initiative that specifically addresses racial injustice is dependent on his working closely with the African American community rather than in isolation.

At the same time, the African American community at large cannot afford to simply stand back to wait and see. We are also responsible both for holding Obama to account in constructive ways and for creating the conditions whereby he might be successful in efforts to support the interests of African Americans. Civil rights activists, notably Al Sharpton, have already forcefully made the case for their own continued relevance (Alston, 2008; Pearson, 2008; Sharpton, 2008). Sharpton says,

> Leaders like me must keep him accountable, because to allow Obama to ignore the plight of black America would fan the flames of racial injustice. . . . We must recognize that without the appropriate consciousness-raising by civil rights leaders, race issues could either doom such a leader to a failed one-term presidency or doom America to remaining hostage to its inglorious racial past. (Sharpton, 2008)

Unlike what some have charged (e.g., Alston, 2008), this is not spoken simply out of rank self-interestedness but from a well-grounded understanding of community and the African American civil rights cause. I suggest that Afrocentric African American academics also have a responsibility to take up the role of engaged public intellectuals (Giroux, 2004; Said, 1994) and action-oriented antiracists (Dei, 1996, p. 25, 2005, p. 12) to continue to shape the discourse around race and to seek out those moments when we can insert critical ideas into the public (not just academic) discourse on race. Furthermore, although Obama may not be ignorant of critical race perspectives, we may not necessarily be able to assume that he has the depth of analysis that Afrocentric and critical race scholars might have. The pressures and contradictions of his present position as well as continual bombardment with the seductive mainstream commonsense discourses of Whiteness to which he is now overexposed are formidable forces against which Obama must stand. The reiteration and rehearsal of critical positions with which he is not unfamiliar and the direct application of these to his situation (as in this journal issue) may well be what it takes to either keep him in a position of community centeredness (if not African centeredness) or bring him to such a position (again). With a president with an intellectual bent, it is not unreasonable to expect that he may indeed be paying attention to what we have to say.

African American entertainers have the ear of the public and influence popular culture well beyond the boundaries of the African American community. They too have a role to play. In a manner similar to what some of them did in the wake of the Hurricane Katrina crisis, they should be raising the salient issues of the day as they affect African Americans. Finally, all African Americans have a responsibility to continue to present their legitimate concerns and their dissatisfaction with the continued deferral and denial of their full citizenship through whatever channels that make themselves available or that can be turned to this purpose. They/we must make clear the urgency of the situation and press the president to address their/our concerns as an integral part of addressing the concerns of "all" Americans.

One thing is certain: This is an opportune moment for African Americans. An African American has managed to win the office of president long before many would have thought was possible just a few short years ago. Furthermore, this particular president has a more impressive history of critical race awareness and action than many might have expected in the first African American president, given the prevailing state of popular race discourse and the compromises that many make to achieve power. In a show of true African community-based agency, African Americans must together grasp the moment and maximize its potential for African liberation.

Notes

1. *We*, in this article, refers to the community of those with a political affiliation with antiracism and Afrocentricity as they are laid out in this article and who agree with the arguments put forth here.
2. In speaking of the African American community, I do not intend to suggest that this is a politically unified monolith. Clearly it is not. Yet within the racially

stratified United States, African Americans are held together by common interests despite the individual understandings, articulations, and levels of fidelity of individual African Americans of or to those interests.

3. In a parliamentary system, such as that in Canada, the prime minister has considerably more power in this regard than the United States president. However, Canada has never had a prime minister who was not White.

4. While this article was in press, Obama made a statement that undermined the relevance of ongoing colonial relations to the current political climate in African nations (see AllAfrica.com, 2009) and another that spoke to the ongoing significance of racial profiling in the United States in the wake of the Henry Louis Gates incident (see Sweet, 2009). Thus, the ambiguity about his position on race continues. Consistent with what I have been arguing in this article, it is not surprising given normalized White dominance and denial that the former statement was eagerly seized on by mainstream media outlets in a bid to blame Africa alone for its plight (see, e.g., Pflanz, 2009; Spillius, 2009)—and Obama needs to be aware of this media tendency whenever he calls for Black responsibility without a corresponding call for White accountability—while the latter statement resulted in questions about his ostensible race neutrality (e.g., George, 2009) and, in some cases, in his being accused of being racist or hating Whites (Associated Press, 2009; Martin, 2009).

References

AllAfrica.com. (2009). *Interview of President Obama by AllAfrica.com: Obama discusses governance, development and upcoming Ghana trip.* Retrieved August 1, 2009, from http://www.america.gov/st/texttrans-english/2009/July/20090708101135emffen0.6657221.html

Alston, J. (2008). Al, Jesse and Barack. *Newsweek, 151*(15), 36-37.

Asante, M. K. (1998). *The Afrocentric idea* (Rev. ed.). Philadelphia: Temple University Press.

Asante, M. K. (1999). *The painful demise of Eurocentrism: An Afrocentric response to critics.* Trenton, NJ: Africa World Press.

Asante, M. K. (2002). Intellectual dislocation: Applying analytic Afrocentricity to narratives of identity. *Howard Journal of Communications, 13*, 97-110.

Asante, M. K. (2007). Barack Obama and the dilemma of power: An Africological observation. *Journal of Black Studies, 38*, 105-115.

Associated Press. (2009, July 29). *Fox News host says Obama is "a racist": Glenn Beck claims president has "a deep-seated hatred for White people."* Retrieved August 5, 2009, from http://www.msnbc.msn.com/id/32197648/ns/politics-more_politics/

Bai, M. (2008, August 6). Is Obama the end of Black politics? *New York Times.* Retrieved March 19, 2009, from http://www.nytimes.com

Bonilla-Silva, E. (2003a). "New racism," color-blind racism, and the future of Whiteness in America. In A. W. Doane, & E. Bonilla-Silva (Eds.), *White out: The continuing significance of racism* (pp. 271-284). New York: Routledge.

Bonilla-Silva, E. (2003b). *Racism without racists: Color-blind racism and the persistence of racial inequality in the United States.* Lanham, MD: Rowman and Littlefield.

Bonilla-Silva, E. (2008, July 15). *The social significance of Barack Obama: Will change happen in Obamerica?* (Message posted to http://contexts.org/obama). Retrieved March 19, 2009, from http://contexts.org/obama/2008/07/15/will-change-happen-in-obamerica/

Brown, M. K., Carnoy, M., Currie, E., Duster, T., Oppenheimer, D. B., & Shultz, M. M. (2003). *Whitewashing race: The myth of a color-blind society.* Berkeley: University of California Press.

Butterfield, F. (1990, February 6). First Black elected to head Harvard's Law Review. *New York Times.* Retrieved March 19, 2009, from http://www.nytimes.com

Carr, L. G. (1997). *"Color-blind" racism.* Thousand Oaks, CA: Sage.

Cose, E. (2007). Opinion: A race away from the past; He isn't a product of the civil-rights movement. Maybe that's why Obama's got a chance. *Newsweek.* Retrieved March 19, 2009, from http://www.newsweek.com/id/70166

Dei, G. S. (1994). Afrocentricity: A cornerstone of pedagogy. *Anthropology and Education Quarterly, 25*(1), 3-28.

Dei, G. S. (1996). *Anti-racism education: Theory and practice.* Halifax, Canada: Fernwood.

Dei, G. S. (1999). The denial of difference: Reframing anti-racist praxis. *Race, Ethnicity and Education, 2*(1), 17-37.

Dei, G. S. (2000). Towards an anti-racism discursive framework. In G. S. Dei, & A. Calliste (Eds.), *Power, knowledge and anti-racism education: A critical reader* (pp. 23-40). Halifax, Canada: Fernwood.

Dei, G. S. (2005). Critical issues in anti-racist research methodologies: An introduction. In G. S. Dei, & G. S. Johal (Eds.), *Critical issues in anti-racist research methodologies* (pp. 1-27). New York: Peter Lang.

Dei, G. S. (2006). "We cannot be color blind": Race, antiracism, and the subversion of dominant thinking. In E. W. Ross, & V. Ooka Pang (Eds.), *Race, ethnicity and education* (Praeger perspectives series; pp. 25-42). Westport, CT: Greenwood.

Dei, G. S. (2008). *Racists beware: Uncovering racial politics in the post modern society.* Rotterdam, Netherlands: Sense.

George, R. (2009, July 24). *Obama's "stupid" response on Gates: A "stupid" response to a question on race.* Retrieved August 1, 2009, from http://www.nbcnewyork.com/news/archive/Skipping-The-Record.html

Giroux, H. A. (2004). Edward Said and the politics of worldliness: Toward a "rendezvous of victory." *Cultural Studies ↔ Critical Methodologies, 4*(3), 339-349.

Hamilton, H. (2009). For Obama, a missed opportunity for a teachable moment. *Race, Racism and the Law.* Retrieved May 14, 2009, from http://academic.udayton.edu/race/ObamaandRacism/Obama07.htm

Hebel, S. (2007a). An interview with Barack Obama: "The most important skill is knowledge." *Chronicle of Higher Education, 54*(12), A24.

Hebel, S. (2007b). Obama, once a leader at Harvard Law, is now a favorite of academe. *Chronicle of Higher Education, 54*(12), A24-A25.

Howard, P. (2009). *The double-edged sword: A critical race Africology of collaborations between Blacks and Whites in racial equity work.* Unpublished doctoral thesis, Ontario Institute for Studies in Education, University of Toronto, Toronto, Canada.

Kailin, J. (1999). How White teachers perceive the problem of racism in their schools: A case study in "liberal" Lakeview. *Teachers College Record*, 100(4), 724-750.

Lipman, P. (1997). Restructuring in context: A case study of teacher participation and the dynamics of ideology, race, and power. *American Educational Research Journal*, 34(1), 3-37.

Logan, E. (2008, August 11). *The social significance of Barack Obama* (Comment 16 posted to http://contexts.org/obama). Retrieved March 19, 2009, from http://contexts.org/obama

Lundy, G. F. (2003). The myths of oppositional culture. *Journal of Black Studies*, 33, 450-467.

Martin, A. (2009, July 24). *Obama's response to Henry Gates incident is affirmative action run amok, says Illinoisan.* Retrieved August 1, 2009, from http://www.pr-inside.com/print1407167.htm

Morrison, T. (1992). *Playing in the dark: Whiteness and the literary imagination.* New York: Vintage.

Murray, M. (2009). *Context of Obama's empathy remark.* Retrieved May 19, 2009, from http://firstread.msnbc.msn.com/archive/2009/05/01/1918695.aspx

Obama, B. H. (1995). *Dreams of my father: A story of race and inheritance.* New York: Three Rivers Press.

Obama, B. H. (2006). *The audacity of hope: Thoughts on reclaiming the American dream.* New York: Three Rivers Press.

Pearson, R. (2008, July 14). *Al Sharpton on responsibility, civil rights* (Message posted to http://www.swamppolitics.com/). Retrieved March 19, 2009, from http://www.swamppolitics.com/news/politics/blog/2008/07/al_sharpton_civil_rights.html

Pflanz, M. (2009, July 11). *Barack Obama tells Africa to stop blaming the West for its woes on historic Ghana visit.* Retrieved August 1, 2009, from http://www.telegraph.co.uk/news/worldnews/northamerica/usa/barackobama/5804828/Barack-Obama-tells-Africa-to-stop-blaming-the-West-for-its-woes-on-historic-Ghana-visit.html

Razack, S. H. (2002). When place becomes race. In S. H. Razack (Ed.), *Race, space, and the law: Unmapping a White settler society* (pp. 1-20). Toronto, Canada: Between the Lines.

Said, E. W. (1994). *Representations of the intellectual: The 1993 Reith lectures.* New York: Pantheon.

Schiele, J. H. (1994). Afrocentricity: Implications for higher education. *Journal of Black Studies*, 25, 150-169.

Sharpton, A. (2008, November 6). *Rev. Al Sharpton: Barack Obama's historic achievement: It's an inspiring day, but civil rights march must continue.* Retrieved March 19, 2009, from http://www.eurweb.com/story/eur48407.cfm

Smith, B. (2007, January 27). *Clinton woos Black vote, targets Obama.* Retrieved March 19, 2009, from http://www.politico.com/news/stories/0107/2402.html

Spillius, A. (2009, July 9). *Barack Obama tells Africa to stop blaming colonialism for problems*. Retrieved August 1, 2009, from http://www.telegraph.co.uk/news/worldnews/africaandindianocean/5778804/Barack-Obama-tells-Africa-to-stop-blaming-colonialism-for-problems.html

Steele, S. (2008). *A bound man: Why we are excited about Obama and why he can't win*. New York: Free Press.

Sweet, L. (2009, July 22). Obama tells Lynn Sweet police acted "stupidly" in arresting Gates (Interview transcript). *Chicago Sun Times*. Retrieved August 1, 2009, from http://blogs.suntimes.com/sweet/2009/07/obama_tells_lynn_sweet_police.html

Tapper, J., & Hinman, K. (2007, February 11). *Obama takes hits, keeps on campaigning: Candidate addresses criticism from foreign leader, and the role race may play in the campaign*. Retrieved March 19, 2009, from http://abcnews.go.com/WNT/Politics/Story?id=2867210&page=1

Trinity United Church of Christ. (n.d.). *Black value system*. Retrieved May 15, 2009, from http://www.trinitychicago.org

Walters, R. (2007). Barack Obama and the politics of Blackness. *Journal of Black Studies*, 38, 7-29.

4

AN IMMIGRANT'S DREAM AND THE AUDACITY OF HOPE: THE 2004 CONVENTION ADDRESSES OF BARACK OBAMA AND ARNOLD SCHWARZENEGGER

Babak Elahi, and Grant Cos

Rochester Institute of Technology

A nother presidential election has passed and left the nation significantly divided. Like 2000, this presidential election left American voters in two significant camps: red states and blue states. Fisher (1973), in his essay on the 1972 presidential campaign, observed,

> The principal cause for concern regarding this year's election is not the individual acts throughout the campaign, but what they symbolically implied. They implied, along with the actual election, a significant statement as to how Americans want to conceive of themselves, the particular myth they want to live by. It was clear at least by the time the Democratic and Republican slates were settled, however compromised they were by how they were determined and would be supported by their constituencies, that the campaign contest would be a struggle between rival definitions of the American Dream. (p. 160)

Are we once again engaged in a similar contest of competing worldviews? Safire (1993), writing on the etymology of the myth, claimed that it "defies definition as much as it invites discussion. As a force behind government philosophy, it seems to be interpreted by most users as a combination of freedom and opportunity with growing overtones of social justice" (p. 18). More specifically, Fisher's analysis pulls out the two main strands of the American dream: a materialistic myth and a moralistic myth. The materialistic myth is "grounded in the puritan work ethic and relates to the values of effort,

Source: American Behavioral Scientist, November 2005; vol. 49, 3: pp. 454-465.

persistence, 'playing the game,' initiative, self-reliance, achievement, and success" (Fisher, 1973, p. 161). At the core of the materialistic myth's ability to explain a way of living is the assumption that its code "assumes that one will pursue one's self-interest, not deny it for the betterment of someone else" (Fisher, 1973, p. 161). In contrast to the unfettered individualism supporting the materialistic myth is the communitarianism of the moralistic myth. Fisher claimed that the moralistic myth is supported by the ideals found in the Declaration of Independence, where "these tenets naturally involve the values of tolerance, charity, compassion, and true regard for the dignity and worth of each and every individual" (p. 161). The important distinction between the two myths is that "where the materialistic myth involves a concept of freedom that emphasizes the freedom *to do* as one pleases, the moralistic myth tends toward the idea of freedom that stresses the freedom *to be* as one conceives himself" (Fisher, 1973, p. 162).

Within the context of the 2004 presidential campaign, there were many instances for candidates, and their surrogates, to articulate the dream. Smith and Nimmo (1991) found that national political conventions were important locales for such messages, given their propensity to serve as sites of "orchestrated" concurrence on the party's platform and candidate. Smith (1990) found that the conventions serve to promote the institutional discourse of the party, specifically, the speeches that the candidates and their surrogates make. It was at the national conventions, we argue, that two instances of this discourse were unveiled. In two prime-time speeches, both Obama (2004) and Schwarzenegger (2004) synthesized the message of their party with its chosen candidate through the imagery of the American dream and an orchestrated inclusiveness. Their speeches are two iterations on transcending these divisions through the identity of the "immigrant" in the mythos of the American dream.

In this article, we provide an overview of the immigrant in American public discourse. A review of this literature enables us to assert that the convention addresses of Obama (2004) and Schwarzenegger (2004) are specific, individual iterations of the American dream. Moreover, these two speeches have a similar theme of "reenchantment" that each speaker infused into the American dream myth via his own immigrant narrative. We argue that these speeches do more than fulfill a traditional role of legitimizing party candidate and platform (Farrell, 1978); they illustrate the clash of mythic bases at the heart of what it means to be an American.

The Immigrant in American Discourse: An Overview

According to Honig (1998), "The myth of an immigrant America depicts the foreigner as ...an agent of national re-enchantment that might rescue the regime from corruption and return it to its first principles, whether capitalist, communal/familial, or consensual" (p. 1). Honig wrote about cultural representations of the immigrant in the United States in the mid-1990s, but her model can be used to examine earlier discursive uses of the immigrant as icon of national renewal. Furthermore, this long-standing discursive use of the figure of the immigrant continues to affect political discourse across the current ideological divide in U.S. politics. Obama (2004) and Schwarzenegger (2004) offered versions of their own life narratives that conform to this "myth of an immigrant America," each attempting to reenchant his party's sense of purity and goodness in a political struggle that has all the earmarks of requiring a "rescue . . . from corruption" (Honig, 1998, p. 1).

Historians of immigration to the United States have suggested that nativistic and xenophobic reaction against immigrants rises and falls in waves corresponding to the shifting demographics of immigration (Bernard, 1998; Feagin, 1997; Jaret, 1999; Johnson, 1997). At the same time, with each wave of anti-immigrant sentiment, we can find a more complex appropriation of the figure of the immigrant to establish or renew the meaning of what it means to be American. From the beginning, legislation against immigration was often matched by symbolic appropriation of the immigrant as icon in iterations of the American dream myth. Thus, although the early republic produced the Alien Act of 1790, its leader also said that "the Bosom of America is open to receive not only the opulent and respectable stranger but the oppressed and persecuted of all Nations and Religions" (as quoted in Perea, 1997, p. 48). In the great era of immigration and immigration restriction in the late 19th century, this paradoxical discourse of legal restriction and rhetorical appropriation was symbolized most clearly in the Statue of Liberty, a sculpture whose meanings were not always those of welcoming immigrants (Perea, 1997). This dual rhetoric comes down through to our own time in the anti-immigration legislation and sentiment of the 1990s and the almost paranoid xenophobia of the post-9/11 Ashcroft era alongside the inclusion of popular representations of immigrants as the essence of American identity in films, literature, and as this article argues, key political speeches in both Democratic and Republican campaigns. Even in times when the foreigner is to be feared, the immigrant fulfills the very essence of the American dream.

Since Crèvecoeur's (1782/1981) *Letters From an American Farmer*, the immigrant as icon has served as a figure of national identity and even national renewal and absolution. Crèvecoeur presented the image of the American as an emigrant who leaves behind the demands of religion, pride, factionalism, and caste to produce something wholly new, to regenerate a new plant in the American soil: "The American is a new man, who acts upon new principles; he must therefore entertain new ideas and form new opinions" (p. 70). The corrupt regime in this early example of the immigrant in American consciousness is less a corrupt American ideology than the stagnating and limiting society the immigrant leaves behind in Europe. Key to this renewal is the importance of property: "He has become a freeholder, from perhaps a German boor. He is now an American, a Pennsylvanian" (Crèvecoeur, 1782/1981, p. 83). It is the freedom that comes with the ownership of property that is key to Crèvecoeur's notion of the American, this new man; the change "from being the slave of some despotic prince, to becoming a free man invested with lands to which every municipal blessing is annexed" is a "great metamorphosis" that "extinguishes all his European prejudices" (p. 83). As we shall see, this model continues to influence Schwarzenegger's (2004) conception of the immigrant as reenchanting the political regime of the right. What is important to note here is that even as early as the 1780s, the immigrant served to confirm America's vision of itself as independent from European corruption in moral and material ways.

With the shift from a mostly rural distribution of immigration in the United States to an urban and industrial concentration of immigrants, the discourse of immigration changed; but even in the debates leading to the far-reaching Immigration Act of 1924, historically called the Johnson-Reed Act or the Natural Origins Act, some voices described the immigrant as a force that would invigorate America. Although proponents of restriction such as Henry Cabot Lodge ultimately won the day, there were voices—as varied as the radical Randolph Bourne and the "Progressive" Teddy Roosevelt—who saw the immigrant as reaffirming American ideals rather than undermining American identity. In his March 16, 1896, speech to the SENATE titled "The Restriction of Immigration," Lodge (1909) argued that the "lower" racial quality of immigrants from Southern and Eastern Europe threatened to destroy "the very fabric of our race" (p. 260). A range of responses opposed to Lodge appropriated the immigrant not as an agent of corruption but rather, as an emblem of reenchantment with American ideals.

For example, Roosevelt (1911/1994), whose political career ran the gamut from restriction to assimilation (but not pluralism), argued for a thoroughgoing Americanization of the immigrant, a process that would also serve to renew old American ideals. Roosevelt stated the case for Americanizing the immigrant most clearly perhaps in an essay titled "Race Decadence," originally published in *Outlook* in April of 1911, where he stated,

> I, for one, would heartily throw in my fate with the men of alien stock who were true to the Old American principles rather than with the men of the Old American stock who were traitors to the Old American principles. (p. 340)

This has been an important assertion for those who wish to marshal the moralistic claims of the immigrant not in favor of the immigrant herself or himself but rather, in favor of materialistic and moralistic ideals of American society.

About this same time, Antin's (1912/1997) *The Promised Land*, a key immigrant autobiography, became a bestseller; her work is a clearer indication of how a liberal political thinker represented her own immigrant identity as a renewal of the American dream more generally. In this sense, she is particularly useful as we look at Schwarzenegger (2004) and Obama (2004), especially the latter, who himself has recently published an immigrant autobiography. Antin's autobiography succeeds at least in part because of her ability to voice the key tenets in the discourse of Americanization. In her narrative of becoming an American, she celebrated American civic faith, reproducing, for example, a poem she wrote in her first years of schooling in America lauding George Washington as the keeper of an American political faith. In her *They Who Knock at Our Gate*, Antin (1914) described her adoption of American ideals in terms that suggest Honig's (1998) notion of the immigrant rescuing America from corruption and returning the nation to its first principles. Antin wrote, "I have chosen to read the story of '76 as a chapter in a sacred history; to set Thomas Jefferson in a class with Moses, and Washington with Joshua; to regard American citizenship as a holy order" (p. 27).

In addition to Washington's and Crèvecouer's (1782/1981) championing of immigration as the essence of America, and to Progressive era uses of the immigrant dream as a renewal of the American dream, the cold war saw the use of immigration as a rhetorical tool for highlighting American exceptionalism. The immigrant dream placed moral weight on religion and liberty in John Kennedy's (1964) *A Nation of Immigrants*, a text whose endorsement of the legal and symbolic opening of the doors of the United States was, in fact, part of a cold war rhetoric in which the hopes and dreams of Hungarian refugees served to renew America's image as the land of the free. This is a rhetoric that Schwarzenegger (2004), in particular, adopted in his speech at the Republican National Convention. More than 40 years before Schwarzenegger was to deliver his speech, Robert Kennedy (1964), in his introduction to his brother's posthumously published book, wrote,

> On his sentimental visit to Ireland in June of 1963, he stood at the spot from which Patrick Kennedy embarked, and said: When my great-grandfather left here to become a cooper in East Boston, he carried nothing with him except a strong religious faith and a strong desire for liberty. (p. 10)

Included in this book is the chapter "The Immigrant Contribution," which concludes with a clear statement of what Honig (1998) described as the immigrant as agent of national reenchantment:

> The *continuous* immigration of the nineteenth and early twentieth century was thus central to the whole American faith. It gave every old American a standard by which to judge how far he had come and every new American

a realization of how far he might go.... Immigration infused the nation with a commitment to far horizons and new frontiers, and thereby kept the pioneer spirit of American life, the spirit of equality and of hope, always alive and strong. (J. Kennedy, 1964, pp. 99-100)

The rhetoric of renewal of faith and life (of the moral and material dream) is clear, and a challenge, perhaps, to the McCarthy era suspicion of immigrants is implicit, for if we turn to an important cultural artifact of the period—Kazan's (1963) film *America! America!*—it becomes clear that Kennedy's praise for the immigrant is but one face of an ambiguous discourse that could just as well have used the immigrant to endorse conservative aims.

Indeed, the ease with which the iconic image of the immigrant could be used to put forward conservative political aims in the 1980s and 1990s may be characterized by the circulation of Reagan's famous use of the metaphor of the shining city on a hill. During this period, the acceleration of globalization and the end of the cold war forced the proponents of the myth of an immigrant America to face such realities as the Mariel Boat Lift of 1980, the shrinking economy of the 1980s, and the culture wars of the 1990s. This period was marked by a kind of backlash against immigration epitomized by books such as Brimelow's (1995) *Alien Nation* that very consciously hark back to the Anglo-Saxonism of a century before and set into law through anti-immigrant legislation at the federal and state levels. The Immigration Reform and Control Act of 1986 and California Proposition 187 (1994) marked this era as a time when Americans were, as Jaret (1999) put it, "troubled by newcomers." According to Jaret, this was a time when even environmentalist arguments were marshaled against immigrants and immigration to the United States.

However, Schwarzenegger's famous predecessor, Reagan, was able to appropriate the image of the immigrant throughout this era as an agent of national renewal and reenchantment. He did so by presenting America through the metaphor first used by Winthrop (1838/2004), Massachusetts' first governor. Reagan's best known use of this metaphor occurred at the end both of the cold war and of his second term (see Reagan, 1989). However, an earlier version of this figure appears in Reagan's (1974) speech announcing his intention to run for the presidency in 1976. In this speech, he used the metaphor in conjunction with praise for immigrants and pioneers. Although the speech refers to Winthrop's idea of America as "a city upon a hill," it places this idea in a number of contemporary and historical contexts, including the place of immigrants, alongside pioneers, as those who made America and, indeed, renewed Winthrop's great ideal:

I have always believed that there was some divine plan that placed this great continent between two oceans to be sought out by those who were possessed of an abiding love of freedom and a special kind of courage. This was true of those who pioneered the great wilderness in the beginning of this country, as it is also true of those later immigrants who were willing to leave the land of their birth and come to a land where even the language was unknown to them. (Reagan, 1974, para. 5)

The key idea in this speech reappears in 1994 when moderate Republican Brian O'Leary (1994) used it to challenge anti-immigration legislation—California Proposition 187—proposed by the conservative wing of his party and endorsed by then California Governor Pete Wilson. In a time when anti-immigration sentiment was increasing—indicated both by this piece of legislation and more broadly in aspects of the Republican "Contract with America"—O'Leary's attack on the conservative wing of his party challenges what he saw as the corruption of a Reagan ideal. Indeed, O'Leary even quoted Reagan's farewell address reference to "the shining city on a hill":

I've spoken of the shining city all my political life, but I don't know if I ever quite communicated what I saw when I said it. But in my mind it was a tall, proud city built on rocks stronger than oceans, windswept, God-blessed, and teeming with people of all kinds living in harmony and peace; a city with free ports that hummed with commerce and creativity. And if there had to be city walls, the walls had doors and the doors were open to anyone with the will and the heart to get here. That's how I saw it, and see it still. (p. B7)

By applying Reagan's comments to the question of immigration, O'Leary attempted to nudge his party away from an extreme conservative reaction against immigration that made the party seem rigid, closed, and even racist.

Now, after 9/11, after Guantanamo, after Abu Ghraib, and during a campaign that seemed, even in its early stages, to have split the nation in two, both parties used their national conventions to reinvigorate themselves and to reenchant the nation. It is not surprising then that both parties used prominent immigrants and their narratives to recuperate the American dream. Schwarzenegger (2004) and Obama (2004), each in his own way, spoke as and for the immigrant as an agent of renewal. With varying emphasis on the moralistic as opposed to the materialistic aspects of the American dream myth, both speakers appealed to certain old American ideas that he as an emblem of his party saw as key to renewing that party and ultimately, reenchanting the nation.

Schwarzenegger at the Republican National Convention

Schwarzenegger (2004) began his speech with a couple of one-liners on acting and the appropriateness of the "True Lies" label for the Democrats' convention. It is in the exordium of his speech that Schwarzenegger framed an immigrant vision of the situation before him and the audience:

> To think that a once-scrawny boy from Austria could grow up to become governor of the state of California and then stand here in Madison Square Garden and speak on behalf of the president of the United States—that is an immigrant's dream. It is the American Dream. (para. 1)

Within this introduction, he underscored the rhetorical moment as the enactment of a grand narrative. Enactment through the taking of his oath of citizenship and the pride he feels as an American and a Republican and the belief that the "country is in good hands."

Schwarzenegger (2004) entered his immigrant dream through a narrative ("When I was a boy, the Soviets occupied part of Austria") of coming to America. He described his experiences as a child and young man in a socialist country, leading to his arrival in the United States in 1968. Schwarzenegger spoke of hearing Richard Nixon speak for the first time, touching on the crucible of Republican dogma:

> I remember I arrived here in 1968. What a special day it was. I remember I arrived here with empty pockets but full of dreams, full of determination, full of desire. The presidential campaign was in full swing. I remember watching the Nixon-Humphrey presidential race on TV. A friend of mine who spoke German and English translated for me. I heard Humphrey saying things that sounded like socialism, which I had just left. But then I heard Nixon speak. Then I heard Nixon speak. He was talking about free enterprise, getting the government off your back, lowering the taxes and strengthening the military. Listening to Nixon speak sounded more like a breath of fresh air. I said to my friend, I said, "What party is he?" My friend said, "He's a Republican." I said, "Then I am a Republican." (para. 5)

It is in this formative moment that Schwarzenegger aligned himself with the party of Lincoln, Teddy Roosevelt, Reagan, and George W. Bush. One cannot help but hear echoes of these earlier statements on the immigrant's dream in his narrative of remaking himself, of leaving behind the rule of a "despotic prince," and of claiming American freedom through the Republican Party. Schwarzenegger clearly used this discursive appeal when he stated, "My family and so many others lived in fear of the Soviet boot" (para. 9). Schwarzenegger used his experience to rescue and redeem the Republican Party by taking it back to one of its first principles—in this case the claim that Republicans up to and including Reagan have been heroes of the cold war, strong opponents of socialism and communism; whereas Democrats have been passive, or worse. In this model, even Nixon is redeemed in the governor's recounting of his immigrant experience. The corruption of the Democratic social-welfare state is presented in contrast to the moral clarity of Republican free enterprise.

Schwarzenegger's (2004) image of himself as a staunch opponent of communism does precisely what Honig (1998) suggested the figure of the immigrant does symbolically for American nationalism—both reenchant and rescue the regime from corruption. With both military and economic scandals such as Abu Ghraib and Enron threatening to derail the Bush campaign, a voice was needed that could make even Nixon— the icon of Republican political corruption in the modern era—look good. The immigrant brings moral clarity; despite the barrier of language, the young immigrant Schwarzenegger could distinguish clearly between a champion of American economic and military power and a defender of socialism.

Obama at the Democratic National Convention

Obama's (2004) keynote address to the Democratic National Convention is also a moment of reenchantment. He echoed the strategy of enactment that Jordan (1976) used some 28 years earlier when she, as keynote speaker, acknowledged her unlikely presence on the stage. Obama proceeded to tell his story, a story grounded in the "larger dreams" of his father, growing up in a humble African existence. Likewise, Obama's mother's family had "big dreams" for her. The connection of their lives and love would create and enact (enchant) the immigrant experience further:

> My parents shared not only an improbable love; they shared an abiding faith in the possibilities of this nation. They would give me an African name, Barack, or "blessed," believing that in a tolerant America your name is no barrier to success. They imagined me going to the best schools in the land, even though they weren't rich, because in a generous America you don't have to be rich to achieve your potential. They are both passed away now. Yet, I know that, on this night, they look down on me with pride. (Obama, 2004, para. 3)

Obama serves as an agent of the moralistic myth of the American dream in its purest sense. Obama is the progeny and result of two American dreamers, knowing that

> I stand here today, grateful for the diversity of my precious daughters. I stand here knowing that my story is part of the larger American story, that I owe a debt to all of those who came before me, and that, in no other country on earth, is my story even possible. (para. 9)

This enactment of the moralistic myth shifts with the second phase of the speech when Obama (2004) acknowledged "the true genius of America, a faith in the simple dreams of its people, the insistence on small miracles" (para. 5); he found these in the obligations he and all Americans have to "future generations." Obama proceeded to shift back and forth between elements of a moralistic, obligatory stance and a materialistic (albeit a Democratic, welfare safety net materialism) stance that emphasized tax breaks to American companies providing jobs to American workers and "the same health coverage our politicians in Washington have for themselves" (para. 9). He shifted into a brief narrative on a young man named Shamus he met at a Veterans of Foreign Wars Hall. In his interaction with the young man, Obama reflected on the devotion and patriotism of the young man: "But then I asked myself: Are we serving Shamus as well as he was serving us?" (para. 10). The question serves as a prompt to introduce Obama's next major idea: our communal obligations to other citizens. Obama explained that John Kerry knows Americans must be prosperous; however, "he knows it's not enough for just some of us to prosper. For alongside our famous individualism, there's another ingredient in the American saga. A belief that we are connected as one people" (para. 11). The moralistic and materialistic stand "alongside" each other in enacting the candidacy of Kerry.

Obama's (2004) final move was in posing the question: "Do we participate in a politics of cynicism or a politics of hope?" Obama stated that

> John Kerry calls on us to hope. John Edwards calls on us to hope. I'm not talking about blind optimism here—the almost willful ignorance that thinks unemployment will go away if we just don't talk about it, or the health care crisis will solve itself if we just ignore it. No, I'm talking about something more substantial. It's the hope of slaves sitting around a fire singing freedom songs; the hope of immigrants setting out for distant shores; the hope of a young naval lieutenant bravely patrolling the Mekong Delta; the hope of a millworker's son who dares to defy the odds; the hope of a skinny kid with a funny name who believes that America has a place for him, too. The audacity of hope! (para. 14)

It is the connection of belief with the action of lifting up voices, with heading to new lands, with enacting the rise of the candidates. From slaves to immigrants to candidates, this is the core of Obama's dream.

Like Antin (1912/1997) before him, Obama (2004) spoke of the need to "reaffirm our values and commitments." In speaking of Kerry's faith and service, Obama spoke of "values and [a] record [that] affirm what is best in us." Describing our time as a "crossroads of history," Obama spoke of the "audacity of hope" and of a country that "will reclaim its promise" in a time of political darkness. Thus, like Schwarzenegger (2004) and like earlier immigrants who spoke to the nation as a whole, Obama expressed the pathos of renewal, of hope, of reaffirmation. He held America up as morally a place of faith and inclusion and as materially a place of equality free from the abuses of military power and corporate control. Obama attempted to renew faith in the United States by challenging those he called the "spin masters" and "negative ad peddlers" who wish to divide America into Black and White, Latino and Asian, Red and Blue. Perhaps the most telling of his responses—and, indeed, the first in a series he presents in the form of a list—Obama stated, "I've got news for them, too. We worship an awesome God in the Blue States" (para. 31). Obama's personal story is one that emphasizes the importance of work and faith—of material production and moral stability—two forces that, again, take us back to the central theme of America made famous by Antin 90 years before: the promised land.

Conclusion

In his *The New York Times* op-ed analysis of Bush's second inaugural address of January 2005, Patterson (2005) presented a dual definition of *freedom* that overlaps with Fisher's (1973) dual definition of the *myth of the American dream*. Patterson argued that Bush used the term *freedom* in a way that oscillates almost imperceptibly between a 19th-century notion of individual liberty and influence and a 20th-century notion of civil liberties and equality. In Fisher's terms, Patterson offers a materialistic and moralistic conception of the rhetoric of freedom. *Freedom* can connote privatized liberty infused with personal power and influence, and in this sense the term "means doing what one wants and getting one's way" (Patterson, 2005, p. A15). Used in the modern liberal sense, *freedom* "emphasizes civil liberties, political participation and social justice," a conception "treasured by foreigners who struggle for freedom in their own countries" and extolled by our government at home (Patterson, 2005, p. A15). According to Patterson, the "problem is that what the president means by freedom, and what the world hears when he says it, are not the same" (p. A15). Patterson argued that the 19th-century version of freedom—the materialistic and privatized—has triumphed in American popular discourse. This version must "now coexist with the more modern version of freedom," and it "does so by acknowledging the latter but not necessarily including it" (Patterson, 2005, p. A15). Bush's genius, Patterson argued, is that he understands this duality in the way the term *freedom* is used and understood. Bush emphasizes what most Americans hear when the term is used—a privatized and materialistic rather than a civic and moralistic sense of freedom. Bush often clothes the former in the garb of the latter.

We suggest that this is part of a wider conservative discourse that uses terms such as *freedom*, *security*, and even the *American dream* in ways that allow the terms to slide back and forth between different rhetorical valences.

Certainly, Bush makes many claims about how "the war on terror" and the PATRIOT Act expand and protect America's moral freedoms—democracy and civil society. However, the rhetorical valence on these claims can slip back into materialistic and individualistic notions of freedom and security as well—continued access to Middle Eastern oil and security for the few. In a similar manner, Schwarzenegger's (2004) discourse of the immigrant dream valorizes the individual immigrant who escapes Communist totalitarianism and adopts and defends American individual freedom, whereas this same discourse can be read as defending a patently materialistic version of the immigrant dream as it is, at the very least, embodied in Schwarzenegger's career as a Hollywood star if not in his policies that favor individual wealth over and above civic and community rights and responsibilities. Obama (2004) is no less deft in his deployment of the immigrant dream narrative as a rhetorical device with a double valence. On one hand, the immigrant dream narrative is about him, but by the end of his speech it is almost as if Kerry has become an honorary immigrant whose life and career (as soldier and as politician) confirm the notion of being American by choice rather than by birth. In this instance, individual wealth and the privileges of being a White man disappear behind Kerry's new identity as honorary immigrant. Indeed, in both its moralistic and materialistic manifestation, the discourse of the immigrant dream allows leaders of both parties to reclaim and revitalize American ideals from corruption, even in the face of national embarrassments such as Abu Ghraib and Guantanamo, and from claims against the Democratic Party's lack of conviction or its candidate's relative position of privilege in relation to those for whom he would speak. More generally, the immigrant icon endorses party loyalty without regret and nationalism without remorse.

References

Antin, M. (1914). *They who knock at our gate: The complete gospel of immigration*. Boston: Houghton Mifflin.

Antin, M. (1997). *The promised land*. New York: Penguin. (Original work published 1912)

Bernard, W. S. (1998). Immigration: History of U.S. policy. In D. Jacobson (Ed.), *The immigration reader: America in a multidisciplinary perspective* (pp. 48-71). Malden, MA: Blackwell.

Brimelow, P. (1995). *Alien nation: Common sense about America's immigration disaster*. New York: Random House.

California Proposition 187. (1994). Retrieved from http://wikisource.org/wiki/California_ Proposition_187_(1994)

Crèvecoeur, H. St.-J. (1981). *Letters from an American farmer and sketches of 18th-century America*. New York: Penguin Books. (Original work published 1782)

Farrell, T. B. (1978). Political conventions as legitimation ritual. *CommunicationMonographs, 45,* 293-305.

Feagin, J. (1997). Old poison in new bottles: The deep roots of modern nativism. In J. F. Perea (Ed.), *Immigrants out! The new nativism and the anti-immigrant impulse in the United States* (pp. 13-43). New York: New York University Press.

Fisher, W. R. (1973). Reaffirmation and subversion of the American dream. *Quarterly Journal of Speech*, *59*(2), 160-167.

Honig, B. (1998). How foreignness "solves" democracy's problems. *Social Text, 16*(3), 1-28.

Immigration Act of 1924. Retrieved from http://www.historicaldocuments.com/ImmigrationActof1924.htm

Immigration Reform and Control Act of 1986, 8 U.S.C. 1101 note. Retrieved February 10, 2005, from http://www.oig.lsc.gov/legis/irca86.htm

Jaret, C. (1999). Troubled by newcomers: Anti-immigrant attitudes and action during two eras of mass immigration to the United States. *Journal of American Ethnic History*, *18*(3), 9-39.

Johnson, K. R. (1997). The new nativism: Something old, something new, something borrowed, something blue. In J. F. Perea (Ed.), *Immigrants out! The new nativism and the anti-immigrant impulse in the United States* (pp. 165-189). New York: New York University Press.

Jordan, B. (1976). *Barbara Jordan: 1976 Democratic National Convention keynote address.* Retrieved from http://www.americanrhetoric.com/speeches/PDFFiles/bjordan_1976DNconvention.pdf

Kazan, E. (Director). (1963). *America! America!* [Motion picture]. United States: Warner Brothers.

Kennedy, J. F. (1964). *A nation of immigrants.* New York: Popular Library.

Kennedy, R. F. (1964). Introduction. In J. F. Kennedy, *A nation of immigrants* (pp. 9-12). New York: Popular Library.

Lodge, H. C. (1909). *Speeches and addresses, 1884-1909.* Boston: Houghton Mifflin.

Obama, B. (2004). *Barack Obama: 2004 Democratic National Convention keynote address.* Retrieved from http://www.americanrhetoric.com/speeches/convention2004/barackobama2004dnc

O'Leary, B. B. (1994, October 7). An initiative even conservatives can hate. *Los Angeles Times*, p. B7.

Patterson, O. (2005, January 22). The speech misheard around the world. *The New York Times*, p. A15. Retrieved January 23, 2005, from http://www.nytimes.com/2005/01/22patterson.1.html

Perea, J. F. (1997). The Statue of Liberty: Notes from behind the gilded door. In J. F. Perea (Ed.), *Immigrants out! The new nativism and the anti-immigrant impulse in the United States* (pp. 44-58). New York: New York University Press.

Reagan, R. (1974, January 25). *Speech announcing presidential intentions for the 1976 election.* Retrieved January 23, 2005, from the Ronald Reagan Legacy Project Web Site: http://www.reaganlegacy.org/ speeches/reagan.announce.president.1.25.74.htm

Reagan, R. (1989). *Farewell speech to the nation following eight years as president, 1989.* Retrieved January 20, 2005, from the Ronald Reagan Legacy Project Web Site: http://www.reaganlegacy.org/speeches/ reagan.farewell.htm

Roosevelt, T. (1994). Race decadence. In M. R. DiNunzio (Ed.), *Theodore Roosevelt: An American mind: A selection from his writings* (pp. 339-344). New York: Penguin. (Original work published 1911)

Safire, W. (1993). *Safire's new political dictionary*. New York: Random House.

Schwarzenegger, A. (2004). *Arnold Schwarzenegger: 2004 Republication National Convention Address*. Retrieved from http://www.americanrhetoric.com/speeches/convention2004/ arnoldschwarzenegger2004rnc

Smith, L. D. (1990). Convention oratory as institutional discourse: A narrative synthesis of the Democrats and Republicans of 1988. *Communication Studies, 41*(1), 19-34.

Smith, L. D., & Nimmo, D. (1991). *Cordial concurrence: Orchestrating national party conventions in the telepolitical age*. Westport, CT: Praeger.

Winthrop, J. (2004). A model of Christian charity. In W. E. Cain (Ed.), *American literature* (Vol. 1, pp. 68–83). New York: Penguin. (Original work published 1838)

Part II

THE ICONIC OBAMA: CONTROLLING THE IDENTITY OF A PRESIDENT

Some Americans saw Barack Obama as the successor to John F. Kennedy and Martin Luther King Jr. Actually, the idea of Obama as a combination of the most iconic Americans of recent times was deeply ingrained in the political rhetoric advanced by his election team. Appropriating the concepts of dreams, promises, and the value of a different time, the candidate would repeat his own mantra, "We have never been just a collection of individuals or a collection of red states and blue states. We are, and always will be, the United States of America," as if by saying it is so, it would be so. Nevertheless, the image of an American president who embodied everyone and who projected a united nation became a powerful icon.

Obama's intellectual appeal was also a part of his image. A public fascinated with Obama's birth, intrigued by his multicultural background and upbringing, found that his Harvard law degree and professorship at the University of Chicago trumped both his Muslim name and the time he spent in Indonesia as a child. Perhaps few American presidents had come to the office with a higher regard for philosophy, international politics, geopolitical realities, scientific discoveries, and the environment. This is why the authors in Part Two explore how Obama's identity adds to his iconic image.

How is his identity generated and sustained? Is he a political pragmatist or a philosophical pragmatist given to appreciating the Chicago School tradition? The scholars in Part Two seek to discover how Obama's blackness was interpreted in the election campaign as well as how President Obama confronted a Faustian bargain in the struggle for a new definition of what it means to be an American.

Many Americans were introduced to candidate Obama through his writings, especially his books *Dreams From My Father* and *The Audacity of Hope*. In these autobiographical volumes, he presents himself to the public and reveals to the readers his thoughts about society, family, success, ethics, and the future of American society. In some senses Obama is the preeminent icon of the age of social media, although his books might be said to have set the stage and prepared the groundwork for his campaign's use of Twitter and Facebook.

5

OBAMA'S POLITICAL PHILOSOPHY: PRAGMATISM, POLITICS, AND THE UNIVERSITY OF CHICAGO

Bart Schultz

University of Chicago

My friends—No one, not in my situation, can appreciate my feeling of sadness at this parting. To this place, and the kindness of these people, I owe every thing.

> —Abraham Lincoln, Farewell Address to the People of Illinois
> (quoted in Michael Burlingame, *Abraham Lincoln: A Life*, 759)

Is it not Abraham Lincoln who has cleared the title to our democracy? He made plain, once for all, that democratic government, associated as it is with all the mistakes and shortcomings of the common people, still remains the most valuable contribution America has made to the moral life of the world.

> —Jane Addams (*Twenty years at Hull House*, 26)

For the world has changed, and we must change with it.

> —Barack Obama, First Inaugural Address

I. Introduction

On November 4, 2008, Barack Obama, the junior senator from Illinois, won the presidential election in the United States of America and thus made history both globally and locally. The first African American to win the presidency, he was also the first president ever with strong bonds to the University of Chicago and to the modern day city of Chicago, with its long and notorious

Source: Philosophy of the Social Sciences, June 2009; vol. 39, 2: pp. 127-173, first published on February 19, 2009.

history of machine politics and corruption. One of Obama's senior political advisors and University of Chicago Law School colleagues, Abner Mikva, who also served as general counsel in the Clinton White House, summed up Obama's victory as also a victory for Chicago: "Really what we'll get out of this is, it will make clear once and for all Chicago is not just full of pork-barrel, sleazy politicians who know only Machine politics . . . We also will have a very special president" (McKinney and Pallasch 2008).

Interestingly, Mikva did not deny that Chicago is full of "pork-barrel, sleazy politicians who know only Machine politics." He simply observed that the city now "also will have a very special president"—someone, presumably, to provide an added and more ethically satisfactory dimension to Chicago politics. Now we know, Mikva seems to suggest, that, *even in Chicago*, the political life can be one of service, inspiration, and hope, a life devoted to the democratic potential and guided by the better angels of our nature, rather than by the temptations of kickbacks from driveway permits and the rewards of cronyism. And this of course is not to mention corrupt governors willing to sell off anything and everything, including the new president's vacated Senate seat.

Mikva, whose own life has been very much devoted to high-minded public service, through such efforts as the "Mikva Challenge" program for introducing youth to the nobler side of public service, is voicing here a very special triumphal note. It is the triumphal note, not only of the tradition of political reform in the city of Chicago, but also of the tradition of political reform that has long marked the University of Chicago, or at least one side of it. This is the tradition stretching from the 1890s down to today, from John Dewey and Jane Addams, through Charles and Robert Merriam, Paul Douglas, Saul Alinsky, and Leon Despres, through Mikva himself, David Greenstone and Cass Sunstein, down to Danielle Allen and Barack Obama. It is the tradition that has always sought, in both theory and practice, to advance democratic deliberation and democracy as "a way of life," to use Dewey's famous expression, to foster a more fully democratic culture that could permeate, reform, and transform narrower forms of political activity. It is a tradition that has had some successes, with settlement houses, community organizing, and independent political opposition to the Chicago Machine. But it is also a tradition that, for the most part, has run against the current, failing to reform the political process, failing to halt or reform unjust urban renewal programs, failing to promote civic friendship across the social, economic, and racial divides built into the very concrete of Chicago, and failing to reform parts of the University itself.

The Obama victory, many now hope, will be the victory of this University of Chicago tradition, and mark, at long last, a winning combination of realism and idealism, of narrow political pragmatism and wider philosophical pragmatism, of faith and doubt, and of rhetoric and action. After all, Obama went from his three years in Chicago as a community organizer (1985–1988) working in Alinskyite fashion, on to Harvard Law School, and then back to Chicago, where he taught at the University of Chicago Law School for twelve years (1992–2004), led an important voter registration drive and served on various foundation boards, and made the successful transition to the electoral politics that would win him the presidency. Chicago and the University of Chicago can lay claim to him, just as he lays claim to them, even if he did spend most of his younger days in Indonesia and Hawaii.

How special is Obama? His is a story unfolding, very much a political work in progress. But it is also very clear to those most familiar with his political trajectory that he has stayed remarkably on message for quite some time, and that his message has been carefully crafted and cultivated from the visions given expression in his books, *Dreams From My Father* (1995) and *The Audacity of Hope* (2006). Bringing together the hope and idealism of the community organizer and the sophistication and strategizing of a seasoned (perhaps lightly seasoned) Chicago politician, Obama does indeed seek believable change—a grassroots, bottom-up revitalization of American democracy, built on the spirit of service and the many efforts of the many, duly aided by the more far-sighted elites. Old dualisms and antagonisms, the familiar battle-lines—these he dusts off with easy elegance, looking for new solutions that work rather than trying to instantiate some fixed ideology. But at heart, for all of his acclaimed cool, he has voiced through one policy position after another an urgent sense that the future is not given us, but must be created in a new mold, for the sake of future generations:

> Thinking about how you provide hope and opportunity to every kid is my biggest motivator. When I see my five-year-old and my two-year-old, it makes me weep because I see children who are just as smart and just as beautiful as they are, who just don't get a shot. It's unacceptable in a country as wealthy as ours that children every bit as special as my own children are not getting a decent shot at life. (Obama, quoted in Mendell 2007, 202–03)

With such a commitment, Obama stands an excellent chance of truly being the "education president"—from his political beginnings to his current exalted status, his strong suit has been educational reform, and he has made that a centerpiece of his platform. But it is education in a very wide sense, embracing everything from expanding Head Start and early education programs, to comprehensive community service programs, to citizenship itself as an educational exercise.[1] This alone would make him the Chicago pragmatist's president. The hopes and integrity of democracy, for Obama, are with democracy as an educating community, in which all citizens share "a willingness to find meaning in something greater than themselves."[2] Citizenship, on this construction, involves much more than conscientious voting and jury duty.

In this essay, I will begin with some general background on pragmatism, reform, and the University of Chicago, and then increasingly bring out the linkage between Obama and the University of Chicago tradition of pragmatic democratic reform and philosophy. Some of these filiations are more indirect than direct, but even so, they provide an important framework for understanding the larger philosophical significance of Obama, who, I shall argue, appears to have taken his playbook and reading of Lincoln from various Chicago pragmatists. For the cosmopolitan, global audience that Obama has now attracted, it is especially important to understand the nature of American pragmatism, political and philosophical, and how Obama was, figuratively at least, "born in Chicago."

II. The Child- and Reform-Centered Pragmatism of Illinois and Chicago

The history of the University of Chicago is in many respects the history of the battle for pragmatism, as both a philosophical and social movement. Although Chicago pragmatism shared much with the larger pragmatist movement of the late nineteenth century, with its antifoundationalism and antiessentialism, it also represented an important expansion of the pragmatist enterprise. John Dewey (1859–1952), for half a century America's best-known and best-loved philosopher, was the acknowledged leader of the Chicago pragmatists, or instrumentalists (to use his favored term), and his emphasis was on uniting science and ethics, including political ethics, via the theory of inquiry and education, along with practical reform. Dewey was very much a formative influence at the University in the 1890s, but so were various of his friends and allies, notably Jane Addams and George Herbert Mead.

This "Chicago School" encompassed philosophy, psychology, pedagogy, and the new social science of sociology, and it was ardently reformist right from the start. Its fundamental practical commitment, if such a description could ever be appropriate to pragmatism, was, in the words of Dewey, to the school as a "social center." That is,

We may say that the conception of the school as a social center is born of our entire democratic movement. Everywhere we see signs of the growing recognition that the community owes to each one of its members the fullest opportunity for development. Everywhere we see the growing recognition that the community life is defective and distorted excepting as it does thus care for all its constituent parts. This is no longer viewed as a matter of charity, but as a matter of justice—nay even of something higher and better than justice—a necessary phase of developing and growing life. Men will long dispute about material socialism, about socialism considered as a matter of distribution of the material resources of the community; but there is a socialism regarding which there can be no such dispute—socialism of the intelligence and of the spirit. To extend the range and the fullness of sharing in the intellectual and spiritual resources of the community is the very meaning of the community. Because the older type of education is not fully adequate to this task under changed conditions, we feel its lack and demand that the school shall become a social center. The school as a social center means the active and organized promotion of this socialism of the intangible things of art, science, and other modes of social intercourse. (Dewey quoted in Bryan and David 1990, 107–08)

Indeed, as Robert Westbrook has shown, in his compelling work on *John Dewey and American Democracy*, both Dewey and Jane Addams were far more radical figures than their somewhat masked public writings revealed. They both sympathized with Labor in the bloody 1894 Pullman Strike, and consistently bemoaned the narrow and divisive materialism of the capitalist class. But,

With regard to one condition of liberty Dewey did, however, take a strong and definite public stand in this period. All members of a democratic society, he declared, were entitled to an education that would enable them to make the best of themselves as active participants in the life of their community. . . . For a child to become an effective member of a democratic community, Dewey argued, he must have "training in science, in art, in history, command of the fundamental methods of inquiry and the fundamental tools of intercourse and communication," as well as "a trained and sound body, skillful eye and hand; habits of industry, perseverance, and, above all, habits of serviceableness." In a democratic community children had to learn to be leaders as well as followers, possessed of "power of self-direction and power of directing others, powers of administration, ability to assume positions of responsibility" as citizens and workers. Because the world was a rapidly changing one, a child could not, moreover, be educated for any "fixed station in life," but schools had to provide him with training that would "give him such possession of himself that he may take charge of himself; may not only adapt himself to the changes which are going on, but have power to shape and direct those changes." (Westbrook 1991, 94)

Dewey got caught up in the efforts to reform the Chicago Schools and, in 1896, was successful in founding the University's Laboratory School, his own effort to put his philosophy into practice. So possessed was he with educational reform that at one point he considered giving up teaching philosophy altogether, except through the vehicle of teaching pedagogy. In this, he was quite different from the perhaps better known "East Coast" pragmatism of Charles Sanders Peirce, William James, and other leading figures from pragmatism's formative period. For Dewey, Peirce was too much the "logician" and James too much the "humanist." Neither carried pragmatism far enough into its natural habitat, the realm of education, which was, in effect, the place for thinking through a fully democratic theory and practice.

But Dewey's pragmatist approach to education worked at all levels. If the early Lab School was aimed at elementary school children, Addams's Hull House, one of the most successful of the Settlement Houses (the model was taken from London's Toynbee Hall, which Addams visited), was directed to adults as well as to children. Dewey devoted a great deal of time and energy to Hull House, regarding it as the very embodiment of his vision of experimentation in democratic community, and Addams, who was also designated as a lecturer at the University, welcomed this alliance. Addams, in such works as *Democracy and Social Ethics*, beautifully encapsulated much of Dewey's social experimentalism:

> For action is indeed the sole medium of expression for ethics. We continually forget that the sphere of morals is the sphere of action, that speculation in regard to morality is but observation and must remain in the sphere of intellectual comments, that a situation does not really become moral until we are confronted with the question of what shall be done in a concrete case, and are obliged to act upon our theory. A stirring appeal has lately been made by a recognized ethical lecturer who has declared that "It is insanity to expect to receive the data of wisdom by looking on. We arrive at moral knowledge only by tentative and observant practice. We learn how to apply the new insight by having attempted to apply the old and having found it to fail. (Addams 1902, 273–74)

For Addams, as for Dewey:

> As the acceptance of democracy brings a certain life-giving power, so it has it own sanctions and comforts. Perhaps the most obvious one is the curious sense which comes to us from time to time, that we belong to the whole, that a certain basic well being can never be taken away from us whatever the turn of fortune. (Addams 1902, 276)

In many ways, as Westbrook demonstrates, Hull House enjoyed a freer and more open public sphere for the exchange of ideas than the University, which had been founded by the combined forces of Rockefeller and Marshall Field and overall had little sympathy with radical democracy, especially when it led to labor unrest. William Rainey Harper, the University's first president, moved steadily in the direction of the more elitist and managerial approach favored by business. As Robin Bachin has argued, in her persuasive work, *Building the South Side: Urban Space and Civic Culture in Chicago, 1890–1919*:

The battle over school reform demonstrates the competing visions that were emerging at Chicago over what form modern American education would take in the wake of the rise of the modern research institutions like the University of Chicago. Harper emphasized business models of consolidation and efficiency for his vision of modern education. His school reform bill reflected the rising belief in the power of centralized coalitions of trained experts to direct all phases of education. Because the University offered the most efficient and professional model for shaping education, Harper sought to bring other educational institutions under its control.

By contrast, Haley, Dewey, and Mead saw the potential for engaged public participation, with decentralized teacher control, as the best course for providing democratic education in modern America. . . . The pedagogical debate further underscored the tensions over civic culture emanating from the University of Chicago. The processes of centralizing education in Chicago, designing the University, and regulating land use all suggested a model of civic engagement different from the one initially invoked by Harper. Rather than seeing the University as a neighbor and partner in shaping knowledge in the city, the administration envisioned a more paternalistic role. Just as the university centralized and consolidated the production and dissemination of knowledge, so too did it try to exert direct control over the process of shaping its physical borders and isolating itself from the rest of the city. These practices were hand in hand, for they illustrated both the physical and the intellectual barriers the University erected as it developed into a leader of higher education both in Chicago and across the nation.

Some critics even compared the tactics of the University of Chicago to those of Standard Oil, arguing that taking over smaller competitors in the realm of education was the equivalent of John D. Rockefeller's trust-building project. By swallowing smaller competitors and supplanting competition with a system of corporate consolidation, the university—like Rockefeller—undermined the democratic ideal. (Bachin 2004, 71–72)

Thus, for all of their success on the community level, both Dewey and Addams represented only one part of the University, not the more dominant "business side." Dewey would leave with the turn of the century, and when he did it was not on happy terms with Harper. Thus, as Bachin concludes, the "more activist and democratic model of civic engagement promoted by Dewey became an auxiliary function of the University rather than a defining component of it." (Bachin 2004, 72). The University, like the country as a whole, was structured more in accordance with something like Walter Lippmann's elitist, managerial conception of limited democracy. Lippmann, who started out as a socialist, steadily moved to a more hierarchical conception of democracy, emphasizing how limited and gullible public opinion needed to be guided and constrained by various forms of elite expertise. He would play the top-down thinly democratic liberal to Dewey's bottom-up thickly democratic liberal, in a crucial philosophical duel that defined the options for American politics in the early twentieth century. Lippmann's *Public Opinion* remains the counterpoint to Dewey's *The Public and Its Problems*.

Still, if this more participatory, Deweyan form of democratic education and community-building became an auxiliary function of the University, it proved to be a lively and enduring one. Mead continued his work at Chicago for decades, and the University had a contingent devoted to its own Settlement, in the Back of the Yards neighborhood eventually made famous by the community organizing of the University's most famous organizer, sociologist/criminologist Saul Alinsky, another chapter in the story of making democracy a way of life in Chicago. And the University's Lab School has throughout proudly proclaimed its Deweyan legacy, even as it has grown and evolved in ways Dewey never could have anticipated. Dewey would surely have been delighted to learn that his experimental school would in due course enroll the children of the first African American President.

Moreover, the more radical, reform elements of the University regularly supported independent reform-minded candidates for city government, unsuccessfully in the case of political scientist Charles Merriam, but successfully in the case of 5th Ward Alderman Leon Despres, who from 1955 on would prove to be one of the most powerful voices on behalf of civil rights, racial equality, and political reform. It was, in the end, Despres, rather than Alinsky, who forcefully (if unsuccessfully) opposed, on grounds of fairness, the university-supported urban renewal plans of the 1950s and 1960s, recognizing that this form of "urban renewal" was indeed, as critics noted, simply a mask for "Negro removal."[3] The University clearly wanted a largely white middle-class residential neighborhood for its surroundings, and it used all of its considerable clout to get exactly that. In recent years, political theorist Danielle Allen has been especially significant in calling attention to the ways in which the University has often failed to act as a good neighbor on the South Side and cultivate the forms of civic friendship that might make for a healthier democracy.[4] The problematic elitism and isolation of the University has, she maintains, unfortunately limited the educational experience the University has had to offer. She founded the Civic Knowledge Project expressly out of the (very Deweyan) belief that scholars and students at the University "need to become civic knowers, that is, people who can learn to decipher the structure of their own world just by observing physical, social, and aesthetic details immediately around them."[5]

As we shall see, Allen's work provides some very helpful analytical material for grasping the significance of Obama's political rhetoric. But before turning to her work, and the work of other recent figures, more must be said about the survival of the Deweyan legacy in the mid-twentieth century, when it took certain forms that would also prove crucial to the shaping of Obama. At this point, it is sufficient simply to underscore, as a prelude, that

Obama's core concerns with educational reform, community service, and bottom-up democracy all reflect the key elements of Deweyan pragmatism. Indeed, his new Secretary of Education, Arne Duncan, former head of the Chicago Public Schools, is also a product of the Lab School and, like Obama, has a very Deweyan focus on teacher quality and educational innovation. Education, in the capacious pragmatist sense, is at the heart of Obama's philosophy and politics, just as it was at the heart of Dewey's, though in good Deweyan fashion his policies are adapted to the times and encourage new forms of experimentation, such as charter schools.

Now, with Despres and Alinsky, the pragmatist sensibility took a very hardball turn. Gone was the high rhetoric of Addams on reconciliation and unity, a distancing from social conflict that even Dewey found hard to follow. With the pacifist Addams, as with the pacifist Martin Luther King, Jr., the emancipation of the oppressed and the emancipation of the oppressor went together—one's tactics needed to allow the opposition to convert. Consider by contrast the lesson in Alinskyean pragmatism that Obama received from his first mentor on the subject, the Alinsky-style organizer Jerry Kellman:

> Marty [Jerry] decided it was time for me to do some real work, and he handed me a long list of people to interview. Find out their self-interest, he said. That's why people become involved in organizing—because they think they'll get something out of it. Once I found an issue enough people cared about, I could take them into action. With enough actions, I could start to build power.
>
> Issues, action, power, self-interest. I liked these concepts. They bespoke a certain hardheadedness, a worldly lack of sentiment, politics, not religion. (Obama 1995, 155)

Alinsky himself had relished conflict and confrontation—when asked if he believed in reconciliation, he explained that yes, once his side had the power and the other side got reconciled to it. Movement created friction and friction created sparks. The organizer could not be afraid of that.

Still, for all of his hard-boiled and decidedly unpacifistic Chicago organizing, Alinsky thought of himself as in the Deweyan tradition:

> To organize a community you must understand that in a highly mobile, urbanized society the word "community" means community of interests, *not physical community*. The exceptions are ethnic ghettos where segregation has resulted in physical communities that coincide with their community of interests, or, during political campaigns, political districts that are based on geographical demarcations.
>
> People hunger for drama and adventure, for a breath of life in a dreary, drab existence. . . . But it's more than that. It is a desperate search for personal identity—to let other people know that at least you are alive. Let's take

a common case in the ghetto. A man is living in a slum tenement. He doesn't know anybody and nobody knows him. He doesn't care for anyone because no one cares for him. On the corner newsstand are newspapers with pictures of people like Mayor Daley and other people from a different world—a world that he doesn't know, a world that doesn't know that he is even alive.

When the organizer approaches him part of what begins to be communicated is that through the organization and its power he will get his birth certificate for life, that he will become known, that things will change from the drabness of a life where all that changes is the calendar. This same man, in a demonstration at City Hall, might find himself confronting the mayor and saying, "Mr. Mayor, we have had it up to here and we are not going to take it any more." Television cameramen put their microphones in front of him and ask, "What is your name, sir?" "John Smith." Nobody ever asked him what his name was before. And then, "What do you think about this, Mr. Smith?" Nobody ever asked him what he thought about anything before. Suddenly he's alive! This is part of the adventure, part of what is so important to people in getting involved in organization activities and what the organizer has to communicate to him. Not that every member will be giving his name on television—that's a bonus—but for once, because he is working together with a group, what he works for will mean something.

Let us look at what is called *process*. *Process* tells us *how*. *Purpose* tells us *why*. But in reality, it is academic to draw a line between them, they are part of a continuum. Process and purpose are so welded to each together that it is impossible to mark where one leaves off and the other begins, or which is which. The very process of democratic participation is for the purpose of organization rather than to rid the alleys of dirt. Process is really purpose. (Alinsky 1971, 123–24)

As one of Alinsky's allies remarked: "Saul felt strongly that you don't patronize people but instead have them experience their own authority and practice their own power. The assertion of personal value is the core of his whole philosophy" (quoted in Horwitt 1989, 383). Abrasive as his tactics were, Alinsky ultimately articulated his position in profoundly Deweyan terms, as an effort to make democracy a way of life and an opportunity for self-creation. For Dewey, democracy was more than a form of government or a means to other ends; it was a "form of moral and spiritual association," the very metaphysics of experience.

Obviously, just on the political face of things, Obama continues this legacy even after moving from community organizing into electoral politics. His experiences as an organizer, as a member of Rev. Jeremiah Wright's Trinity United church, as a supporter of Harold Washington—all involved charged experiences of bringing people into action and into their identities. The move to organizing a highly successful get-out-the-vote drive in the early nineties and promoting educational reform (especially through Deweyan strategies for improving teacher quality) were also very much in the pragmatist mode. Obama headed the Chicago Annenberg Challenge from 1995–2002, a huge effort to reform the public school system, and sat on the boards of the Woods Foundation and the Joyce Foundation, both with deep commitments to community organizing and educational reform. And like both Dewey and Alinsky, Obama has long been prepared to organize the middle class too, challenging its identification with the super rich and working to align it with the more disadvantaged.

Indeed, it could also well be said that like Dewey, Obama found the business of enhancing democratic education and participation a seamless web of electoral and nonelectoral activity. New publics and public spheres needed to be formed, yes, but no pragmatist should ever take a hard, dogmatic line on what government can or cannot do or what the agent of change should be. To suppose that the public and the private are somehow eternally fixed spheres is to fall into another old and untenable dualism, like mind versus matter, or faith versus reason. Obama goes to Kenya in search of roots, attends Harvard Law School, and then returns to Chicago more determined than ever to work with what works, rather than a preconceived ideological position. In the mid-1990s, when running successfully for the Illinois State Senate, he is constantly telling community organizers that to have a serious impact they need to get involved in politics.[6] But he carries the same searching questions with him, even as he confronts even harsher realities:

> What is our community, and how might that community be reconciled with our freedom? How far do our obligations reach? How do we transform mere power into justice, mere sentiment into love? The answers I find in law books don't always satisfy me—for every *Brown v. Board of Education* I find a score of cases where conscience is sacrificed to expedience or greed. And yet, in the conversation itself, in the joining of voices, I find myself modestly encouraged, believing that so long as the questions are still being asked, what binds us together might somehow, ultimately prevail.
>
> That faith, so different from innocence, can sometimes be hard to sustain. Upon my return to Chicago, I would find the signs of decay accelerated throughout the South Side—the neighborhoods shabbier, the children edgier and less restrained, more middle-class families heading out to the suburbs, the jails bursting with glowering youth, my brothers without prospects. All too rarely do I hear people asking just what it is that we've done to make so many children's hearts so hard, or what collectively we might do to right their moral compass—what values *we* must live by. Instead I see us doing what we've always done—pretending that these children are somehow not our own. (Obama 1995, 438)

Like Dewey, Obama finds the test of his philosophy, its meaning and application, in the fate of future generations, future generations who must perforce be brought into the deliberative democratic dialogue through imagination and empathy. Civic knowledge and education for democracy as it should be means providing people, especially young people, with the opportunities to cultivate their humanity in this larger sense. And in this context, the old social contractarian talk must be left behind, as the pragmatists urged. We are not in a relationship of reciprocal agreement with the future. The language of Locke and Jefferson has been reconstructed in a very different idiom. Obama's rhetoric carries in its very structure just such a message. This, and various broad themes of Obama's pragmatism, can be illuminated by reading Obama's speeches as exercises in that politics of hope championed by Richard Rorty, the philosopher who did more than anyone in the late twentieth century to revive interest in Deweyan pragmatism.

III. Many Speeches, One Voice

What—what is that American promise? It's a promise that says each of us has the freedom to make of our own lives what we will, but that we also have obligations to treat each other with dignity and respect.

It's a promise that says the market should reward drive and innovation and generate growth, but that businesses should live up to their responsibilities to create American jobs, to look out for American Workers, and play by the rules of the road.

Ours—ours is a promise that says government cannot solve all our problems, but what it should do is that which we cannot do for ourselves: protect us from harm and provide every child a decent education; keep our water clean and our toys safe; invest in new schools, and new roads, and science, and technology.

Our government should work for us, not against us. It should help us, not hurt us. It should ensure opportunity not just for those with the most money and influence, but for every American who's willing to work.

That's the promise of America, the idea that we are responsible for ourselves, but that we also rise or fall as one nation, the fundamental belief that I am my brother's keeper, I am my sister's keeper.

That's the promise we need to keep. That's the change we need right now. (Obama, Acceptance Speech at the Democratic National Convention in Denver, August 28, 2008)[7]

Obama's acceptance speech at the Democratic National Convention moved artfully between the sense of "promise" as a ground for expectation and "promise" as a specific pledge, as a saying that is a doing. One and the same "American promise" is something that apparently "makes us fix our eye not on what is seen, but what is unseen, that better place around the bend" and something that gets made "to my daughters when I tuck them in at night and . . . that you make to yours." The candidate in fact made sparing reference to "democracy" in any serious political philosophical sense, opting instead to inspire with talk of an "American promise" redolent of the aspirational, imaginative element uniting everything from the March on Washington to the bedtime stories told to Malia and Sasha. Dreams that you can believe in, not dreams to be deferred. A promise that can still be kept. In rhetorical terms, this is an artful move from forensic or juridical oratory concerning the past, through epideictic or demonstrative oratory concerning the present, to that deliberative or hortative oratory concerning the future, choices to be made together. With Obama, the accent is always on the latter, the future as consensus and climax.

And tellingly, although the speech manifestly invoked the language and imagery of the social contract tradition, which in its Lockean version has been so crucial to the American political tradition, it did so via pure resonance, without buying into any of the suspect political theoretical machinery of the notion of a social contract, original or hypothetical.

For this is indeed a special form of promise, a promise that bends without ever being finally broken, a promise that can be both made to and kept by the people, a promise that in some magical way is almost its own fulfillment, keeping hope alive. After all, the time horizon on this promise appears to be that long arc of the universe tending toward justice. The allusion to the harsher perspective of a Langston Hughes was fleeting and in faintly invidious contrast to the words of King's "I Have a Dream" speech: "The men and women who gathered there could've heard many things. They could've heard words of anger and discord. They could've been told to succumb to the fear and frustrations of so many dreams deferred." Instead, they heard King's Ralph Ellisonian message that "in America, our destiny is inextricably linked, that together our dreams can be one." And "'We cannot walk alone,' the preacher cried. 'And as we walk, we must make the pledge that we shall always march ahead. We cannot turn back.'" The quotation marks fall as the candidate makes the preacher's words his own. "America, we cannot turn back." We cannot walk alone, turn back, continue the politics of the past (eight years), etc.

Obama knows "the cynicism we all have about government." But he also knows that "Change happens—change happens because the American people demand it, because they rise up and insist on new ideas and new leadership, a new politics for a new time." It is up to us to keep our brothers, our sisters, and the promise of America. Again, this is the rhetoric of the deliberative, of the future tense, which defines the present and gets us over the past.

And Obama's acceptance speech not only happily represents his commitment to the deliberative mode of persuasive discourse. It also displays most of his favored rhetorical devices, especially his seeming addiction to anaphora (repeating words or groups of words at the beginning of successive clauses), parallelism and isocolon, allusion, Lincolnesque dubitatio (downplaying his own talents as a rhetorician), and a singular form of antanaclasis, which repeats a word in different senses but with a serious ethical point rather than a punning intention. His remarkable grasp of kairos, seizing the persuadable moment, is of course evident, but so is his deviation from the classical rhetorical forms in his ability to sound the note of the preacher, of a Martin Luther King, Jr., without actually sermonizing or even citing much biblical scripture. Obama's major speeches tend to allude to or indirectly invoke biblical scripture through a secular or political scripture, though the words of King or Lincoln. Adroit at logos, ethos, and pathos, he appeals to logic, character, and emotion in turns, but always with the stress on the evidence that the improbable is possible, that character is in the making, an experiment, and that the making involves empathy and service, especially to future generations. The rhetoric is part and parcel of a pragmatist outlook that denies that character is destiny, that destiny is fixed, and that democratic social experimentation to see what works is somehow a thing of the past, rather than the very future of America.

If only the revisionist pragmatist public intellectual Richard Rorty, another product of the University of Chicago College and a great booster of Deweyanism, had lived to see this version of Achieving Our Country. In his book of that title, Rorty had taken his point of departure from James Baldwin's line:

> If we—and now I mean the relatively conscious whites and the relatively conscious blacks, who must, like lovers, insist on, or create, the consciousness of the others—do not falter in our duty now, we may be able, handful that we are, to end the racial nightmare, and achieve our country, and change the history the world. (Rorty 1998, 12–13)

Here is the defining moment, and the handful has become a seeming multitude. Rorty's Baldwin was not the angry Baldwin who, like Richard Wright, moved to France to escape American racism. For Rorty,

> National pride is to countries what self-respect is to individuals: a necessary condition for self-improvement . . . just as too little self-respect makes it difficult for a person to display moral courage, so insufficient national pride makes energetic and effective debate about national policy unlikely. Emotional involvement with one's country—feelings of intense shame or of glowing pride aroused by various parts of its history, and by various present-day national policies—is necessary if political deliberation is to be imaginative and productive. Such deliberation will probably not occur unless pride outweighs shame. (Rorty 1998, 3)

Rorty would have loved the deep historical irony of having the most truly cosmopolitan presidential candidate the United States has ever seen opening up the very University of Chicago liberal/pragmatist way he had searched for—reweaving our solidarity and/or national pride to help us achieve our country, just when it so desperately needs achieving. Forget the carping and whining of the literary Academic Left and get with the real people, including those in Law School and economics departments. Basketball is a perfectly legitimate substitute for bowling; in fact, it is harder for people to do it alone.

Clearly, Obama may well confirm Rorty's diagnosis and prognosis:

> Emphasizing the continuity between Herbert Croly and Lyndon Johnson, between John Dewey and Martin Luther King, between Eugene Debs and Walker Reuther, would help us to recall a reformist Left which deserves not only respect but imitation—the best model available for the American Left in the coming century. If the intellectuals and the unions could ever get back together again, and could reconstitute the kind of Left which existed in the Forties and Fifties, the first decade of the twenty-first century might conceivably be a Second Progressive Era. (Rorty 1998, 56)

On that score, Obama is trying—he loves the word "Progressive" and FDR, Kennedy, and King all loom large—though he will have to aim for the second decade of the twenty-first century. One only hopes that he will turn out to be even more progressive than he is on the matter of income inequality. He needs to undo much more than the damage of the last eight years. And this, of course, is not even to mention the global poor, the billion plus constituency that suffers from U.S. policy but scarcely manages to secure so much as a passing reference in the Democratic candidate's acceptance speech. The biggest problems of justice confronting the world today do not make appropriate campaign material for the major parties.

To be sure, Obama is concerned with global justice. But the favored tropes of his rhetoric are very much in line with Rorty's emphasis on national pride and deliberative rhetoric, or rather restoring national pride by tapping into the American ideal and possible future, rather than the American reality. He is himself perhaps the best vehicle for just such a restoration. His speeches overflow with quotations from or allusions to King and Lincoln, and these are all of a theme—out of the many, one, as a choice we must make:

> If there is anyone out there who still doubts that America is a place where all things are possible; who still wonders if the dream of our founders is alive for our time; who still questions the power of our democracy, tonight is your answer.
>
> It's the answer told by lines that stretched around schools and churches in number this nation have never seen, by people who waited three hours

and four hours, many for the very first time in their lives, because they believed that this time must be different; that their voice could be that difference.

It's the answer spoken by young and old, rich and poor, Democrat and Republican, black, white, Latino, Asian, Native American, gay, straight, disabled and not disabled—Americans who sent a message to the world that we have never been a collection of Red States and Blue States: we are, and always will be, the *United States of America.*

It's the answer that led those who have been told for so long by so many to be cynical, and fearful, and doubtful of what we can achieve to put their hands on the arc of history and bend it once more toward the hope of a better day.

It's been a long time coming, but tonight, because of what we did on this day, in this election, at this defining moment, change has come to America. (Obama, Victory Speech in Grant Park, Chicago, November 4, 2008)

All things considered, the Obama victory speech was very sober. Again, there was the characteristic anaphora and parallelism, the downplaying of the juridical and the fusing of the epideictive to the deliberative. Again, there was the political sermonizing invocation of King's moral arc of the universe; again, there was the aura of Lincoln, as the father of the second American founding and the architect of the American ideal of union as the defining vision in achieving our country; again, there was the confrontation with cynicism, though this time around, the "change has come to America." The questions are still posed, but the doubts can now be defeated. The arc of the universe does not seem quite so long, at least looking forward.

But the speech itself does not stand still, cannot rest with this perspective. As in his old days as a community organizer on Chicago's South Side, Obama is compelled, even driven, to provide the immediate postmortem, whether it be of defeat or of victory. And even at the moment of ultimate victory, he could not resist, very much like Lincoln, segueing into a mode of tired sobriety (still with hope for the future), albeit in a collective tone:

I know you didn't do this just to win an election and I know you didn't do it for me. You did it because you understand the enormity of the task that lies ahead. . . . The road ahead will be long. Our climb will be steep. We may not get there in one year or even one term, but America—I have never been more hopeful than I am tonight that we will get there. I promise you—we as a people will get there.

There will be setbacks and false starts. There are many who won't agree with every decision or policy I make as President, and we know that government can't solve every problem. But I will always be honest with you about the challenges we face. I will listen to you, especially when we disagree. And above all, I will ask you to join in the work of remaking this nation the only way it's been done in America for 221 years—block by block, brick by brick, calloused hand by calloused hand.

What began 21 months ago in the depths of winter must not end on this autumn night. This victory alone is not the change we seek—it is only the chance for us to make that change. And that cannot happen if we go back to the way things were. It cannot happen without you.

So let us summon a new spirit of patriotism; of service and responsibility where each of us resolves to pitch in and work harder and look after not only ourselves, but each other. Let us remember that if this financial crisis taught us anything, it's that we cannot have a thriving Wall Street while Main Street suffers—in this country, we rise or fall as one nation; as one people. (ibid.)

Thus, the speech seemingly contradicts itself, at least in some pragmatic sense: change has come to America, but this victory is "not the change we seek." The arc of the universe is still long, and what's more, now seems to involve an uphill climb. We still cannot go back, but must go forward, and in a new spirit. The "promise" of America and of Obama is still there in all its complexity and ambiguity. The voice of the old community organizer, understanding that change comes one step at a time and the struggle always continues (and that citizen mobilization, democracy in the streets, is crucial), weaves through the speech on the way to a quotation from Lincoln: "We are not enemies, but friends; though passion may have strained it must not break our bonds of affection." Then a call for help, addressed especially to those "whose support I have yet to earn," followed by words "to all those watching tonight from beyond our shores." It is a message and an apology: "tonight we proved once more that the true strength of our nation comes not from the might of our arms or the scale of our wealth, but from the enduring power of our ideals: democracy, liberty, opportunity, and unyielding hope." The conclusion: "For that is the true genius of America—that America can change. Our union can be perfected. And what we have already achieved gives us hope for what we can and must achieve tomorrow."

So, America has changed, can change, and must change—the ideals may endure and inspire hope of perfection, but America as an ideal is not an ideal of static perfection. The future shapes our present and our past. Like all good pragmatists, Obama always finds the anti-Platonic voice, even as he is about to cry "God Bless America." Like Dewey's "A Common Faith" or Cornell West's oratorical pragmatism, Obama, especially since breaking with the church of Rev. Jeremiah Wright, appears to find his God in the democratic faith, in the ever shape-shifting genius of the people. The eternity promised is that of future generations of people on earth. If the universal vision suggests the permanent, the particularity of the people suggests the transient. This sense was powerfully invoked in Obama's 2008 Father's Day address at the Apostolic Church of God, in a rare performance that began with a bit of scripture and concluded with a characteristic play on the word "Father," trading on the earthly and heavenly, but at the deepest level preached this anaphoric confessional:

> And what I've realized is that life doesn't count for much unless you're willing to do your small part to leave our children—all of our children—a better world. Even if it's difficult. Even if the work seems great. Even if we don't get very far in our lifetime.

This has ever been the paradoxical position of pragmatism. Pragmatism was the first and only truly original American contribution to philosophy, and as a philosophy, it has always been viewed as peculiarly American, somehow carrying on its sleeve the American ideal—for Obama, the Bob the Builderism of "Yes We Can," because "when Americans come together, there is no destiny too difficult or too distant for us to reach." Yet at the very same time, the universalizing, Platonizing, Christianizing elements of Americanism are the very things pragmatism usually seeks to undercut, albeit in ways that avoid the old dualisms. Against the declaration of self-evident truth in the Declaration of Independence, pragmatists hold that accepted "truths" are always provisional, experimental, and open to revision. As Christopher Hayes put it, in his helpful but rather slight essay on Obama "The Pragmatist":

> Pragmatism as a school of thought was born of a similar [to Lincoln's] spirit of reconciliation. Having witnessed, and in some cases experienced firsthand, the horror of violence and irreconcilable ideological conflict during the Civil War, William James, Charles Peirce and Oliver Wendell Holmes were moved to reject the metaphysical certainty in eternal truths that had so motivated the abolitionists, emphasizing instead epistemic humility, contingency and the acquisition of knowledge through practice—trial and error. . . . The crux of pragmatism, and indeed democracy, was a rejection of the knowability of foreordained truths in favor of "variability, initiative, innovation, departure from routine, experimentation. (Hayes 2008)

With Dewey, the model of the school as social center, and of ethical knowledge, was effectively a model for epistemology as a whole—society was one big school, or rather, one big research team, and participatory and deliberative democracy the most effective form of education, of inquiry and problem-solving, of "learning by doing," as his slogan had it. "Intelligence," for Dewey, is "social intelligence," as much a community function as democracy itself, which to be realized involves so much more than mere majoritarian voting mechanisms and constitutional protections. The purpose of American democracy is not to aggregate consumer preferences on the political side, but to create a forum for deliberation and participation, for listening to one another, talking to one another, and taking action together. And society cannot evade the responsibility for developing democratic citizens capable of this.

Thus, nothing is written in stone, the "quest for certainty" needs to be abandoned, and old views always need to be reconstructed in light of changing historical realities, though some views do seem to work better than others. As Hilary Putnam has put it: "That one can be both fallibilistic *and* antiskeptical is perhaps *the* basic insight of American pragmatism" (Putnam 1995, 21). Putnam, by the way, is a better interpreter of Dewey than Rorty, who resolutely failed to appreciate Dewey's degrees of epistemological realism.

Such negotiations between the transient and the permanent are—like the Deweyan emphasis on education and future generations—quite evident in Obama's crucial speech on race, "A More Perfect Union" (March 18, 2008); in some ways the single best source for his rhetoric. Addressing the controversy brought on by Rev. Jeremiah Wright's inflammatory comments about the racism of the United States, Obama, appropriating the staging and symbolism of the Constitution Center in Philadelphia, began with the Constitution:

> The answer to the slavery question was already embedded within our Constitution—a Constitution that had at its very core the ideal of equal citizenship under the law; a Constitution that promised its people liberty and justice and a union that could be and should be perfected over time.

But, the emphasis is on "perfected over time," and words without actions do not reality make:

> And yet words on a parchment would not be enough to deliver slaves from bondage, or provide men and women of every color and creed their full rights and obligations as citizens of the United States. What would be needed were Americans in successive generations who were willing to do their part—through protests and struggles, on the streets and in the courts, though a civil war and civil disobedience, and always at great risk—to narrow the gap between the promise of our ideals and the reality of their time.

As always, the arc is long, the road steep, the answer in union:

> This was one of the tasks we set forth at the beginning of this presidential campaign—to continue the long march of those who came before us, a march for a more just, more equal, more free, more caring and more prosperous America. I chose to run for president at this moment in history because I believe deeply that we cannot solve the challenges of our time unless we solve them together, unless we perfect our union by understanding that we may have different stories, but we hold common hopes; that we may not look the same and we may not have come from the same place,

but we all want to move in the same direction—toward a better future for our children and our grandchildren.

Although the speech is headed toward associations with King and Lincoln, Obama turns back, in a moment of double indirection, to quote his own words, from *Dreams from My Father*, to describe his version of the religious experience, as he found it at Trinity, Rev. Wright's church:

> People began to shout, to rise from their seats and clap and cry out, a forceful wind carrying the reverend's voice up into the rafters. And in that single note—hope!—I heard something else: At the foot of that cross, inside the thousands of churches across the city, I imagined the stories of ordinary black people merging with the stories of David and Goliath, Moses and Pharaoh, the Christians in the lion's den, Ezekiel's field of dry bones. Those stories—of survival and freedom and hope—became our stories, my story. The blood that spilled was our blood, the tears our tears, until this black church, on this bright day, seemed once more a vessel carrying the story of a people into future generations and into a larger world. Our trials and triumphs became at once unique and universal, black and more than black. In chronicling our journey, the stories and songs gave us a meaning to reclaim memories that we didn't need to feel shame about—memories that all people might study and cherish, and with which we could start to rebuild (Obama 1995, 294).

From there, the narrative moves with empathy through the black experience and the white, and then through the path of the past to the path of the possible future, in which people recognize the pain and sacrifice of the past, but move on:

> I would not be running for President if I didn't believe with all my heart that this is what the vast majority of Americans want for this country. This union may never be perfect, but generation after generation has shown that it can always be perfected. And today, whenever I find myself feeling doubtful or cynical about this possibility, what gives me the most hope is the next generation—the young people whose attitudes and beliefs and openness to change have already made history in this election.

Obama then concludes with another artful repetition, of the story of Ashley, which he had told when speaking at King's church, Ebenezer Baptist in Atlanta, on King's birthday. Ashley, a young, white campaign worker in South Carolina, joined the campaign because her own difficult childhood experiences of sacrifice to help her ailing mother had led her to want to help "the millions of other children in the country who want and need to help their parents, too." She tells her story at a roundtable discussion, moving around the room to ask the others why they are supporting the campaign:

finally they come to this elderly black man who's been sitting there quietly the entire time. And Ashley asks him why he's there. And he does not bring up a specific issue. He does not say health care or the economy. He does not say education or the way. He does not say that he was there because of Barack Obama. He simply says to everyone in the room, "I am here because of Ashley."

The moral:

> "I'm here because of Ashley." By itself, that single moment of recognition between that young white girl and that old black man is not enough. It is not enough to give health care to the sick, or jobs to the jobless, or education to our children. But it is where we start. It is where our union grows stronger. And as so many generations have come to realize over the course of the 221 years since a band of patriots signed that document right here in Philadelphia, that is where the perfection begins.

From the many, one, from the particular, the universal, and from the transient, the permanent. We live in the particular and the transient, but we live by the universal and the permanent. Except that, as with the word "promise," Obama works the word "perfection" into something worthy of Stanley Cavell, taking antanaclasis to a new level of political significance. "Perfection," on his reading, is not like "pregnant" or "best," etc. "This union my never be perfect, but generation after generation has shown that it can always be perfected"— which means, it seems, not "perfected" as in achieving "perfection," but "perfected" as in "improved." The transitive verb form here does not mean "To bring to perfection or completion." It is rather the means by which Obama pragmatizes the American Dream. Perfection, whatever it may be, is so far off and so much the business of future generations, that we are left, for all practical purposes, afloat on our makeshift raft of belief and democratic experimentation. No one will live to see the Promised Land. The road is too long, too steep. But life, especially democratic life, just is hope, in all its audacity. Perfecting is enough for us. And as William James would add, we have every right to experiment, to try on this outlook and see where it goes and what it produces.

Some might think that this is pragmatism through the back door, rather than the kind of thing promoted by Dewey et al. As Rorty insists, when noting the link between Dewey, the philosopher of democracy, and Walt Whitman, the poet of democracy:

> Both Dewey and Whitman viewed the United States as an opportunity to see ultimate significance in a finite, human, historical project, rather than in something eternal and nonhuman. They both hoped that America would be the place where a religion of love would finally replace a religion of fear.

They dreamed that America would break the traditional link between the religious impulse, the impulse to stand in awe of something greater than oneself, and the infantile need for security, the childish hope of escaping from time and chance. They wanted to preserve the former and discard the latter. They wanted to put hope for a casteless and classless America in the place traditionally occupied by knowledge of the will of God. They wanted that utopian America to replace God as the unconditional object of desire. They wanted the struggle for social justice to be the country's animating principle, the nation's soul. (Rorty 1998, 17–18)

But Rorty is surely right that "Forgetting about eternity, and replacing knowledge of the antecedently real with hope for the contingent future, is not easy." How could he have denied the power of Obama's effort, very much in the mood of Whitman, Dewey, and Rorty himself, to marshal the future transcendental for the present pragmatic? This is the very approach Rorty sought, and Obama, far more effectively than Cornell West, has achieved the rhetorical pragmatism, self-creation, and Americanism that Rorty described. The substance of the speechcraft, as well as the structure, points up this lesson, and there is still more to the substance.

IV. The Love of a King, the Politics of a Lincoln

We are not enemies, but friends. We must not be enemies. Though passion may have strained, it must not break our bonds of affection. The mystic chords of memory, stretching from every battlefield, and patriot grave, to every living heart and hearth-stone, all over this broad land, will yet swell the chorus of the Union, when again touched, as surely it will be, by the better angels of our nature.

—Abraham Lincoln, First Inaugural Address

Obama's speechcraft, it should be stressed, was something developed on the campaign trail, and rather late in the day, after his period as a community organizer. Although, as we shall see, many of the characteristic themes and topics represent very long-standing concerns, his rhetorical style in presenting them was only honed to perfection during his successful race for the U.S. Senate starting in 2003, though this was still well before his current team of speechwriters, including the young Jon Favreau, came on the scene. A key player in the process was his political consultant David Axelrod (another product of the University of Chicago), the man who would eventually play a crucial role in Obama's presidential campaign. As David Mendell's biography of Obama puts it:

"My involvement was a leap of faith," Axelrod said. "Barack showed flashes of brilliance as a candidate during the early stages of the campaign, but there were times of absolute pure drudgery. . . . His speeches were very theoretical and intellectual and very long. But I thought that if I could help Barack Obama get to Washington, then I would have accomplished something great in my life."

To counter Obama's shortcomings as a candidate, Axelrod did two things. He urged Obama to think more in terms of people and their stories rather than pure policy, and he stressed the importance of this advice to Obama's other close adviser—Michelle Obama.

Axelrod told Obama to visualize the people he had met and would be meeting on the campaign trail, to try to bring their stories to life, to "invoke more humanity in his speeches." . . . "In a classic way he grew under the tutelage of the people he was meeting out on the stump and realized that he was internalizing their everyday concerns and problems and realizing what the whole was about," Axelrod said. "It clicked in his head and he became a much better candidate over time. His learning curve is great. Once he realized that he was not taking orals at Harvard he became a better candidate."

This maturation process is not dissimilar to that of many great politicians. Again, John F. Kennedy was a poor speechmaker and even worse glad-hander at the beginning of his political career. But after coaching from aides and his own observations on the campaign trail, Kennedy developed into one of the great presidential orators . . . (Mendell 2007, 178-79)

Axelrod has also explained that his coaching sessions with Obama were like "musicians riffing together" (Mendell 2007, 224).

Mikva, too, has noted that Obama was not, early on, a very effective speaker—he was too professorial and abstract. Although Obama sometimes claims that his public speaking was greatly improved by his teaching experience at the University of Chicago, it is very clear that he struggled hard to get beyond that pedagogical model. He worked very hard, first to speak more effectively to the black audiences on Chicago's South Side—"Obama spent countless hours in Chicago's African-American churches digesting the cadence of a preacher's rhythm and the themes that stoke an African-American crowd" (Ibid, 227)—and then, later, under Axelrod's coaching, to transmute that style into a larger call for unity through the personal and the particular. The first of these transformations occurred during his earlier phase of political development (roughly 1994–2000), when running for state office and then (unsuccessfully) for Congressman against black political icon Bobby Rush, a former Black Panther who has controlled the first Congressional district in Chicago for many years. As Mendell observes, the "I am my brother's keeper" themes came to the fore at that point, and such "addressed from Obama were mostly secular and political in nature, but he made sure to pepper them with hints of the Bible, Christian orthodoxy and borrowed phrases from the nation's African-American civil rights icon, the

Reverend Martin Luther King Jr." (Ibid, 227) It was at this time that Obama began repeating the King mantra "The arc of the moral universe is long, but it bends toward justice," adding "but it doesn't bend on its own. It bends because you put your hand on that arc and you bend it in the direction of justice" (Mendell 2007, 227).

But as Jerry Kellman, the Alinskyian community organizer who brought Obama to Chicago in the first place, after his graduation from Columbia and early public interest work in New York in 1985, has observed:

> Barack has become the expectation of his people, and in that sense he is similar to King. As I know Barack, he will carry that as a weight, but he will carry that burden with great seriousness....I think he knows that if he wants to go where he wants to go in politics, he has to speak for more than the black community. But I think the rest of his life, he will take on that burden of being that person who changes the situation for African-Americans" (Ibid., 74).

However, speaking for more than the black community has not been the chief problem for Obama. His voracious reading in political theory and history, particularly under the philosopher Roger Boesche at Columbia, was never particularly Afro-Centric. He is familiar with philosophers and theologians, from Nietzsche to Niebuhr, in a way that is decidedly unusual for an American politician, and is much more of a true intellectual than even that darling of the Democratic liberal intellectuals, Adlai Stevenson, another son of Illinois (one might also mention former Senator Paul Simon in this context, a huge force in Illinois politics whose untimely death came just before his planned endorsement of Obama in the 2004 Senate race). And as a recent issue of the *University of Chicago Magazine* had it, in a story on "How U of C is Barack Obama?" that quoted the conservative columnist and alum David Brooks: "Around U of C people Obama is pretty U of C. Meaning cerebral, reasonably Socratic, always emphasizing the complicated nature of any question." Dean of the College John Boyer also weighed in:

> Obama reminds Boyer of Paul Douglas, a Chicago economics professor and social reformer alongside Jane Addams who went to Washington in 1949 as an Illinois Senator: "Paul Douglas was an iconic activist here, a lefty professor at a time when it was unpopular," he says. "Both men were in the machine but not of the machine." (Gibson 2008, 45).

Moreover, Boyer added "Axelrod is a creature of the College," noting his "analytic skills, his disciplined approach to problem-solving." Indeed, the side of both men that shows how they "know the world"—especially the world of Chicago machine politics—but are never reduced to it seems very much in line with the legacy of Douglas, Simon, Stevenson, Despres, et al.

The point here, however, is that more of Obama's big negotiations have come from modulating his other worldly side into his this worldly side, assembling the materials of his philosophical self-creation in ways that served his more theorized than realized purposes. Thus, although he has gone on record as explaining that his most important philosophical influences were Gandhi, King, and Lincoln, it is manifest that in his political realization, increasingly evident in his speeches, the politics of the first two gets subordinated to the politics of the third.

Indeed, the constant stream of references, quotations, and allusions to King and Lincoln in Obama's speeches can obscure some fundamental differences important for understanding his pragmatism.

On King, for example, Obama can sound in deep harmony, especially with King's key message, so brilliantly expressed in his sermon on "The Man Who Was a Fool":

> All men are caught in an inescapable network of mutuality, tied in a single garment of destiny. Whatever affects one directly affects all indirectly. I can never be what I ought to be until you are what you ought to be, and you can never be what you ought to be until I am what I ought to be. (King 1963, 7)

But if King's belief in the interdependence of all life links seamlessly to Obama's on service, there is a vast divide when it comes to politics. As Coretta Scott King observed, "'Christ gave us the goals,' he would often say, 'and Mahatma Gandhi provided the tactics.'" King's distance from the mainstream political process and embrace of the pacifist, direct action tactics of Gandhi do indeed point to something deeply puzzling about Obama's commitments. One cannot imagine him writing what King wrote, in the "Letter from a Birmingham Jail":

> But as I continued to think about the matter I gradually gained a bit of satisfaction from being considered an extremist. Was not Jesus an extremist in love—"Love your enemies, bless them that curse you, pray for them that despitefully use you." Was not Amos an extremist for justice—"Let justice roll down like waters and righteousness like a mighty stream." Was not Paul an extremist for the gospel of Jesus Christ—"I bear in my body the works of the Lord Jesus." Was not Martin Luther an extremist—"Here I stand; I can do none other so help me God." Was not John Bunyan an extremist—"I will stay in jail to the end of my days before I make a butchery of my conscience." Was not Abraham Lincoln an extremist—"This nation cannot survive half slave and half free." (King 1992, p. 94)

What is Obama's extremism? If anything, an extremism of hope—that "audacity" of hope of which his second book speaks, taking the expression from the Rev. Wright. But it is an extremism that, like Lincoln's and unlike King's, is tied to democratic mobilization to change the electoral process, rather than the pacifist direct action that King directed against the going political and legal institutions. Obama's roots in community organizing were never in the same mode as King's, drawing rather on the more secular influence on King represented by Saul Alinsky's form of community organizing. On the other side, he could never really adopt the hard-nosed confrontationalism of Alinsky's followers, and sought refuge in the imagery and spirituality of the civil rights organizers. As he put it in *Dreams from My Father*:

> Such images [from the civil rights movement] became a form of prayer for me, bolstering my spirits, channeling my emotions in a way that words never could. They told me (although even this much understanding may have come later, is also a construct, containing its own falsehoods) that I wasn't alone in my particular struggles, and that communities had never been a given in this country, at least not for blacks. Communities had to be created, fought for, tended like gardens. They expanded or contracted with the dreams of men—and in the civil rights movement those dreams had been large. In the sit-ins, the marches, the jailhouse songs, I saw the African-American community becoming more than just the place where you'd been born or the house where you'd been raised. Through organizing, through shared sacrifice, membership had been earned. And because membership was earned—because this community I imagined was still in the making, built on the promise that the larger American community, black, white, and brown, could somehow redefine itself—I believed that it might, over time, admit the uniqueness of my own life. (Obama 1995, 135)

It is the unity, not the confrontation, in these images that inspires Obama, a unity he also felt and witnessed in the electoral victories in the 1980s of Chicago's first African American mayor, Harold Washington. This is the theme uniting *Dreams from My Father* and *The Audacity of Hope,* a work that is both a reflection on his political achievements and a resource for a great deal of his speechmaking, past and present. *Audacity* explains Obama's take on the civil rights movement at length, and in singularly pregnant terms, when addressing the long history of American racism going back to the Founders:

> How can I, an American with the blood of Africa coursing through my veins, choose sides in such a dispute? I can't. I love America too much, am too invested in what this country has become, too committed to its institutions, its beauty, and even its ugliness, to focus entirely on the circumstances of its birth. But neither can I brush aside the magnitude of the injustice done, or erase the ghosts of generations past, or ignore the open wound, the aching spirit, that ails this country still.

The best I can do in the face of our history is remind myself that it has not always been the pragmatist, the voice of reason, or the force of compromise, that has created the conditions for liberty. The hard, cold facts remind me that it was unbending idealists like William Lloyd Garrison who first sounded the clarion call for justice; that it was slaves and former slaves, men like Denmark Vesey and Frederick Douglass and women like Harriet Tubman, who recognized power would concede nothing without a fight. It was the wild-eyed prophecies of John Brown, his willingness to spill blood and not just words on behalf of his visions, that helped force the issue of a nation half slave and half free. I'm reminded that deliberation and the constitutional order may sometimes be the luxury of the powerful, and that it has sometimes been the cranks, the zealots, the prophets, the agitators, and the unreasonable—in other words, the absolutists—that have fought for a new order. Knowing this, I can't summarily dismiss those possessed of similar certainty today—the antiabortion activist who pickets my town hall meeting, or the animal rights activist who raids a laboratory—no matter how deeply I disagree with their views. I am robbed even of the certainty of uncertainty—for sometimes absolute truths may well be absolute.

I'm left then with Lincoln, who like no man before or since understood both the deliberative function of our democracy and the limits of such deliberation. We remember him for the firmness and depth of his convictions—his unyielding opposition to slavery and his determination that a house divided could not stand. But his presidency was guided by a practicality that would distress us today, a practicality that led him to test various bargains with the South in order to maintain the Union without war; to appoint and discard general after general, strategy after strategy once war broke out; to stretch the Constitution to the breaking point in order to see the war through to a successful conclusion. I like to believe that for Lincoln, it was never a matter of abandoning conviction for the sake of expediency. Rather it was a matter of maintaining within himself the balance between two contradictory ideas—that we must talk and reach for common understandings, precisely because all of us are imperfect and can never act with the certainty that God is on our side, and yet at times we must act nonetheless, as if we are certain, protected from error only by providence.

That self-awareness, that humility, led Lincoln to advance his principles through the framework of our democracy, through speeches and debate, through the reasoned arguments that might appeal to the better angels of our nature. (Obama 2006, 97–98)

This is, to be sure, the ultimate pragmatist stance—namely, to avoid being dogmatic even about pragmatism. And Obama is in the finest Chicago pragmatist tradition in this appropriation of Lincoln. But the point here is that this negotiation between King and Lincoln has Obama flatly on the side of

Lincoln. Community organizing has met electoral compromise, and pragmatism in the narrow sense has met pragmatism in the larger philosophical sense.

As Andrew Delbanco notes, in a perceptive essay on Obama, "His books are 'how-to' books about his own exemplary success at competing with others in the marketplace, but they are also conversion narratives about his discovery that serving others is the only way to save himself" (Delbanco 2008, 22). But this "service" floats across many different tactics, without drawing the sharp boundaries between direct action and politics that both Alinsky and King (and the founders of CORE, the Congress of Racial Equality) drew.[8] And it is precisely because of this that Obama can become, in effect, the hope of the Mikva Challenge—someone bringing the ethical attractions of service back to electoral politics. This is as much Harold Washington as King, and more Lincoln than Washington. As Delbanco rightly argues:

> One feels in Obama's books as well as his speeches the presence of that iconic American, Abraham Lincoln, whom he sometimes names and sometimes namelessly invokes. In *The Audacity of Hope*, he tells of having once received a rebuke ("not entirely undeserved") for presumptuously likening himself in print of Lincoln. On his first visit to the White House as a freshman senator, he tells us, Lincoln appeared to him as a ghostly figure "pacing the hall, shouldering the weight of a nation," the moral and political genius who managed to maintain "within himself the balance between two contradictory ideas. . . ."
>
> This description of Lincoln as a man of self-doubt yet with an unswerving sense of mission is as instructive as it is insightful. Obama seems to have composed his public life in conscious emulation of Lincoln. He announced his candidacy in Springfield and delivered his speech on race in Philadelphia, where Lincoln, en route to his first inauguration, gave a great speech on the Declaration of Independence as American's secular scripture. In his victory speech on the night of clinching the Democratic nomination, Obama incorporated or played variations on several phrases from Lincoln—"the last full measure of devotion," "the last best hope of earth," "the better angels of our nature."
>
> To some, it all seems calculated and hubristic, and they will no doubt continue to detect in his style a self-involved inwardness. But, to me, it feels like heartfelt homage from someone with a keen sense of the complexities and commonalities of human experience. (Delbanco 2008, 22)

Delbanco is surely correct on many counts. Some, notably James Fallows, have suggested that Obama the presidential debater was a far cry from the Obama who debated in 2004 with a wry sense of fun and wit (Fallows 2008). But a broader comparison of Obama's self-presentations, in his speeches, books, interviews, etc. suggests that, whatever his sense of fun, his message has remained remarkably constant and consistent in its Lincolnesque pragmatism, the pragmatism of this worldly doubt and action. The gravity and more restrained expression, like the heightened oratorical skills, were timely additions to Obama's talents, coming relatively late in the day. Like the strategic repetitions in his speeches, quotations of or allusions to his own earlier words, they provide a subtext of constancy and stability through all the self and nation reconstructing and creating.

Indeed, the Rortyean style appropriation of Lincoln as the source of personal and political self-creation is about as much of a constant in Obama as anything. As his Springfield "Declaration of Candidacy" speech wound to its conclusion, the identification was forthright:

> By ourselves, this change will not happen. Divided, we are bound to fail.
> But the life of a tall, gangly, self-made Springfield lawyer tells us that a different future is possible.
> He tells us that there is power in words.
> He tells us that there is power in conviction.
> That beneath all the differences of race and region, faith and station, we are one people.
> He tells us that there is power in hope.
> As Lincoln organized the forces arrayed against slavery, he was heard to say: "Of strange, discordant, and even hostile elements, we gathered from the four winds, and formed and fought to battle through."
> That is our purpose here today.
> That's why I'm in this race.
> Not just to hold an office, but to gather with you to transform a nation.

The positive fits of anaphoric word play only accentuate how Obama, like Rorty, Dewey, and Addams (whose father was friends with Lincoln) seeks comfort and inspiration from Lincoln, especially when the doubt and self-doubt start to gnaw. And in fact, it is well worth stressing in this context that Obama's own favorite speech from among his productions is the one that he delivered to a Chicago antiwar rally in October of 2002. It was a risky speech, since it was politically risky at that time to oppose Bush's Iraq policy, and Obama made it all the riskier, given his audience, by going out of his way, in his usual anaphoric mode, to distance himself from anything smacking of Gandhi's or King's pacifism:

> What I am opposed to is a dumb war. What I am opposed to is a rash war. What I am opposed to is the cynical attempt by Richard Perle, Paul Wolfowitz and other armchair, weekend warriors in this administration to shove their own ideological agendas down our throats, irrespective of the costs in lives lost and in hardships borne. What I am opposed to is the attempt by political hacks like Karl Rove to distract us from a rise in the uninsured, a rise in the

poverty rate, a drop in the median income—to distract us from corporate scandals and a stock market that has just gone through the worst month since the Great Depression.

That's what I'm opposed to. A dumb war. A rash war. A war based not on reason but on passion, not on principle but on politics. (quoted in Mendell 2007, 175)

The big divide, with Gandhi and King on one side and Lincoln on the other, comes with, not just the philosophy of direct action to bring social change, but with the pacifist philosophy of direct action—against a more eclectic, less absolutist, electorally open set of strategies. He was indeed "left then with Lincoln." Obama never underestimates the power of words, especially Lincoln's words. And those words are not the words of an absolutist pacifism.

And of course, it is just here that one finds the materials for understanding both the wider and narrower senses of Obama's pragmatism. After all, Lincoln was one of the figures that pragmatists from Dewey to Rorty most wanted to appropriate. Consider Rorty's account, in *Achieving Our Country*:

The contrast between national hope and national self-mockery and self-disgust becomes vivid when one compares novels like *Snow Crash* and *Almanac of the Dead* with socialist novels of the first half of the century— books like *The Jungle, An American Tragedy,* and *The Grapes of Wrath.* The latter were written in the belief that the tone of the Gettysburg Address was absolutely right, but that our country would have to transform itself in order to fulfill Lincoln's hopes. Transformation would be needed because the rise of industrial capitalism had made the individualist rhetoric of American's first century obsolete.

The authors of these novels thought that this rhetoric should be replaced by one in which America is destined to become the first cooperative common wealth, the first class-less society. This America would be one in which income and wealth are equitably distributed, and in which the government ensures equality of opportunity as well as individual liberty. This new, quasi-communitarian rhetoric was at the heart of the Progressive Movement and the New Deal. It set the tone for the American Left during the six decades of the twentieth century. Walt Whitman and John Dewey . . . did a great deal to shape this rhetoric. (Rorty 1998, 8–9)

Indeed, as Rorty goes on to explain, in words redolent with resonance with Obama's political language:

I think there is no point in asking whether Lincoln or Whitman or Dewey got America right. Stories about what a nation has been and should try to be are not attempts at accurate representation, but rather attempts to forge a moral identity. The argument between Left and Right about which episodes in our history we Americans should pride ourselves on will never be a contest between a true and a false account of our country's history and its identity. It is better described as an argument about which hopes to allow ourselves and which to forgo.

As long as our country has a politically active Right and a politically active Left, this argument will continue. It is at the heart of the nation's political life, but the Left is responsible for keeping it going. For the Right never thinks that anything much needs to be changed: it thinks the country is basically in good shape, and may well have been in better shape in the past. It sees the Left's struggle for social justice as mere troublemaking, as utopian foolishness. The Left, by definition, is the party of hope. It insists that our nation remains unachieved. . . . Whitman and Dewey were among the prophets of this civic religion. They offered a new account of what America was, in the hope of mobilizing Americans as political agents. (Rorty, 14–15)

In this sense, then, Obama is clearly of the Left, of the party that hopes because it sees the need for change. The broad tone is that of this school of Progressivism, though without the overt references to any form of economic socialism or economic democracy. Obama, like the British political philosophers of the generation prior to Dewey—e.g., Henry Sidgwick and T. H. Green—obviously prefers a form of ethical socialism, a civic ethic of service to the common good as one of the best means to one's own good, without thinking that this necessarily translates into any actual form of economic socialism.

Moreover, as stated above, Obama's own rhetorical tactics fit this Rortyean mode of rhetorical hope-making extremely well. Like Rorty's somewhat opportunistic retelling or reconstruction of the western tradition of philosophy, Obama's retelling or reconstruction of American political history and his own life story are, avowedly, moves in the effort to forge a moral identity, not to represent something already given. The "community I imagined was still in the making"—and he is helping to construct it, assembling the materials of a useable past in the light of the future. This is indeed only a "quasi" or democratically qualified form of communitarianism (much like Dewey's). It is precisely the type of antiessentialist pragmatism, applied to racial identity as well as other forms of identity, that Tommy Shelby and Eddie Glaude have persuasively defended in recent years (see, especially, Shelby 2005 and Glaude 2007). Thus, the ruthless appropriation of the solidarity of the sixties civil rights movement, but not the pacifist direct action, or "extremism," and of the grass roots mobilizing of the community organizing tradition, but without the opposition to or disdain for electoral politics, are suggestive of the creative reconstruction that Obama represents and that Rorty would have adored. And this is not to mention the identification with Lincoln's self-doubt in the service of decisive action to overcome deep social divisions. It is the type of pragmatist reconstruction that at times can seem a bit like a self-esteem movement for the nation as a whole, with its accentuation of the positive and the possibilities of the future. Yes We Can!

However, Obama is the political figure genuinely in line, not only with recent pragmatist critics of racial essentialism and identity politics, but also with the strands of Lincolnesque pragmatism that made Dewey, Addams, and then Rorty and many others think Lincoln needed to be appropriated in the first place. His speechmaking and political rhetoric unfailingly invoke this legacy. He has been sworn in as president by placing his hand on the Lincoln bible, after coming to Washington by train in conscious emulation of Lincoln. His farewell to the people of Illinois echoed Lincoln's words, quoted at the beginning of this essay, and if one wants an advance guide to the key words and lines he will invoke during any important moment or event, one can do no better than to turn to accounts of what Lincoln said or did at some parallel point in his career. It was a genuine surprise that his Inaugural Address, as president, harked back to Washington rather than Lincoln in its chosen end quotation, but even in doing so, the stagesetting and cadences (and the familiar anaphora) were Lincoln's: "This is the source of our confidence—the knowledge that God calls on us to shape an uncertain destiny." The speech was shorter on direct quotations than any other major Obama speech, and clearly meant as an exercise in direction rather than indirection, with Obama using his own voice, a voice of sobriety befitting the times. The opening line was worthy of Lincoln: "I stand here today humbled by the task before us, grateful for the trust you have bestowed, mindful of the sacrifices borne by our ancestors." It was indeed a Lincolnesque "New Birth of Freedom," but one with especially strong resonances to another favored Obama source, Emerson's "Self-Reliance.'"

All of which might suggest some complications to my analysis. For, like Lincoln, but seemingly unlike Dewey, there is in Obama's thinking a streak of cosmic sadness, of resignation. Obama's reading list includes, like Lincoln's, much Shakespeare. It also includes Reinhold Niebuhr, often regarded as another arch counterpoint to Deweyan pragmatism, one who shared more of Lincoln's depressive sense of human failing. The sense of sin and human weakness, of predatory self-interest, that Niebuhr highlighted in his work, as a contrast to Deweyan optimism, needs to be fitted to the larger pragmatist framework. But this is best done by bringing out yet more of the connection between Obama and the University of Chicago. For once again, it is the Chicago pragmatist tradition that best explains and exemplifies the core elements of Obama's philosophy. Chicago pragmatism has always found much to be sad about.

V. Depressive Pragmatism

The various facets of Obama's Chicago pragmatism mentioned thus far—his emphasis on democratic, progressive education and future generations, on bottom-up politics and community service, on democracy as a way of life or culture of deliberation and participation, on combining direct action and electoral action, on experimentalism and fallibilism, on America as hope and the land of self-creation rather than fixed identities, etc.—do not fully capture the tensions and apprehensions of his philosophical orientation or the richness of the Chicago pragmatist tradition. But to better appreciate the significance of that tradition, it is necessary to turn to some of its more recent proponents, theorists, and activists who, like Rorty, have given that legacy such ongoing relevance.

In her moving work, *Talking to Strangers: Anxieties of Citizenship since Brown v. the Board of Education,* the afore cited Danielle Allen, formerly both a professor of political science and dean of the humanities at the University of Chicago, defends a form of political rhetoric ("talking to strangers") that, she maintains, can help build up the forms of civic friendship and trust crucial to a healthier democratic culture. Drawing on recent work on both the theory and practice of democracy, especially the work on democracy and social capital made famous by Robert Putnam (another direct influence on Obama), Allen claims that the pervasive distrust and alienation that has distorted American politics, and that is especially evident in the tensions of racial politics, stems in part from the failure to recognize the enabling sacrifices made by various groups of citizens, especially people of color. Drawing heavily on Ellison's novel *Invisible Man* and the touching, courageous sacrifice made by Elizabeth Eckford in the famous battle to integrate Little Rock's Central High School, she points to various ways, including rhetoric, by which the sacrifices of peoples rendered invisible by the political culture might be recognized and reconciliation achieved, with a much enhanced circulation of knowledge across various racial, ethnic, and social barriers. America, she holds, underwent a new founding during the civil rights era, but we have yet to complete the work of building civic friendship that the civil rights movement began.

Allen's vision has also been shaped by her background in classics and her work with Josiah Ober on ancient Athenian democracy. The more participatory, direct form of democracy that marked ancient Athens was characterized in part by a more fluid circulation of knowledge across different knowledge communities, such that political life reflected a richer and more inclusive social intelligence, at least for citizens. Adapting that lesson to our very different circumstances, Allen nonetheless holds that it is possible to improve democracy as a way of life here and now by cultivating new citizenly habits of trust, friendship, and communication that share something of the ancient model of civic friendship. And in this, she certainly shares much with the Deweyan legacy, though without explicitly acknowledging the overlap between her democratic theory and that of, say, *The Public and Its Problems*. Like Dewey, she casts democracy in cultural terms, as a set of background habits and practices that create the context for certain types of institutional arrangements. When applying her views through concrete institutional reforms, such as the creation of the University of Chicago's Civic Knowledge Project, she in effect cast her model of democratic friendship in highly Deweyan terms as the most effective mobilization of social intelligence.

But of special interest here is Allen's case for political rhetoric as a vehicle for facilitating these new citizenly habits and richer conception of civic knowledge. To her mind, and contra such conservative or neoconservative political theorists as the Straussians, rhetoric, properly understood, "is not a list of stylistic rules but an outline of the radical commitment to other citizens that is needed for a just democratic politics." It is "the art not of rousing people to immediate or unthinking action but of putting as persuasive an argument as possible to an audience and then leaving actual choices of action to them" (Allen 2004, 141). Even so, she does formulate a list of suggestions for equipping ourselves to change our habits:

In order to generate trust, a speaker should

— aim to convince 100 percent of her audience; if she finds herself considering rather how to carry a majority, she is acting in a fashion that over the long term will undermine democracy;
— test herself by speaking to minority constituents whose votes she does not need;
— once she has found the limits of her ability to persuade, she should think also about how to ameliorate the remaining disagreement and distrust;
— "separate the people from the problem" by (i) developing external standards and universal principles for assessing problems and (ii) recognizing that dealing with the people means engaging with specific features of their subjective situation;
— be precise about which emotions are at stake in a particular conversation;
— seek to transform conditions of utility into experiences of good-will;
— recognize that reciprocity is established over time and that enough trust has to be generated to allow this process to proceed;
— recognize that the most powerful tool for generating trust is the capacity to prove that she is willing to make sacrifices even for the strangers in her polity;
— be aware too that she is trustworthy only if she can point to a *habit* of making sacrifices for strangers and not merely to a single instance;
— recognize that where there is no trust, a great sacrifice will be necessary to sow the first seeds of trust, which can develop only over time

through repeated interactions in which citizens have opportunities to
test each other;
— give her audience opportunities for judging (accepting or rejecting) her
arguments;
— be willing to have any member of the polity respond to her arguments;

In order to prepare the way for the generation of trust, a listener should

— separate a speaker's claims about facts from the principles on which her
conclusions are based; assess both;
— ask whether a speaker has a history of making pragmatically correct
decisions;
— ask who is sacrificing for whom, whether the sacrifices are voluntary,
and honored; whether they can and will be reciprocated;
— ask whether the speaker has spoken as a friend;
— insist on opportunities to judge political arguments;
— judge.

Here then are some new habits to try on. Rhetoric is relevant not only in the
halls of the legislature and in the courtrooms but wherever any stranger has
to convince another of anything. Any interaction among strangers can generate trust that the polity needs in order to maintain its basic relationships.
If citizens keep in mind these guidelines for speaking and listening to their
fellow citizens, they will import the expertise of ordinary friendship into the
political realm, and political friendship will grow out of that. Political
friendship thus generated sustains a democratic polis by helping citizens to
accept decisions with which they may disagree. But friendship must be
mutual. (Allen 2004, 157–58)

In a great many respects, Obama's rhetoric fits this model. In his major
speeches, his campaign tactics, and in his presidential debate performances, he has
been conspicuous in his efforts to speak to a wider range of citizens, generously
acknowledge the strengths of his opponents, and reach out to those not won over.
His candid confessions, acknowledgements of his own weaknesses, and magna-
nimity toward opponents have often succeeded, in classical rhetorical fashion, in
persuading people of the strength of his character and convictions, not their weakness. By and large, though not completely, refusing to go in for personal attacks
on his opponents, he has reserved most of his remarks about character for soul-
searching discussions of his own strengths and weaknesses. And like Allen, Obama
appeals to self-interest mostly in a much more exalted sense than material self-
interest. Finding oneself through service, through devotion to the common good,
especially for future generations—that is the message he resolutely sticks to, so
much so that when he talks of sacrifice, it is less of the sacrifices he has made and
more of how the sacrifices of others have enabled him to hope and succeed. His

message, like Allen's, is the Ellisonian one, the vivid empathizing with and recognition of sacrifice. And it is very much the message that he shares with his most important partner, his wife Michelle (née Robinson), a product of Chicago's South Side who has also worked for the University. Her work in community relations has also often sounded the Dewey-Allen note: "'We have so much more in common as people,' she told *People* magazine in 2007. 'It's just that we don't cross paths enough as communities'" (quoted in Mundy 2008, 119).

Ironically, however, Allen's account, which fits Obama so well in so many ways, has it that a key problem in the American effort to cultivate new citizenly habits is the fixation on oneness, on unity, the *e pluribus unum* that celebrates maximal agreement and obscures the loss and sacrifice that the real world of democracy entails. She urges a common democratic faith that settles for wholeness, achieving reconciliation between winners and losers through better habits of genuinely reciprocal civic friendship, rather than fantasies of having somehow overcome all difference and loss in oneness.

Perhaps in practice Obama is not quite as distant from Allen on this point as it would seem, at first blush. But it is impossible not to acknowledge his extraordinary commitment to the rhetoric of oneness, of unity. Americans may be "a people of improbable hope," but their aspirations—to "'live free from fear and free from want . . . speak our minds and assemble with whomever we choose and worship as we please'—are bigger than anything that drives us apart." We can "answer our destiny and remake the world once again" only through unity. Consider his remarks on Martin Luther King, Jr. day, 2009:

> Today, we celebrate the life of a preacher who, more than 45 years ago, stood on our national mall in the shadow of Lincoln and shared his dream for our nation. His was a vision that all Americans might share the freedom to make of our lives what we will; that our children might climb higher than we would.
>
> Dr. Martin Luther King's was a life lived in loving service to others. As we honor that legacy, it's not a day just to pause and reflect—it's a day to act. Today, ordinary citizens will gather together all across the country to participate in the more than 11,000 service projects they've created using USAservice.org. And I ask the American people to turn today's efforts into an ongoing commitment to enriching the lives of others in their communities, their cities, and their country.
>
> Tomorrow, we will come together as one people on the same mall where Dr. King's dream echoes still. As we do, we recognize that here in America, our destinies are inextricably linked. We resolve that as we walk, we must walk together. And as we go forward in the work of renewing the promise of this nation, let's remember King's lesson—that our separate dreams are really one.[9]

And this of course is simply another side of the language of Lincoln, which above all was devoted to the rhetoric of union. As helpful as Allen's analysis is for filling in the details of and updating the rhetorical pragmatism that Rorty theorized and Obama practices, it has some enormous gaps, one of the most problematic of which is her complete disregard for the role of Lincoln in American political rhetoric and democratic practice. Despite her emphasis on the new founding of the civil rights movement, her detailing of the ideal of oneness moves away from actual American political history to deal with theorists from Hobbes to Habermas, who have had very little actual influence on American political culture. Yet Lincoln was the architect of the second American covenant, and Obama's recognition of his importance, like Rorty's, has been a mainstay of the pragmatist reconstruction of the American political tradition. Intriguingly, the crucial mediation between oneness and wholeness was theorized by another University of Chicago pragmatist political scientist, whose work bridged the period from Alinsky to Allen—J. David Greenstone.

Greenstone, an extraordinarily creative political scientist who died in 1990 at the tragically young age of 52, had a profound effect on both the Department of Political Science and the College at the University of Chicago. He had traveled an unusual academic path from a specialization in American labor politics and educational policy to a focus on the broader philosophical and cultural dimensions of the American political tradition, developing along the way a passionate interest in the philosophy of Ludwig Wittgenstein that shaped his analysis of the languages and practices of American political life, highlighting (like Allen) the importance of habits and background contexts for their interpretation. Remarkably, Greenstone appreciated the deep filiations between Wittgensteinian philosophy of language and American pragmatism long before Rorty and his followers did. And even more remarkably, he had spelled out, long in advance of *Achieving Our Country*, something very like Rorty's take on Deweyan (or Wittgensteinian) pragmatism and its links to the figure of Lincoln. In his posthumously published book, *The Lincoln Persuasion: Remaking American Liberalism* (1993), some of the crucial points are made in the following passage:

> The point is not that Lincoln's enthusiasm for institutions overrode his belief in individual development; on the contrary, as a devotee of Whig culture, Lincoln believed that the improvement of individual and society were almost inseparably joined. He considered the collective activities of past and present generations to be morally worthy, because they were indispensable for the cultivation of individual human reason. In his most interesting discussion of this question, at the height of the slavery crisis in 1859, Lincoln examined the connection between the "habit" of ratiocination and "the most important discoveries and inventions," that is, between *reflection* and

experiment. In his view, the process of rational inquiry was essentially communal. Not only was "the inclination to exchange thoughts with one another . . . probably an original impulse of our nature" but, especially when language becomes written, it was this exchange—sometimes across generations—that enabled "different individuals to . . . combine their powers of observation and reflection, greatly [facilitating] useful discoveries and inventions. . . . What one observes . . . he [then] tells to another . . . [and a] result is thus reached which neither *alone* . . . would have arrived at."

This view casts in a progressive and egalitarian form the familiar Whig belief in the importance of social and historical development. Anticipating the arguments of the late-nineteenth-century Pragmatists, Lincoln emphasized the importance of a community of inquiry and practice that depended on both socially established habits and socially shared language. As a number of authors have suggested, Emerson can be seen as a link between the Puritans' focus on nature as God's handiwork and the Pragmatists' emphasis on naturalism. Similarly, Lincoln represents a link between the Puritans' focus on society and the Pragmatists' emphasis on community and scientific collaboration. Lincoln's argument about the nature of this community is indicative of perhaps his most fundamental justification for unionism; it is an argument that echoes that of the tenth Federalist paper: the full exercise and development of human reason requires not the intimacy of a small, morally homogeneous community, but the diversity and freedom of a geographically and temporally extended republican society.

For Lincoln, in other words, there was a symbiotic relationship between individual development and the institutional life of a community. Lincoln thought that only a regime devoted to improving the capacities of its members for self-development could rightfully be called the Union. His emphasis on the social dimensions of inquiry, however, also suggests the converse: that the humanitarian cause of individual improvement could flourish only in a republican society large and complex enough to sustain human inquiry and progress. (Greenstone 1993, 277–78)

Sadly, the fuller account of the transition from Lincoln to the pragmatists that Greenstone planned to publish was never completed. But his interpretive line was clearly articulated in some brilliant articles completed before he shifted his attention to Lincoln. Thus, in "Dorothea Dix and Jane Addams: From Transcendentalism to Pragmatism in American Social Reform" (1979), Greenstone argued:

By Jane Addams's time, a clearly weakening belief in moral certainty and moral community had created a political and intellectual crisis that threatened the viability of the social reform tradition to which Dix had made such signal contributions. On one side, interest-oriented liberals could quite easily rally to a new social Darwinist rationale for a self-interested politics. But if the standards tradition was to continue to invoke human rationality (acting prior to or independent of sense experience) as a warrant for developing each individual's moral and intellectual capacities, then that rationality would have to be redefined.

Pragmatism provided a philosophic response to this problem. On a Pragmatist view, the claim that the universe is unfinished and that we cannot attain final truth, or that our knowledge of particular objects is never complete, does not reduce the status of human rationality. Rather, these claims make rationality all the more important. If these claims are valid, human knowledge (including the interpretations that render sense experience meaningful) is radically dependent on an active process which seeks to define objects more clearly by moving from hypothesis, through experiment and confirmation, to still further hypothesis.

Addams's achievement was to connect epistemology to ideology, to link the Pragmatists' new account of rational thought to the theory and practice of social reform and social service. In that sense, she helped introduce into American social and political thought both a new version of and a new justification for the reformer's traditional vision.

None of this is to say that Addams successfully resolved the reformers' great problem: that the contradictions within a society might be simply too great to respond to the appeals to conscience and moral standards so central to the reform tradition. If this problem can be solved, and perhaps it can, it may require moving beyond the somewhat abstract and optimistic features of Dewey's Pragmatism to the related but more critical and concrete philosophy of Ludwig Wittgenstein. (Greenstone 1979, 553–54)

As these passages demonstrate, Greenstone's interpretation of the American political tradition contested the view, long associated with Louis Hartz, that there was a single dominant, and highly Lockean, American political ideology. Greenstone was more impressed by what he called the "bi-polarity" in American liberalism, the ways in which the larger political culture had in fact always suffered versions of the same tensions marking democratic theory and practice that the University of Chicago had. Against something more akin to classical rights or interests-based liberal individualism, one could always find a counterforce shaped by a passion for moral and democratic reform that could not fit that paradigm. To be sure, this counterforce, in the larger drama of American history, went through many transformations, from a more conscience based, Transcendentalist version to a more this worldly pragmatist one. In a sense, Greenstone, like Allen, seizes on the illusions of oneness, and the difficulties of achieving even wholeness. But unlike Allen, and very much like Rorty, he brilliantly reconstructed and revived the pragmatist gambit of making Lincoln the pivotal figure in this transition. Lincoln's vision of Union was that of a community built on habits of civic friendship, true, but it was also of a diverse, multicultural community of inquirers—in key respects, a forerunner of Deweyan democratic community, in which people cultivate their humanity and apply their social intelligence in social experiments aimed at solving the problems they face together, and this without any transcendental guarantees of success or even being on the right path.

Thus, Greenstone was prescient in his appreciation of how Dewey and Addams hung together, how their epistemological and philosophical positions could be helpfully updated through later philosophical developments (Wittgenstein and other philosophers of language, notably Donald Davidson), and how in the American context, the living reality of pragmatism owed a crucial debt to the legacy of Lincoln. Although Greenstone did not use the word "rhetoric" in the way he might have, his keen appreciation for the language of politics and its cultural, habitual context amounted to the same thing. Like Allen, he did not share the invidious Straussian comparison between rhetoric and philosophy, despite having shared an academic Department with Strauss himself. And it is also worth mentioning that he knew the Alinsky approach to democratic activism intimately.

Now, the larger point here is of course that this Lincoln, Greenstone's Lincoln, is the Lincoln of Obama. There have been a great many academic and nonacademic efforts to come to terms with the Lincoln legacy, and they have run a very wide gambit, from Lincoln as Great Man, to Lincoln as opportunist, to Lincoln as racist, etc. But surprisingly little of this interpretive work has had the philosophical sophistication of the pragmatists, both early and late, from Addams and Dewey to Greenstone and Obama. And with philosophers, at least, Lincoln has magnetized pragmatists like no other political figure, no doubt because of his deeply experimental temper in grappling with the deeply divisive problems of forging democratic community. What Obama has found in Lincoln just is what the pragmatists have always found in him, and this has been a type of pragmatism long associated with the University of Chicago. It is a vision of a democratic community as an educating community, as an experimental, open community of inquiry that through participation mobilizes our collective intelligence and problem-solving abilities.

And crucially, what this reading of Lincoln opens up is a form of Deweyan pragmatism that can address the charge advanced by Niebuhr—namely, that the Deweyan democratic faith goes too far in its repudiation of the notion of sin and human weakness. It is a charge that largely dissolves on examination. After all, experiments, social or scientific, can fail, and the powers of quick adaptation and alert intelligence could not be realized without a compelling candor about the limitations of the world.

But no serious reader of *Twenty Years at Hull House* or Dewey's political works could come away thinking that these authors lacked contact with the world's harsh cruelties. Again, Westbrook has sounded the right note, bringing out the ways in which Niebuhr and Dewey in fact shared many of the crucial views:

Dewey was not an optimist and Niebuhr was not a pessimist. Both made a point of distinguishing their position from each of these views of human destiny. Each, albeit in very different language, advanced a view of experience and nature which warned against both the pride and arrogance of optimism and the despair and abasement of pessimism. Both were members of the party of humility and faith. Dewey no less than Niebuhr could caution that "humility is more demanded at our moments of triumph than at those of failure" and advise "a sense of our dependence upon forces that go their way without our wish and plan." And Niebuhr no less than Dewey could declare his faith in an ethical ideal that tightly wedded self-realization and community. "By the responsibilities which men have to their family and community and to many common enterprises," he said, "they are drawn out of themselves to become their true selves." (Westbrook 1991, 529–30)

Contrary to Niebuhr's often more or less slanderous misrepresentations, Dewey knew full well the cruel and depressing realities of worldly politics, including very worldly Chicago politics. He simply wondered why anyone was supposed "to believe that every man is born a sonofabitch even before he acts like one, and regardless of how and why he becomes one?" (Westbrook 1991, 530). True, Niebuhr took a much bleaker view of the possibilities for real-world democracy, but on this count, both Dewey and Obama, like Lincoln, discovered in the world a much richer practice of citizenship as demanding service and recognizing the need for sacrifice—Obama's Inaugural Address, like Lincoln's Gettysburg Address, expressly linked the key notion of service to the sacrifices made by members of the military. For both, the aspiration to Oneness is built on the recognition of sacrifice and the sadness and setbacks of our uncertain destiny. Henry Louis Gates, Jr. and John Stauffer put it well in a recent *New York Times* editorial:

> Lincoln's great achievement, in the eyes of posterity, was really the outcome of his ingrained pragmatism. The Emancipation Proclamation was born of a certain opportunism . . . and is not a lesser thing for it. Perhaps there is a lesson for Mr. Obama here: those who invoke high ideas and scorn compromise often bring themselves into disrepute. Those whose actions are conditioned by an exquisite sense of frailty, by an understanding that it's more important to avoid the worst than to attain the best, may better serve those ideals in the end. (Gates and Stauffer 2009)

Has Obama actually read Greenstone? Allen? Rorty? At one level, it scarcely matters. Just as his daughters, as students at the Lab Schools, absorb Deweyanism as a matter of course, the intellectual air he breathed both as an organizer and at the University was simply filled with these ideas—ideas that one of his leading advisors, Cass Sunstein, was directly involved in developing. Until his recent move to Harvard, Sunstein held appointments in both the Law School and the Department of Political Science at the University of Chicago, and he was a close colleague of Greenstone's, one whose own work on deliberative democracy—e.g., *The Partial Constitution* (1993) or *Republic.com* (2001)—has long been positively steeped in Deweyanism, especially Deweyan worries about the dangers of self-insulation and atomistic individualism. Sunstein's work, which merits an essay in itself, in effect traces the more deliberative, reformist side of Greenstone's liberal bipolarity back to Madisonian roots, and forcefully critiques, on grounds of both Constitutional law and political tradition, constructions of American liberalism as mere preference or interest aggregation. Especially with respect to the changes to political communication wrought by the information age and the Internet, Sunstein's works represent the best update of Deweyan pragmatism since Rorty. *Republic.com* builds much of its case on Dewey's words: "No man and no mind was ever emancipated merely by being left alone" (Sunstein 2001, 192).

Sunstein knows Obama very well indeed, labeling him a "Chicago" liberal, and explaining, in words suggesting Dewey's challenge to the quest for certainty:

> In the 2000 campaign, Bush proclaimed himself a "uniter, not a divider," only to turn out to be the most divisive President in memory. Because of his own certainty, and his lack of curiosity about what others might think, Bush polarized the nation. Many of his most ambitious plans went nowhere as a result.
>
> As president, Barack Obama would be a genuine uniter. If he proves able to achieve great things, for his nation and for the world, it will be above all for that reason. (Sunstein 2008)

Sunstein, whom Obama has now tapped to head the Office of Information and Regulatory Affairs, was part of the faculty consulting group that assembled *The Lincoln Persuasion* for publication after Greenstone's untimely death. Even if Obama has never read this book, he has clearly been exposed to its ideas many times over from colleagues who were part of the community of inquirers who produced it. And this is not to mention Axelrod, a product of Greenstone's Department of Political Science (he chaired it when Axelrod began his studies) and Greenstone's College (he was Master of the Social Sciences Collegiate Division when Axelrod graduated).

Still, it is true that Greenstone's influence on political philosophy, especially in its American context, and Chicago pragmatism generally, has not been as widely appreciated as it should have been. This is one of those University of Chicago legacies that takes a bit more local knowledge to appreciate.

But perhaps now, as the new generations of political philosophical interpreters struggle to make sense of a presidency that has already been declared historic, there will be a renewed appreciation for that less than dominant side of the University of Chicago's political history that has always struggled to make its voice heard. The arc of the rhetorical universe has indeed been long. But at last it is clear that with Obama, whatever his fondness for and admiration of Gandhi and King, it is the rhetoric of Lincoln that matters most, and moreover the rhetoric of Lincoln is the rhetoric of pragmatism. How fitting that the nation is celebrating the Lincoln Bicentennial at the very same moment it is welcoming the most Lincolnian president since Lincoln himself. Praise song for the day, the words of the poet.

Notes

1. See Obama et al. (2008).
2. Inaugural Address, January 20, 2009.
3. See Despres (2005).
4. See especially the "Epilogue" to her *Talking to Strangers* (2004).
5. See http://civicknowledge.uchicago.edu/files/Origins.pdf.
6. See De Zutter (1995) and Obama's contribution to the book *After Alinksy: Community Organizing in Illinois* (1990).
7. All references to Obama's speeches are to the authorized versions included in *Change We Can Believe In* (2008) or on the official Obama Web site, http://www.barackobama.com/index.php.
8. See, for example, "The Civic Knowledge Project Remembers 1942-43," at http://mahimahi.uchicago.edu/media/ckp/1942-3_768k.mov.
9. http://my.barackobama.com/page/community/post/stateupdates/gGxH9J.

References

Addams, Jane. 1902. *Democracy and social ethics*. New York: Macmillan.

———. 1910. *Twenty years at Hull House with autobiographical notes*. New York: Macmillan.

Alinsky, Saul, 1971, *Rules for radicals: A practical primer for realistic radicals*. New York: Random House.

Allen, Danielle S. 2004. *Talking to strangers: Anxieties of citizenship since Brown v. Board of Education*. Chicago: University of Chicago Press.

Bachin, Robin. 2004. *Building the South Side: Urban space and civic culture in Chicago, 1890–1919*. Chicago: University of Chicago Press.

Bryan, M. L. M., and Allen F. David, eds. 1990. *100 years at Hull House*. Bloomington: Indiana University Press.

Burlingame, Michael. 2008. *Abraham Lincoln: A life*. Baltimore, MD: Johns Hopkins University Press.

Delbanco, Andrew. 2008. Deconstructing Barry: A literary critic reads Obama. *New Republic*. July 9.

Despres, Leon. 2005. *Challenging the Daley machine: A Chicago alderman's memoir*. Chicago: Northwestern University Press.

Dewey, John. 1927. *The public and its problems*. New York: H. Holt & Co.

———. 1990. The school as social center. In *100 years at Hull House*, edited by M. L. M. Bryan and Allen F. David. Bloomington: Indiana University Press.

De Zutter, Hank. 1995. What makes Obama run? *Chicago Reader*. December 8.

Fallows, James. 2008. *Atlantic*. Rhetorical questions. September.

Gates, Jr., Henry Louis, and John Stauffer. 2009. A pragmatic precedent. *New York Times*. January 18.

Gibson, Lydialyle. 2008. Elemental Obama. *University of Chicago Magazine*. 101 (1): 45.

Glaude, Eddie. 2007. *In a shade of blue*. Chicago: University of Chicago Press.

Greenstone, J. David. 1979. Dorothea Dix and Jane Addams: From transcendentalism to pragmatism in American social reform. *Social Service Review* 53 (4): 527–59.

———. 1993. *The Lincoln persuasion: Remaking American liberalism*. Princeton, NJ: Princeton University Press.

Hayes, Christopher. 2008. The pragmatist. *Nation*. December 10.

Horwitt, Sanford. 1989. *Let them call me rebel: Saul Alinsky, his life and legacy*. New York: Vintage Books.

King, Jr., Martin Luther. 1963. *Strength to love*. New York: Harper & Row.

———. 1992 [1986]. *I have a dream*. San Francisco: Harper.

Lippmann, Walter. 1922. *Public opinion*. New York: Harcourt, Brace and Company.

McKinney, Dave, and Abdon M. Pallasch. 2008. Locally, it's all good: Obama in White House helps city's Olympic bid. *Chicago Sun-Times*. November 5.

Mendell, David. 2007. *Obama: From promise to power*. New York: Amistad.

Mundy, Liz. 2008. *Michelle*. New York: Simon & Schuster.

Obama, Barack H. 1990. Why organize? Problems and promise in the inner city. In *After Alinksy: Community organizing in Illinois,* edited by Peg Knoepfle. Springfield, IL: Sangamon State University Press.

———. 1995. *Dreams from my father: A story of race and inheritance*. New York: Times Books.

———. 2006. *The audacity of hope : Thoughts on reclaiming the American dream*. New York: Crown.

Obama, Barack H., and Obama for America. 2008. *Change we can believe in: Barack Obama's plan to renew America's promise*. New York: Crown Books.

Putnam, Hilary. 1995. *Pragmatism*. Oxford: Blackwell.

Rorty, Richard. 1998. *Achieving our country: Leftist thought in twentieth-century America*. Cambridge, MA: Harvard University Press.

Schultz, Bart. 2008. The Civic Knowledge Project remembers 1942-43. http://mahimahi.uchicago.edu/media/ckp/1942-43_768k.mov.

Shelby, Tommy. 2005. *We who are dark*. Cambridge, MA: Harvard University Press.

Sunstein, Cass R. 1993. *The partial constitution*. Cambridge, MA: Harvard University Press.

———. 2001. *Republic.com*. Princeton, NJ: Princeton University Press.

———. 2008. The Obama I know. March 5. http://www.huffingtonpost.com/cass-r-sunstein/the-obama-i-know_b_90034.html.

University of Chicago Magazine. 2008. September-October.

Westbrook, Robert. 1991. *John Dewey and American democracy*. Ithaca, NY: Cornell University Press.

6

BARACK OBAMA AND THE POLITICS OF BLACKNESS

Ron Walters

University of Maryland

O n Sunday, March 11, 2007, Senator Barack Obama of Illinois took his
presidential campaign to Brown Chapel in Selma, Alabama, where he
was the keynote speaker on the occasion of the 42nd anniversary of "Bloody
Sunday," the event that ushered in the 1965 Voting Rights Act. This was
more than a normal campaign event for him; it would be not only a commemoration of a historically important civil rights march that took place in
1965, it would help answer the question of whether he was "Black enough"
to appeal legitimately for the Black vote as an African American candidate
for president of the United States.

The drama of this occasion, however, was heightened by the fact that
Obama's competitor and the front-runner for the Democratic nomination
for president, New York senator Hillary Clinton, would not be left out of
the competition for the Black vote and requested to speak simultaneously in
Selma at the First Baptist Church. In a February 2007 *Time*/Associated Press
poll, Clinton led Obama 41% to 17%, with John Edwards close behind
at 16%. But by the end of February, Clinton's lead had narrowed to 36%
to 24%, with Al Gore at 14% and Edwards 12% (Balz & Cohen, 2007).
The shift in ratings among the two leaders in February was due largely to
the growth of Black support for Obama: In the earlier poll, Blacks favored
Clinton 60% to 20%, but in the later poll, Obama had pulled ahead, at 44%
to Clinton's 33% (Balz & Cohen, 2007). Thus, it seemed that for many Black
voters, Obama had begun to prove his Blackness.

Source: Journal of Black Studies, September 2007; vol. 38, 1: pp. 7-29, first published on
July 18, 2007.

The Public Controversy Over Obama's Blackness

Reading Barack Obama's (1995) first book, *Dreams From My Father*, one becomes aware that it is virtually the story of his journey into functional Blackness. Having grown up in America except for 3 years, the experiences Obama presents of cultural exclusion, vilification with the "N word," and association with and socialization into the racial confusions of Black youth build a predicate for his search for community. Thus, he wrote, when he was ready to begin to function seriously as an adult,

> I knew it was too late to ever claim Africa as my home, and if I had come to understand myself as a black American, and was understood as such, that understanding remained unanchored to place. What I needed was a community, I realized, a community that cut deeper than the common despair that black friends and I shared when reading the latest crime statistics, or the high fives I might exchange on a basketball court. A place where I could put down stakes and test my commitments. (p. 115)

In other words, Obama answered a question raised on the same page in a letter from his father, who instructed him to "know where you belong," and he proceeded to resolve the issue by accepting his identity as an African American with its attendant commitments, and he set out to test them functionally as a leader of the Black community.

This grounding in Blackness gave Obama the requisite sensitivity to the problems of the Black community and strategies used to address them. However, the deployment of his talents in a distinctly moderate legislative institution that demands collegiality and negotiation among dissonant forces to achieve anything creates in him a practical politician's approach. Thus, we learn in *The Audacity of Hope* (Obama, 2006, pp. 231-259) that although he is sensitive to the fact that part of the attraction of Whites to him is that he represents a "postracial" era, he is cautious about that in light of the obvious racism still rampant in most theaters of American life; how we close the gap with Whites in achievement is as much a factor of the continuing enforcement of our civil rights as it is the adoption of negative behaviors that impede progress; and because White guilt has lost its currency as an instrument of change, perhaps universalistic policies should be pursued in an effort to lift the remaining boats stuck in the mire of poverty and oppression. In short, it is the game of seeking tactical advantage, given the prevailing winds, rather than sailing against them to make the most dramatic changes in America's racial course possible.

The question of Obama's "Blackness" initially caused considerable comment, because some thought that it was an inappropriate issue, a point countered by writers who appeared to be culturally Black nationalist and thus hostile to the prospect of his candidacy as an untraditional "African American." For example, Stanley Crouch, a Black columnist for the *New York Daily News*, wrote in a November 2006 article about Obama that "other than color, Obama did not—does not—share a heritage with the majority of black Americans, who are descendants of plantation slaves." And although my objection to the following statement is outside the context of this article, Crouch went on to qualify his initial observation: "Of course, the idea that one would be a better or a worse representative of black Americans depending upon his or her culture or ethnic group is clearly absurd." This plainly limits the force of his observation to the rather simple fact that Obama's heritage is different, which makes his identity different, leaving open its political meaning.

Then, Debra Dickerson (2006), a Black writer with *Salon*, an online magazine, added her voice, appearing to say much of the same thing:

> "Black," in our political and social reality, means those descendants from West African slaves. Voluntary immigrants of African descent (even if they are descended from West Indian slaves) are just that, voluntary immigrants of African descent with markedly different outlooks on the role of race in their lives and politics.

However, Dickerson's point was that the attribution of Blackness to Obama is something of a shill in that he is being used as a substitute for a traditional, or "real," Black person as a more acceptable version. She wrote that in "swooning" over Obama, "you're not embracing a black man, a descendant of slaves. You're *replacing* the black man with an immigrant of recent African descent of whom you can approve without feeling either guilty or frightened." As such, she wrote, that amounts to a methodology of getting over slavery: "Lumping us all together . . . erases the significance of slavery and continuing racism while giving the appearance of progress."

The chorus of objections to Crouch's (2006) and Dickerson's (2006) views by media and various Black Americans supporting Obama's campaign was substantial. Typical of the responses was that of a CBS News reporter, who asked,

> What does "not black enough" mean, anyway? Are you more black if you grew up in an all-black neighborhood, and less black if you grew up around a mix of cultures? Is hair part of the equation? If it's natural, does that make you more black?
>
> Is blackness measured in percentages, so that any white person in one's gene pool dilutes one's purity? So if you're half-black, you're mulatto; one-quarter black: a quadroon, one-eighth black: an octoroon? Do we really want to go back to that time in our history? (Giles, 2007)

Marc Hansen (2007), a reporter for the *Des Moines Register*, strongly opined that it was "ridiculous" to doubt Obama's "blackness." However, Hansen exhibited his distance from the Black community when he suggested that he had never heard former Representative Harold Ford Jr. of Tennessee questioned as to the quality of his Blackness, given the conservative cast of Ford's views. Another reporter, with the *San Francisco Chronicle*, considered the idea of attempting to determine Obama's cultural authenticity "ugly business," writing that it "is both the most ridiculous and the most destructive issue I've seen in the last decade of watching politics" (Millner, 2007).

Nevertheless, such criticisms amount, in my view, to an unsophisticated conception of the political meaning of "Blackness" as an essential concept of Black identity, bounded by skin color, biology, history, and culture. In fact, there are different kinds of Black people in America, a Black diaspora if you will, a fact that increasingly complicates the use of categories in America that were originally meant for the majority of Blacks with a history that stretches back to ancient Africa and includes the legacy of slavery and postslavery oppression. Witness the recent complication in the higher education community among some who observe that at certain Ivy League institutions, a disproportionate majority of "Blacks" are in fact the sons and daughters of Africans born on the continent. Indeed, this issue has come to the fore because of the rapid growth of the African-born population. Census data show that in the nearly 100 years between 1891 and 1980, fewer than 200,000 African-born residents came to America, but in the period from 1990 to 1999 alone, there were 346,416 (Austin, 2006). In the most recent census decade, however, this number has rocketed to nearly 500,000, or double the previous amount. Those who are charged with administering affirmative action programs of course face both the moral and political propriety of the selection of such enrollees as minority "stand-ins" for American-born Blacks as a contribution to the category of statistics known as "peoples of color." And although this category is used for various reasons, including to give the impression that an institution is "colorblind," it also violates the original intent of affirmative action as a method of creating equal opportunities for Americans of African descent.

In any case, I consider the views of both Dickerson (2006) and Crouch (2006) to be excessively particularistic and narrow, in that as they recognize the special history of Black Americans, they also appear to close off the opportunity of those who have different kinds of "Black" identity to share the experiences of community. In his comments, Crouch regarded such pan-African views as "naive" and wrote that

> if he [Obama] throws his hat in the ring, he will have to run as the son of a
> white woman and an African immigrant. If we then end up with him as our

first black president, he will have come into the White House through a side door—which might, at this point, be the only one that's open.

This work acknowledges the caution reflected in the Crouch–Dickerson perspective and that of others about his campaign, while examining the link between the meaning of Obama's identity and the nature of Black political behavior in the end.

Validity of the Black Perspective

It is an immutable reality that a uniquely "Black" identity was created in America (whatever it is called in each historical era) as the result of historical ties and cultural practices. This culture, although marked by oppression in America, also exhibits the same richness of cultural complexity containing social triumph and public achievement as any other. Professor Roger Wilkins wrote of this:

> Every oppressed community, or any community that thinks of itself as a community has drawn lines and says certain behavior puts you outside the community. For Black Americans who live in a society where racism exists, it is legitimate to set parameters. In arguing how best we struggle, there is some political and intellectual behavior in which you engage that keeps you from being a black person. (quoted in Williams, 1991, p. 1)

Several studies have confirmed the validity of the use of the identifying term *Black* by most individual Black Americans, the coherence of group racial identity as a cultural entity, and the importance of such shaping factors as education and confrontation with racism (Helms, 1990; Thompson, 1990). And while acknowledging the debates about factors that mitigate an essentialist concept of "Black culture," such as hybridity, immigration, class, and others, there is still substantial coherence to the concept in behavioral terms to lend substantial legitimacy to its use as an evaluative tool in political behavior.

The problem addressed here involves who retains rights to access this unique in-group concept and the complexity that poses for representational leadership in the local and national arenas. The logic of Wilkins's inference is that even someone from another culture of African descent might find it difficult to easily broach traditional parameters and assimilate easily into American Black culture.

I found in researching *Pan Africanism in the African Diaspora* (Walters, 1986, pp. 54-88) that the attempt of some Black Americans who went to Ghana to identify as traditional "Africans" in the excitement of the independence era of the 1960s was also often marked with derision by indigenous Africans and ultimately failure. Similarly, the communities of Black people living in the diasporas of America, London, Latin America, and the Caribbean have the same intercultural difficulties of relating to each, as previous research on West Indian and Black Americans has shown (Foner, 2001).

Here, the strength of the acculturation of the incoming Black group to the traditional group already in place is important to a person from the incoming group being able to effect legitimate interest representation. For example, to the degree that African-born Blacks are able to experience the range of American-style social dynamics, with similar forms of oppression and victory (the realization of police racism by the family of West African Amadou Diallo, who was murdered in Brooklyn several years ago, or the participation of Washington, D.C., cab drivers from Africa in the local elections), they may over time develop similar perspectives on public issues. Indeed, researchers have shown that a foundation for legitimizing representation by nontraditional African descendants is that Black Americans have more positive attitudes toward immigrant Africans than other immigrant groups (Thornton & Taylor, 1988).

Thus, it is legitimate that Black Americans raise questions about "Blackness" as an objective issue, because it is the core concept that defines the basic cultural identity of Black people. That is why the cultural identity of Barack Obama evoked such confusion. He appeared to be of African descent, but the cultural markers to which traditional American Blacks were exposed presented him as someone born of a White American mother and a Kenyan father and raised in Hawaii. Also, the fact that he had lived for a while in Indonesia complicated the matter further. In short, his identity omitted many of the cultural markers with which Blacks are more familiar to the extent that it has promoted a curiosity of "cultural fit" that in turn has become an issue of political trust.

Political studies have traditionally shown that complications of trust ultimately affect political behavior (Hetherington, 2005). And although these studies have shown that because of the negative consequences of racism in American society, Blacks' trust in the political system has been less than that of Whites, there is also evidence, from a study by Professor James Avery (2006), that "trust among African Americans follows more from racial group consciousness than from short-term political and policy evaluations" (p. 654). Thus, the perceived lack of credibility in Obama's group or cultural identity affects the confidence of many potential Black voters in his political accountability to their agenda.

In this context, whether Obama looks Black, or who his ancestors were, matters, but ultimately less than his commitment to Black interests, and Blacks have historically been cautious about the issue of group representation. For instance, in 1976, when Jimmy Carter asked for Black support, he was largely unknown in the Black community, and therefore there was considerable initial reticence to support him, as a former Georgia governor. Andrew Young, a trusted aide to Dr. Martin Luther King Jr., mayor of

Atlanta, and a member of the U.S. House of Representatives, then brokered Black support through the "King wing" of the Black leadership, creating a valid cultural stamp of approval (Jennings, 1992, p. 172; Stone, 1977).

Another source of cultural caution is that Blacks have been misled by skin politics. When Clarence Thomas was nominated as associate justice of the U.S. Supreme Court in 1991 and there arose some Black opposition, there were also credible voices in the Black community promoting the notion that because he was physically Black, his conservative policy posture would change over time to reflect mainstream Black interests, and thus Blacks should "give the brother a chance" (Thomas, 2001, pp. 358, 479). However, once nominated, Thomas has become a constant irritant to the attempts of Black leaders to foster aspects of civil rights.

Such caution may be warranted, in fact, because of Obama's universalistic perspective on policy issues. This style of discourse was characterized by Obama himself in an interview with Steve Inskeep (2007) of National Public Radio, when he said, "There has always been some tension between speaking in universal terms and speaking in very race-specific terms about the plight of the African American community. By virtue of my background, I am more likely to speak in universal terms." However, Inskeep cited a contrasting view from an interview between Representative Bobby Rush of Chicago (a former political opponent) and National Public Radio correspondent Juan Williams, in which Rush said bluntly, "I'm a race politician and he's not. I don't compromise. I don't step back. I don't try to deny. I'm proud to be an African American." But when Steve Kroft (2007) of CBS News asked Obama how important race was to his identity when he was growing up and at what point he decided he was Black, Obama responded, "Well, I'm not sure I decided it. I think, you know, if you look African-American in this society, you're treated as an African-American. And when you're a child in particular, that is how you begin to identity yourself." Most important was his statement that he was "rooted in the black community, but not defined by it" (Kroft, 2007).

The universalistic perspective is supported by former Virginia governor Doug Wilder, who has said that neither he nor Obama views politics through a strict prism of race. In the several conversations between Wilder and Obama, Wilder said, "One thing we discussed is that there are no such things as 'black issues.' Health and education are not black issues. Improvement of job opportunities is not a black issue" (Curiel, 2007). Of course, my view rejects this assertion, because even though both Virginia Union (a Black university in Richmond) and the University of Virginia (in Charlottesville) both need higher education funding, the historic lack of adequate funding for Virginia Union due partially to a racial rationale is by definition a "Black issue." This definition of issues specific to the Black community follows wherever their interests are disproportionately represented.

Nevertheless, Wilder's perspective as a candidate seeking statewide office or governing is compelling: As with David Dinkins, former mayor of New York City, and other Black candidates vying to represent large minority Black geographical areas such as states, Black voters have been challenged to adopt a sophisticated posture to support their campaigns. If the candidates had previously established confidence among Black voters, based on their historical and cultural experience in the Black community, Black voters would most likely reciprocate by allowing the candidates to run on liberal universal themes, because there would be an unspoken understanding that such candidates could not be expected to run "Black campaigns." The question here may be how close Obama's campaign agenda will approximate those issues.

Black Political Accountability

Some analysts have misunderstood the difference between direct and indirect representation of Black interests, as reflected in the difference between candidates such as Reverend Jesse Jackson or Reverend Al Sharpton and traditional presidential campaigns. For traditional candidates, Blacks often must construct a test of political accountability. However, some members of the media, such as commentator Arianna Huffington (2007), for example, have asserted that the reticence of some civil rights leaders, such as Sharpton, to embrace Obama amounted to a "hazing ritual," the source of which is jealousy and ego. However, let me pose an equally valid motivation on the basis of the integrity of the quest for political accountability. Civil rights and political leaders have been relied on by the Black community to vet anyone who presents himself or herself before the community for its support. Political accountability is used to ensure that the issues most directly relevant to the Black community are raised at the highest level of politics in exchange for Black voter influence.

Never was this clearer than in the 2000 election cycle, when Senator Joe Lieberman of Connecticut was selected as Al Gore's running mate on the Democratic ticket. There had been some questions about Lieberman's position on affirmative action, suggesting that he had, in the past, opposed it or proposed that it become class based (Brazile, 2004, pp. 252-256). In any case, accountability was demanded by Representative Maxine Waters of California, and at the Democratic National Convention that year, Lieberman was questioned by leaders of the Black Democratic Caucus in a closed session about his views on affirmative action before receiving the support of the Black delegates. When he assured Black leaders of his fidelity to this policy, they encouraged others to support him.

A Nontraditional "Black" Campaign

None of the questions about community trust and the consequent confidence in the nature of the link between policy issues and their presidential campaigns were raised in the cases of Jackson and Sharpton, because their campaigns arose from within the Black community. They had been familiar to Blacks before these elections, serving them in various ways as heads of highly visible organizations in the field of civil rights. But by arising from within the Black community, they also arose at the periphery of the American electorate, a fact that defined the nature of the campaigning and the style, agenda, and audience addressed. In *Freedom Is Not Enough* (Walters, 2005, pp. 133-148), I evaluated both the 1984 and 1988 presidential campaigns of Jackson, because I considered them to be the most important mobilizations of the Black community in presidential politics to date, and fashioned a loose-knit "Jackson model" from their key aspects. Given the characteristics of the Jackson campaigns, I have concluded that Obama's campaign will not be able to use critical aspects of this model.

The Jackson campaigns shared several major features:

1. A candidacy motivated essentially to empower the Black electorate: Obama's motivation as presented in his campaign announcement is to respond to the national desire for new leadership, fueled by American opposition to an unpopular war, rather than Jackson's dedication to the "boats stuck on the bottom of society" as the rationale for his campaign.
2. Campaign mobilization dedicated to foster immediate social change as well as win votes: Obama's campaign style is in the mode of a traditional voter-appeal mobilization, with no substantial side benefit offered for supporters or unique groups of supporters. Jackson used his campaign to bring public attention to the social justice causes of various groups in the process of appealing for votes.
3. Collaboration with the Black civic culture to affect voter registration as well as voter turnout: Obama's campaign stops do not feature the element of voter registration; rather, he is competing for the electorate as configured. Jackson sought to expand the electorate as an empowerment strategy for minority groups and as a way of boosting the possibilities of an untraditional candidacy.
4. A policy focus that was a vehicle for the assertion of Black interests: Obama's policy aims, although liberal to progressive, are more universalistic and lack concentrated attention to the Third World or issues that are associated strongly with underrepresented American groups. Jackson, on the other hand, championed progressive policies toward Cuba, the Palestinians, Nicaragua, the Middle East, and Africa, as well as civil rights for women, small farmers, gays, Blacks, and other dispossessed groups.

Adopting a Traditional Campaign Posture

Therefore, the assessment above raises a more important question than Obama's biology in asking to what extent the location from which his campaign arises in the center of the electorate will be compatible with the policy interests of the Black community. In other words, will the style of his campaign and the policies he supports permit the interests of the Black community to compete successfully in the internal space within his campaign with the strong structural forces necessary to retain the ability to attract White voters and major financial contributors? I present below some indications of this contentious dynamic, reflected in his avoidance of direct encounters with controversial racially characterized issues.

Obama (2004) was introduced to the American people for perhaps the first time on a national stage as a key speaker at the 2004 Democratic National Convention. In that role, he discussed the inner city in a way acceptable to centrists, saying,

> Go into any inner city neighborhood, and folks will tell you that government alone can't teach our kids to learn. They know that parents have to parent, that children can't achieve unless we raise their expectations and turn off the television sets and eradicate the slander that says a black youth with a book is acting white.

As he closed his remarks, which were wrapped in the symbolic patriotism of the founders, flag, and country, he produced a rhetorical flourish, saying,

> I say to them tonight, there's not a liberal America and a conservative America—there's the United States of America. There's not a black America and a white America and a Latino America and Asian America—there's the United States of America.

The exercise of self-direction among Blacks is a well-accepted fact, essentially because it has been the major resource of Black advancement. However, Obama did not address the balance that is necessary by calling to attention the public policy responsibility to enrich Black neighborhoods so that the exercise of individual responsibility may bear the maximum fruit. It would be left to Al Sharpton to deliver a speech that called up the legacy of civil rights as the ground on which they both stood, and while acknowledging the importance of self-direction in his own family, Sharpton (2004) also pointed to the failures of public policy in the founders' vision of America's promise: "The promise of America says we will guarantee quality education for all children and not spend more money on metal detectors than computers in our schools."

Second, Hurricane Katrina created one of the most awesome scenarios of devastation the nation had ever seen, and the equally awesome maelstrom of human damage created an emotional moment of historical proportions because of the depth of the neglect of the government's response in a situation that affected Blacks disproportionately. A CNN poll revealed that 60% of Blacks believed that their race was implicated in the slow response of government, and 63% believed that poverty was also a factor ("Reaction to Katrina," 2005). Yet Senator Obama (2005) responded that he did not believe the slow response of the government to be racially based, that it was "colorblind." Several days later, he said that although

> it was apparent on the first day that blacks were disproportionately impacted . . . it was important to frame how we think about that issue. I was outraged and heartbroken by what happened and felt anxious. I felt like I needed to do something. (Zeleny, 2005, p. 1)

However, as his chief adviser, David Axelrod, and others warned him to remain silent and avoid injecting himself into a racially charged issue, he felt that he had to respond publicly, as Axelrod would say, out of a sense of responsibility, both as a senator and "as an African American" (Zeleny, 2005, p. 1). In the end, Obama would characterize the dismissive attitude of the administration in the Katrina crisis as one related to class:

> It is way too simplistic just to say this administration doesn't care about black people. I think it is entirely accurate to say that this administration's policies don't take into account the plight of poor communities and this is a tragic reflection of that indifference. (Zeleny, 2005, p. 1)

It would be up to the reporter in this case to observe that although the issue of race was squarely presented in the public sphere, Obama's response was cautious in avoiding a direct encounter with the subject.

Third, another *Chicago Tribune* reporter wrote about the question of Obama's Blackness, couching this inquiry in the context of criticism of the principles that guided his church, Trinity United Church of Christ in Chicago. Trinity, with a congregation of nearly 9,000 people, was headed by one of the most celebrated preachers in the Black community, Reverend Jeremiah Wright Jr. The church had been criticized by conservative talk show host Sean Hannity of Fox News as pursuing a program of "Blackness" that was "separatist" insofar as it unashamedly honored and practiced a set of principles known as the "Black value system."

A March 2, 2007, interview of Wright by Hannity on the Fox News program *Hannity & Colmes* allowed Wright to explain that the Black value system is a set of principles and work committed to the liberation of the Black family and the Black community from the oppressive circumstances under which it exists. Nevertheless, the view of Hannity reflected that of other conservative critics, who accused the church of practicing a "cultist" or even racist doctrine ("Obama's Pastor," 2007). Although Obama was surprised that conservatives expressed criticism of his religion, considering the conservative aspects of his church's doctrine of self-reliance and self-help, his sensitivity to the criticism led him to disinvite Wright to the announcement of his candidacy for president.

Finally, on the cold, snowy day of February 10, 2007, Obama announced his candidacy for the Democratic nomination for president. His speech was given on the steps of the old state office building, a small building in Springfield, Illinois, where Abraham Lincoln once said, referring to slavery, that "a house divided against itself cannot stand." Obama used this powerful symbolism to strike a modern parallel, both to himself as a gangly young lawyer and to the divisions that beset the nation, reflected in the war in Iraq. One is hesitant to include race because there is no reference to American racial problems in the 20-minute speech. In fact, one reporter noted that Obama "did not make a single reference to the color of his skin. . . . Not once did the words 'black' or 'African-American' pass Mr. Obama's lips" (Baldwin, 2007). Rather, he highlighted his role at the cusp of a new generation, like John Kennedy, and set forth his desire to lead a process of transformation in resolving some of the most vexing problems of health care, education, the economy, the tyranny of oil, and ending the war in Iraq by bringing the troops home by March 2008 (Obama, 2007).

At the exact time of his announcement, a group of nationally regarded Black leaders and intellectuals were participating in The State of Black America townhall meeting, an annual forum, at Hampton University in Virginia sponsored by talk show personalities Tom Joyner and Tavis Smiley. The gathering had been invited there in honor of the celebration by the State of Virginia in honor of the 400th anniversary of the English landing at Jamestown and the construction of the colony that began the American experiment. In light of the fact that the Virginia General Assembly had also expressed its "profound regret" for slavery, this venue was considered a likely site for Obama's announcement. Indeed, one of the agenda items was to consider the viability of Obama's candidacy for president.

However, Obama canceled his appearance, an act that produced a mixed chorus of both support and criticism by participants related both to the chosen site for his announcement and his race-neutral agenda. Some feelings paralleled those of a North Carolina funeral director who participated in the Hampton meeting: "The focus of what's represented here needs to be the agenda of anybody who's running" (Bogues, 2007). Obviously, what had emerged by that time was caution within the Obama campaign about his association with racially controversial issues, which were represented by the balance of issues addressed at Hampton.

In this sense, Obama has suffered from such questions about his Blackness not only because of the lack of familiarity of American Blacks with him personally but because his campaign arose in the middle of the electorate, and as such, he contributed to questions about trust and confidence and thus to issues of accountability, to some extent, by political positions that he himself has taken. These positions were not only symptomatic of the emergence of his campaign; they may also be material to the reason why his campaign arose in the middle of the electorate, because their racial neutrality may have given Whites more confidence that Obama would represent their interests effectively.

Adopting the Structural Requisites of Campaigning

Another major deviation from the Jackson model is structural in the sense that Jackson's fund-raising activities were strikingly limited, amounting to $3.5 million in 1984 and nearly $10 million in 1988; in the 2008 election cycle, the expected amount needed to campaign effectively is between $50 million and $100 million, with the total amount of the presidential campaign amounting to nearly $500 million per candidate for each of the major political parties through the general election (Kuhnhenn, 2007). In January 2007, Obama began his exploratory bid for president with an estimated $6.4 million available to his political action committee, Hopefund, an amount nearly twice as large as raised in 1984 by Jackson (Conrad, 2007). Somewhat later, analysts at the respected *National Journal* estimated Obama's fund-raising potential to be about $20 million by the end of 2007, somewhat less than the $25 to $30 million Hillary Clinton could raise and John Edwards's $15 million (McAuliff & Kennedy, 2007).

In March 2007, the fund-raising efforts of Obama were competitive with those of Hillary Clinton, as he crisscrossed the country at fund-raising events sponsored by his campaign or supporters, typically raising $100,000 to $500,000 at luncheons and over $1 million at large events (Wilkinson, 2007). One particularly notable event featuring Hollywood executives, such as famed movie producer Steven Spielberg, and progressive actors, such as George Clooney, Eddie Murphy, and Barbara Streisand, netted Obama $1.3 million. The news value of this event, however, was that David Geffen, also of DreamWorks, broke with Hillary Clinton in a dramatic way because of her centrist policy positions ("Sen. Barack Obama Pulls in $1.3 Million," 2007).

The political cost of these funds may not be as great to Obama, because they emerge from sources aligned with his own liberal views. Also, fund-raising among people in the tech industry may have little cost because they are not generally policy attentive (Hart, 2007). However, the Obama campaign raised considerable funds in several cities in Florida, with fund-raising stops in March (Times Wires, 2007). Perhaps to prepare him to appeal to centrist

Jewish groups in states such as Florida, Obama opposed the formation of the Palestinian unity government in a speech before the American Israel Public Affairs Committee (AIPAC) in Chicago, saying,

> We should all be concerned about the agreement negotiated among Palestinians in Mecca last month. The reports of this agreement suggest that Hamas, Fatah and independent ministers would sit in a government together, under a Hamas prime minister, without any recognition of Israel, without a renunciation of violence, and with only an ambiguous promise to "respect" previous agreements. . . . We must tell the Palestinians this is not good enough. (Siegel, 2007)

Press reports indicated that support for Obama's campaign from AIPAC was not offered, perhaps because in his maiden speech in Iowa, although he acknowledged a belief in the security of Israel, he also attracted considerable criticism for the view that "nobody is suffering more than the Palestinian people" (Beamont, 2007). Still, fund-raising reports show that he had collected $110,000 from pro-Israel sources as of June 2006, largely from the Chicago-based Pritzker family, which owns the Hyatt chain of hotels. AIPAC's treasurer, Lee Rosenberg, is also a member of Obama's finance committee (Cohler-Esses, 2007).

In the search for funds, Obama has also attracted sources of enormous wealth, such as billionaires Sheila Johnson (the African American cofounder of Black Entertainment Television) and George Soros, and he has used the fund-raising expertise of well-known financial giants such as Goldman Sachs and the European firm Credit Suisse. Although the exact political effect of support from such a group of financiers is not clear, it may bode a substantially moderate course in public policy for Obama, except perhaps where Soros is concerned. Soros, who gave over $35 million in the 2004 elections to defeat George Bush, is an antiwar political progressive who regards Obama as a "very honest and fine person" and a "transformational figure with a fresh voice" (White & Luce, 2007). But Soros (2007) also believes that a foreign policy that attempts to exclude Hamas is folly.

In any case, the surprise was that when the first quarter's fund-raising results were announced, Obama had raised only $1 million less than Hillary Clinton ($26 million to $25 million), with some analysts believing that in fact, Obama had won this first contest, given the fund-raising prowess of Bill Clinton. Moreover, Obama raised this amount from a base of 100,000 contributors, compared with 50,000 for Clinton (Philips, 2007). In any case, this was 2.5 times more than Jesse Jackson raised in his best effort, the campaign of 1988, no doubt a fact that gave Jackson far more flexibility with respect to issues and will give Obama far less.

Presidential Elections and the Blackness Criteria

The game of politics asks two questions: How many votes can you mobi-lize, and on what issue basis? In answering these questions, Blacks should have a single criterion for all candidates, be they Black or White: What policy proposals do the candidates present that are as close as possible to Black interests, and how do they deploy a positive campaign relationship that pro-motes the strongest electoral mobilization in the Black community? These are the keys to effecting power in the political system, but it means that both the cultural and political definitions of Blackness are critical.

Culturally, to provide Blacks with confidence-building material, Obama has to campaign effectively within the Black community on both the cultural and political levels. The cultural and political familiarity that he establishes will create the currency that will enable Black voters to positively link his identity to his program. Here, he begins the cultural presentation with strong assets: He is of African descent, he married a Black woman, he belongs to a Black church, and he lives in a racially integrated community. This cultural context alone defines him as very different from the normative Black conservative and creates the expected access and level of association with the Black community that is the starting point for accountability for any Black politician.

This also places the meaning of Obama's Selma visit into context. His deliberate attempt to connect with the legacy of Black struggle there is pre-sumptively regarded as more powerful than what did not occur at Hampton University at The State of Black America. In Selma, Obama asserted that he "stood on the shoulders" of the civil rights movement; that it was material in allowing his father to come to America, without which he would not have been born; and that it was the responsibility of his "Joshua generation" to carry the movement into the next century (Boyd, 2007).

Although his visit to Selma greatly strengthened the cultural and political definition of Obama's Blackness, his January 29, 2007, visit to New Orleans was also important, because in his second visit to the city, he was highly critical of the Bush administration's efforts 17 months after Katrina, say-ing that "there was not a sense of urgency" because there was "not one word . . . in the State of the Union address" and that it was "shameful" to give the impression that the country was forgetting about New Orleans (Dorning, 2007). The day after his visit to New Orleans, Obama submitted legislation on the war in Iraq, calling for a phased redeployment, with the majority of American troops to be withdrawn from the war effort by March 2008 (Strickland, 2007). He has also supported the Senate version of the minimum wage legislation and other issues of social significance.

His opposition to racism was presented forcefully in mid-April in the midst of the firing of Don Imus, the high-profile "shock jock" radio and TV host, who characterized the Rutgers University women's basketball team, which played for the national championship, as consisting of "nappy-headed hos." In an interview with ABC News, Obama indicated that he would not return to Imus's show and supported his removal (Tapper, 2007).

Politically, Barack Obama also has a formidable record as a liberal state senator in the Illinois legislature for 7 years that must be considered in defining his "political Blackness." For example, he was known as a consistently liberal senator, voting to raise the minimum wage, increase the earned income tax credit for low-income working families, end tax breaks for businesses, and repeal the state's 5% tax on gasoline. He earned a 100% vote from Planned Parenthood for his support of abortion rights; sponsored the Health Care Justice Act, studying ways to affect a statewide universal health care system; sponsored a requirement that law enforcement video-tape interrogations of suspected criminal offenders; and many other things ("Obama Record," 2007). Of course, there are also some aspects of his record on the conservative-leaning side, but these are far fewer in number and scope.

As a U.S. senator, although Obama has a 100% voting record on issues defined by the National Association for the Advancement of Colored People and a liberal voting record overall, he has described none of the issues he has supported as "Black issues" (National Association for the Advancement of Colored People, 2007; "The U.S. Congress Votes Database," 2007). However, as liberal issues, they approximate the interests of the Black community: Polling data show strong interest in the issues of Hurricane Katrina relief, Iraq withdrawal, the minimum wage, and others that might be described as such. In other words, in his public positions, Obama has come close to the public support of issues about which the Black community feels strongly.

The lack of resolving these issues has a cost, for like other social dynamics in America, race alters the playing field to some extent. For instance, there is an item in the polling data that recalls the Jackson model: Despite the lead Obama achieved among Blacks, there is some evidence that they have less confidence that he will be elected. The March poll of *The Washington Post* cited above reveals that when Blacks are asked who has the best chance of getting elected president, Obama scores 21%, John Edwards 22%, and Hillary Clinton 50% (Balz & Cohen, 2007). I believe this result obtains not because they perceive that he is less "Black" but because of other factors, such as a lack of confidence that Whites will vote for him, his lack of equal political experience with other candidates, or their perception that he cannot raise the requisite funds to be competitive. For although Obama led in February polls 44% to 33% among Blacks over Hillary Clinton, an April poll showed a 53% to 36% rebound by Clinton, creating the nagging feeling that Obama has not yet conquered the issue of his "Blackness" ("Poll: Presidential Races," 2007).

This suggests that the resolution of the issue of Obama's Blackness is the key to answering the question of whether most Blacks, especially the traditional American contingent, which is the largest, will acquire the confidence that he will carry their interests effectively into the campaign for president and therefore move his favorable rating among Blacks above the 80% range that is typical of Black political cohesiveness. In fact, confirmation that the Blackness issue is not yet resolved is found in the April CNN poll, demonstrating a sustained 51% to 35% lead for Clinton. But what was most striking was that 88% of Blacks appeared to hold the view that Clinton "understands the problems of people like me," whereas 77% held that view of Obama ("Poll: Presidential Races," 2007). This implies that Clinton is perceived as more politically "Black" than Obama.

Conclusion: Political Blackness Matters More

I have endeavored here to suggest that there is legitimacy to the issue of Barack Obama's Blackness insofar as its perceived strength or weakness regulates the political behavior of Blacks toward his appeal for support. His attempt to represent the Black community as one of his constituencies creates the test of accountability, which applies equally to him as it does to other candidates. Even as other Black candidates mounted campaigns for president from a more familiar location from within the Black community, proof that they were not exempt from the requirement of accountability resides in the criticism of Al Sharpton's campaign funding, and this test was also the basis of support for White candidates, as indicated above.

So, with respect to Obama's prospects for achieving the maximum "political Blackness" in the form of support from the Black community, I conclude that at least three major variables emerge from this discussion that may prevent his campaign from achieving the high level of Black support enjoyed by Jesse Jackson in the 1980s. They relate to a weaker link between Obama's cultural and political "Blackness," the structural requirements of the location of his campaign, and the existence of substantive competition from other candidates (an issue I have not had the opportunity to fully discuss).

First, the record shows that beyond his physiology, Obama has established a credible record of both assimilation into the Black community and political representation, which stands as a credible claim for Black political support. However, his "Blackness" is weakened by his tendency to exercise considerable caution with respect to strong support of symbols and issues of Blackness. As he indicated, this is consistent with his penchant to cast issues in universal terms, even if they are pitched from a liberal base.

Second, the distance between the structural requirements of the "Jackson model" and the centrist location from which Obama's campaign has arisen poses considerations that may demand a more race-neutral, or moderate, cast to his campaign issues, reminiscent of those of former Virginia governor Doug Wilder or former New York City mayor David Dinkins, as cited above. Thus, the distance between the Jackson model and Obama's campaign means that although Obama may not be able to represent issues current in the Black community with the strength desired, as a liberal politician, he could adopt positions much closer to the Black community than other candidates. This overall judgment flows from the balance between those issues presented above that he has previously adopted and those about which he has taken a cautious position.

Third, preliminary election polling indicates that for the first time, there could be a considerable split in the Black vote among major Democratic candidates. At this point, in early spring, polling data suggest the presence of serious competition between Obama and Clinton for the Black vote. However, Edwards attracts a much lower share of the Black vote (12% in the March poll and 5% in the April CNN poll), and rumors continue that Al Gore may make himself available to run for president, adding considerably more pressure on the cohesiveness of Black voters.

Therefore, the issue of Blackness, when reduced to both culture and politics, is not, as described by one conservative journalist, something coined by "'60s ideologues," a "narrow set of attitudes and experiences that were said to make up the black identity" (Staples, 2007). Indeed, one wonders how such a person would describe the cultural identity to which he or she belongs if Blackness is not at its core. Moreover, in political terms, the Black community is the most coherent voting bloc in American politics, averaging 85% support for Democratic presidential candidates from 1980 to 2000. So to argue that "Blackness" is an outmoded form of cultural identity begs the question of what cultural conception will provide the coherence and unity for Black political participation to achieve equivalent political power for Blacks in the 21st century.

The political posture of the Obama campaign that is addressed to identify with the Black community, but not to be totally defined by it, is part of the objective situation that it faces. However, this reality will also force upon it the constant project of negotiation that, in this case, may complicate the evaluation of many Blacks and prevent it from attracting the dominant share of the Black vote. And although many Black voters will deploy their sophisticated stance to support Obama, or do so because of the attractiveness of electing the "first Black president," still it is unlikely that this campaign will be unable to substantially evade the question every "Black" politician must resolve. Whether Harvard trained, exceedingly cosmopolitan, or not, the test of accountability is the extent to which the community with which a candidate identifies will be fundamentally served by his or her politics. Thus, Obama's campaign poses an interesting test, not only of his wider electoral viability, but of the value and effectiveness of political accountability as a value in the Black community itself.

References

Austin, A. (2006, May 8). Are Africans in America African Americans? *Black Directions*, 2(2). Available at http://www.thorainstitute.com/2006/05/black-dire ctions-vol-2-no-2.html

Avery, J. M. (2006). The sources and consequences of political mistrust among African Americans. *American Politics Research*, 34(5), 653-682.

Baldwin, T. (2007, February 12). Obama seeks "stay fresh" formula as he tries to widen appeal. *The Times*. Available at http://www.timesonline.co.uk/tol/news/ world/us_and_americas/article1368652.ece

Balz, D., & Cohen, J. (2007, February 28). Blacks shift to Obama, poll finds. *The Washington Post*, p. A1.

Beamont, T. (2007, March 12). Up-close Obama urges compassion in Mideast. *The Des Moines Register*. Retrieved from http://www.desmoinesregister.com/apps/ pbcs.dll/article?AID=2007703120330

Bogues, A. (February 11, 2007). Obama's dreams stir interest at HU event. *Daily Press*, p. 1A.

Boyd, H. (2007, March 8). Politicking in Selma: Obama and Clinton mark their turf. *The New York Amsterdam News*. Available at http://www.amsterdamnews.com/ News/article/article.asp?NewsID=76780&sID=4

Brazile, D. (2004). *Cooking with grease: Stirring the pot in American politics*. New York: Simon & Schuster.

Cohler-Esses, L. (2007, March 9). Obama pivots away from dovish past. *The Jewish Week*. Available at http://www.thejewishweek.com/news/newscontent.php3?artid= 13766

Conrad, D. (2007, February 15). *Obama: The senator with the Midas touch*. Available at http://obama.senate.gov/news/060215-obama_the_senator_with_ the_midas_touch/index.html

Crouch, S. (2006, November 2). What Obama isn't: Black like me on race. *New York Daily News*. Available at http://www.nydailynews.com/opinions/2006/11/02/2006- 11-02_what_obama_isnt_black_like_me_on_race.html

Curiel, J. (2007, March 11). The year of keeping up with Obama: Democrat candidates courting Black voters. *San Francisco Chronicle*. Available at http://www.sfchron- iclemarketplace.com/cgi-bin/article.cgi?f=/c/a/2007/03/11/ING1IOH2Q11.DTL

Dickerson, D. J. (2006, December 22). Colorblind: Barack Obama would be the great Black hope in the next presidential race—if he were actually Black. *Salon*. Available at http://www.salon.com/opinion/feature/2007/01/22/obama/index_np.html

Dorning, M. (2007, January 30). Obama rips U. S. effort after Katrina. *Chicago Tribune*. Available at http://www.chicagotribune.com/news/politics/chi-0701300049 jan30,0,7783635.story

Foner, N. (2001). The Jamaicans: Race and ethnicity among migrants in New York City. In N. Foner (Ed.), *New immigrants in New York* (Rev. ed., pp. 195-217). New York: Columbia University Press.

Giles, N. (2007, March 4). What exactly is "Black enough"? Nancy Giles ponders the question everyone seems to be asking. CBS News. Available at http://www.cbsnews.com/stories/2007/03/04/sunday/main2534119.shtml

Hansen, M. (2007, February 22). "Ridiculous" to doubt Obama's "Blackness." *Des Moines Register*, p. 1.

Hart, K. (2007, March 19). Local tech executives open wallets for Obama. Washingtonpost.com. Available at http://blog.washingtonpost.com/posttech/2007/03/obama_taps_into_tech_community.html

Helms, J. E. (1990). *Black and White racial identity: Theory, research, and practice.* Westport, CT: Greenwood.

Hetherington, M. J. (2005). *Why trust matters: Declining political trust and the demise of American liberalism.* Princeton, NJ: Princeton University Press.

Huffington, A. (2007, March 15). Thank you, sir, may I have another? Sharpton puts Obama through a political hazing ritual. *The Huffington Post.* Available at http://www.huffingtonpost.com/arianna-huffington/thank-you-sir-may-i-hav_b_43513.html

Inskeep, S. (2007, February 28). Obama to attend Selma march anniversary. National Public Radio. Available at http://www.npr.org/templates/story/story.php?storyId=7630250

Jennings, J. (1992). *The politics of Black empowerment: The transformation of Black activism in urban America.* Detroit, MI: Wayne State University Press.

Kroft, S. (2007, February 11). Candidate Obama's sense of urgency. CBS News. Available at http://www.cbsnews.com/stories/2007/02/09/60minutes/main2456335.shtml?source=RSSattr=60Minutes_2456335

Kuhnhenn, J. (2007, March 14). Presidential camps spend more than ever. *USA Today.* Available at http://www.usatoday.com/news/elections/2007-03-14-3848955441_x.htm

McAuliff, M., & Kennedy, H. (2007, March 18). For '08, it's life in the cash line: Prez seekers on run for 250G, every day. *The New York Daily News.*

Millner, C. (2007, March 2). The definition of political absurdity. *San Francisco Chronicle.* Available at http://www.sfgate.com/cgi-bin/article.cgi?f=/c/a/2007/03/02/EDGT1OD JHH1.DTL&hw=barack+obama+black+enough&sn=007&sc=586

National Association for the Advancement of Colored People. (2007). *How Congress voted: Civil rights federal legislative report card: 109th Congress 2005 & 2006: January 4, 2005 through December 9, 2006.* Available at http://www.naacp.org/pdfs/109th_final_report_card3.pdf

Obama, B. (1995). *Dreams from my father: A story of race and inheritance.* New York: Times Books.

Obama, B. (2004, July 27). *Keynote address.* Delivered at the 2004 Democratic National Convention, Boston. Available at http://www.pbs.org/newshour/vote2004/demconvention/speeches/obama.html

Obama, B. (2005, September 6). *Statement of Senator Barack Obama on Hurricane Katrina relief efforts.* Available at http://obama.senate.gov/statement/050906-statement_of_senator_barack_obama_on_hurricane_katrina_relief_efforts/index.html

Obama, B. (2006). *The audacity of hope: Thoughts on reclaiming the American dream*. New York: Crown.

Obama, B. (2007, February 10). Full text of Senator Barack Obama's announcement for president. Available at http://www.barackobama.com/2007/02/10/remarks_of_senator_barack_obam_11.php

Obama record may be gold mine for critics: Eight years as state senator were full of controversial votes, including abortion and gun control. (2007, January 17). CBS News. Available at http://www.cbsnews.com/stories/2007/01/17/politics/main2369157.shtml

Obama's pastor: Rev. Jeremiah Wright. (2007, March 2). *Hannity & Colmes*. Available at http://www.foxnews.com/story/0,2933,256078,00.html

Philips, K. (2007, April 16). Campaign cash, details, details. The Caucus. Available at http://thecaucus.blogs.nytimes.com/tag/campaign-cash

Poll: Presidential races tighten on both sides. (2007, April 27). CNN.com. Available at http://www.cnn.com/2007/POLITICS/04/16/poll.2008/index.html

Reaction to Katrina split on racial lines. (2005, September 13). CNN.com. Available at http://www.cnn.com/2005/US/09/12/katrina.race.poll/index.html

Sen. Barack Obama pulls in $1.3 million in Hollywood fundraiser. (2007, February 21). Fox News. Retrieved from http://www.foxnews.com/wires/2007Feb26/0,4670,Presidentialfundraising,00.html

Sharpton, A. (2004, July 28). Text of Al Sharpton's address to the Democratic National Convention. *The Washington Post*. Available at http://www.washingtonpost.com/wp-dyn/articles/A21903-2004Jul28.html

Siegel, J. (2007, March 9). Barack Obama steps up bid for Jewish backing. Forward.com. Available at http://www.forward.com/articles/barack-obama-steps-up-bid-for-jewish-backing

Soros, G. (2007). On Israel, America and AIPAC. *The New York Review of Books*, 54(6). Available at http://www.nybooks.com/articles/20030

Staples, B. (2007, February 11). Decoding the debate over the Blackness of Barack Obama. *The New York Times*. Available at http://www.nytimes.com/2007/02/11/opinion/11sun3.html?ex=1328850000&en=1e1beeebd5c954e9&ei=5088&partner=rssnyt&emc=rss

Stone, C. (1977, January). Black political power in the Carter era. *The Black Scholar*, 8, 6-16.

Strickland, K. (2007, January 30). Obama's Iraq plan. MSNBC.com. Available at http://firstread.msnbc.msn.com/archive/2007/01/30/45227.aspx

Tapper, J. (2007, April 11). Obama: Fire Imus. ABC News. Available at http://www.abcnews.go.com/Politics/story?id=3031317&pages=1

Thomas, A. P. (2001). *Clarence Thomas: A biography*. San Francisco: Encounter.

Thompson, V. S. (1990). Factors affecting the level of African American identification. *Journal of Black Psychology*, 17(1), 19-35.

Thornton, M. C., & Taylor, R. (1988). Intergroup perceptions: Black American feelings of closeness to Black Africans. *Ethnic and Racial Studies*, 11, 139-150.

Times Wires. (2007, March 19). Obama comes to Tampa. *St. Petersburg Times*. Available at http://sptimes.com/2007/03/19/Hillsborough/Obama_comes_to_Tampa.shtml

The U.S. Congress votes database: Members of Congress: Barack Obama. (2007). Available at http://projects.washingtonpost.com/congress/members/o000167/

Walters, R. (1986). *Pan Africanism in the African diaspora.* Detroit, MI: Wayne State University Press.

Walters, R. (2005). *Freedom is not enough: Black voters, Black candidates and American presidential politics.* Lanham, MD: Rowman & Littlefield.

White, B., & Luce, E. (2007, March 8). Obama takes on Clinton for Wall St cash. MSNCBC.com. Available at http://www.ft.com/cms/s/277c3936-cce8-11db-a938-000b5df10621.html

Wilkinson, H. (2007, February 27). Obama's appeal keeps donors coming: Downtown breakfast raises up to $500,000. *The Enquirer.* Retrieved from http://news.enquirer.com/apps/pbcs.dll/article?AID=/20070227/NEWS01/702270408

Williams, L. (1991, November 30). In a 90's quest for Black identity, intense doubts and disagreement. *The New York Times,* p. 1.

Zeleny, J. (2005, September 12). Judicious Obama turns up volume. *Chicago Tribune,* p. 1.

7

BARACK OBAMA'S FAUSTIAN BARGAIN AND THE FIGHT FOR AMERICA'S RACIAL SOUL

Christopher J. Metzler

Georgetown University

If Obama's election means anything, it means that we are now living in post-racist America. That's why even those of us who didn't vote for Obama have good reason to celebrate.

—Dinesh D'Souza

To say that the election of Barack Hussein Obama in 2008 to the presidency of the United States of America was a watershed moment in the geopolitical racial milieu of the world is to state the obvious. But stating and analyzing the obvious are not the same things. The year 2008 will always be historic in a country whose shameful, bitter, divisive, violent, destructive struggle with racism at the hands of the government and the citizenry remains unresolved. America's so-called peculiar institution (enslavement) continues its shameful legacy (Reed, 2007). The White House is occupied by a Black man and race-baiting continues.

If the rhetoric of the Obama victory is eerily familiar, it is because we have been here before. The March on Washington, the civil rights movement, and the Million Man March all rhetorically and symbolically promised lasting change in the way that America practiced racism. The symbol, it seems, continues to outweigh the substance. The election of President Obama provides an opportunity to apply a theoretical, contextual framework to race and racism, which seeks to eliminate the racial thinking that has enveloped the president's election and its aftermath.

Source: Journal of Black Studies, January 2010; vol. 40, 3: pp. 395-410.

Obama's Election Viewed Through the Prism of Critical Race Theory

Critical race theory (CRT) has not spread into popular discourse about the continuing significance of race. Because of this, President Obama's election has led to a vacuous rhetorical discussion of race that has been anointed "postracial." The discourse has deliberately and uncritically pronounced the single event of his election as uncontroverted proof that America has exorcised its racial demons and, as a result of this electoral exorcism, has banished the demons to the inner sanctum of hell. This is a major problem addressed in the CRT framework:

> Because there is no currently viable alternative to an ambivalent liberal vision of race, on the one hand, and an inadequate vision of racialism, on the other, many progressive voices in the [Black] community tend to gravitate toward the racialist view. For all of its faults, racialism at least acknowledges the persistence of racism (albeit it in an essentialist and exclusionary way). Without a counter vision of race that does not fall into the nebulous world of liberal ambivalence and apology, the dangers of racialist politics for communities of color will continue to go unheeded, even in light of the deep contradictions that such politics produces. (Crenshaw, Gotanda, Peller, & Thomas, 1995, p. xxxii)

Discussions about progress on civil rights in America often gain fuel from the landmark *Brown v. the Board of Education* case of 1954, which outlawed segregation in public schools. The Supreme Court's pronouncement in *Brown*—that separate is inherently unequal—provided juridical, political, and psychological nourishment to a movement starved by judicially sanctioned race discrimination. Emboldened by an increasingly activist Court, Congress supplemented *Brown* with the Civil Rights Act of 1964, which outlawed discrimination in employment, and the Voting Rights Act of 1965, which protected Black suffrage.

To be sure, these legislative and judicial actions were significant attempts to address the racism that continued to relegate Blacks to the status of nonhumans. However, these events, for all their symbolic and legislative potency, were imperfect because they were enacted as a reaction to a political situation that sought a political solution to provide Blacks with protection from discrimination, without seeking to understand or address the racial foundation upon which America was built.

The reality is that America was built literally and figuratively on the backs of enslaved Africans and on the dispossession of Native Americans whose only crime was the color of their skin. Thus, any substantive legislative solution to this crime would require an elimination of the legacy of White supremacy that is built into the American psyche. For White supremacy has not been excised from our national core, and the election of President Obama, without more, will not accomplish this.

Moreover, for all the good that *Brown*, the Civil Rights Act, and the Voting Rights Act did, they did an equal amount of harm. First, *Brown* ensured that Black children and White children could be in the same classroom, but it did nothing to ensure that their opportunities for learning would be equal (Bell, 1976). And there are parallels between the narratives in *Brown* and the one developing as a result of the election of President Obama that simply cannot be ignored. The main narrative is that Obama will avoid addressing race unless his political survival depends on it. He knows that the majority of the Black electorate will support and defend him to the bitter end and demand very little in return. It is with whom he must enter into a diabolic racial pact.

Second, *Brown* was seen as a waypost in the struggle for civil rights, just like Obama's election is seen in the post–civil rights era. Second, the promise of *Brown* has not been realized, as schools still remain largely segregated on the basis of race, with Black students still failing at an alarming rate. While *Brown* is law, schools are still segregated based on race, and a significant percentage of Black elementary school children still cannot read (Chaddock, 2004). Second, what we have learned so far in the young presidency of Obama is that many see it as being capable of fulfilling the dream of equality.

Chicago Sun-Times columnist Mary Mitchell (2007) endows then Senator Obama with near omniscience:

> Besides being immensely gifted, Obama has intimate knowledge of the best and worst of black and white relationships and our often-intolerant behavior toward each other. He has an intimate understanding of the attitudes that keep Americans from capitalizing on their differences. And he knows that racial apprehensions aren't always driven by racism, but often by irrational fears on the part of whites, and deep-seated pain on the part of blacks. (Mitchell, 2007, paras. 4-5)

Of course, Mitchell offers much too simplistic an analysis of racism, choosing to construct a narrative based on interpersonal relationships without regard for policy and practice. It is this type of racial thinking that sees the event of Obama's election as the endgame and not a means to eliminate racism. Moreover, the model that Mitchell is using to analyze racism in the age of Obama was developed and subsequently failed in the 1960s era because it confused symbolic activities with durable change. It is this model that has created the space for the promulgation of "postracial" absurdity.

Like *Brown*, the Civil Rights Act of 1964, in the minds of many, meant the end to the struggle. What was there to fight for when the Court said that we are equal? The flaw in this argument is that judges can simply decree an end to the enduring power of White supremacy by deciding individual discrimination cases. In 1934, Dr. Ralph Bunche (1971) said,

> The burden of proof is always upon him. For the interpretation and realization of these rights he is forced to appeal to the Supreme Court. Thus, the Negro has been compelled to substitute the complicated, arduous and expensive process of litigation for the ballot box. What other groups are able to do for themselves, the Negro hopes the judiciary to do for him. There is more than ample evidence in the decisions of the supreme tribunal of the land on questions involving the rights of the Negro to dispute the possibility of any general relief from this quarter. (p. 59)

Many scholars in the civil rights movement saw the Voting Rights Act as ending the last bastion of discrimination by protecting the right of Blacks to vote: "The Voting Rights Act codified the right of protected minority groups to an equal opportunity to elect candidates of their choice, although its language disclaims the rights to racial representation by members of the racial groups proportionate to population" (Guinier, 1993, p. 1589).

We traded struggle for promises and engagement for complacency. Whites could point to legal protections and rewrite the narrative once again. The new narrative would read something like "We have given you freedom from slavery, outlawed discrimination so that you can live, work, and travel anywhere you want to. Suffrage is yours, and yet you still can't succeed?" The Obama election has provided the occasion to augment the narrative with the following: "We have given you a Black president. What else do you want?"

CRT was born out of the reality that the formal and legalistic approach to civil rights in America began but did not end the conversation about how Blacks experience racism and how Whites have the privilege of opting out of the conversation unless it provides succor to their own self-interest.

The slavish dedication to formal equality could not stop the 1964 riots in Harlem and Bedford-Stuyvesant of New York; the 1965 riots in the Watts section of Los Angeles; the murder of Malcolm X in New York; the several dozen riots, including ones in Newark and Detroit; and the 1968 assassination of Martin Luther King Jr. and the attendant race riots. Formal equality, because of its desolate rhetoric, could not stop the erection of physical and mental ghettos that would enslave entire generations of Blacks.

The reality of race and racism in America is that it is largely a narrative that began with enslavement and was simply rewritten *for* Blacks, not by Blacks. In the age of Obama, many Blacks, including the president, have not rewritten the narrative. Instead, they have opted to pick up and continue the narrative.

No one contests the symbolism of President Obama's election. What is contested is the role of race and racism in his election, his reluctance to engage in race in any meaningful way, and whether his election as the first Black president of the United States will be relegated to a mere symbolic footnote in the racial historical discourse. Crenshaw and colleagues' *Critical Race Theory: The Key Writings That Formed the Movement* (1995) provides a framework for interrogating these matters.

> The task of *Critical Race Theory* is to remind its readers how deeply issues of racial ideology and power continue to matter in American life. Questioning regnant visions of racial meaning and racial power, critical race theorists seek to fashion a set of tools for thinking about race that avoids the trap of racial thinking. Critical Race Theory understands that racial power is produced by and experienced within numerous vectors of social life. Critical Race Theory recognizes, too, that political interventions which overlook the multiple ways in which people of color are situated (and resituated) as communities, and individuals will do little to promote effective resistance to, and counter-mobilization against, today's newly empowered right. (p. xxxii)

Electoral decisions that claim to be "color-blind," such as the election of President Obama, are as steeped in racist ideology as the ones that predated the civil rights era in that they continue the frontal assault on the racial reality and thinking that permeate much of American social and political institutions without acknowledgment or apology.

CRT and the Evolving Racial Narrative of Obama's Election

What we have learned about Obama and race is that he avoids the issue altogether or addresses it when it threatens his political interests. As a candidate, he addressed race only when Black liberation theology was introduced in the person of Obama's former pastor, the Reverend Jeremiah Wright, unnerving his White base of support. In this regard he is not different from any politician who acts to eliminate threats to the power he seeks. But, rightly or wrongly, his decisions cannot be divorced from a racial discursive in which Whites seek to protect their racial privilege and Blacks seek more access to that privilege.

The racial discursive was on full display with Reverend Wright when journalist Christopher Hitchens (2008) wrote the following:

> The issue of race has been present throughout the contest for the Democratic nomination, and it's bubbling to the surface as the comments of Barack Obama's pastor, the Rev. Jeremiah Wright, have come under scrutiny. . . . An ABC News review of dozens of Rev. Wright's sermons, offered for sale

by the church, found repeated denunciations of the U.S. based on what he described as his reading of the Gospels and the treatment of [Black] Americans. . . . So if the savvy Obama campaign knew Wright was a problem a year ago, why did the Illinois senator, a parish member for two decades, wait until last week to disassociate and denounce the minister's inflammatory statements? (para. 4)

And so it was that the media found its racial voice. The candidate that was "postracial" had now become preracial, currently racial, polar racial, and racialized. It seemed as if Barack had gotten his Black back.

Sensing a looming political crisis, Obama delivered a major address on race in Philadelphia. Among the highlights, Obama said that Wright's statements were controversial and divisive and racially charged. He added that the White community must start acknowledging that what ails the African American community does not exist only in the minds of Black people, that the legacy of discrimination and current incidents of discrimination, while less overt than in the past, are real and must be addressed.

The reality is that his speech on Wright was designed to placate Whites since he assumed, perhaps correctly, that Blacks understood that the racial thinking of Whites demanded that Obama not be seen as the "angry Negro" that Whites had rejected in previous presidential primaries (read: Jackson and Sharpton). Thus, the racial narrative that he would employ to "save the dream" would propitiate Whites even at the expense of forcing Blacks to employ racial thinking without the promise of payback for that thinking. At the speech in Philadelphia, candidate Obama (2008) said,

> I can no more disown him than I can disown the Black community. I can no more disown him than I can my White grandmother. These people are a part of me. And they are a part of America, this country that I love.

Some praised the speech, others ignored it, and the media overanalyzed it. However, afterward, Obama once again caused some Whites to ask whether he had gotten too Black; when speaking on a Philadelphia sports show, he said,

> The point I was making was not that Grandmother harbors any racial animosity. She doesn't. But she is a typical White person, who, if she sees somebody on the street that she doesn't know, you know, there's a reaction that's been bred in our experiences that don't go away and that sometimes come out in the wrong way, and that's just the nature of race in our society. (Barack Obama interview, *610 WIP Morning Show*)

So, who is a "typical" White person? Larry King, *The Huffington Post*, Jonah Goldberg of *The Nation*, and others wondered. "Seriously, Barack

Obama basically called all White people racist. . . . Is this guy kidding?"
(Marsh, 2008). Here again, Whites who were so comfortable pretending that
Obama is not Black have had to address the fact that he is. In a postracial
America, this is a source of discomfort for the color-blind advocates. They
did not have to look far or wait long for their answer. Pat Buchanan (2008)
spoke for "typical" White people with crystal clarity:

> First, America has been the best country on earth for [Black] folks. It was
> here that 600,000 [Black] people, brought from Africa in slave ships, grew
> into a community of 40 million, were introduced to Christian salvation, and
> reached the greatest levels of freedom and prosperity [Blacks] have ever
> known. . . . Second, no people anywhere has done more to lift up [Blacks]
> than [White] Americans. Untold trillions have been spent since the '60s on
> welfare, food stamps, rent supplements, Section 8 housing, Pell grants, stu-
> dent loans, legal services, Medicaid, Earned Income Tax Credits and poverty
> programs designed to bring the African-American community into the
> mainstream. Governments, businesses and colleges have engaged in dis-
> crimination against [White] folks—with affirmative action, contract set-
> asides and quotas—to advance [Black] applicants over [White] applicants.
> Churches, foundations, civic groups, schools and individuals all over
> America have donated time and money to support soup kitchens, adult
> education, day care, retirement and nursing homes for [Blacks]. We hear the
> grievances. Where is the gratitude?

Regardless of whether one agrees with Buchanan's conservative credentials or his ideology, he says those things that White people in a postracial America say only in private and shy away from in public. His views
are often those expressed by Whites when they talk about race among themselves. The "typical" White person in a postracial America situates racism in
the past; embraces formal equality; believes that America has done so much
for Blacks and yet Blacks never seem to think that it is enough; walks on
eggshells around Blacks for fear of saying something offensive; believes in
interracial dating so long as it is not their son or daughter who is marrying
Black; does not see him- or herself as racialized but basks in White privilege;
believes that Blacks use race as an excuse for failure, that Blacks who are successful are the exception; believes that pretending that race does not matter
makes it true; and still harbors and makes decisions based on the powerful
marker of race that is imbedded in American racial reality. As Crenshaw
(1988) correctly notes,

> popular struggles are a reflection of institutionally determined logic and
> a challenge to that logic. People can demand change only in ways that
> reflect that logic of the institutions they are challenging. Demands for
> change that do not reflect the institutional logic—that is, demands that

do not engage and subsequently reinforce the dominant ideology—will probably be ineffective. (p. 1367)

The verisimilitude of the narritive is that, despite their assertions to the contrary, many Whites first considered Obama's race and then either decided to pretend it did not matter and, as a way of liberating themselves from their own racial thinking, voted for him anyway. Many Whites, including self-professed liberals, view Obama's election as linear in that there was slavery, there was Jim Crow, there was a civil rights movement, and there is now a Black president. They reason that Whites ought to be rewarded for their willingness to forget the past and give a Black man the keys to America. They also argue that they see no real and signifcant differences between the president and themselves; they would rather focus on what they have in common with him, including his White lineage.

The decision by many Blacks to vote for President Obama is no less steeped in racial thinking. For them, his election has an enduring fable that will not soon fade from memory. While many Whites voted for Obama as a way to move beyond race, many Blacks voted for him as a way to vindicate the entire Black race. Of course, Whites do not vote for Whites to vindicate the White race, since by virtue of their skin color—and White privilege and White supremacy—they do not need vindication.

Some Blacks may explain their votes by arguing that Obama's election proves that Blacks are capable of leading the free world. That is, many Blacks bought into that highly racialized view of Black inferiority and also voted for Obama in part because Whites deemed him acceptable. Of course, this is not to suggest that Black pride at Obama's election is not genuine. In fact, the opposite is true. It *is* to suggest that far too many Blacks in this election employed the trap of racial thinking that, according to CRT, continues to be a challenge for us despite the historical and social upheaval that has resulted in a less formal racism but a no less racially pernicious America.

Barack Hussein Obama's Bargain With White America

Obama is what I have called a "bargainer"—a Black who says to Whites, "I will never presume that you are racist if you will not hold my race against me." Whites become enthralled with bargainers out of gratitude for the presumption of innocence they offer. Black bargainers relieve White anxiety about Whiteness, and for this gift of trust, bargainers are often rewarded with a halo of sorts. Obama's postracial idealism told Whites the one thing they most wanted to hear: America had essentially contained the evil of racism to the point at which it was no longer a serious barrier to Black advancement. Thus, Whites became enchanted enough with Obama to become his political base.

It was Iowa—95% White—that made him a contender. Blacks came his way only after he won enough White voters to be a plausible candidate (Steele, 2008).

Regardless of whether one agrees with his philosophy on race, Steele (2008) makes a valid point. Despite the exuberance that has come from Blacks as a result of Obama's election, there is very little empirical evidence to suggest that he was their first choice. In fact, public opinion polls suggested that Blacks would be voting in overwhelming numbers for Hillary Clinton. Obama's resounding acceptance by White Iowans was the racial cover that many Blacks needed to erase the lingering doubt about him, thus raising the centroidal question of why, despite emancipation, did many Blacks still need Whites to validate their choices? Some will argue that the question was not about needing Whites to validate Obama but rather, was he electable? This argument is a distinction without a difference. If Blacks believed that he was electable, then why did many wait for the decision from Iowa? We have voted for losing White candidates before, and we did not need White validation (read: Carter, Mondale, Dukakis, Gore, and Kerry).

Stanley Crouch (2006) of the *New York Daily News* captured the racial thinking endemic to the Obama election:

> So when [Black] Americans refer to Obama as "one of us," I do not know what they are talking about. In his new book, "The Audacity of Hope," Obama makes it clear that, while he has experienced some light versions of typical racial stereotypes, he cannot claim those problems as his own—nor has he lived the life of a [Black] American.

Moreover, have the badges and incidents of slavery so encumbered us that we see racial thinking as our destiny?

On the issue of race, the president has indeed proven, as Steele suggests (2008), to be a bargainer. He rarely, if ever, willingly raises his own race or the racial problems that continue to plague America as an issue. Thus far, he has made no substantive policy pronouncement on race, nor has he signaled that he is any more sensitive to issues of race than his White male predecessors. For many Whites who continue to be uncomfortable with the reality of race as well as with their continuing complicity with racial thinking, this is comforting. They have a deal. They believe that the civil rights movement and its aftermath have all but eliminated racism, save a few egregious cases of outright racial vitriol. The president's election means that they will not have to take responsibility for racism, since they were not slaveholders and did not engage in the creation of racism. Thus, Obama will protect them from taking up the "White man's burden" of race. Since he has done nothing to disabuse them of this notion, they believe that he is in fact a "postracial" Black man whose White background and Ivy League pedigree will relegate racism to a historical relic.

Thus, the election of the nation's first Black president must be analyzed in the context of the racial provincialism that still permeates American discourse. President Obama's election is not a single event that is divorced from racial subordination and subjugation. His election, like the civil rights movement, is both a continuation and a departure from the silhouette of race. It is not "postracial," because America is still a racialized society and he has done nothing to change the narrative. In fact, since his political interests are served by a continuation of the "postracial" narrative, he has encouraged it.

This "postracial" narrative suggests that Obama is a president who happens to be Black, aiding in the cultural transformation that started with *Brown* and that many hope will end with Obama. The problem of course is that "postracial" posturing is relatively unconcerned with the fact that racism in America is not an event in American history that was eradicated by this self-serving, fictional, romanticized narrative suggesting that race simply does not matter.

CRT allows us to understand that President Obama is a Black president, complete with the social significance of Blackness. The racial narrative of his presidency in its historical context is a color-conscious one. According to CRT, color-consciousness makes Blacks subjects and not objects, thus having the potential to take away the potency and seeming permanence of the White definitions of Blackness. It also allows for an analysis of how Blacks as a people have survived the physical and psychological damage inflicted on them while remaining contributing members of a society that did not want them, and it acknowledges the contribution of Black culture, not simply as windows on "the race question," but as distinct (if varied) voices and traditions worthy of study in their own right (Gotanda, 1991).

CRT understands that the racial DNA of America is inextricably linked to power. It also gets sustinance from the fact that Whites can proclaim their fidelity to the theory of equality as long as it does not affect them or fundamentally alter their grip on power or put them at a social or economic disadvantage.

Interest Convergence and the Election of President Barack Obama

CRT also relies on the interest convergence principle, which posits that for Blacks in America to become substantively equal with Whites, their interests must converge. Bell (1995) posits that Whites may support social justice and equity-oriented policies and practices yet still cling to the notion that they do not have to give up their privileged position that comes as a result of their Whiteness. Bell is joined in his critique by Castagno and Lee (2007), who explain the reality of Black and White interest convergence by postulating that those in the majority will advance social justice agendas "when such advances suit" their own self-interests.

Racial apologists such as Thernstrom and Thernstrom (1999) want to be seen as taking the "middle ground" on race. They do so by telling conservatives that they can seem to embrace race yet keep White privilege. That is, they can have Black friends, live in the inner city, and advocate for change without having to admit their complicity and benefit in White privilege. They write that liberals are a part of the problem because they want Whites to feel guilty about racism. Liberals, according to the logic of the racial apologists, are afraid to admit that there has been change, because Whites will become too complacent and revert to the days of racial hostility.

Thernstrom and Thernstrom (1999), knowingly or otherwise, demonstrate the kind of self-serving logic inherent in interest convergence logic. They seem to suggest that it is in the best interests of conservatives to admit that America has had an ugly racial history (read: history as past event). Doing so, they reason, means that with admission comes no responsibility for remedy in any social policy that does not converge with the interests of Whites. Liberals, they argue, have a convergent interest with other Whites in admitting dramatic change. Thus, the racial logic they employ sees Blacks as subjects of racism with White interests as the ultimate tool of subjugation. Moreover, CRT catechizes that the history of race in America is not a single tale but an ongoing narrative in which Black equality succeeds only where it converges with White interests.

Of course, before Obama, there were Sharpton and Jackson, neither one of whom succeeded. Unpacking racial logic suggests that since Sharpton and Jackson are not Ivy League–educated or as willing to openly and notoriously converge with the interests of Whites as Obama, neither one would be validated as capable by Whites.

With social psychologists at Tulane University, University of Washington researchers surveyed 74 college undergraduates 10 days before and a week after November's election. Those who answered the online survey were mostly White and overwhelmingly female. Four out of five supported Obama. The results: 71% of Obama voters and 75% of supporters of Republican senator John McCain said there was less need for continued racial progress. The students also showed less support for policies aimed at reducing racial inequality. That support fell by 62% among Obama supporters and 67% among McCain supporters ("Support for Racial Equality," 2009).

A recent *New York Times*/CBS poll concluded that race relations are improving in the wake of the election of President Obama. According to the survey, about 66% of Americans said that race relations are generally good, compared with 53% in July of last year. Fifty-nine percent of African Americans, along with 65% of Whites, now characterize the relationship between Blacks and Whites in America as "good." The *New York Times* proclaimed with glee, "Barack Obama's presidency seems to be altering the public perception of race relations in the United States" (Castagno and Lee, 2007).

CRT suggests that interest convergence theory can be used to analyze the poll results. It also warns that Black advocates for substantive racial equality should not cower for fear of interrogating the first Black president about how he plans to deal with race. Also, it means that Whites who support President Obama should ask themselves whether that support is in exchange for his "bargain" not to engage in any meaningful way on the issue of race.

President Obama has had the opportunity to address race substantively several times, and each time he demurred, perhaps sensing a lack of interest convergence. When Attorney General Eric Holder said that on the issue of race, America is a "nation of cowards," the president balked, saying, "I think it's fair to say that if I had been advising my attorney general, we would have used different language" (Cooper, 2009, para. 1). The president, of course, did not address the substance of the attorney general's comments, nor did he tell us what different language he would have chosen. Once again, he chose to pick up and continue the dominant narrative on race without apology.

As president, Obama nominated Sonia Sotomayor as the first Latina to the Supreme Court of the United States. She was immediately race-baited for her comment, "I would hope that a wise Latina woman with the richness of her experiences would more often than not reach a better conclusion than a white male who hasn't lived that life" (Savage, 2009, para. 3). And once again, the president was race-baited. Rather than put the justice's comments in the context of a decidedly racial America, he demurred, choosing instead to have the justice backtrack on her comments. The biggest racial polemic that hit the president was the one in which Harvard professor Henry Louis Gates accused police of racially profiling him and arresting him at his home. The president first declared that the police had "acted stupidly." Sensing the same threat to his presidency as in the Wright imbroglio, Obama backed down and invited the officer and Gates to the White House for a beer. Sensitive to the visual aspect of the racial narrative, the president ensured racial balance by also inviting Vice President Biden to join them. The decision by the president to engage on the topic of race—and then disengage—is both a reminder and a warning of the fallacy of his "postracial" logic. The "beer summit" resolved nothing and once again relegated discussions of racism to interpersonal clashes that can be solved by talk, no action, and no responsibility.

Conclusion

The history of the impact of race on the 2008 U.S. presidential election has yet to be written; however, in a "postracial America," the fact that Obama is Black restricts rather than expands his ability to implement racially substantive policies. The racial calculus in America means that the president must tread lightly on race lest he lose the support of those Whites who claim to be "postracial." Some Whites and some Blacks voted for Obama because he is, in their view, within the "acceptable" role of Sidney Poitier in *Guess Who's Coming to Dinner*.

The response to the civil rights movement was the removal of formal barriers and symbolic manifestations of subordination. Thus, "Whites only" notices and other obvious indicators of the social policy of racial subordination disappeared—at least in the public sphere. The disappearance of these symbols of subordination reflected the acceptance of formal equality, signaling the demise of White supremacist rhetoric as expressing America's normative vision. In other words, it could no longer be said that Blacks were not included as equals in the American political vision.

Obama's election proves that Blacks are included in the American political vision. What it has not proven is whether he sees his election any differently from the election of a White president. In theory, he should not. In reality, his decision to ignore race or relegate it to a historical relic will have dire consequences, as he has begun to find out. He can ignore this truth at his own peril.

Given that America is a racialized society, we need to address the question of how this fact affects the decisions that we all make, rather than seek to castigate people for making racialized decisions. Avoiding discussions about racism and its continuing significance in all aspects of American life is akin to the person who has a terminal illness and pretends that if he or she ignores it, it will go away. CRT, then, urges us to examine Obama's election in context and not simply conclude that it is the event that will close the racial question.

Thus, the "postracial" discourse that has occupied so much of our intellectual and political discourse since the election of President Obama does not maintain a progressive outlook that examines the reality, texture, and contours of race in America. It seems as if we are destined to repeat the claptrap of the civil rights vision, which promised much, frustrated many, and on the issue of race, delivered less than it promised.

References

Bell, D. A., Jr. (1976). Serving two masters: Integration ideals and client interests in school desegregation litigation. *Yale Law Journal, 85,* 470.

Bell, D. A., Jr. (1995). *Brown v. Board of Education* and the interest convergence dilemma. In G. N. K. Crenshaw (Ed.), *Critical race theory: The key writings that formed the movement* (pp. 20-28). New York: New Press.

Buchanan, P. (2008, March 21). *A brief for Whitey.* Retrieved April 10, 2009, from http://www.buchanan.org/blog/?p=969

Bunche, R. (1971). A critical analysis of the tactics and programs of minority groups. *Journal of Negro Education, 5,* 59-65.

Castagno, A. E., & Lee, S. J. (2007). Native mascots and ethnic fraud in higher education: Using tribal critical race theory and the interest convergence principle as an analytic tool. *Equity & Excellence in Education, 40*(1), 129-157.

Chaddock, G. R. (2004). *Beyond integration: Better teaching is post-'Brown' frontier.* Retrieved July 19, 2009, from http://www.csmonitor.com/2004/0517/p01s03-legn.html

Cooper, H. (2009, March 7). Attorney General chided for language on race. *The New York Times.*

Crenshaw, K. (1988). Race, reform and retrenchment: Transformation and legitimation in antidiscrimination law. *Harvard Law Review, 101,* 1331-1387.

Crenshaw, K., Gotanda, N., Peller, G., & Thomas, K. (Eds.). (1995). *Critical race theory: The key writings that formed the movement.* New York: New Press.

Crouch, S. (2006, November 2). What Obama isn't: Black like me. *New York Daily News.*

Gotanda, N. (1991). A critique of "Our constitution is color-blind." *Stanford Law Review, 44*(1), 1-68.

Guinier, L. (1993). Groups, representation and race-conscious districting: A case of the emperor's clothes. *Texas Law Review, 71,* 1589.

Hitchens, C. (2008, January 7). *Identity crisis: There's something pathetic and embarrassing about our obsession with Barack Obama's race.* Retrieved April 10, 2009, from http://www.slate.com/id/2181460

Marsh, T. (2008, March 20). *Obama: Grandmother "typical White person."* Retrieved April 10, 2009, from http://www.huffingtonpost.com/taylor-marsh/obama-grandmothe-typic_b_92601.html

Mitchell, M. (2007, January 17). *Obama might be the candidate who can bridge the racial divide.* Retrieved July 18, 2008, from http://www.suntimes.com/news/politics/obamacommentary/215777,CST-NWS-mitch18.stng

Obama, B. (2008). *Transcript of Obama's speech.* Retrieved July 10, 2008, from http://www.cnn.com/2008/POLITICS/03/18/obama.transcript/

Reed, P. D. (2007). From the Freedmen's Bureau to FEMA: A post-Katrina historical, journalistic, and literary analysis. *The Journal of Black Studies, 37,* 555-567.

Savage, C. (2009, May 14). A judge's view of judging is on the record. *The New York Times.*

Steele, S. (2008, November 5). Obama's post-racial promise [Opinion]. *Los Angeles Times.*

Support for racial equality may be victim of Obama's election. (2009, March 23). *University of Washington News.* Retrieved October 15, 2009, from http://uwnews.org/article.asp?articleid=48160

Thernstrom, A., & Thernstrom, S. (1999). *America in Black and White: One nation, indivisible.* New York: Touchstone.

Part III

THE LESSONS OF THE OBAMA PRESIDENTIAL ELECTION

The vagaries of political campaigning never cease to dog the steps of a candidate. Political scientists, communicationists, sociologists, and psychologists have quickly seized upon the optimism in the Obama campaign as one of the central themes of his strategy. With his own self-conscious audacity, Barack Obama challenged the American nation to view itself through his optimistic eyes. If it were necessary for him, as a product of a white woman and a black man, to plot his own course through life as an optimist, what could prevent others in this society from possessing similar desires for hope?

The scholars in Part Three analyze the lesson of optimism and establish both its boundaries and prospects. Obama's motto "Yes We Can" resounded from one campaign stop to the next during a time when American society was in the deep throes of an economic recession brought about by a runaway financial sector. Furthermore, the self-image of the American nation had been damaged by the seemingly endless wars in Afghanistan and Iraq. The strategy of the Obama campaign was to grab hold of the despair that was seeping into the soul of the nation and turn it into a call for victory. Thus, "Yes We Can" awakened the natural desire for hope.

Clearly, as the scholars in this section demonstrate, the rhetoric of hope was packed with energy, capacity, and destiny. Those who wanted to join the historic journey to a new future were ready to leap onto the rising tide of hope repeated in Obama's message. The nation was seduced by an optimism that was considered to be the answer to the financial crisis, the economic downturn, and the wars in Afghanistan and Iraq. Thus, domestic issues were interpreted through the lens of hope, but there were also international issues and problems that had to be managed at the same time. American political scientists, Africologists, sociologists, and communicationists saw in Obama's campaign rhetoric a definite message to the international community. America was not going to be a bully on the world stage; it would engage the international community as partners in the prosecution of democratic reforms, international security, and the search for peace. Consequently, his campaign for the presidency appeared to have a dimension that was usually lacking in the American presidential campaign: an appeal to the world community. Obama, more than any other presidential candidate in America's history, was a fresh voice and, of course, face for world politics. Crowds came to see him in Berlin and Paris and other international cities as he was campaigning to be president of the United States. In the end, as the scholars in Part Three show, it was a politics of hope that shaped the character of the presidential campaign.

8

FACING BARACK HUSSEIN OBAMA: RACE, GLOBALIZATION, AND TRANSNATIONAL AMERICA

Radhika Parameswaran

Indiana University, Bloomington

As I walk past a row of magazines in a chain bookstore 2 days after the inauguration ceremonies in January 2009, I witnessed a barrage of close-up images of President Obama's face plastered on an array of covers that spanned a spectrum of taste cultures, from *People* magazine to *The Atlantic Monthly*. Inviting readers to engage in the politics of presidential intimacy, the deluge in such mass market portraits of Obama's face momentarily inscribed him within normative cultural scripts of feminine subjectivity. The camera's fine-grained aesthetic fascination with Obama's face—deploying physiognomy as the window into his personality and identity— reminded me of the continual supply of women's faces in the commercial world of global advertising that bridge the gap between commodity and fantasy. Emulating the brand power of female celebrity in the transnational consumer sphere, Obama's face, as one report in *Advertising Age* claimed, had the power to launch a global makeover for Brand America's tainted face: "After years of suffering a reputation as a menacing bully, suddenly America had a new countenance" (Wentz, 2008). An advertising professional and presidential historian, also quoted in this article, offered his hopes for refurbishing America's reputation on the global stage, "We've put a new face on America and that face happens to be African-American" (Wentz, 2008).

Beyond the facade of celebrity branding, Obama's historically significant ascendance—one that purportedly gives the nation a new face—compels us to parse and probe the politics of racial identity in the global imaginary. In the

Source: Journal of Communication Inquiry, July 2009; vol. 33, 3: pp. 195-205, first published on March 23, 2009.

aftermath of the inauguration ceremonies and Obama's election to president in November 2008, news media recorded the euphoric reactions of citizens around the world. The implications of Obama's victory for the analytic and lived categories of race, gender, class, and nation have very clearly rippled well beyond the national stage. What does it mean when terms such as "African American" or "Black American" or "Black" enter the lexicon of presidential identity in the context of America's enduring construction as a transnational cultural and political space? What work does the intense focus on Obama's racial identity do to challenge the amnesia over race in academic discourses on globalization? What particular configurations of Blackness did the Obama story incite in relation to a global reading and viewing public? I explore these questions in this article not from the vantage point of an expert on race or Black identity in the United States, but as an academic, who teaches on gender, race, and media more broadly and studies cultural globalization and South Asia, and as a South Asian immigrant, who has tried to make sense of race, ethnicity, and culture as I travel back and forth between India and America.

Globalization and Race

Appadurai's canonic and oft-cited essay, "Disjuncture and Difference in the Global Economy," describes the social and economic processes that constitute globalization as a series of flows in cultural representations (mediascapes), ideas and value systems (ideoscapes), people (ethnoscapes), currencies and capital (financescapes), and mechanical and informational technologies (technoscapes). Appadurai (1990) explained that the term *ethnoscapes* refers primarily to the landscape of moving groups and persons (tourists, immigrants, refugees, exiles, guest workers) whose travels across and within borders shape the politics of nations. Critiquing Appadurai and other scholars who have made similar arguments about the flexibilities and mobilities contained in globalization's shifting and flowing ethnoscape, scholars of race, class, and globalization have pointed to the social experiences that become muted and recede to the background in such visions of portable ethnomodernity. Johar Schueller (2007) wrote that the prominence of migrancy to the North from the South in some theories of globalization ignores the "majority of the world's labor that is not migrant" and it dismisses the salience of local resistances:

> Whether conceptualized as Hardt and Negri's multitude against empire, Appadurai's mass migration of workers, or Anthony Appiah's cosmopolitanism as perspective based on the ability to travel, transiency is central to all these formulations . . . because globalization theories have stressed the decentered flow of capital and cultural goods, as well as migrancy, they have tended to dismiss any local movements as reactionary. (p. 7)

Furthermore, questioning the idea that globalization happens to those living outside of the United States, Johar Schueller advocates for models of globalization that bring postcolonial theory into a productive conversation with critical race studies: "The theoretical impetus of this book—to bring postcolonial theory and critical race studies together—might well appear contradictory, particularly because postcolonial theory in its universalist and globalist guises simply absorbs the specific functioning of racism into a narrative of diaspora and migration" (p. 3). Similarly, Jackson (2006) draws our attention to the ways in which "theories of globalizing 'flows' and transnational scapes" are limited in how much they can "account for the entrenched and institutionalized non-flowingness and ine-*scap*ability of race in contemporary American society—and all around the world" (p. 193).

The inflections in globalization theories toward ethnicity have oriented scholars to engage with culture, nation, and heritage as lenses to understand social identity rather than race, a concept that remains tethered in a problematic fashion to the terrain of the United States. Insisting on the importance of finding ways to insert race into the vocabularies and terminologies of globalization, Thomas and Clarke (2006) begin their edited volume, *Globalization and Race: Transformations in the Cultural Production of Blackness*, with the following statement:

> While scholarly analyses of globalization have proliferated, and while there have been recent attempts within the social sciences to consider the articulations among ethnicity, gender, and sexuality within a global frame of analysis, race and processes of racialization are not usually considered central issues in academic discussions of global economic and political transformations. (p. 1)

These authors also speculate on the reasons for the relative absence of race and constructions of racial identity in scholarship on globalization in the social sciences and humanities:

> Invoking race in a global context seems to conjure up Western experiences of difference or generalized concepts such as white racial supremacy, concepts that reek of a kind of ontological approach to whiteness and blackness—an absolute truth about racial difference everywhere—that the constructionist approach disavows. (p. 2)
>
> The disconnect between our de-essentialization of race and our fetishization of the global, therefore, seems rooted in the difficulty of making an argument that gives race explanatory power once it has been established that race operates differently in different contexts. (p. 2)

By studying how "people traditionally classified as 'black' or of 'African descent' are actively transforming racial meanings," these authors contend that we can gain a better understanding of "new forms of subjectivity, cultural practice, and political action that also move us beyond racism" (pp. 2-3). Extending Thomas and Clarke's discussion further, I also argue that race in communication and media studies has become anchored to questions of national history and domestic concerns of U.S. institutions and state policy rather than a phenomenon that has relevance in the international arena. Jackson refers to this unspoken amnesia about race and globalization when he writes that "certain provincializing assumptions within American anthropology today (and within American ideologies more generally) might imagine globalism to be far better spied in other parts of the world," with the result that U.S. academics can often end up ignoring globalization's intersections with the problems of race, gender, and class in their own backyards and neighborhoods (p. 190). Thomas and Clarke's prescriptions to study race in the context of globalization include the need for "studies of racial process to be more attuned to the ways changing relations of power globally have generated innovative alliances" (p. 19) and for work that shows how "blackness does not just index race; it also indexes gender, class, ethnicity, sexuality, religion, labor, nationality, transnationality, and politics" (p. 9).

Global Citizenship and the Rise of Obama: Producing and Reducing Race

In November 2005, I arrive at the international airport in Mumbai, India, one late night, and take a cab to my destination. The friendly and talkative cab driver, who had expressed his desire to migrate to America two minutes after I seated myself, now began pummeling me with practical questions about the viability of the American dream. He asked me where he should think about moving once he gets to America. I tell him about the difficulties of balancing income with cost of living and opportunities for community life (contact with other Indian immigrants, food choices, and religious affiliation) in the United States, giving him examples drawn from my own circle of Indian friends and acquaintances. After listening carefully, the driver said, "Well, I do know where I should *not* go, the place where all those poor people got stuck due to the cyclones and rain. And, most of them were not *gora* [White/foreigner], were they? The place did not look very different from the slums in Mumbai." Later, after we had talked about Hurricane Katrina for a while, he requested me to write down "New Orleans" on a piece of paper so he would remember the place he should avoid.

As I traveled within India and answered similar queries about the Third World conditions of Black citizens living in the First World, it became clear to me that images of Hurricane Katrina delivered through the mediascape of instantaneous television news had brought a hitherto hidden American racioscape to life for some people in India, a racioscape of poverty and disenfranchisement that disrupted the global hegemony of the American dream. It is precisely this sense of a global "Third Worldness" that Rodriguez (2007) alluded to when he drew analogies between the victims of Katrina and the dark-skinned Ayta community in the Philippines, which experienced similar struggles with displacement and destruction when the Mount Pinatubo volcano erupted in 1991. Media coverage of Hurricane Katrina made visible to a global audience a racial community that was rendered physically and socially immobile—referring back to Jackson's ine-*scap*ability of race—in an America whose participation in globalization is increasingly based in creating an uberconsumer market utopia for goods and services produced elsewhere.

If Hurricane Katrina's visual repertoire of race did the work of globalizing a particular version of Blackness—its historical containment within marginal structures of class in the United States—President Obama's ascent to a political office whose whiteness seemed impossible to dismantle, circulated a different story of race. How did Obama's racial identity do the work of redefining Blackness and expanding its boundaries to encompass a more global sensibility? Obama's widely publicized biography inscribed Blackness within a hybrid cosmopolitan sensibility, one that meshed American insiderness with an international outsiderness, and hence, cemented his identity as a global citizen. From his Kenyan father to his White American maternal family and his life in Hawaii and Indonesia, Obama's subjectivity, as African writer and political columnist Wa Ngugi (2008) noted, represents a "mosaic of cultures and experiences" to make him among the world's first political leaders to "fit snugly into the skin of globalization with all its promises and contradictions." Obama's triumph provoked the media to stretch the skin of race to accommodate the identities of non-Western people, who are not typically viewed as a race. Using the terminology of race instead of culture or ethnicity to describe the global communities that responded to Obama's triumph (Dickey, 2008), a *Newsweek* report carries the headline, "Reflecting on race barriers, Obama's breakthrough provokes a *global race* to capitalize on, and build on, his win." This *global race* that surfaced in solidarity with Obama spanned a Bedouin sheikh in an Israeli village, a politician of Turkish descent in Germany, Hungarian citizens, and a low-caste Indian woman politician.

Following a similar narrative trajectory, *The Boston Globe*'s archive of photographs on the inauguration ceremony, part of a series titled, "The Big Picture," registers visually the wide sweep of President Obama's global endorsement. Pictures of groups of people watching the inauguration ceremony on television in France, Iraq, Afghanistan, Mexico, Kenya, and Bosnia Herzegovina document the cultural production of Blackness as global celebrity in the realm of electoral politics, a departure from the more widespread global commodification of American Black masculinity in the arenas of sports and entertainment. In image after image, television, along with Obama, occupies the role of heroic protagonist, uniting global audiences in their act of witnessing a key event in America's history. In one particularly moving photograph, the glowing bluish light of a television screen illuminates the faces of young Black men in one of the poorest quarters in Nairobi, Kenya, transfixed as they watch Obama (not visible in this photo) being sworn in as president. Linking Africa to America and homeland to the Black diaspora, this picture of television's global reach projects a discourse of global racial solidarity crossing the boundaries of class and nation.

A kitschy *youtube* video offers another variation of Obama worship, one that translates his celebrity status and his Black identity into the popular idioms of the global language of Bollywood. Set to the soundtrack of a song from *Mela* (2000), "Bollywood Obama" blends images of Obama delivering public speeches and conversing with ordinary Americans on the campaign trail with Bollywood film clips that show young Indians dancing energetically and swaying to the beat of the music. In one scene, as Obama begins to speak, his open mouth fills up with an image of ornately dressed young Indian women enacting the familiar erotics of Bollywood's musical fantasies. Other visual signifiers—the Indian flag juxtaposed with Obama speaking, Obama's face overlaid with henna markings, the word "Obama" streaming across the Taj Mahal—do the work of transforming Obama into a global *desi* (South Asian) icon. Ironically, as one *youtube* commentator noted, "Obama's Blackness intersects here with a lyric that describes the hero's desire for a 'gori', a light-skinned beautiful woman." In the United States, Obama enjoyed overwhelming support from the Indian American community, with some supporters even arguing that Obama's victory paved the way for Indian Americans to aspire to the presidency: "Obama's inauguration means a new day in America especially for Indian-Americans, now any Indian-American can truly dream of occupying the highest office in the land or the most powerful position in the world whether their name is Bob, Bobby or Baljit" ("Obama Has Truly Energized," 2009). Here, Obama's unusual name (Obama has described himself as a "skinny kid with a funny name"), paired alongside his Blackness, becomes a source of empathetic identification.

Obama's cosmopolitan "global Blackness" and his funny name, however, turned into a domestic liability at times forcing him to walk a rhetorical tightrope of diplomacy during his 2008 campaign. Controversies over Obama's official religion—Islam or Christianity—precipitated conflicts between his national identity as an authentic American and normative discourses of religious and racial identity in the United States. Rumors that Obama, whose middle is Hussein, had been raised a Muslim and attended religious schools or madrasas in Indonesia were debunked by news media, but nevertheless fueled an Islamophobia whose currents had been swirling in the public sphere in a post 9/11 America. Obama's repeated pronouncements that he was *not* a Muslim only seemed to reinforce the demonization of Muslims as alien others, the pagan, and barbaric "Orientals" of Europe's colonies who could not claim their identities as American citizens. Stepping into the fray to help Obama and challenge Islamophobia, another Black leader, Colin Powell, who endorsed Obama stated that "he is not a Muslim, he's a Christian. He's always been a Christian. But the really right answer is, what if he is? Is there something wrong with being a Muslim in this country? The answer's no, that's not America."

Later, as the controversy faded, Obama toned down his rhetoric of "I am not a Muslim," and instead began articulating his plans to change the Bush foreign policy regime in Iraq and his willingness to engage in dialogue with Muslim leaders. Khalil (2008) noted that Obama "represents a phenomenon that has drawn global attention and captivated the minds of Muslims around the world as he wages a spirited campaign to become the next president of the United States." Khalil registers here the support that Obama generated in a global Muslim community that had mobilized in opposition to the Bush administration's "war on terror" campaign and the military intervention in Iraq. Khalil recognizes the ways in which Obama's racial and religious identities converged in the global Muslim community's sympathy for him: "Internet campaigns exploited Obama's alleged Muslim links by portraying America as a 'racist country' whose citizens and politicians would never permit Obama to win because he is *black and has Muslim roots*. The effort was misleading, but nonetheless garnered the candidate even more sympathy in the Muslim world." Even as Obama's middle name registered his family's contacts with Islam in Africa and Indonesia, a Christian minority that has endured persecution in an Islamic nation *also* mobilized Obama's *Christian* identity to make their cause visible in the global arena. A *Boston Globe* photograph of Pakistani Christian children holding portraits of Obama during a prayer ceremony in Islamabad, Pakistan, generated lively debate on the blog Sepia Mutiny about the impact of Hindu and Islamic fundamentalism on South Asia's Christian populations.

Recalling Thomas and Clarke's advice to problematize Blackness in the context of global spaces as inciting new alliances and indexing social registers outside of race, we can see that Obama's biography radiated outward in the global mediasphere to challenge a hegemonic notion of Blackness as quintessentially American. His expansive racial identity traversed multiple continents and touched different world religions (including his father's atheism) even as his White American grandparents and dark-skinned African American wife from Chicago, Michele Obama, allowed him to shore up his authentic American identity.[1] Yet it is also important to consider here the consequences of these global representations of solidarity in the wake of Obama's achievement of the "American dream" for American nationalism and for race *in* America.

The "American dream" and the "American way of life," as Grewal (2006) notes, are persuasive ideological constructs that circulate in varied transnational contexts to produce shifting global allegiances that in turn revive the idea of America as a mythical national space of unbridled freedom and democracy:

> As a superpower and policeman, a multicultural nation as well as a site of hierarchical racial and gendered formations, America the nation-state, along with American nationalism, produces identities within many connectivities in a transnational world, whether as the source of imperial power or as a symbol of freedom and liberty. (p. 196)

Grewal examines the uneven production of racial, gendered, and multicultural subjects in post-9/11 America to map the continuation and fulfillment of earlier neoliberal nationalist ideologies in the global popular and consumer spheres. Focusing on the outpouring of international support for America after 9/11, Grewal argues that the emergence of this new transnational solidarity "contributed to the formation of an 'American exceptionalist' nationalism that was the dominant discourse after 9/11" (p. 206). A new internationalist alliance of the civilized against the barbaric in this moment affirmed the exceptional status of America and its democratic promise of the "American dream" for a transnational public.

Although nuanced very differently from the condolences and sympathy that poured in from all parts of the world after 9/11, the global solidarity that emerged in conjunction with Obama's election to the presidency, and in particular the responses to his triumph as a *Black man* in America, also fueled neoliberal American exceptionalist nationalism in the arenas of racial progress and equality (Rodriguez, 2008). Multiple currents outside and inside America, including the global reach of hip hop and rap music's commercial renderings of Black resistance, and Obama's own nationalist rhetoric bolstered this transnational investment in American colorblind nationalism. Obama has been careful to balance his inspirational and unifying nationalism with strong disclaimers about the weaknesses of America, but the selective repetition and amplification of particular rhetorical statements, "There is not a Black America and a White America and a Latino America and Asian America, there's the United States of America," and "If there is anyone out there who still doubts that America is a place where all things are possible; who still wonders if the dream of our founders is alive in our time . . . tonight is your answer," on television news and in popular biographies also provoked celebratory proclamations of a postracial America (Hsu, 2009; Marquand & Pommerau, 2008; Mazrui, 2008). When interviewed for a story in the *Christian Science Monitor*, Pap Ndiaye, an academic in Paris, said that "Obama has restored belief in the American dream" and that

Obama's success put "France on the hot seat" (Marquand & Pommerau, 2008). A German citizen in the same story argues that Obama's victory could be a lesson for Germany on the value of migrants and that America's shining moment would hasten the opening up of Germany.

The circulation of these discourses that position America as a nation where upward mobility is unrestricted for Black Americans evacuates questions of class (education and family background) from Obama's own biography and disavows the institutional and historical structures of race and class that displaced hundreds of poor Black citizens after Hurricane Katrina. Pinkney's hyperbolic anger against the hypocrisy of the "Obama spectacle" ignores some of the productive ways in which Obama's story of ascent destabilized the hegemonic equation between Blackness and Americanness (Pabst, 2006), but his strong plea to dispute the "installment of Obama" as ushering in a "postracial era in the nation" deserves careful attention. Pinkney (2008) noted that the enormous challenges of joblessness, poor health care, failing public education, and homelessness that affect the lives of ordinary "people of all colors and ethnicities" perverts not only the idea of the "American dream," but even more importantly, Dr. Martin Luther King Jr.'s dream of economic and social justice for those living in the peripheries of American prosperity.

Recentering America: The First Black President in a Decentered Nation?

During my visit to India in November 2008 after Obama won the elections, relatives and academics (Obama supporters) asked me repeatedly, "What is he going to do? How is this man going to meet these expectations of hope and change? What will happen to America?" These questions highlight the changing conditions of a global economic context—America's relations with the emerging market nations of India and China—that surround Barack Hussein Obama's historic election. Obama's status as the first Black president dramatized the accessibility of the American dream at a time when a host of economic developments threaten the security of America's taken-for-granted position in the global economy. Capturing the flavor of these shifting currents, an Indian magazine proclaims boldly that India is "Taking over the world." *Outlook* magazine's triumphant cover portrait (November 6, 2006) in which the faces of four successful Indian entrepreneurs replace the sculpted faces of the four former U.S. presidents on the iconic Mount Rushmore Memorial seeks to reverse the earlier hierarchies of First World–Third World economic relations. Zakaria's analysis of a post-American world, a world in which America has to contend with the "rise of the rest," points to the third great shift in modern history, the first being the rise of the Western world, the second the rise of the United States, and the third contemporary moment when America may dominate in the military and political arenas, but "along every other dimension—industrial, financial, social, cultural—the distribution of power is shifting, moving away from American dominance" (Zakaria, 2008). In the midst of this economic decentering of America, Obama's successful bid for the presidency generated debates about how America could recenter itself through a program of change in the global economic, foreign policy, environment, and military arenas.

The Onion's satirical story headlined "Black Man Given Nation's Worst Job"(2008) provokes reflection on the historical context of Black labor and achievement in America even as it illuminates the challenges that lie ahead: "African-American man Barack Obama, 47, was given the least desirable job in the entire country . . . As part of his duties, the black man will have to spend four to eight years cleaning up the messes other people left behind." Some of Obama's bold campaign promises to redistribute economic power in an increasingly class-divided America earned him the slur from right-wing media outlets of being an "international socialist" (Kincaid, 2008), a label that presents another ripe subject for exploring the historical articulations of race and labor in the global economy that emerged in the midst of Obama's candidacy. This article's brief exploration of the Obama story's implications for Black identity in the global mediasphere points to the rich opportunities that lie ahead for scholars to examine representations and transformations of race, nation, and globalization in the next several years to come.

Note

1. See the *Wall Street Journal* report by Kaufman and Fields (2008) for an insightful examination of Obama's standing in the Black community. Black women interviewed in this story praise Obama for choosing Michelle Obama—a dark-skinned and professionally successful Black woman—as his wife.

References

Appadurai, A. (1990). Disjuncture and difference in the global cultural economy. *Public Culture*, Spring, 1-24.

Black man given nation's worst job. (2008, November 5). Retrieved January 25, 2009, from http://www.onion.com

Dickey, C. (2008, November 2008). Reflecting on race barriers: Obama's breakthrough provokes a global race to capitalize on, and build on, his win. *Newsweek*. Retrieved January 26, 2009, from http://lexisnexis .com

Grewal, I. (2006). *Transnational America: Feminisms, diasporas, neoliberalisms.* Durham, NC: Duke University Press.

Hsu, H. (2009, January/February). The end of white America. *The Atlantic Monthly*, pp. 46-55.

Jackson, J. (2006). Gentrification, globalization, and georaciality. In K. M. Clarke & D. Thomas (Eds.), *Globalization and race: Transformations in the cultural production of blackness* (pp. 188-205). Durham, NC: Duke University Press.

Jain, U. (Producer), & Darshan, D. (Director) (2000). Mela [Motion picture]. India: Venus Records and Tapes Pvt. Ltd.

Kaufman, J., & Fields, G. (2008, August 23). Black in a new light—Sen. Obama's candidacy sparked a debate about identity in the African American community. *Wall Street Journal*. Retrieved January 26, 2009, from http://global.factiva.com

Khalil, Y. (2008, June 16). Obama's appeal in the Muslim world. *Christian Science Monitor*. Retrieved January 2, 2008, from http://www.csmonitor.com

Kincaid, C. (2008, February 14). *Obama's international socialist connections*. Retrieved January 14, 2008, from http://www.aim.org

Marquand, R., & Pommereau, I. (2008, November 7). With Obama's victory, Europe's minorities sense new possibilities. *Christian Science Monitor*. Retrieved February 3, 2009, from http://www.csmonitor.com

Mazrui, A. A. (2008, September). *The black Atlantic from Othello to Obama: In search of a post-racial society*. Conference paper presented at "From Eurafrique to Afreurope: Africa and Europe in a new century," Stellenbosch, South Africa.

Obama has truly energized the community: Indian Americans. (2009, January 20). Retrieved January 25, 2009, from http://www.livemint.com

Pabst, N. (2006). Mama, I'm walking to Canada: Black geopolitics and invisible empires. In K. M. Clarke & D. Thomas (Eds.), *Globalization and race: Transformations in the cultural production of blackness* (pp. 112-132). Durham, NC: Duke University Press.

Pinkney, L. (2009, January 22). *The Obama spectacle: History, hypocrisy, and empire*. Retrieved February 3, 2009, from http://www.blackcommentator.com

Rodriguez. D. (2007). The meaning of disaster: Under the dominance of white life. In *What lies beneath: Katrina, race, and the state of the nation* (pp. 133-156). Boston: South End.

Rodriguez, D. (2008, November 10). *The dreadful genius of the Obama moment*. Retrieved January 13, 2008, from http://racewire.org

Schueller, M. J. (2007). *Locating race: Global sites of postcolonial citizenship*. New York: State University of New York Press.

Taking over the world. (November 6, 2006). *Outlook* magazine.

Thomas, D., & Clarke, K. M. (2006). Introduction: Globalization and the transformation of race. In K. M. Clarke & D. Thomas (Eds.), *Globalization and race: Transformations in the cultural production of blackness* (pp. 1-36). Durham, NC: Duke University Press.

Wa Ngugi, M. (2008, October). *What is America to me? Thoughts on the US presidential elections*. Retrieved January 6, 2009, from http://www.blackcommentator.com

Wentz, L. (2008, November 10). An instant overhaul for tainted Brand America. *Advertising Age*. Retrieved January 26, 2009, from http://lexisnexis.com

Zakaria, F. (2008, May 12). The rise of the rest. *Newsweek*. Retrieved January 29, 2009, from http://www.newsweek.com

9

THE AUDACITY OF HOPE

Dewey Clayton

University of Louisville

Barack Obama's Formal Introduction

Something unique occurred at the Democratic National Convention in Boston, Massachusetts, in July 2004: An African American candidate for the U.S. Senate from Illinois gave the keynote address. He was only the third African American to deliver such a speech at a major political party convention. In that address, Barack Obama declared that there is no Black America or White America—only the United States of America. Obama electrified the convention hall as well as the American public with that speech. In what has been described as a message of hope, Obama made an appeal to Americans to unite across racial lines and party lines.

Since that keynote address, Barack Obama has become the political superstar of the Democratic Party. He campaigned across the country throughout the fall of 2006 for Democratic candidates. Everywhere he went, there were large crowds in attendance—Black, White, brown, young, old, male, and female. On February 10, 2007, Obama announced his candidacy for president of the United States of America in Springfield, Illinois.

This act was unprecedented on several levels. Obama is the only African American in the U.S. Senate (and only the third African American senator since the Reconstruction). Having been elected in 2004, he has served only 2 years of his first term. His Republican opponent in the Illinois Senate race was Jack Ryan, a White man who was forced out of the race after tawdry details about his divorce were made public (Curry, 2006). Only 3 months before the general election, the Republicans chose Alan Keyes, a social conservative who was living in Maryland at the time. Obama had been a surprise winner in the Illinois 2004 Democratic primary. In early opinion polls before the

Source: Journal of Black Studies, September 2007; vol. 38, 1: pp. 51-63, first published on July 10, 2007.

primary, Obama trailed multimillionaire businessman Blair Hull and Illinois Comptroller Dan Hynes. Obama's candidacy was boosted by an advertising campaign featuring images of the late Chicago Mayor Harold Washington (the first Black mayor of Chicago) and the late U.S. Senator Paul Simon (who was White), the support of Simon's daughter, and political endorsements by the *Chicago-Tribune* and *Chicago Sun-Times*. From a crowded field of seven candidates, Obama received more than 52% of the vote in the March 16, 2004, primary ("Primary Election Results," n.d.).

In August 2004, with less than 3 months before Election Day, Keyes accepted the Illinois Republican Party's nomination to replace Ryan. Through three televised debates, Obama and Keyes took different positions on stem cell research, abortion, gun control, school vouchers, and tax cuts. In the general election on November 2, 2004, Obama received 70% of the popular vote to Keyes's 27% ("America Votes 2004," n.d.).

Obama became only the fourth African American to make a serious bid for the White House as a major party candidate. New York Congresswoman Shirley Chisholm ran in 1972, the Rev. Jesse Jackson ran in 1984 and 1988, and the Rev. Al Sharpton ran in 2004—all as Democrats. Obama's political career began just over 10 years ago. He was elected to the Illinois Senate in 1996. In 2000, he lost a primary bid for the U.S. House of Representatives to Democratic incumbent Bobby Rush, who had accused Obama of not being "black enough" (Fauntroy, 2007). Obama won reelection to the state senate in 2002, running unopposed.

Background

Barack Obama was born on August 4, 1961, in Honolulu, Hawaii, to Barack Hussein Obama Sr. (born in Nyanza Province, Kenya) and Ann Dunham (born in Wichita, Kansas). His father was an African man from Kenya and his mother was a White woman from Kansas. When Barack Obama Jr. was 2 years old, his parents separated and were later divorced. His father went on to Harvard University to pursue his PhD degree and later returned to Kenya. His mother married a foreign exchange student from Indonesia, and they had one daughter. The family moved to Jakarta in 1967, where Obama attended local schools from age 6 to 10. He returned to Hawaii and lived with his maternal grandparents from 5th through 12th grade. His father died in an automobile accident in Kenya when Obama was 21 years old, and his mother died of cancer when he was 34. Obama received his bachelor's of arts degree from Columbia University and later entered Harvard Law School. He was the first Black president of the *Harvard Law Review* and received his JD degree in 1999. He is married to Michelle Robinson Obama, an African American, and they have two daughters (Senior, 2006).

The 2008 Presidential Race

The 2008 presidential race has been heralded as unprecedented. After 217 years of major presidential nominees who were, without exception, White and male, the 2008 election offers voters quite a variety of candidates. Thus far, the announced Democratic candidates include New York Senator Hillary Clinton, a White female; Governor Bill Richardson of New Mexico, a Latino male; former North Carolina Senator John Edwards; and Senator Barack Obama.

In early trial heat polls in 2007, Obama trailed Hillary Clinton for the Democratic nomination but ran nearly as well as Clinton in general election matchups against the leading Republican candidates (see Table 1). A key question for this presidential election is whether the American voters are finally willing to vote for a qualified African American candidate for president. In a Pew Research Center publication titled *Can You Trust What Polls Say About Obama's Electoral Prospects?* (Keeter & Samaranayake, 2007), the authors pointed to two important trends that may suggest Americans are now ready. They cited a *Newsweek* poll conducted in 2006 that found that only 3% of Americans said that they were not willing to vote for a qualified African American candidate. The Gallup Organization has been asking a version of this question since 1958, when a majority (53%) responded that they would not vote for an African American candidate. In 2003, in contrast, 92% said they would vote for an African American candidate for president, whereas only 6% said they would not (Keeter & Samaranayake, 2007). Second, Gallup noted that polling undertaken in campaigns in which Blacks run against Whites are doing a better job of accurately predicting the results of those elections than in the past when hidden racial biases skewed the results.

The "Bradley effect" led to inaccurate voter opinion polls in some American political campaigns between a White and a non–White candidate

Table 1   Democratic Primary Preference (%)

	Clinton	Obama	Edwards	Gore
February	36	24	12	14
January	41	17	11	10
December	39	17	12	10

'08 Matchups							
Clinton vs.	Giuliani	Clinton vs.	McCain	Obama vs.	Giuliani	Obama vs.	McCain
49	47	50	45	45	49	47	45

Source: ABC/*Washington Post* Poll: '08 Election. January 19, 2007. http://abcnews.go.com/images/US/1029a1'08Election.pdf; *Washington Post*-ABC News Poll February 22-25, 2007. February 27, 2007. http://www.washingtonpost.com/wp-srv/politics/polls/postpoll_022607.htm

in the past. The effect has occurred when a statistically significant number of White voters tell pollsters in advance of an election that they are either undecided or likely to vote for the Black candidate but exhibit a different behavior when actually casting their ballots. White voters who stated that they were undecided broke in statistically large numbers toward the White candidate, and many of the White voters who said that they were likely to vote for the Black candidate cast their ballots for the White candidate. This reluctance to give accurate polling has extended to postelection exit polls as well. Researchers have theorized that some White voters have felt a societal pressure not to declare their support for a White candidate in such a race, fearing that by doing so, they might appear to others to be racially prejudiced (Cose, 2006). The term *Bradley effect* originated with the 1982 gubernatorial race in California between a Black mayor, Tom Bradley, and his White opponent, George Deukmejian. The polls leading up to the election consistently showed Bradley with a lead. However, Bradley narrowly lost the race. Postelection results showed that a smaller percentage of White voters actually voted for Bradley than those who said they planned to vote for him, and voters who were categorized as "undecided" voted for Deukmejian (Cose, 2006).

A New Face and a New Message

Much of Obama's appeal is his ability to transcend race. Indeed, in his keynote address at the Democratic Convention in 2004, he stated,

> The pundits like to slice and dice our country into Red States and Blue States; Red States for Republicans, Blue States for Democrats. But I've got news for them too. We worship an awesome God in the Blue States, and we don't like federal agents poking around in our libraries in the Red States. We coach Little League in the Blue States and yes, we got some gay friends in the Red States. There are patriots who opposed the war in Iraq and patriots who supported the war in Iraq. We are one people, all of us pledging allegiance to the Stars and Stripes, all of us defending the United States of America. ("2004 Democratic National Convention Keynote Address," 2007)

Obama has a charismatic style that connects with people and rises above racial stereotypes. But there is still much skepticism as to whether an African American can win the U.S. presidency. Obama won his Senate seat against an African American who had only recently become a resident of the state. Harold Ford Jr., a Black Democrat and U.S. representative from Tennessee, and Michael Steele, a Black Republican attorney general from Maryland, both lost to White candidates in the general election in their respective states in 2006.

Furthermore, demographics may prove problematic for an African American candidate. Stated *The New York Times* columnist Adam Nagourney (2006),

> Black Americans are concentrated in about 25 states—typically blue ones, like New York and California. While black candidates cannot assume automatic support from black voters, they would at least provide a base. In states without large African American populations, the candidates' crossover appeal must be large.

In addition, Senator Hillary Rodham Clinton, the current Democratic front-runner, presents a formidable challenge to Senator Obama. And that challenge comes from both White voters and African American voters. A Gallup Poll in September 2006 showed a steady rise in the number of people who were willing to elect a woman or African American as president one day. But many political observers feel that the country is ready to elect a White woman for president before electing a Black. White women have made greater strides in public office than Blacks: The current Congress has 71 women, one of whom is the first speaker of the U.S. House of Representatives. There are 43 African Americans in the U.S. Congress. There are nine female governors but only one African American governor, Deval Patrick of Massachusetts. Women account for 51% of the population, whereas African Americans account for only 12.7%. Some political observers see this as a sign that most Americans are comfortable with White women in the role of chief executive officer. Jesse Jackson, civil rights leader and former presidential candidate, has said that "All evidence is that a white female has an advantage over a black male—for reasons of our cultural heritage" (Nagourney, 2006). According to Geraldine Ferraro, the first woman to run as a major party vice presidential candidate, "It's more realistic for a woman than it is for an African American. . . . There is a certain amount of racism that exists in the United States—whether its [sic] conscious or not it's true" (Nagourney, 2006). Black South Carolina state Senator Robert Ford, who has endorsed Hillary Clinton for president, has stated that the country isn't ready to vote for an African American as president and that everyone running on the Democratic ticket next year would lose because Barack Obama would drag the ticket down. Obama responded in February 2007 when speaking at Claflin University, a historically Black institution in Orangeburg, South Carolina, by saying,

> I know this . . . that when folks were saying we are going to march for our freedoms, somebody said you can't do that. When somebody said let's sit at the lunch counter, somebody said we can't do that . . . I don't believe in this can't do, won't do, won't even try style of leadership. Don't believe in that. . . . Yes, we can. (Mitchell, 2007)

Table 2   African American Support of Clinton Versus Obama (%)

	Clinton	Obama
February	33	44
January	60	20
December	60	20

Source: ABC/*Washington Post* Poll: Election 2008-2/25/07. February 25, 2007. http://abcnews.go.com/images/US/1031a3Election.pdf

Ironically, Obama's early support by many White Americans created unease among some in the African American community. In fact, some early polls showed Obama trailing Hillary Clinton among African American Democratic voters. A January 2007 *Washington Post*–ABC News poll found that 20% of Black voters polled supported Obama for president whereas 60% supported Clinton (see Table 2).

Some African Americans have questioned Obama's blackness. Black author Debra Dickerson stated, "Obama isn't black in an American racial context. He married black. He acts black. But there's a lot of distance between black Africans and African Americans" (Swarns, 2007). Others have pointed to Obama's heritage and the fact that he did not embody the experiences of most African Americans whose ancestors had endured slavery, segregation, and the quest for civil rights. Stanley Crouch, a Black newspaper columnist, stated, "When black Americans refer to Obama as 'one of us,' I don't know what they are talking about" (Nagourney, 2006). Both Jesse Jackson and Al Sharpton, former African American presidential candidates, initially declined to endorse Obama, but Jackson has since changed his position and announced his endorsement of Obama's candidacy (Bellandi, 2007). Professor Ronald Walters, who was an adviser to Jesse Jackson's presidential campaigns and heads the African American Leadership Institute at the University of Maryland said, "He's going to have to win over some African Americans. They have a right to be suspicious of people who come into the country and don't share their experience" (Nagourney, 2006).

The Source of Obama's Appeal Among White Voters

Michael Fauntroy, a political scientist at George Mason University, noted, "In the wider American society, there are some African Americans . . . who are seen as transcending race and for lack of a better phrase, 'don't scare white people'" (Curry, 2006). Obama is a member of the post–civil rights generation of African American politicians and is not identified with leaders such as Jesse Jackson or Al Sharpton, who may be polarizing to White voters.

Obama, however, describes himself as an African American and has said that growing up he yearned to be accepted as a Black man. Emil Jones Jr., the president of the Illinois state senate and an early mentor of Obama's, says he is frustrated by Black voters who question Obama's heritage. "As a state legislator, Obama had the support of voters in his district, which is 67 percent black" (Swarns, 2007). Furthermore, several members of the Congressional Black Caucus, including civil rights pioneer John Lewis (D-GA); Jesse Jackson Jr. (D-IL), the son of the Rev. Jesse Jackson; and Artur Davis (D-AL), have announced their support of Obama's presidential bid (Swarns, 2007).

In early February 2007, Senator Joseph Biden (D-DE), a White presidential candidate, added fuel to the debate on race and the presidency when on the day that he announced his own candidacy for the presidency described Obama as "the first mainstream African-American who is articulate and bright and clean and a nice-looking guy." He subsequently apologized for his remarks (Swarns, 2007). Donna Brazile, campaign manager for Al Gore's presidential bid in 2000 and Democratic consultant, later said she was deluged with e-mail messages from people who wanted to volunteer for Obama's campaign and that most of the requests were from Whites (Nagourney, 2006).

By late February 2007, there appeared to be a sizable shift among African Americans about their impressions of Obama. A *Washington Post–ABC News Poll* showed that Clinton's and Obama's support among White voters changed little since December 2006, but the shifts among Black Democrats were dramatic. Throughout December 2006 and January 2007, in *Washington Post–ABC News* polls, Clinton led Obama among African Americans by 60% to 20%. However, in the late February poll, Obama held a narrow advantage among African Americans, 44% to 33% (Balz & Cohen, 2007; see Table 2).

The Civil Rights Legacy

One of Obama's first real jobs after graduating from Columbia University was that of a community organizer on the Southside of Chicago. In an interview with *The New Republic* magazine, Obama stated that the civil rights movement had inspired him. "Through organizing, through shared sacrifice, membership had been earned. Obama wanted to join the club" (Lizza, 2007, p. 24). He said that Bob Moses and John Lewis, members of the Student Nonviolent Coordinating Committee during the 1960s, were his role models of that time. In his book *The Audacity of Hope* (Obama, 2006), he reflected on how his mother instilled in him the values she saw in the civil rights movement: tolerance, equality, and standing up for the disadvantaged.

Impasse at Selma 2007

In February 2007, presidential candidate Barack Obama announced that he would deliver the keynote address at a service at the Brown Chapel A.M.E. Church commemorating the 1965 civil rights march across the Edmund Pettus Bridge in Selma, Alabama. Not to concede anything to Obama, presidential candidate Hillary Clinton announced that she would be attending the commemoration and speaking at First Baptist Church. Clinton's husband, former President Bill Clinton, was scheduled to be inducted into the Hall of Fame at the National Voting Rights Museum in Selma that Sunday as well. Although Senator Clinton originally had planned to accept the award on behalf of her husband, at the last minute she announced that he would be attending the ceremony. Both candidates spoke at churches not far from one another. Both candidates also reflected on how the Selma march made it possible for them to become presidential candidates. However, the appearance of former President Clinton for the event, given his popularity among Black voters (after all, he had been dubbed the "first Black president"), was a strong signal from the Clinton camp that candidate Clinton was not ceding the African American vote to Obama (Kornblut, 2007). Moreover, the appearance of both candidates in Selma on the anniversary of "Bloody Sunday" signaled the importance of the African American vote in the upcoming Democratic primaries.

During his speech, Barack Obama sought to establish his connection to Selma in 1965, when he was only 3 years old, and to 2007, when he is a candidate for president of the United States. He referred to members of his generation who were too young to march in the streets but still are required "to fulfill that legacy, to fulfill the obligations and the debt that we owe to those who allowed us to be here today" (Kornblut & Whoriskey, 2007). In addition, Obama proclaimed "the civil rights movement inspired his African father to move from Kenya to seek an American education and eventually marry his white mother" (Kornblut & Whoriskey, 2007).

Racial Politics in America

In Virginia in 1989, L. Douglas Wilder became the first elected African American governor in the history of this country. When asked about his prescription for success years later, Wilder remarked, "Don't run to make history as an African American candidate, run to be the best qualified candidate for the job" (Schaller, 2006, p. 69).

Racial politics has been front and center in American politics since the 17th century. Even modern-day politicians use race to appeal to the prejudices and fears of voters. Richard Nixon abandoned the Republican Party's antislavery roots when in 1968 he appealed to White voters using racially coded language such as "B-U-S-I-N-G." Jimmy Carter, the Democratic nomi-nee in 1976, used the term *ethnic purity* in depicting White ethnic enclaves and neighborhood schools. George Bush Sr., the Republican nominee in 1988, used the infamous "Willie Horton" advertisement to suggest that his Democratic opponent was soft on crime. Even Bill Clinton, the Democratic nominee in 1992, attacked the Rev. Jesse Jackson's Rainbow Coalition for its invitation to rap singer Sister Souljah to distance himself from African American voters (Glick, 2004).

Some White candidates still feel the need to appeal to White voters along racial lines and drive a wedge between Black and White voters in this coun-try. In the 2006 U.S. Senate race in Tennessee, with only a few weeks to go in a very tight election, the Republican National Committee ran an adver-tisement linking Democratic candidate Harold Ford with a White Playboy bunny at a Playboy party. The advertisement played on Southern White fears that Ford, a single African American male, if elected senator might date their daughters. Ford lost.

The history of racial politics and racially polarized voting in this coun-try has made many Blacks cautious about Barack Obama's chances of win-ning the presidency. Obama has said, "I think there is a protectiveness and a skepticism within the African American community that is grounded in their experiences. But the skepticism doesn't mean there is a lack of support" (Nagourney, 2006).

The Presidential Campaigns of Jesse Jackson

The presidential campaigns of the Rev. Jesse Jackson in 1984 and 1988 may be key to the maturation process of White voters today. When Jackson first ran for president in 1984, a Gallup Poll showed that 18% of Whites said that they would not vote for a Black man for president even if he were qualified and a party nominee. Jackson was unable to transcend race in his presidential election bid in 1984 or 1988. But according to political observers, his campaign helped to reshape the contours of American poli-tics. Journalist Fay Joyce (1984) observed, "Jackson gained so much respect in the 1984 presidential election that he made the 'idea of a serious black presidential candidacy' much more acceptable" (p. A1). City Councilman John Lewis of Atlanta, speaking about Jackson's presidential bid, noted, "He's creating a climate for some black man or black woman to come along and be elected President of the country" (Joyce, 1984, p. A1). Moreover, Jackson mounted a very successful effort to increase voter registration levels of African Americans throughout the country, and he is credited with having a significant impact on African American turnout at the polls in 1984 and 1988 (Tate, 1991).

Is Obama a Viable Candidate?

The question remains in the minds of many Americans: Is Barack Obama a viable candidate? Unlike Senator Hillary Clinton, who has a huge war chest and extensive contacts, Obama lacks experience. Can he attract the huge sums of money that are required to mount a successful presidential bid? Federal Election Commission (FEC) Chairman Michael Toner has said that the 2008 presidential election will be the most expensive in history. Toner has estimated that the race will be a $1 billion election and that a serious candidate will need to raise $100 million by the end of 2007 (Hallow, 2006). Obama has shown success comparable with Clinton in fund-raising. In the first quarter of fund-raising, the Clinton campaign announced raising $26 million, whereas the Obama campaign announced it had raised $25 million. Obama's fund-raising came from more than 100,000 donors, more than half of them through the Internet (Pickler, 2007).

In a *Washington Post*–ABC News poll conducted on January 19, 2007, among the leading Democratic contenders, Senator Obama trailed Senator Clinton 41% to 17% among likely Democratic voters. Although Clinton is the early front-runner, the first Democratic caucus isn't until January 14, 2008, and the political landscape may change considerably by then. And there are early signs that Clinton is feeling some heat from Obama. Hollywood executive David Geffen cohosted a fund-raiser for Obama in February 2007 that reportedly raised more than $1 million. Geffen, once a close ally of the Clintons, was quoted in *The New York Times* as disparaging Hillary Clinton and questioning whether she could win the presidency in 2008. The Clinton camp called on Obama to "denounce the remarks, remove Mr. Geffen from his campaign and return his money" (Preston, 2007).

Barack Obama has stated that he will not accept donations from federal lobbyists or political action committees for the campaign. When Obama started to collect private contributions for a general election account, he asked the FEC if he could return the money later if he decided to take public funds. In response, the FEC is allowing presidential candidates to take private contributions for a general election campaign even if they decide to accept public funding (McCormick, 2007).

A Historic Candidacy in the Making

Newsweek magazine depicted Barack Obama and Hillary Clinton on its cover for the week of December 25, 2006, to January 1, 2007, with the caption "The Race Is On, But Is America Ready for Either One?" In many ways Barack Obama is a unique candidate, which is why many Democrats and Republicans view him as a viable one. Obama has compiled a liberal record in his 2 years in the Senate. Some observers see his limited résumé as a plus because his opponents will have less of a record to use against him.

Obama also may benefit from an actual decline in racially saturated issues such as crime and welfare. Journalist Peter Beinart (2007) argued that Obama's ability to garner Black support and to promise to bridge America's cultural divide would have been impossible 25 years ago. Today, asserted Beinart, "It is at the heart of Obama's appeal." Beinart maintained that American politics has not transcended race but that defying White stereotypes of Blacks no longer requires moving as far to the right as it once did.

David Bositis, senior research associate at the Joint Center for Political and Economic Studies and an expert on Black elected officials, says the race between Obama and Clinton "is no David versus Goliath." According to Bositis, Obama has a substantial organization and the ability to raise money (personal communication, March 9, 2007). Mayor Richard Daley of Chicago and his brother, William Daley, a former commerce secretary, have endorsed him. Numerous celebrities, including talk show host Oprah Winfrey and actor George Clooney, are supporting him. Donna Brazile has summed up Obama's historic run for the United States presidency as follows: "Barack will tell us that we don't have to go back to being just a white America or a black America, that we can now become something else together. That's the promise of his campaign, and his challenge" (Swarns, 2007).

References

2004 Democratic National Convention keynote address. (2007). *Wikisource, the Free Library.* Retrieved March 29, 2007, from http://en.wikisource.org/w/index.php?title=2004_ Democratic_National_Convention_keynote_address&oldid=317938

America votes 2004: U.S. Senate/Illinois. (n.d.) *CNN.com.* Retrieved March 21, 2007, from http://www.cnn.com/ELECTION/2004/pages/results/states/IL/S/01/index.html

Balz, D., & Cohen, J. (2007, February 28). Blacks shift to Obama, poll finds. *The Washington Post*, p. A01.

Beinart, P. (2007). Black like me. *The New Republic.* Retrieved March 8, 2007, from http://www.tnr.com/doc.mhtml?i=20070205&s=trb020507

Bellandi, D. (2007). Jesse Jackson endorses Obama run. *Time.* Retrieved April 12, 2007, from http://www.time.com/time/nation/article/0,8599,1605410,00.html

Cose, E. (2006). The "Bradley effect." *Newsweek.* Retrieved April 12, 2007, from http://www.msnbc.msn.com/id/15366427/site/newsweek/

Curry, T. (2006, December 13). Obama seeks to settle racial doubts. *MSNBC.com.* Retrieved March 9, 2007, from http://www.msnbc.com/id/16177866/print/1/displaymode/1098

Fauntroy, M. (2007, January 30). Is he Black enough? *The Huffington Post.* Retrieved April 12, 2007, from http://www.huffingtonpost.com/michael-fauntroy-phd/is-he-black-enough_b_40048.html

Glick, T. (2004, February 19). Racism and presidential elections since 1964: A short history. *ZNet.* Retrieved March 9, 2007, from http://www.zmag.org/content/showarticle.cfm?ItemID=5011

Hallow, R. Z. (2006, December 20). Road to White House may cost $1 billion. *The Washington Times*. Retrieved April 12, 2007, from http://washingtontimes.com/national/20061220-121843-2600r.htm

Joyce, F. S. (1984, April 13). Jackson candidacy is giving new shape to politics in U.S. *The New York Times*, p. A1.

Keeter, S., & Samaranayake, N. (2007). *Can you trust what polls say about Obama's electoral prospects?* Retrieved March 9, 2007, from http://pewresearch.org/pubs/408/can-you-trust-what-polls-say-about-obamas-electoral-prospects

Kornblut, A. E. (2007, March 2). At site of '65 march, an '08 collision. *The Washington Post*, p. A01.

Kornblut, A. E., & Whoriskey, P. (2007, March 5). Clinton, Obama link Selma march to present. *The Washington Post*. Retrieved March 7, 2007, from http://www.barackobama.com/2007/03/05/clinton_obama_link_selma_march.php

Lizza, R. (2007, March 19). The agitator: Barack Obama's unlikely political education. *The New Republic*, pp. 22-29.

McCormick, J. (2007, March 1). FEC rules on presidential campaign funding. *Chicago-Tribune*. Retrieved March 21, 2007, from http://www.chicagotribune.com/news/nationworld/chi-070301elect,1,1372893.story?track=rss&ctrack=1&cset=true

Mitchell, M. (2007, February 18). Black man can't win? Think again, Obama says in South Carolina stop. *Chicago Sun-Times*. Retrieved March 30, 2007, from http://infoweb.newsbank.com/iw-search/we/InfoWeb/?p_action=print&p_docid=11760FB

Nagourney, A. (2006, December 10). The pattern may change, if... *The New York Times*. Retrieved March 21, 2007, from http://www.nytimes.com/2006/12/10/weekinreview/10nagourney.html?ex=1175140800&en=9878655ef0cda5da&ei=5070

Obama, B. (2006). *The audacity of hope*. New York: Crown.

Pickler, N. (2007, April 4). Obama rivals Clinton in fundraising, rakes in $25 mil. *Chicago Sun-Times*. Retrieved April 12, 2007, from http://www.suntimes.com/news/elections/326247,obama040407.article

Preston, M. (2007, February 21). Clinton, Obama camps mix it up verbally. *CNN.com*. Retrieved March 24, 2007, from http://www.cnn.com/2007/POLITICS/02/21/clinton.obama/index.html

Primary election results. (n.d.) *Chicago-Tribune*. Retrieved March 21, 2007, from http://www.chicagotribune.com/news/specials/elections/primary/

Schaller, T. (2006). *Whistling past Dixie*. New York: Simon & Schuster.

Senior, J. (2006, October 2). Dreaming of Obama. *New York Magazine*. Retrieved April 12, 2007, from http://nymag.com/news/politics/21681/

Swarns, R. L. (2007, February 2). So far, Obama can't take Black vote for granted. *The New York Times*. Retrieved March 21, 2007, from http://query.nytimes.com/gst/fullpage.html?res=9905E3DE123FF931A35751C0A9619C8B63

Tate, K. (1991). Black political participation in the 1984 and 1988 presidential elections. *American Political Science Review*, 84, 1159-1176.

10

OBAMA AND THE WHITE VOTE

Todd Donovan

Western Washington University

The presidential candidacy and election of Barack Obama produced many intriguing claims about the place of race in American politics. Prominent among these was the idea that Obama's election constituted a shift to a "post-racial" era where race plays little role in the electoral prospects of African American candidates. There are theoretical and empirical reasons for questioning this assumption, and the 2008 presidential election presents a unique opportunity to test how race affected support for an African American candidate in a majority white electoral setting. That election also provides an opportunity to test how white voters responded when presented with the choice between a white and a black candidate as the potential Democratic nominee. This article illustrates that there was something specific about the relationship between a state's racial context and Obama's appeal relative to Hillary Clinton that structured where the Democrats gained or lost vote share from 2004 to 2008. Racial context may have structured whites' attitudes about Obama relative to Clinton, and state-level distributions of these attitudes affected how much better (or worse) the 2008 Democratic candidate did relative to the 2004 Democratic candidate. Analysis of survey data also demonstrate that the racial context of congressional districts may have conditioned whether white voters supported Obama or John McCain.

Candidate Race, State Racial Context, and Voting

Social science has demonstrated that African American candidates often receive a small fraction of the white vote (Reeves 1997), particularly in the American South (Davidson and Grofman 1994). Experimental research demonstrates that racial animus on the part of some whites operates independently

Source: Political Research Quarterly, December 2010; vol. 63, 863-874, first published on August 4, 2010.

of political considerations in candidate evaluations (Reeves 1997, 89) and that for some whites the mere mention of racial policies can aggravate preexisting negative stereotypes of blacks[1] (Sniderman and Piazza 1993, 104; see also Heerwig and McCabe 2007). Racial attitudes, moreover, have been shown to affect voter choice between white presidential candidates (Kinder and Sanders 1996; Mendelberg 2001).

Although there are prominent examples of African American candidates winning in electorates that are majority white,[2] such cases have been relatively rare (Grofman, Handley, and Niemi 1992, 134). The history of race and voting in the South demonstrates particularly high levels of racially polarized voting (Lublin 1997a; Davidson and Grofman 1994; Engstrom and McDonald 1981). This causes African American candidates to depend heavily on support from African American voters in majority (or near-majority) minority districts to win elections (Lublin 1997b). There is general consensus in this literature that a substantial proportion of whites, particularly in the South, have a low probability of supporting African American candidates (Lublin 1999; Cameron, Epstein, and O'Halloran 1996; Swain 1993; Brace et al. 1988).

Given all this, what role might race have played in shaping the 2008 presidential election results? Studies have found a minority of Americans might not support an African American presidential candidate. One study from the 1980s estimated that 16 percent of voters would oppose a black presidential candidate on the basis of race (Sigelman and Welsh 1984). Although contemporary opinion polls found 90 percent saying "yes" when asked, "If your party nominated a African American for president, would you vote for him if he were qualified for the job?" list experiments suggest social desirability response effects may inflate positive responses by 20 percent (Heerwig and McCabe 2007).

Theory and empirical studies also demonstrate that white voters' racial attitudes and white voters' evaluations of black candidates may operate differently in different places, since racial context can play a role in conditioning the relationship between candidate race, whites' attitudes, and voting. The racial threat thesis, or white backlash hypothesis, proposes that whites are more likely to fear social, economic, or political advances by minorities when they reside in jurisdictions where the minority group's population share is larger. As classic examples of this, V. O. Key (1949) found conservative (segregationist) candidates fared best in southern counties with the highest African American populations; and Blalock (1957) found greater discrimination against African Americans in southern counties with larger nonwhite populations (also see Branton and Jones 2005). The threat thesis assumes that at some level of geography, people are aware of the racial context of their surroundings and respond to that context. Wong (2007) demonstrates that Americans overestimate the percentage of minority residents in the United States but also shows that perceptions of the size of an area's African

American population is modestly associated with the actual (proportionate) size of the group in an area. This article employs measures of racial context from both the state level and congressional district level to examine if racial context affected white voters' attitudes and behavior in 2008.

Contemporary studies of how racial context might affect political outcomes have yielded mixed results. A number of studies fail to support the threat thesis (Voss 1996, 2001), while others do provide support (Giles and Evans 1986; Giles and Hertz 1994; Giles and Buckner 1993; Behrens, Uggen, and Manza 2003; Rocha and Espino 2009). Many of these results are driven by the racial context of the American South, although there is evidence that the racial threat mechanism explains patterns in election results outside of the South (Tolbert and Grummel 2003). Scholars specify the causal mechanism of the threat thesis differently,[3] but a straightforward read of Key's (1949) thesis suggests group size is the relevant factor. The racial threat thesis illustrates how the effect of racial context might structure the relationship between candidate race and voting and suggests that the likelihood that a white voter might support a black candidate is not randomly distributed geographically.

Race and the 2008 Election

If a racial threat mechanism operated in 2008, or, similarly, if white voters' racial attitudes that work against African American candidates are spatially concentrated in conjunction with larger African American populations, we would expect that the appeal of Obama as a candidate would operate differently in states according to the racial context of the state. Forecasting models generally predicted that a generic Democratic candidate would do well in 2008 (Campbell 2008). Obama's 4.6 percent improvement over the 2004 Democratic vote was close to what several models predicted.[4] As Table 1 illustrates, the Democratic vote swing from 2004 to 2008 was uneven across the states. The largest Democratic gains over 2004 were in nonsouthern states with small African American populations, and the larger losses were in southern and border states. Despite a deteriorating economy that predicted substantial vote loss for the Republican party, Obama ran weaker in several states in 2008 than John Kerry did in 2004.

What role did candidate race and state racial context play in 2008? During the 2008 campaign, claims about the role of race and electoral support for Obama came in many forms, some of which were clearly contradicted by the election results. Early in the primaries, a number of Obama's detractors suggested he was not "black enough" to win the Democratic nomination (Crouch 2006). Obama was tipped as being a weaker general election candidate than Hillary Clinton because "the Hispanic voter . . . has not shown a lot of willingness to support black candidates" (Rodriguez 2008; see also Barreto and Ramirez 2008). As media scrutiny of Rev. Jeremiah Wright

Table 1   States with Greatest and Least Swing Democrat, 2004–2008 (in percentages)

Hawaii	17.8
Indiana	10.7
North Dakota	9.0
Nebraska	8.9
Montana	8.7
Vermont	8.6
Delaware	8.6
Utah	8.3
New Mexico	7.9
Nevada	7.3
U.S. average	4.6
Alaska	2.4
Kentucky	1.8
Arizona	0.6
Oklahoma	−0.1
Massachusetts	−0.1
West Virginia	−0.6
Tennessee	−0.7
Alabama	−1.0
Louisiana	−2.3
Arkansas	−5.6

peaked during the lead-up to the April 22 Pennsylvania primary, Sen. Clinton suggested that Obama was unelectable, in part because he relied so heavily on support from African Americans (Reid 2008).[5] In May, after Sen. Clinton won the Indiana primary and lost the North Carolina primary, she noted how Obama's support was weakening among "hard working Americans— white Americans" (Kiely and Lawrence 2008). Clinton supported the claim that she had stronger support among "swing, working class voters" by citing opinion polls from Kentucky and West Virginia (Kiely and Lawrence 2008).

In November, Obama won 53 percent of the popular vote, with an estimated 43 percent of the white vote and 67 percent of the Latino vote.[6] Obama's vote share roughly matched what preelection polls predicted.[7] Obama won a higher share of the Latino vote than Al Gore or John Kerry,[8] and exit polls estimated white voters' support for Obama was slightly greater than for John Kerry in 2004 or Al Gore in 2000.

Obama won, then, with substantial support from white voters. The *New York Times* headline announcing the election result proclaimed, "Racial Barrier Falls in Decisive Victory," and prominent critics of the Voting Rights Act claimed that Obama's victory signaled a postracial era for voting. Abigail Thernstrom and Stephan Thernstrom argued that "the myth of racist white voters was destroyed by this year's presidential election" and that "aggressive federal interference in state and local districting decisions enshrined in the Voting Rights Act should therefore be reconsidered."[9] Justice Clarence Thomas echoed a similar theme in 2009, arguing that a key section of the Voting Rights Act used to justify majority-minority districting was no longer constitutional because the historic context of race and politics had changed so much since 1965.[10] Thernstrom (1995) had long contended that racism by whites in contests between a white and black candidate was a thing of the past and that contemporary instances where African American candidates are denied victory in settings where the electorate is majority white are idiosyncratic anomalies (Reeves 1997, 7). But how much does Obama's election suggest that something has changed in terms of the role of race in voting?

Accounting for Racial Context and Voter Attitudes in 2008

The question of how race and racial context may have affected how voters responded to Obama is assessed here in three steps. The first is by applying the racial threat thesis to examine the relative appeal to whites of Obama versus Clinton as potential Democratic candidates. Second, Obama's relative appeal to whites is then used to model where the Democratic nominee gained and lost vote share over 2004 in the general election. Finally, survey data are employed to test how racial context affected white voters' support for Obama in the general election.

The unique nature of the 2008 Democratic nomination contest provides an opportunity to compare the relative appeal of a white (Clinton) versus a black (Obama) Democratic presidential candidate. Nearly two months into the voting phase of the nomination contest (late February), it was clear that McCain would be the Republican nominee, but the outcome of the Democratic race was still in doubt. The collapse of the financial system was several months away, and racial innuendo about Obama was a regular part of campaign discourse.

In January, Sen. Clinton used the King holiday as a venue for suggesting that it took a (white) president to get civil rights legislation enacted. Later that month, former president Clinton attracted attention by comparing Obama's South Carolina victory to Rev. Jesse Jackson's failed campaign (Harden 2008). Nation of Islam Minister Louis Farrakhan was reported to have endorsed Obama on February 24. At the same time, a photo of Obama dressed in traditional Somali robes circulated on the Internet with rumors that Obama was Muslim (Raum 2008). Conservative talk show hosts and some Republican officials were using Obama's middle name (Hussein) when referring to the candidate, and some referred (incorrectly) to the Somali robes as "Muslim" dress (Vo 2008). On February 25, Obama's campaign manager David Plouffe responded to the Somali photo by claiming that Clinton was practicing "the most shameful, offensive, fear-mongering we've seen from either party in this election" (Baldwin 2008). In a nationally televised debate the next day, Obama was asked about Farrakhan and controversial statements made by Rev. Wright and was criticized by Sen. Clinton for his handling of the Farrakhan "endorsement" (*New York Times* 2008). Intentionally or not, the "race card" was on the table.

State-level measures of how white voters responded when presented with a choice between a potential white (Clinton) or black (Obama) Democrat candidate in a contest against John McCain, taken in this late February context, provide valuable information about where and why a black presidential candidate may meet greater acceptance or resistance. Such information is not perfect for assessing this. Obama and Clinton crafted different themes, targeted different constituencies with their messages, and, obviously, were of different genders. Yet they were identical on the most critical predictor of vote choice (party) and highly similar in general policy liberalism.[11] Gender was clearly a factor affecting choices between the two Democratic candidates, but it plays much less of a role when the choice is presented as either a Democrat or a Republican. The distribution of gender also has rather limited variance across states and, thus, is unlikely to explain differences in how the candidates were evaluated across the states. A cross-state comparison of aggregated responses to survey questions asking hypothetical head-to-head match-ups of Obama versus McCain and Clinton versus McCain thus provides a rare means for getting leverage on how white voters in different settings responded to an African American presidential candidate.

Data and Analysis: The Relative Appeal of Obama or Clinton to Whites

State-level measures of candidate support (Obama vs. McCain and Clinton vs. McCain) were measured in all fifty states in late February 2008. Survey USA conducted random digit dial surveys in nearly every state from February 26 to 28.[12] Given that nearly all the data were collected by the same firm, using the same methods, at the same time, any potential measurement error associated with survey methodology should be constant across states.

The hypothetical general election appeal to white voters of Obama as a Democrat, compared to Clinton as a Democrat, is expressed in Table 2 as the difference between Obama's or Clinton's lead in head-to-head match-ups in late February 2008. The range of differences across states in the relative appeal of Clinton versus Obama is substantial. For example, Clinton trailed McCain among white voters in the Utah survey by 43 percent, while Obama trailed McCain among whites in the same survey by just 16 percent, a 27 percent advantage for Obama relative to Clinton in Utah. At the other

Table 2   Difference between Obama and Clinton among White Voters in Head-to-Head Match-Ups against John McCain, by State, February 2008 (in percentages).

Utah	27
Hawaii	26
North Dakota	23
Vermont	22
Nebraska	22
Idaho	21
Alaska	20
Illinois	17
Iowa	15
Wyoming	14
U.S. average	1.4
Florida	−12
Mississippi	−13
Kentucky	−13
Louisiana	−15
Alabama	−16
Ohio	−19
Tennessee	−21
Oklahoma	−22
West Virginia	−24
Arkansas	−38

Survey USA (SUSA) state samples, data collected February 26–28. Ohio SUSA data collected February 15–17. Alaska data from Rassmussen poll. Approximately 500-600 respondents per state.

extreme, Clinton led McCain by 4 percent among whites in Arkansas and Obama trailed McCain by 34 percent, a 38 percent deficit for Obama. There is some support here for Sen. Clinton's claim that she may have had stronger general election support among whites, but mainly in southern and border states. Obama, however, enjoyed large advantages among whites relative to Clinton in northern and western states—including many states where Democrats have been weak as general election candidates.

What, then, explains why Clinton and Obama had such widely different (hypothetical) general election appeal to white voters across the states? The racial threat thesis suggests that the racial context of a state should be a key feature in structuring how some white voters would respond to Obama's candidacy. Obama's relative appeal to whites is expected to be less in states with larger African American populations. Conversely, Obama would have more opportunities to make inroads with white voters in heavily white states, as these voters are expected to be less likely to have negative reactions to an African American candidate and to the racial innuendo associated with Obama. Figure 1 displays

Figure 1   Relationship between state population African American and Obama advantage (disadvantage) over McCain relative to Clinton among white voters

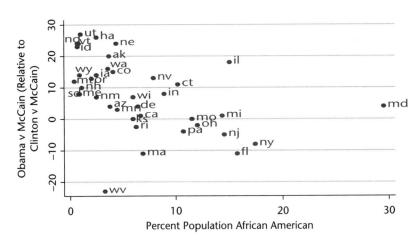

Values above the zero-level on the y-axis are states where Obama polled better among whites than Clinton in head-to-head match-ups against McCain. Values below the zero-level are states where Clinton polled better among whites than Obama in match-ups against McCain.

a scatterplot of the relationship between state racial context and Obama's relative advantage (disadvantage) as a candidate compared to Clinton ($r = -.41$). Points above the zero-level are where Obama polled relatively better than Clinton among whites in head-to-head match-ups against McCain. Conversely, points below the zero line are where Clinton polled better against McCain than Obama did. The pattern in Figure 1 is consistent with the racial threat hypothesis, but there are rival hypotheses. Clinton (or Obama) may have had a larger (or smaller) potential for support in each state due to the base of the Democratic vote or political liberalism of a state. Variation in economic conditions across the states could also structure differing levels of support for the candidates. Economic distress affected some states more severely than others early in 2008. A candidate making more explicit economic appeals may thus have had greater success in states where the economy was performing poorly.

These rival hypotheses are tested in Table 3. The racial threat hypothesis may be better tested with data aggregated at a lower geographic level (e.g., county, census tract) for more accurate measurement of racial context. However, robust measures of white voters' attitudes about the rival Democratic candidates are available at the state level, so models are first estimated with state-level data. Economic conditions were specified using several state-level measures from February 2008, including unemployment level,

Table 3 Obama's Appeal to White Voters, Relative to Clinton

	All states			Nonsouthern states	
Democratic vote (Kerry), 2004	−0.16	−0.15	−0.21	−0.10	−0.14
	(0.20)	(0.21)	(0.22)	(0.23)	(0.22)
Percentage state population African American	−0.46	−0.68	−0.48	−0.65	−2.7
	(0.18)	(0.40)	(0.48)	(0.34)	(0.94)
Percentage African American squared	—	0.01	0.01	—	0.08
		(0.01)	(0.01)		(0.03)
Unemployment	−0.86	−0.72	−0.77	−0.87	1.1
	(1.4)	(1.4)	(1.4)	(1.5)	(1.6)
Southern state	—	—	−5.1	—	—
			(6.3)		
Constant	21.6	21.4	23.7	20.6	18.4
	(9.8)	(9.8)	(10.3)	(10.3)	(9.8)
Adjusted R^2	.13	.13	.11	.10	.28
Number of cases	50	50	50	39	39

Ordinary least squares (OLS) regression coefficients, with standard errors in parenthesis. Dependent variable is difference between Obama and Clinton in head-to-head match-up with John McCain.

change in unemployment, change in housing prices, and change in real disposable income.[13] Racial context is represented both as a linear and a nonlinear function of the size of a state's African American population. Bullock (1976) and Longshore (1982) contend that racial animus and perceptions of a minority group as a threat climb until the racial context is around 40 percent African American. Up to that point or some similar threshold, whites may become increasingly concerned that traditional social relations are threatened by the minority group. Beyond a threshold, however, whites may be more accustomed to not having majority status, so the effect of racial context on whites' attitudes and behavior levels off. The nonlinear specification assumes the limiting effect that racial context has on white support for an African American candidate increases as the African American population increases, then flattens out beyond some threshold point. This nonlinear specification may also better reflect the skewed distribution of racial population densities in the United States.[14]

The racial context models are estimated with data from all fifty states using a separate intercept for southern states and are also estimated with only data from nonsouthern states.[15] Alternate models were estimated with controls for a baseline level of Democratic vote in the previous (2004) presidential election and with controls for state ideology and percentage of the state that is urban.[16] Similar models estimating white support for Obama with individual-level data and measures of a respondent's congressional district racial context are reported in a subsequent section of this article.

A number of estimations of the Obama/Clinton differential among whites using state-level economic measures produced null results and are not reported in Table 3.[17] There was a significant, inverse bivariate relationship between state unemployment and Obama's advantage over McCain relative to Clinton among whites, so this economic indicator is included in the multivariate models. The relationship between unemployment and Obama's margin over Clinton disappears, however, when the effect of state racial context is included in the multivariate models. Previous support for a Democratic presidential candidate (Kerry) in a state (reported in Table 3) and the liberalism of the state's citizens and congressional delegations (not reported here) were also poor predictors of where Obama was a stronger (or weaker) candidate than Clinton in a hypothetical match-up against McCain.

There is a significant relationship between state racial context and white support for Obama versus Clinton. In the fifty state sample, we see an inverse linear relationship between the size of a state's African American population and Obama's appeal (relative to Clinton) among whites. This effect is not significant, however, when a dummy variable for southern states is included. When the analysis is constrained to nonsouthern states, the size of a state's African American population explains more than one-quarter of cross-state variation in the relative appeal of Obama to Clinton among white voters. Clinton's potential appeal to white voters as a Democratic candidate in the 2008 general election was stronger than Obama's in states with the largest African American populations, whereas Obama's appeal to whites was greatest in states with the fewest African Americans. The nonlinear specifications suggest a linear decline in Obama's appeal among whites associated with larger African American populations eventually leveled off in states with the largest African American populations (as suggested in Figure 1).

Racial Context, White Voters, and the General Election

We now use these measures of opinions from the primaries to assess where Obama made general election gains among white voters as a Democratic presidential candidate in 2008. In this section, we test how the relative appeal to white voters of a black versus white Democratic candidate explained where the Democrats gained or lost vote share from 2004 to 2008. Following this, we utilize individual-level opinion data to assess if white voter support for Obama was reduced in areas (congressional districts) that had higher African American populations.

Since state racial context conditioned how white voters responded to an African American candidate (Table 3), we expect that Obama made above-average gains in states where he was relatively more appealing to white voters and below-average gains in states where he was less appealing to whites (as measured in the February survey data). Again, there are rival hypotheses. First, the state's preexisting political context could mute any effect of the Democrats' nominating an African American candidate. The state's baseline (2004) level of support for a Democratic presidential candidate may thus wash out any effect of the Obama/Clinton differential among whites that was measured in February. Second, economic conditions played out differently across the states, and the Democrats' advantage in 2008 associated with the deteriorating economy could have been magnified in states where conditions were worse. Third, an African American candidate could have produced a net advantage for Democrats in states with more African American voters.

Table 4 reports the results of several lagged endogenous variable ordinary least squares (OLS) estimates of change in state-level Democratic vote share from 2004 to 2008 that are designed to test these rival hypotheses. Not surprisingly, the Kerry vote in 2004 is a powerful predictor of a state's Obama vote in 2008. Depending on the specification, the models estimate a near-perfect linear relationship between state vote Democrat in 2004 and state vote Democrat 2008. Again, state-level measures of economic conditions fail to add anything to the models, but there are important, indirect effects of state racial context. Regardless of specification, the measure of the state-level Obama/Clinton difference in appeal to white voters from February 2008 is significant and positive. Obama thus ran stronger in November in states where he was relatively more appealing to whites than Clinton and weaker where Clinton was relatively more appealing to whites than Obama. Recall that results from Table 3 demonstrated that variation in Obama's relative appeal to whites as a Democratic candidate (compared to a white Democratic candidate) decreased as the size of a state's African American population increased. Table 4 demonstrates that for each additional 1 percent advantage in head-to-head comparisons with McCain that Obama had over Clinton among white voters, he is estimated to have received an additional 0.23 percent (when all states are included) or an additional 0.20 percent (in nonsouthern states) share of a state's vote in the general election. This is above and beyond effects associated with the Democratic share of the state vote in 2004.

Table 4 also illustrates effects of racial context on where Democrats gained or lost vote share in 2004 another way. When we do *not* account for how a state's white electorate shifted Democrat from 2004 to 2008[18] (first and fourth columns), the effect of whites' attitudes about Obama (relative to Clinton) is reduced substantially[19] but remains significant. Change in the Democratic share of the white vote (from 2004) is a significant predictor of where the 2008 Democratic presidential candidate gained (or lost) votes over 2004. The fact that this measure suppresses the effect of whites' attitudes about Obama suggests white voters were more likely to move toward the Democrats in 2008 in places where whites found Obama relatively more

Table 4   Change in Democratic Share of State Popular Vote, 2004-2008

	All states			Nonsouthern states		
State Democratic vote (Kerry), 2004	1.08	1.05	1.04	1.08	1.07	1.05
	(0.05)	(0.04)	(0.04)	(0.05)	(0.05)	(0.05)
Obama/Clinton difference among white voters	0.23	0.18	0.17	0.20	0.15	0.16
	(0.03)	(0.03)	(0.03)	(0.04)	(0.04)	(0.04)
State unemployment	−0.02	0.15	0.06	−0.19	−0.09	−0.15
	(0.28)	(0.26)	(0.27)	(0.33)	(0.30)	(0.30)
Percentage state population African American	—	—	0.08	—	—	0.10
			(0.06)			(0.07)
Change in white vote Democratic, 2004-2008	—	0.24	0.27	—	0.24	0.26
		(0.07)	(0.07)		(0.09)	(0.09)
South	—	—	−1.4			
			(1.2)			
Constant	0.2	0.2	0.6	1.4	1.0	1.4
	(2.3)	(2.0)	(2.1)	(2.4)	(2.2)	(2.2)
Adjusted R^2	.93	.94	.94	.93	.94	.95
Number of cases	50	50	50	39	39	39

Ordinary least squares (OLS) regression coefficients, with standard errors in parenthesis.

appealing than Clinton.[20] Thus, whether we account for the effect of white support for Obama indirectly (via whites' attitudes about Obama that are structured by the racial context of the state), or more directly (with exit poll measures of state-level change in white voters' support for a Democrat), the results suggest that the Democrats' state-level gains and losses over 2004 were driven by the white electorate's responses to Obama. The importance of this can also be seen by comparing models in Table 4 that omit or include a measure of the size of the state's African American population. Unlike the measures of whites' attitudes, this adds little to our understanding of where Democrats gained or lost vote share in 2008.

Thus far, the analysis has relied on aggregate measures of whites' attitudes and behavior. Public opinion data provide another vehicle for testing the effects of racial context—one where we have direct measures of white voters' reported attitudes and behavior. Table 5 presents an individual-level test of how racial context may have affected white support for Obama in 2008, using data from the preelection wave of the American National Election Study (ANES). White support for Obama is modeled here with logistic regression as being conditioned by the racial composition of the survey respondent's congressional district. The ANES sampled white voters in 110 different congressional districts. This provides for a wider range of variation in racial

Table 5   Estimate of White Voters' General Election Support for Obama, 2008

Percentage district population African American	−0.056 (0.02)
African American population squared	0.001 (0.000)
Democrat	1.2 (0.21)
Republican	−0.93 (0.13)
Liberal	0.79 (0.29)
Conservative	−0.97 (0.29)
Age	−0.016 (0.00)
Education	−0.03 (0.04)
Female	0.16 (0.18)
Respondent is worse off financially	0.06 (0.07)
Born-again Christian	−0.35 (0.19)
Southerner	−0.25 (0.19)
Latino	0.44 (0.24)
Household income	0.005 (0.01)
Thinks national economy worse	0.37 (0.13)
Does not approve Bush handling Iraq war	0.52 (0.06)
Number of cases	1,171
Pseudo R^2	.45

2008 American National Election Study data. Preelection poll.
Logistic regression estimates, robust standard errors clustered by congressional district (reported in parenthesis). Dependent variable = 1 if respondent intended to vote Obama, 0 if McCain or other).

context (compared to state-level data) and allows us to match respondents more directly to the racial geography they reside in. A respondent's propensity to support Obama was modeled as a linear function of the size of the respondent's district's African American population (not reported) and as a nonlinear function of the district's racial composition. Either functional form is significant, but the nonlinear results are reported because these better reflect the skewed racial geography of America and because we expect a ceiling effect of racial threat beyond some threshold at which a minority population becomes relatively large. The estimates reported in Table 5 include controls for standard factors that influence the vote: partisanship, ideology, age, gender, region (southern or not), religion, ethnicity (Latino), income, evaluations of economic conditions, and evaluations of the war in Iraq.

Overall, the results for the control variables are not surprising. Democrats, liberals, younger voters, Latinos, people who viewed the national economy as worse than a year before, and people who disapproved of President Bush's handling of the Iraq War were more likely to say they supported Obama. Republicans, conservatives, born-again Christians, and southerners were more likely to say they would vote for McCain. With all these factors accounted for, racial context remains a significant factor in explaining where white voters were more (or less) likely to support Obama in 2008.

Figure 2   Probability of a white voter supporting Obama, 2008

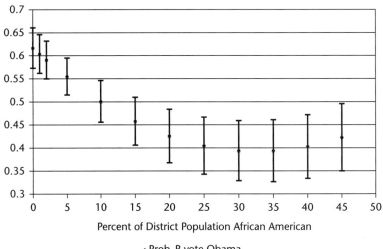

Percent of District Population African American

◆ Prob. R vote Obama

Predicted probabilities with standard errors of the predictions as bars. Predictions generated
from Clarify simulations using estimates reported in Table 5. Probability of supporting Obama
for a white non-Hispanic, nonsouthern, politically independent woman of median age and
education who gave the modal responses to questions about Iraq and the economy.

The substantive meaning of the estimates reported in Table 5 are illustrated in Figure 2, which displays the predicted probability that hypothetical
voter would support Obama depending on the racial context of the respondent's congressional district. The figure displays the probability of supporting Obama for a moderate, non-Hispanic white, nonsoutherner, politically
independent woman of median age, income, and education who gave the
modal responses to questions about Iraq and the economy. The estimated
probability of such a voter supporting Obama is displayed across different racial contexts, with the standard error of each estimate represented by
error bars above and below the estimate. The figure demonstrates the clear,
significant association between white voter support for Obama and racial
context. Other things being equal, our hypothetical white voter living in a
district with a low proportion of African Americans is estimated to have a
relatively high probability of supporting Obama. In a district that was 5 percent African American (50 percent of whites lived in districts where African
Americans were less than 5.8 percent of the population), a white voter is
estimated to have a .55 probability of supporting Obama. The estimated
probability declines significantly for the same white voter living in districts

with larger proportions of African Americans. Whites living in areas with more than 10 percent African American population are predicted to vote for McCain. These results are consistent with patterns found in the state level data analyzed in Tables 3 and 4 and are consistent with the idea that racial context affected how white voters responded to Barack Obama.

Discussion

Race was clearly a factor in the 2008 presidential election. Independent of innuendo about Obama that was associated with his race, there are reasons to expect that some white voters might still find it difficult to support an African American candidate for president. Results presented here are consistent with the racial threat thesis: other things being equal, some whites living in places with more African Americans were more likely to prefer Clinton to Obama when presented with hypothetical match-ups against John McCain. These sentiments, in turn, were associated with how and where the Democrats made electoral gain or lost vote share over 2004.

This said, these results do not establish that white voters' evaluations of Obama were grounded in racism; nor do they establish that a white Democratic candidate would have received a greater share of the popular vote in 2008. But the evidence here suggests that attitudes about the candidates associated with racial context structured the 2008 election map. Moreover, down-ticket voting in some southern and border states showed notable gains for white Democratic candidates, suggesting that a nontrivial proportion of people who voted for white Democratic candidates in other statewide contests did not support Obama. In states where Obama underperformed relative to the 2004 vote, support for many other Democratic statewide candidates increased or held steady in 2008 compared to previous election cycles. The 2008 vote for Democratic U.S. Senate candidates increased by 30 percent in Mississippi, 11 percent in Kentucky, 6 percent in Louisiana, 2 percent in Oklahoma, and 1 percent in West Virginia over 2002.[21] Democratic gubernatorial candidates posted gains of 10 percent in Missouri, where a Democrat regained control of the governor's office, and 5 percent in West Virginia, where a Democrat was reelected.

Obama's relatively weak showing in these states (relative to John Kerry in 2004) may reflect long-term trends that would have worked against any Democratic presidential candidate, trends that happened to correspond with state racial context. Figure 3 demonstrates that the presidential vote in many southern and border states relative to the national average had been trending Republican prior to 2008. Statewide Democratic candidates in these states who were relatively successful in 2008 were also generally more conservative than Obama and, thus, likely had a different appeal in these states than Obama did. This race-neutral perspective might explain why trends working

Figure 3   State vote for Democratic presidential candidates, deviation from
national popular vote total: 1984-2008

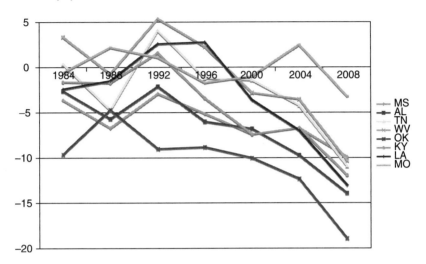

Calculated from Federal Election Commission records.

favorably for white Democrats in southern and border states, and working
favorably for Obama in states with smaller African American populations,
corresponded with Democratic presidential vote share *loss* in many of these
states in 2008. However, Figure 3 illustrates that the decline in Democratic
presidential vote share in some of these states (relative to the national average)
from 2004 to 2008 was steeper than in previous years. Given the ideological
similarity of Obama and Kerry, a race-neutral perspective is not very effective
for explaining the difference between Obama's and Kerry's electoral fortunes
in these states. The results presented in this article suggest that this difference
may be grounded in white voters' attitudes that are structured by the racial
context of these states.

What, then, of claims that American voters are beyond race and that some
key applications of the Voting Rights Act need to be reconsidered? This analysis of the 2008 election suggests that larger African American populations
correlate with whites' evaluating candidates in a manner that depressed white
support for an African American candidate, particularly in areas where the
Voting Rights Act has justified the use of majority-minority districts. Obama
did post substantial gains over the Democratic Party's vote share in 2004
by increasing the Democratic share of the white vote. These gains, however,
came more from racially homogeneous states, where race was likely less of a
factor in affecting how white voters evaluated candidates.

Declaration of Conflicting Interest

The author declared no conflicts of interest with respect to the authorship and/or publication of this article.

Funding

The author received no financial support for the research and/or authorship of this article.

Notes

1. As example, simply mentioning "affirmative action" prior to a question increased from 26 to 43 percent the number of whites who agreed that "blacks are irresponsible" (Sniderman and Piazza 1993, 104).
2. Examples include David Dinkins (New York City), Harold Washington (Chicago), Norm Rice (Seattle), Tom Bradley (Los Angeles), Douglas Wilder (Virginia), and Deval Patrick (Massachusetts).
3. Some studies represent context by measuring the size of multiple racial/ethnic groups (Tolbert and Hero 1996). Others measure the prospects for majority group–minority group interactions or levels of segregation (Oliver and Wong 2003; Kinder and Mendelberg 1995; Rocha and Espino 2009).
4. McCain's actual vote share was 1 percent less than the average of nine models reported. One postelection analysis of forecasting models concluded that Obama should have received 58.7 percent but that 11 percent of the electorate "could not bring itself to vote for a black candidate" (Lewis-Beck and Tien 2009).
5. President Bill Clinton echoed the theme after Obama's victory in the January 28 South Carolina primary.
6. CNN exit poll data.
7. The Real Clear Politics average prior to election day had Obama at 52.1 percent and McCain at 44.5 percent. The result was Obama 52.9 percent, McCain 45.6 percent.
8. CNN exit poll data.
9. http://online.wsj.com/article/SB122637373937516543.html?mod=googlenews_ wsj, November 11, 2008.
10. *Northwest Austin v. Holder et al.*, 577 U.S. (2009). Thomas argues that state-sponsored discrimination is gone and that absent "the violence, intimidation, and subterfuge that led Congress to pass Section 5," the section is no longer constitutional. Thomas's dissent reflects arguments found in Thernstrom (2007).
11. Clinton and Obama had identical Americans for Democratic Act (ADA) voting scores in 2007 and 2006.
12. Each state sample included approximately six hundred respondents, with sampling errors of +/− 4 percent. The Ohio Survey USA (SUSA) data were collected two weeks earlier. There was no SUSA survey of Alaska. Results from a Rasmussen poll are used for Alaska.
13. Bureau of Labor Statistics, Bureau of Economic Analysis, and Federal Housing Finance Agency data, reported in the *Wall Street Journal*.
14. Many voters are distributed in states with low proportions of African Americans, while smaller proportions reside in states with higher populations of African Americans.

15. Southern states are defined as the states that formed the Confederacy.
16. Controls for state ideology included data from Richard Fording's update of data originally published in Berry et al. (1998) and *National Journal* measures of the liberalism of the state's 2007 U.S. House delegation. Results reported in Table 3 are unchanged when these controls, and percentage of state urban, are included. Results are not affected by eliminating candidate's home states (Arkansas and Hawaii) from the data set.
17. Likewise, a control for the median age of the state's population was not significant.
18. White vote for the Democratic candidates is measured with reported exit poll data.
19. From .20 to .15, or 25 percent, in nonsouthern states.
20. A model estimating percentage of a state's whites voting Democrat in 2008 as a function of percentage of whites voting Democrat 2004, and the Obama/Clinton differential, shows this to be the case ($b = .21$; $p = .001$ for the Obama/Clinton measure; $R^2 = .85$).
21. It was down 3 percent in Alabama and 12 percent in Tennessee.

References

Baldwin, Tom. 2008. Democrat race blighted by row over turban picture. *Times of London*, February 26.

Barreto, Matt, and Ricardo Ramirez. 2008. The Latino vote is pro-Clinton, not Anti-Obama. *Los Angeles Times*, February 7.

Behrens, Angela, Chris Uggen, and Jeff Manza. 2003. Ballot manipulation and the "menace of negro domination": Racial threat and felon disenfranchisement in the United States, 1850-2002. *American Journal of Sociology* 109 (3): 559-605.

Berry, William, Evan Ringquist, Richard Fording, and Russell Hanson. 1998. Measuring citizen and government ideology in the American states, 1960-93. *American Journal of Political Science* 41:327-48.

Blalock, Hubert M. 1957. Percent non-white and discrimination in the South. *American Sociological Review* 22 (6): 677-82.

Brace, Kimball, Bernard Grofman, Lisa Handley, and Richard Niemi. 1988. Minority voting equality: The 65% rule in theory and practice. *Law and Policy* 10 (1): 43.

Branton, Regina, and Bradford Jones. 2005. Reexamining racial attitudes: The conditional relationship between diversity and sociological environment. *American Journal of Political Science* 49 (2): 359-72.

Bullock, Charles. 1976. Interracial contact and student prejudice: The impact of southern school desegregation. *Youth and Society* 7:271-309.

Cameron, Charles, David Epstein, and Sharyn O'Halloran. 1996. Do majority-minority districts maximize substantive black representation in Congress? *American Political Science Review* 90 (4): 794-812.

Campbell, James E. 2008. Editor's introduction: Forecasting the 2008 national elections. *PS: Political Science and Politics* 41 (October): 679-82.

Crouch, Stanley. 2006. What Obama is not: Black like me. *New York Daily News*.

Davidson, Chandler, and Bernard Grofman. 1994. *Quiet revolution in the South*. Princeton, NJ: Princeton University Press.

Engstrom, Richard, and Michael D. McDonald. 1981. The election of blacks to city councils. *American Political Science Review* 75 (2): 344-54.

Giles, Michael, and Melanie Buckner. 1993. David Duke and black threat: An old hypothesis revisited. *Journal of Politics* 55:702-13.

Giles, Michael, and Arthur Evans. 1986. The power approach to intergroup hostility. *Journal of Conflict Resolution* 30:469-86.

Giles, Michael, and Kaenan Hertz. 1994. Racial threat and partisan identification. *American Political Science Review* 88 (2): 317-26.

Grofman, Bernard, Lisa Handley, and Richard Niemi. 1992. *Minority representation and the quest for voting equality*. Cambridge: Cambridge University Press.

Harden, Toby. 2008. Barack Obama's win is rebuke for Bill Clinton. *Daily Telegraph*, January 28.

Heerwig, Jennifer, and Brian McCabe. 2007. Social desirability bias in estimated support for a black presidential candidate. Manuscript, Department of Sociology, New York University.

Key, V. O. 1949. *Southern politics in state and nation*. New York: Knopf.

Kiely, Kathy, and Jill Lawrence. 2008. Clinton makes case for wide appeal. *USA Today*, May 8.

Kinder, Donald, and Tali Mendelberg. 1995. Cracks in American apartheid: The political impact of prejudice among desegregated whites. *Journal of Politics* 57: 402-24.

Kinder, Donald R., and Lynn Sanders. 1996. *Divided by color: Racial politics and democratic ideals*. Chicago: University of Chicago Press.

Lewis-Beck, Michael, and Charles Tien. 2009. Race blunts the economic effect? The 2008 Obama forecast. *PS: Political Science and Politics* 42 (1): 21-21.

Longshore, Douglas. 1982. School racial composition and white hostility: The problem of control in desegregated schools. *Social Forces* 61:73-78.

Lublin, David. 1997a. The election of African Americans and Latinos to the US House of Representatives, 1972-1994. *American Politics Quarterly* 25 (3): 269-86.

Lublin, David. 1997b. *The paradox of representation*. Princeton, NJ: Princeton University Press.

Lublin, David. 1999. Racial redistricting and African American representation: A critique of "Do majority-minority districts maximize substantive black representation in Congress?" *American Political Science Review* 93 (1): 183-86.

Mendelberg, Tali. 2001. *The race card*. Princeton, NJ: Princeton University Press.

New York Times. 2008. Transcript: The Democratic debate in Cleveland. February 26.

Oliver, J. Eric, and Janelle Wong. 2003. Intergroup prejudice in multi-ethnic settings. *American Journal of Political Science* 47:67-82.

Raum, Tom. 2008. Analysis: Debate unlikely to change race. *Associated Press*, February 27.

Reeves, Keith. 1997. *Voting hopes of voting fears: White voters, black candidates and racial politics in America*. Oxford: Oxford University Press.

Reid, Tim. 2008. Hillary Clinton fights in secret to show Barack Obama is unelectable. *Times of London*, April 4.

Rocha, Rene, and Rodolfo Espino. 2009. Racial threat, residential segregation, and policy attitudes of Latinos. *Political Research Quarterly* 62 (2): 415-26.

Rodriguez, Gregory. 2008. Quote from Clinton staffer Sergio Bendixen. *Los Angeles Times*, January 28.

Sigelman, Lee, and Susan Welsh. 1984. Race, gender and opinion toward black and female presidential candidates. *Public Opinion Quarterly* 48 (2): 467-75.

Sniderman, Paul, and Thomas Piazza. 1993. *The scar of race*. Cambridge, MA: Harvard University Press.

Swain, Carol. 1993. *Black faces, black interests: The representation of African Americans in Congress*. Cambridge, MA: Harvard University Press.

Thernstrom, Abigail. 1995. Racial gerrymanders come before the Court. *Wall Street Journal*, April 12, p. A15.

Thernstrom, Abigail. 2007. Section 5 of the Voting Rights Act: By now, a murky mess. *Georgetown Journal of Law and Public Policy* 54:41-78.

Tolbert, Caroline, and John Grummel. 2003. Revisiting the racial threat hypothesis: White voter support for California's Proposition 209. *State Politics and Policy Quarterly* 3 (2): 183-202.

Tolbert, Caroline, and Rodney Hero. 1996. Race/ethnicity and direct democracy: An analysis of California's illegal immigration initiative. *Journal of Politics* 58:806-18.

Vo, Kim. 2008. Muslims say faith used as scare tactic against Obama. *San Jose Mercury News*, February 29.

Voss, D. Stephen. 1996. Beyond racial threat: Failure of an old hypothesis in the New South. *Journal of Politics* 58 (4): 1156-70.

Voss, D. Stephen. 2001. Following the false trail: The hunt for white backlash in Kentucky's 1996 desegregation vote. *State Politics and Policy Quarterly* 1:62-80.

Wong, Cara. 2007. "Little" and "big" pictures in our heads. Race, local context and innumeracy about racial groups in the United States. *Public Opinion Quarterly* 71 (3): 392-412.

Part IV

THE LIMITS OF GOVERNANCE IN OBAMA'S ADMINISTRATION

Part Four introduces readers to the complexities of governance in a highly industrialized, technologically oriented, heterogeneous society with a history of racial inequities. Governing is never like campaigning. The lessons needed to master the tactics for gaining an election victory are often different from the ones that must be learned and mastered to maintain a position and to sustain a movement. The limits of governance confront every person who holds the highest office in the land. It is as if the new president walks into the White House and is handed a briefing paper that literally changes his entire image of the job he was seeking. However, as the authors of the articles in Part Four understand, President Obama would never be able to accomplish much of what he promised and would not be able to effect the changes that some had expected. The reality of governing is different from the pathway to the office.

Many scholars questioned the gap between the expectations and the genuine ability of the president to gain support from other stakeholders in the American government. A president serves at the pleasure of the people, alongside members of Congress and a Supreme Court of lifetime judges. This is the complicated scenario faced by any president. The researchers in Part Four tackle the issues of Obama's whiteness and blackness, but they also suggest that it was impractical to call for a black president to be post-racial or to overcome the dilemma of power. Obama would have to face the same dilemmas as other presidents, and the fundamental dilemma would always be that the president does not govern alone.

As these researchers suggest, demands have been made upon Obama that were in line with the normal obligations of the presidential office, but there have also been inordinate and unholy demands made of him because he was a black man. He will be unable to live up to all of these demands, and as some have argued, he should not have to consider those demands that are made on him simply because of his biology or culture. Both as a candidate and as the president, Obama has been asked to demonstrate his appreciation for the African American struggle, the labor movement, the white male fear of the erosion of power, the female anxiety over voting for a black male candidate over Hilary Clinton, and the rising influence of the Latino community. The fact that he has been able to achieve some measure of success in these areas means that he has struck a note for rewiring the American polity as a comprehensive collective society, and not as a disunited, dispirited, and separate people.

11

OBAMA: THE NEW CONTOURS OF POWER

Jerry Harris

Committees of Correspondence for Democracy and Socialism

Carl Davidson

DeVry University, Chicago

Amerrican progressives have won a major victory in helping to defeat John McCain and placing Barack Obama in the White House. The far Right has been broadly rebuffed, the neoconservative war hawks displaced, and the diehard advocates of neoliberal economics are in thorough disarray. Of great importance, one long-standing crown jewel of white supremacy, the whites-only sign on the Oval Office, has been tossed into the dustbin of history.

Behind the political victory is the historic cultural shift rooted in the Civil Rights struggle. Not only was a Black man elected president, but one whose name shouts its Third World otherness. Those of us whose initial political experience was the Civil Rights movement, with its reactive wave of racist violence and hatred, have been deeply moved by the Obama victory. Moreover, Obama's personal history is grounded in the multicultural and global reality of today's world. Born in Hawaii, the most Third World of all US states, and spending his early years in Indonesia adds to Obama's universal appeal as an important symbol of multicultural globalisation. In this, he reflects the sensibilities of today's youth and the first glimpse of US society in a new century.

The depth of the historical victory was revealed in the jubilation of millions who spontaneously gathered in family homes, neighbourhoods and downtowns across the country, as the media networks called Obama the winner. When President-Elect Barack Hussein Obama took the platform in Chicago to deliver his powerful but sobering victory speech, millions of

Source: Race & Class, April 2009; vol. 50, 4: pp. 1-19.

Americans of every race and age literally danced in the streets and wept with joy, celebrating the achievement of a dramatic milestone in a 400-year struggle, and anticipating a new period of hope and possibility.

While celebrating Obama's election is important, a more critical task is understanding the shift in power and the political character of the emerging hegemonic bloc. What are the social forces put into motion by the ever-worsening economic crisis, the failures of neoliberal globalisation and the gathering demographic changes in US society? What sectors of the capitalist class will the new administration represent and what tensions are already evident inside this alliance, particularly between the hierarchy of elites and the social base? We'll attempt to answer these and other questions as we explore Obama and the new contours of power.

The defeated bloc

First, we need to review the defeated ruling bloc that John McCain attempted to ride to power. Ironically, his stiff war-bruised body seemed the perfect symbolic representation of the battered Iraq occupation and broken economic model he sought to lead. In this bloc, the most influential sectors were the military/industrial complex and low-road global speculators firmly entrenched in Wall Street. Of all US industries, the military/industrial complex is the least globalised, receiving the majority of its profits from government contracts.[1] Its war culture is steeped in patriotic chauvinism, and neoconservatives as the industry's ideological frontmen rallied around McCain.

As for global speculators, Treasury Secretary Hank Paulson is a fine representative. As ex-chairman of Goldman Sachs, he pushed financial deregulation and cross-border integration that spread the economic crisis to banks and institutions worldwide. Paulson's initial $700 billion bail-out package was proposed with no legal or constitutional oversight, reflecting his own unrelenting faith in unregulated free markets. But not all globalists are in the Paulson mode. Differences erupted during the Asian meltdown in 1997 and continue to be the current lines of demarcation. As analysed in 2000 by William Robinson and Jerry Harris:

> the free-market conservatives call for a complete global laissez-faire based on an undiluted version of the Washington consensus. The neoliberal structuralists want a global superstructure that could provide a modicum of stability to the volatile world financial system ... and the neoliberal regulationists call for a broader global regulatory apparatus that could stabilise the financial system as well as attenuate some of the sharpest social contradictions of global capitalism in the interest of securing the political stability of the system.[2]

Since 1980, Reagan/Thatcher free-market conservatives have led the globalist bloc and, although accepting some structural and regulatory constraints, they expanded the widely speculative markets that crashed so spectacularly in 2008. Neoliberalism was aided and abetted by the Third Way politics of Bill Clinton, Tony Blair and others whose polices represented a centre/right alliance between free-market fundamentalists and structuralists. This alliance was sustained during the Bush administration, as neoliberals continued to follow the philosophy of Milton Friedman with blind faith. As Friedman succinctly wrote: 'Few trends could so thoroughly undermine the very foundations of our free society as the acceptance by corporate officials of a social responsibility other than to make as much money for their stockholders as possible.'[3] As the era's popular saying went, 'greed is good'. But by 2007, as the depths of the economic crisis became clearly revealed, the structuralists began to abandon their neoliberal dogma and, in 2008, split with the conservatives and rallied to Obama.

McCain's social base came from the fundamentalist religious movement and right-wing anti-immigrant nationalists. During the campaign, the right-wing media, exemplified by the Fox News Hannity-Limbaugh machine (two talk-show hosts), escalated their overtly chauvinist, immigrant-baiting, red-baiting, terror-baiting, anti-Black and anti-Muslim bigotry to a ceaseless fever pitch. Christian moral superiority blended with nativism and warrior patriotism has been wedded to the Republican Party since Richard Nixon's racist Southern strategy. To stay in power, all hegemonic blocs must maintain legitimacy with their social base. But these links became a leaden chain around McCain's neck, forcing him to accept Sarah Palin over Joe Lieberman as his vice-presidential pick. Acquiescing to the most reactionary wing of his alliance forfeited McCain's appeal to independents. Palin energised the base, but the only area where Republican votes increased was in the heart of the old slave-state South. This presents a bleak future for the Republicans, now torn between movement fundamentalists and the economic conservative but socially moderate wing. Moreover, Reagan-era conservatives admit their ideology lacks any new ideas and faces stagnation.[4] Nevertheless, McCain won some 57 million votes and, with a deepening crisis, the Right can make a comeback if Obama fails to meet expectations.

The new hegemonic bloc

The hegemonic bloc in formation around Obama is broad and deep, containing the possibility of a generational shift in political orientation. Neoliberal ideology has reigned over capitalism for thirty years but the crisis has stripped bare its dominant narrative. All can now see that the emperor has no clothes, and even free-market guru Alan Greenspan admitted to 'a state of shocked disbelief'.[5] The elite of the new bloc are neo-Keynesian globalists attempting to redefine liberalism for the twenty-first century in both ideology and policy. This unites broad sectors of the capitalist class. The centre has shifted left, creating new dialogue and new debates. Government job programmes, infrastructure spending, expanded federal support to states, greater environmental investments and regulation of financial markets have suddenly all become mainstream. Ideas rarely spoken of by major news outlets now appear on magazine covers and daily talk shows. A new New Deal has become the common expectation of millions. Obama made such ideas the centre of his campaign, a highroad strategy of capital investments in production, job creation, green technology, health care for all and a withdrawal from Iraq. Politically, Obama is a pragmatic centrist without the ideological sensibilities of the 1960s, yet his vision is often driven by some core progressive values. It was these values, more than his politics, which drew massive support from minorities, youth and unions. This progressive social base is well to the left of the neo-Keynesian elite and the resulting tension will certainly be the centre of struggle within the new bloc.

As Antonio Gramsci has powerfully demonstrated, most power elites maintain their rule through more than armed force and economic coercion, deploying a range of 'softer' tools to maintain their dominance, which are political, economic and cultural. To form a hegemonic bloc, factions of the capitalist class need a social base in the population, drawing this into partnership and coalitions through intermediate civil institutions and mass movements, such as the anti-abortion or anti-immigration movements on the Right and the anti-war and environmental movements on the Left. Keeping a bloc together requires compromise and concession with the base in order to maintain legitimacy. In fact, in democracies, culture and ideology are most often the most important tools. The blocs are historic; they develop over time, are shaped by the times, and also have limited duration. When external and internal crises disrupt them and lead to stagnation, a new 'counter-hegemonic' bloc takes shape, with a different alignment of economic interests and social forces, to challenge and take leadership. The crisis of war and economic failure set the conditions for such a challenge, taking shape within the Obama campaign from above and below. Militant activity from below creates the possibilities for more meaningful reforms than first conceived by the elites. This was true during the Great Depression, the Civil Rights era, and such possibilities exist again today. It was the abandonment of any social base by an increasingly conservative Democratic Party that made Democrats a minority for thirty years. Meanwhile, the Republicans and neoliberal capitalists achieved dominance by building a new bloc in alliance with the dynamic reactionary social movements that arose in the late 1970s and 1980s, and in turn succeeded in pushing the centre to the right.

The ruling-class core of the emerging hegemonic bloc is made up of the old corporate liberals, and former neoliberals badly shaken by the extent of the economic crisis. Globalists of this sector were never Milton Friedman fundamentalists. Most advocated structural limitations of the free market while still promoting the main pillars of neoliberalism, such as privatisation of state assets, greater mobility for cross-border capital, the deregulation of financial markets and IMF structural adjustments for Third World economies. Even now, they still maintain faith in expanding global trade by breaking down national barriers and supporting other free-market principles. But the crisis has forced them to look to government as a major economic actor and focus their attention on the social problems of the working class, thereby turning to Keynesian solutions.

Almost all of Obama's cabinet come from this sector of capital. Lawrence Summers is a good example of how such neoliberals have jettisoned some of their baggage and moved to the left. Summers, who in 1998 purged Joseph Stiglitz from the World Bank for his biting criticisms of globalisation, now sounds more like his former nemesis. Recently Summers wrote: 'Companies come to have less of a stake in the quality of the workforce and infrastructure in their home country when they can produce anywhere. Moreover businesses can use the threat of relocating as a lever to extract concessions regarding tax policy, regulations and specific subsidies. Inevitably the cost of these concessions is borne by labour.' Summers proposes three solutions: preventing a 'race to the bottom' by closing tax havens and instituting progressive taxation; raising global regulatory standards; and protecting labour rights.[6] As the crisis deepened, Summers' approach continued to evolve and he now calls for a large government stimulus package focused on job creation.

Another Obama appointee is Paul Volcker, former chairman of the Federal Reserve under Ronald Reagan and a pioneer in financial deregulation. But what does Volcker say today? 'Simply stated, the bright new financial system for all its talented participants, for all its rich rewards, has failed the test of the market place.'[7] And for men like Volcker, the market place is the arbiter of all reality.

Timothy Geithner, head of the Federal Reserve Bank of New York and Obama's pick for Treasury Secretary, is another appointee from this wing of neo-Keynesian globalists. Speaking to the Council on Foreign Relations in January 2007, Geithner expressed a deep faith in the global financial system, stating that 'improvements in risk management and capital cushions and a variety of other changes to the system have made the system more stable and more resilient ... macroeconomic policy is really substantially better around the world'. At the same time, referring to Summers' fears over declining legitimacy for globalisation, Geithner stated:

> This political challenge of sustaining support for global economic integration and for fiscal sustainability will be more difficult in the United States because of what's happened to the broader distribution of income and to economic insecurity. This very long-term increase in economic inequality, the slow pace in growth in real wages ... the increase in the volatility of

income that's come with the increased flexibility of the U.S. economy and the greater exposure of households to the risk in financing retirement, and the burden of paying for health care – these broad forces substantially complicate what would already be a daunting set of political challenges, economic challenges.[8]

This combination, a belief in neoliberal globalisation alongside concern over the loss of political support and legitimacy due to expanding inequality, has driven this wing of capitalists to join the newly emerging hegemonic bloc, and defines their neo-Keynesian approach. As with Franklin Roosevelt, they realise the system has to change to be saved.

This has produced a new mainstream consensus at the top; policy ideas from yesterday's left are today's centre. In an op-ed to Obama, the Peterson Institute for International Economics argued that the crisis offers the US the 'opportunity to transform the economy by moving resources (capital and people) out of financial services and into manufacturing, technology, and other activities based on "real" (i.e. nonfinancial) innovation'.[9] Furthermore, former chief economist of the IMF Simon Johnson, speaking for the Peterson Institute in his testimony to the US Congress, laid out a high-road strategy for recovery. His short-term programme advocated four points: 1) direct aid to state and local governments, much of which would be spent on schools and health care; 2) extended unemployment benefits; 3) expanded food-stamp aid; and, 4) loan modifications for distressed homeowners. Johnson's long-term programmes included investment in basic infrastructure, job retraining, expanded student loans, expanded small business loans and investment in alternative energy. Johnson estimated that the package should cost $450 billion and be spread out over three to four years.[10]

How does this compare to policy suggestions from the liberal-progressive wing of the new hegemonic bloc? A number of outstanding voices here were early repentant critics of globalisation. While remaining supporters of expanding trade and transnational integration, Nobel prize-winning economists Joseph Stiglitz and Paul Krugman have, for the past decade, called for greater financial regulation and attention to global inequalities. Although having limited representation in the Obama administration, progressives exert constant pressure through their voice to the broader public. Krugman suggests the global slump can be fixed, at least in part, with public works' spending. As he says: 'The answer, almost surely, is good old Keynesian fiscal stimulus.'[11] Stiglitz, much like Johnson, calls for investments in infrastructure, education and energy technologies, financial help to state and local governments, taxing the rich and renegotiating mortgages so that people can stay in their homes.[12]

Moving to the Left, we hear similar policy ideas. Calling for a $200 billion stimulus package, the Institute for Policy Studies advocates investments in renewable energy, refinancing mortgages to keep people in their homes and aid to state and local governments. It also suggests an end to tax havens, increasing corporate taxes and a new securities transaction tax.[13] The Center for Study of Working Class Life issued a report on economically distressed workers with policy recommendations for creating 3.3 million new jobs and a stimulus package of $220 billion. The Center called for aid to states, universal health care, new infrastructure projects, pro-labour reform legislation, immigration reform and expanding credit for business. Suggestions for distressed families included extending unemployment benefits, school lunch and food-stamp programmes and housing subsidies.[14] Well-known author Mike Davis writes: 'A good start for progressive agitation on Obama's left flank would be to demand that his health-care reform and aid-to-education proposals be brought front and centre as preferential vehicles for immediate macro-economic stimulus', reminding us that 'core public employment is, hands-down, the best Keynesian stimulus around'.[15] Lastly, the Apollo Economic Recovery Act advocates a fundamental redesign of the energy and transportation systems using sustainable technologies. In it, the Apollo Alliance (a national coalition of labour, business, environmental and community leaders) projects a stimulus package costing $262bn that would create two million new jobs.[16]

Another important sector consists of what conservative David Brooks called the 'rising class of information age analysts', working in electronics, communications, law and finance. As Brooks points out: 'Socially liberal knowledge workers naturally want to see people like themselves at the head of society, not people who used to run Halliburton and who are supported by a vast army of evangelicals.'[17] Situated within these strata is an expanding group of green entrepreneurs with growing influence in the rising hegemonic bloc. In 2007, more than $5 billion of US venture capital was invested in clean energy technology. This constituted close to 20 per cent of all venture capital, up from just 2 per cent eight years before. In 2008, the trade show of the American Wind Energy Association attracted 12,000 people and 770 exhibitors. Daniel Kammen, an adviser to Obama and director of the Renewable and Appropriate Energy Laboratory at the University of California, Berkeley, says solar, wind and renewable energy could create 5 million new jobs by 2030. In the Midwest, there is growing hope that the industry can help replace disappearing industrial jobs. For example, wind turbine production needs both skilled engineers and skilled blue-collar workers. Al Gore is the best known representative of this capitalist sector, and certainly demands will be made for government investment, subsidies and tax breaks.

As we can see, there is great similarity between all these programmes, no matter what part of the political spectrum they originate from. All are high-road industrial policies that are closely aligned with Obama's own call for creating 2.5 million jobs with a $500 billion stimulus package in the first two years of his administration. This package grew to 3 million jobs and $700 billion as the crisis grew and would pass aid to state and local governments to invest in infrastructure projects and green technologies, which would include work on schools, sewer systems, mass transit, electrical grids, dams and other public utilities. The green programme covers jobs dedicated to creating alternative fuels, windmills and solar panels as well as building energy-efficient appliances. Obama also promises to bring broadband access to schools and hospitals: currently the US ranks fifteenth in the world for broadband use.

Although there is broad agreement on policy aims, the devil will be in the detail. Struggle over what programmes are a priority, where and how money is spent and whether reforms have structural depth or are simply temporary fixes, all this and more will be points of conflict. Given that the majority of Obama's cabinet and advisers come from the most conservative wing of the new bloc, the importance of a well-organised and mobilised base will be key in winning progressive reforms.

The progressive base

The most important and active sectors of the base are anti-war youth, minorities and union activists. In terms of voting results, 97 per cent of Blacks, 67 per cent of Latinos, 63 per cent of Asian Americans and 45 per cent of whites cast their ballots for Obama. Among white union members, 67 per cent voted for Obama.[18] Among youth, Obama took 65 per cent of the vote. There was also an upsurge in voting patterns: Blacks voted in greater numbers by 14 per cent, Latinos by 25 per cent and young people aged between 18 and 29 by 25 per cent. This played a key role in winning over swing states and giving Obama his victory. In New Mexico, the youth and Latino vote surged by 71 per cent; in Ohio, 27 per cent more Blacks came out; in North Carolina, the Black vote increased by 23 per cent and the youth vote by 33 per cent; and, in Florida, Blacks voted in greater numbers by 19 per cent and Latinos by 27 per cent.

The large number of white voters, especially union voters, is also significant. The election in 1982 of Harold Washington, the progressive Black mayor of Chicago, is an interesting marker for comparison. Washington was a life-long Democrat but took on the Richard Daley machine in an election where race became an explosive element. Like Obama, Washington's election was the impetus for massive new voter registration and participation. Deserted and opposed by the regular Democratic Party machine, he put a volunteer army of 10,000 on to the streets of Chicago. Washington won two elections but with never more than 18 per cent of the white vote, and Chicago was a union town. The fact that Obama could carry 45 per cent of the white vote nationally indicates a significant change in American political culture.

Obama was able to awaken, organise and mobilise an incredible force of what grew into an army of more than 3 million volunteers. Obama started with his local coalition in Chicago, the Black community, 'Lakefront liberals' from the corporate world, and a sector of labour, mainly service workers. Obama's initial attraction was his early opposition to the Iraq war and his participation in two mass rallies against it, one and another before it began and an other after the war was under way. This both awakened and inspired a large layer of young anti-war activists, some active for the first time, to join his effort to win the Iowa primary. The fact that he had publicly opposed the war before it had begun distinguished him from Hillary Clinton and John Edwards, his chief opponents. These young people also contributed to the innovative nature of his organisation, combining grassroots community organising with the mass communication tools of internet-based social networking and fundraising. Many had some earlier experience organising and participating in the World Social Forum in Atlanta 2007, which energised nearly 10,000 young activists. Those who came forward put their energy to good use. Had Obama not won Iowa, it is not likely we would be talking about him today.

The Iowa victory quickly produced another major advance. Up until then, most African-American voters favoured Hillary Clinton, and were dubious about a Black candidate's chances. But Iowa is one of the 'whitest' states in the country, and Obama's win changed their minds. In short order, Obama gained wide support in Black communities across the country, inspiring even more young people, more multinational and more 'Hip-Hop', to emerge as a force. Black women in their churches and Black workers in their unions joined with the already engaged younger Black professionals who were seeking a new voice for their generation. A wing of trade unions most responsive to Black members came over, setting the stage for Obama's next challenge, winning the Democratic primaries against Clinton.

This now put the ranks of organised labour in the critical position. Even though they represented only a minority of workers, they had wider influence, including among white working-class families who were for Clinton, and leaning to McCain. Both national coalitions, the AFL-CIO and Change to Win, did the right thing, and in a big way. They knew McCain was their 'clear and present' danger. So they mobilised their resources and members on the streets, especially in the 'white working-class' battleground areas in critical electoral states, and among Latino voters in the West. They won a wide majority of union households and, although they did not get a majority of white working-class voters for Obama, they brought the spread down to single digits. In many areas, they did better with Obama than John Kerry had done four years earlier. It was enough to put Obama over the top.

Each sector of the base had its own way to organise, its own networks, culture and motivations. These overlapped to one degree or another, united to one degree or another, but they were not the same by a long shot.

First, the local Obama offices were mainly run by the Obama youth, twenty-somethings, many of them young women, who worked their hearts out, sixteen hours a day, seven days a week, for months on end. They were deployed in a vast array of 'neighborhood teams', with old teams often generating new ones, connected via the social networking of their own blogs, email, cell phones and text messaging. Each team knocked on hundreds, if not thousands of doors, and tracked it all on computers. The full-time leaders were often 'parachuted in' from distant states, skilled mainly in mobilising others like themselves. But add up dozens, even hundreds of teams in a given county, and you're making a serious difference.

The Black community's campaign was more indigenous, more traditional, more rooted, more deeply working class. It made use of the Black church's social committees, tenant groups and civic organisations, who widely united. Many day-to-day efforts were in the hands of older Black women who knew everything about everybody, and had decades of experience in registering and getting out the vote. In some parts of the country, there were other nationalities working this way – Latino, Asian, Native American – and they found the way to make common cause with the African American community, rebuffing GOP efforts to appeal to anti-Black racism or narrow nationalism as a wedge. Some of the older people in these communities learned how to use computers, and sent regular contributions to Obama via PayPal in small amounts. Multiply one of these experienced community-based women organisers by 50,000 or 100,000 more just like her in another neighbourhood or town, and something new and serious was going on.

Organised labour also carried out its campaign in its own way. Its workers had substantial resources for meeting halls, phone banks and the traditional campaign window-signs, yard-signs, buttons, T-shirts, stickers, banners, professionally done multicoloured flyers directly targeted on the top issues of union members and the wider working class. They put it together as an almost industrial operation, well planned and with a division of labour. Top union leaders came in, called mass meetings and, in many cases, gave fierce, no-nonsense speeches about 'getting over' fear of Black candidates and asserting the need for workers to vote their class interests. The central offices produced walking maps of union member households and registered voter households, political district by political district, broken right down to how many people were needed for each door-knocking team to cover each district or neighbourhood. They printed maps with driving directions. They had tally sheets for interviewing each voter, boxes to check, to be scanned and read by machines when turned in. The hundreds of member-volunteers came to each hall, raffles were held for free gas cards, and when you got back and turned in your tallies, free hot dogs and pizza. Sometimes busloads and car caravans went to other nearby states, to more 'battleground' areas. They often shared their halls with the Obama kids, and tried not to duplicate efforts. It was powerful to see, and it worked. There's nothing to replace a pair of union members standing on the porches of other working-class families, talking things over.

The emergence of the Latino vote is an important development in the American political landscape. This has been building for some time. One important point was the Justice for Janitors campaign launched by the Service Employees Union. This was one of the most vigorous and militant union efforts in recent years and was focused on the mainly Latino work-force who cleaned large corporate office buildings. It was particularly strong in Los Angeles where it helped lead to the election of Antonio Villaraigosa as the city's first Latino mayor. Although Bush had increased the Latino vote for Republicans to 44 per cent, the anti-immigration sector of the right-wing alli-ance destroyed any chance of making this a strategic enlargement of their hege-monic bloc. Attacks on immigrants grew as part of the post 9/11 security push, with increasing raids, more miles of border fences and a xenophobic response to Comprehensive Immigration Reform (originally the McCain-Kennedy Bill). These growing attacks led to the unprecedented mobilisation of millions for the immigration marches on May Day in 2006 and 2007 under the slogan 'Today we march; tomorrow we vote.' This growing political organisation and consciousness led directly into a massive mobilisation during the elections, at first mainly for Clinton, and then for Obama in the general election.

This wide progressive base of support has its own priorities that align with the neo-Keynesian elites. Moreover, building working alliances with the more solidly Keynesian factions who advocate broader conceptions of the green economy and high-road industrial strategy are good. At the top of the progressive agenda are new jobs and new industries. People are espe-cially motivated by practical plans for green jobs in alternative energies and major infrastructural repair, schools and support for students, debt relief and protections for their economic security in face of the Wall Street crash. Immigration reform and pro-labour legislation such as the Employee Free Choice Act are also key issues. Regarding health care, many unions and local government bodies are signing on to Single-Payer health care (under which care is financed by only one source of money for paying health-care provid-ers), but some will accept other plans, wisely or not, as a step in that direction or an improvement over the current set-up.

In overwhelming numbers, people who voted for Obama want an end to the war in Iraq. But it needs to be understood that they have a different character from the traditional Left-led anti-war rallies. Demands to end the war are deeply connected with supporting the troops, getting them home and out of harm's way, supporting veterans across the board, and a view of the war as an offence to patriotism. They hate the waste of lives of people from families they know; and they hate the waste of resources and huge amounts of money. Ending the war is stressed as the way to lower taxes and revive the economy by spending for projects at home. People will denounce oil barons, but you'll hear very little expressed in terms of anti-imperialism or solidarity with various other liberation struggles around the world. 'We were lied to getting us into this', and 'we have our problems to solve here' – those are the underlying themes and watchwords.

Obama has to deliver on all of these issues to maintain legitimacy. For the new hegemonic bloc to consolidate its hold on power, real solutions must be found for capitalism's current crisis. This means concessions to the base and the possibility of pushing the elite's agenda beyond its neo-Keynesian conceptions. But beyond the stage of national problems looms the global economic and security crisis to which Obama must also respond. Here, too, much needs to be done and much is expected.

Globalisation and war

The new hegemonic bloc must craft an economic response not only to the US crisis but to the global crisis. Here the debates parallel the lines drawn nationally between the neoliberal and neo-Keynesian wings of trans-national capital. From the beginning of financial globalisation, free-market fundamentalists have controlled the dominant position in building the new system of accumulation. In the closing days of the Bush administration, they stood firm during the G-20 meeting in Washington, fighting against creating any new international market regulator with cross-border author-ity. But there is growing consensus for greater regulatory control, the extent of which will be a major debate within and without the Obama adminis-tration. Even globalisation's most ardent supporters recognise the depth of the crisis and the need for change. As Martin Wolf commented in respect of the Federal Reserve's rescue of the huge investment bank Bear Stearns: 'Remember Friday March 12, 2008: it was the day the dream of global free-market capitalism died.'[19]

Because the US was the central proponent of global neoliberalism it is now the target of criticism and anger. Jeffrey Garten of the Yale School of Management writes:

> the US should jettison its habit of making financial policy as if it were cocksure of what it is doing. Indeed, it should be humbled by the magnitude of its inepti-tude in overseeing financial markets. [The US] should consider a wholesale

restructuring of the financial system in all its global dimensions ... a challenge of massive proportions that will require the re-examination of everything ... However, it is time for the US to figure out how to lead by building a consensus, rather than moving unilaterally or trying to shove its own discredited biases down other people's throats.[20]

Open debate has even broken out inside the International Institute of Finance, a leading global association of transnational banks and insurance companies. The IIF, chaired by Josef Ackermann of Deutsche Bank, called for a relaxation of accounting rules on asset valuation. In response, Goldman Sachs and Morgan Stanley threatened to leave the association, calling the proposals 'Alice-in-Wonderland accounting'.[21] Such language and open disagreement is rarely seen in this tight-knit world and indicates the depth of the on-going debates over a proper regulatory structure.

Representing the neo-Keynesian wing of transnational capitalism, Obama's economic team is in the best position to lead reform efforts. Harvard economist Dani Rodrik notes the 'remarkable turnaround in the intellectual climate' among mainstream economists. As he writes: 'Today the question is no longer, "Are you for or against globalisation?" The question is, "What should the rules of globalisation be?" The cheerleaders' true sparring partners today are not rock-throwing youths but their fellow intellectuals.' As Rodrik points out, the model of liberalisation and economic integration of the 1980s and 1990s 'is unsustainable. If globalisation is to survive, it will need a new intellectual consensus to underpin it. The world economy desperately awaits its new Keynes.'[22]

But globalisation needs more than one brilliant economist. Standing in the way of a common solution is the national character of the crisis as it hits one country after another. To maintain local legitimacy transnational capitalists must come up with solutions that benefit their nationally based working class. As each country has its own set of actors and conditions, designing a global response may be beyond the current stage of globalisation. C. Fred Bergsten, head of the Peterson Institute, points to this very problem: 'The globalization of the crisis means we need a globalization of responses, but most of the responses will be national. For all the institutions we have, we don't have the right institutions to do this.'[23] Still, Bergsten is attempting to confront the challenge and his editorial in the *Washington Post* called for a global stimulus programme, a coordination of national efforts to recapitalise banks, and a global policy guaranteeing unlimited insurance on bank deposits.

A key factor for any global solution will be the inclusion of the powerful emerging economies of the South. Growing sectors of transnational capitalists have been accepting the need to bring China, India, Brazil and other countries into the inner circles of decision making. This will be easier to accomplish under the multilateral approach of the Obama globalists than the Bush unilateralists. Even World Bank president Robert Zoellick and IMF chief Dominique Strauss-Kahn have spoken on the need to give more say to the South in their respective institutions.

This is a necessary recognition of a changed world. As Goldman Sachs points out, 'Since 2001, the US share of world gross domestic product has fallen from 34 percent to 28 percent, while that of the BRICs [the economies of Brazil, Russia, India, China] has risen from 8 percent to 16 percent. China's reserves have rocketed from $200bn to $1,800bn, Brazil's from $35bn to $200bn, Russia's from $35bn to $500bn and India's from $50bn to $300bn. World oil consumers have transferred more than $3,000bn to exporters.'[24] Given such economic strength, the influence of the South becomes part and parcel of globalisation's institutional power.

But just as the neo-Keynesian elite will be challenged by a progressive base inside the US, so, too, will it be challenged by the Third World perspective of the South. At a meeting of the General Assembly at the United Nations in September 2008, there was an outpouring of anger against the US, with many countries referring to the harsh neoliberal advice meted out during previous hard times. UN General Secretary Ban Ki Moon called for a Green New Deal in which 'Governments have a huge role' and for world leaders to 'help redirect resources away from the speculative financial engineering at the root of today's market crisis and into more productive, growth-generating and job-creating investments for the future'. Moon pointed to China's green capital investments as the first steps in a 'wholesale reconfiguration of global industry'.[25]

China's profile as a world leader is certainly becoming more pronounced. The *New York Times* reported that: 'Chinese officials are expressing their disdain in forums around the world' for US-style neoliberalism, suggesting that the Chinese style of management would serve the developing world better.[26] Furthermore, China took the global lead in being the first to announce a massive stimulus package aimed at low-income housing, infrastructure, environmental protection and technological innovation. This was followed with Obama's announcement of a stimulus package and then French president Nicholas Sarkozy's plan along similar lines. China's $586bn plan was unveiled at the meeting of G-20 finance ministers in Brazil where it received high praise from President Lula da Silva of Brazil. But neither China nor Brazil are calling for a retreat from globalisation. They are far too integrated into the world economy to turn their backs on transnational capital. Instead, they are demanding more power to determine the rules of the game. In fact, China's top bank regulator Liu Mingkang joined western globalists in calling for new international standards and regulatory systems for the world's integrated financial markets.

The old military/industrial hegemonic bloc would look upon all of this as a fundamental challenge to US supremacy. But the neo-Keynesian globalists seem ready to accept the new conditions and make the necessary strategic adjustments. As Stiglitz points out: 'U.S. credibility and the credibility of U.S. financial markets is zero everywhere in the world.'[27] Under such circumstances, neo-Keynesian globalists have become eager to recognise what Fareed Zakaria calls 'the birth of a truly global order'. As he points out, in every dimension except the military, 'industrial, financial, educational, social, cultural – the distribution of power is shifting, moving away from American dominance'.[28] Richard Haass, president of the influential Council on Foreign Relations, is another political insider advocating that the US adjust to new world realties. According to Haass: 'The unipolar era, a time of unprecedented American domination, is over. It lasted some two decades, little more than a moment in historical terms.' Instead, Haass sees a world of 'nonpolarity' in which power is distributed and decentralised.[29]

This assessment was underlined by the latest 'Global Trends' report, produced every four years by the National Intelligence Council, which represents all sixteen American intelligence agencies. As the report states, 'the United States' relative strength – even in the military realm – will decline and U.S. leverage will become more constrained'. Within the next twenty years, 'the U.S. will find itself as one of a number of important actors on the world stage [playing] a prominent role in global events' but not able to dominate as in the past.[30]

Given this perception of global conditions, Obama's security policy will move to multilateralism and nation building as its central effort. This will mean a shift to soft power which relies on multilateral diplomacy, economic reconstruction and political solutions. Admiral James Stavridis, head of SouthCom (US Southern Command, responsible for all US military activity in South and Central America), gives voice to this emerging policy, 'I don't need Humvees down here, I don't need high-priced fighter aircraft. I need the inter-agency and I need to hook up with private-public ventures … like Operation Smile, Doctors Without Borders and the American Red Cross.'[31] This approach has been advocated for the last six years in foreign policy and security circles in opposition to the military unilateralism of the Bush White House. As Zbigniew Brzezinski succinctly stated, 'the war in Iraq is a historic, strategic and moral calamity'.[32]

But none of this means an end to military efforts. Unfortunately, there will in all likelihood be a reduced but long-term military presence in Iraq, including limited combat duty and more troops sent to Afghanistan. The war against the Taliban and al-Qaida will be the biggest and most controversial foreign policy challenge for Obama. Although most Americans still view the effort in Afghanistan as a just war against those who attacked the US, the experience in Iraq has dampened support for combat, and this majority is shrinking. Additionally, Afghanistan, with a population close to 33 million has about 5 million more people than Iraq and is larger by 82,000 square miles, with a geography more adaptable to guerrilla warfare. The Taliban is based among the Pashtun, the largest ethnic group and close to 42 per cent of the population. Between Pakistan and Afghanistan, there are 45 million Pashtuns whose tribal identity is stronger than the colonial border drawn by the British. More problematic is that the tribal areas of Pakistan are now part of a broader war. One of the few military advantages the US has is air power, but its use is responsible for a large number of civilian deaths, thereby alienating the population and driving people into the arms of the insurgency. All this has resulted in a growing number of US foreign policy elites recognising that a military solution is impossible. But the balance between military force and political compromise is still being debated inside both the US and NATO.

Defense Secretary Robert Gates seems to be aware of the dangers of military occupation. In December, when commenting on sending more troops to Afghanistan, he stated: 'The history of foreign military forces in Afghanistan, when they have been regarded by the Afghan people as there for their own interests, and as occupiers, has not been a happy one. The Soviets couldn't win in Afghanistan with 120,000 troops. And they clearly didn't care about civilian casualties. So I just think we have to think about the longer term in this.'[33] Although a Bush appointee who oversaw the surge strategy, Gates was part of the Baker-Hamilton Iraq Study Group that called for a military drawdown and a regional political settlement. In fact, his own views on how to conduct the war are closer to Obama's than Bush's.

Recently, new thinking on the regional conflict was laid out in an article by Barnett Rubin and Ahmed Rashid in *Foreign Affairs* in which they argue that 'the next U.S. president must put aside the past, Washington's keenness for "victory" as the solution to all problems, and the United States' reluctance to involve competitors, opponents or enemies in diplomacy'.[34] This means a regional solution that would include Pakistan, India, Iran, Russia and China.

As the authors write:

Lowering the levels of violence in the region and moving the global community toward genuine agreement on the long-term goals there would provide the space for Afghan leaders to create jobs and markets, provide better governance, do more to curb corruption and drug trafficking, and overcome their countries' widening ethnic divisions [and] have a more meaningful dialogue with those insurgents who are willing to disavow al Qaeda and take part in the political process.[35]

All this is in keeping with the soft-power approach of multilateral globalism, but it is far easier said than done. If the military solution becomes dominant, Afghanistan will be Obama's Iraq.

Conclusion

The election of Obama has displaced neoliberal global speculators, neo-conservatives and the far Right. There is the real possibility of a progressive historic shift with a new emerging hegemonic bloc consisting of a multi-class alliance. The Obama forces at the top are linked to the neo-Keynesian sector of global capital. This leadership is trying both to consolidate its power against its rivals and maintain a degree of unity and struggle among the contending poles and centres of power within it. The business community has split into productive versus speculative capital, with an important sector seeking an industrial policy based on job growth and green technologies. Internationally, the push towards a multipolar world order that seeks stability through political compromise is struggling against an opposing strategy of military dominance. The task of progressives is to grow the strength of the multinational working class and broader community of allies, pushing from below an expanding agenda of social justice and peace. The future is open, outcomes are still unclear. Yet the possibility of a better world is within our grasp. But only a well organised and mobilised grassroots movement of millions can hope to win lasting and progressive structural change.

References

1   Jerry Harris, 'The US military in the era of globalisation', *Race & Class* (Vol. 44, no. 2, 2002).
2   William Robinson and Jerry Harris, 'Towards a global ruling class: globalization and the transnational capitalist class', *Science & Society* (Vol. 64, no.1, spring 2000), p. 43.
3   Milton Friedman, *Capitalism and Freedom* (Chicago, University of Chicago Press, 1962), p. 135. See also Michael Skapinker, 'Virtue's reward', *Financial Times* (28 April 2008), p. 8.
4   David Frum, 'Republicans must change to win', *Financial Times* (5 July 2008), p. 11.
5   David Kotz, 'Shocked disbelief', <www.truthout.org/110208B?> (3 November 2008).
6   Lawrence Summers, 'A strategy to promote healthy globalisation', *Financial Times* (5 May 2008), p. 9.
7   See John Plender, 'The return of the state', *Financial Times* (21 August 2008), p. 9.
8   Timothy Geithner, 'Developments in the global economy and implications for the United States' (New York and Washington, Council on Foreign Relations, 11 January 2007).

9   Peter Boone, Simon Johnson and James Kwak, 'An economic strategy for Mr. Obama', <www.petersoninstitute.org/publications> (11 November 2008).

10 Simon Johnson, 'Faltering economic growth and the need for economic stimulus', testimony before the Hearing of the US Congress Joint Economic Committee on Faltering Economic Growth and the Need for Economic Stimulus, <www.petersoninstitute.org/ publications> (30 October 2008).

11 Paul Krugman, 'What to do', <www.truthout.org/1130008Y?> (1 December 2008).

12 Joseph Stiglitz, 'Reversal of fortune', <www.truthout.org/103108R?> (3 November 2008).

13 Sarah Anderson, John Cavanagh, Chuck Collins, Dedrick Muhammad and Sam Pizigati, 'A sensible plan for recovery' (Washington, Institute for Policy Studies, 7 October 2008).

14 Michael Zweig, Junyi Zhu and Daniel Wolman, 'Economic stimulus and economically distressed workers' (New York, Center for Study of Working Class Life, University of New York Stony Brook, 29 September 2008).

15 Mike Davis, 'Why Obama's Futurama can wait, schools and hospitals should come first in any stimulus package', <www.tomdispatch.com> (19 November 2008).

16 Elena Foshay, 'Data points: economic outcomes of the Apollo Economic Recovery Act', Apollo News Service (6 December 2008).

17 David Brooks, 'Obama's money class', New York Times (1 July 2008).

18 Paul Ortiz, 'On the shoulders of giants: Senator Obama and the future of American politics', Truthout/perspective, <www.truthout.org> (25 November 2008).

19 Martin Wolf, 'The rescue of Bear Stearns marks liberalisation's limit', Financial Times (26 March 2008).

20 Jeffrey Garten, 'Think globally on financial regulation', Financial Times (4 April 2008).

21 See Francesco Guerrera, 'Goldman set to sever IIF links', Financial Times (23 May 2008).

22 Dani Rodrik, 'No cheers for globalisation', Guardian (31 July 2008).

23 Mark Landler, 'Global fears of a recession grow', New York Times (7 October 2008).

24 Robert Hormats and Jim O'Neill, 'A new world faces the next leader', Financial Times (27 June 2008), p. 9.

25 Ban Ki Moon, 'We need a big green jobs machine', San Francisco Chronicle (26 November 2008), p. B-9.

26 Edward Wong, 'Booming, China faults U.S. policy on the economy', New York Times (17 June 2008).

27 Quoted in ibid.

28 Fareed Zakaria, 'The post-American world', New York Times (6 May 2008).

29 Richard Haass, 'What follows American dominion?' Financial Times (16 April 2008), p. 11.

30 Scott Shane, 'Global forecast by American intelligence expects Al Qaeda's appeal to falter', New York Times (21 November 2008).

31 See Demetri Sevastopulo, 'Here, we are not launching missiles, we are launching ideas', Financial Times (2 July 2008), p. 6.

32   Zbigniew Brezezinski, 'Four steps towards calming the chaos in Iraq', *Financial Times* (2 February 2007).

33   Elisabeth Bumiller, 'In Afghanistan, Gates talks of troop increases', *New York Times* (11 December 2008).

34   Barnett Rubin and Ahmed Rashid, 'From Great Game to grand bargain', *Foreign Affairs* (November/December 2008).

35   Ibid.

12

BARACK OBAMA AND THE DILEMMA OF POWER: AN AFRICOLOGICAL OBSERVATION

Molefi Kete Asante

Temple University

Barack Obama, the junior senator from Illinois, is running for the Democratic nomination for president. A great discourse has ensued about the Obama candidacy because he is the first African American to gain such widespread popular support so soon in the campaign. Indeed, he is the first candidate in history to receive secret service protection so early in the primary campaign, gaining such protection on April 3, 2007, because of serious threats against his person by numerous detractors.

An Afrocentric examination of the political campaign and presidential prospects of Senator Obama begins with an interrogation about the nature of the political process in relationship to history, location, the American imperium, and the dilemma of power in a racial politic (Asante, 1998; Mazama, 2003). Any intense interrogation of Obama's concept of himself as an African American locates him in a particular space and time. One can read his autobiographical writings and make an assessment of his person in the light of his acculturation. Clearly he understands that, given his upbringing and his social and political education, African people in the United States have been moved off of all economic, social, cultural, and political terms. The fact that African Americans operate, so to speak, on someone else's terms and in someone else's political and intellectual space, if African Americans do not claim space and intellectual grounds, should be clear to Obama. Thus, Obama, as a part of the African American community, has participated in the pursuit of agency in the midst of a society where being Black has meant struggle for justice and reciprocity. Afrocentrists have always charged the

Source: Journal of Black Studies, September 2007; vol. 38, 1: pp. 105-115, first published on July 18, 2007.

victims of violence and oppression with complicity to their status as victims because they have not confronted racial and social crimes. To change one's situation, it is necessary to change one's consciousness. Obama's sense of agency is itself an Afrocentric act. The idea is that he must view himself as an actor not as a spectator to the making of history. This is the critical aspect of the political road of Obama. He has not been a silent partner to the political process and therefore, as a Black person, has shown an understanding of the theory of agency, that is, the idea that African Americans must be viewed as agents rather than spectators to historical transformation.

In the analysis of political discourse, Afrocentricity enters the critique of social and racial hegemony after a series of attempts by some Western writers to advance critical methods of the construction of reality in the context of White culture alone. But it is rare that we have been able to discover a satisfactory critique of the hegemonic paradigm or grand narrative of White racial domination or the assumption of political privilege by Whites. It is here that Afrocentricity provides us with a theoretical and philosophical way to grasp the role of an Obama candidacy in the context of the American society.

How Obama approaches his own rendezvous with destiny will manifest itself in light of questions of displacement, economic inequality, fragmentation, problems of race, and other issues in the course of the campaign. But all actions by the candidate will have to be viewed through the light of the political process itself. An African American candidate would have, one would expect, a much more difficult time establishing herself or himself as viable fund-raiser. To be sure, this was the one area where other Black candidates ran into trouble with the political process. They were not able to raise huge amounts of money. This has not been the case with the Obama campaign.

During the first quarter of the political primary campaign in 2007, Obama raised more than 25 million dollars to run for president. This was second only to the amount raised by Senator Hillary Clinton of New York among Democrats. African Americans have engaged in the political process on a wider basis than ever since the Voters Rights Act of 1965. Although it may be fashionable to speak of the Romantic Era of Reconstruction—a 12-year interlude in America's racist 19th century—as a point of departure when discussing the political prospects and achievements of Blacks, it is clearly not in the category of the period after the 1960s.

During the Reconstruction, African Americans were elected to state legislatures, the Senate, and Congress because of the newly acquired right to vote. Indeed, among Blacks elected to office were two who represented the state of Mississippi in the Senate, the same body where Obama now serves. Hiram Revels was in the Senate for a partial term in 1870 to 1871, and Blanche Kelso Bruce served a full term from 1875 to 1881. Scores of African Americans were elected as state treasurers, lieutenant governors, clerks, and state legislators. In fact, one lieutenant governor, P. B. S. Pinchback, served as governor of Louisiana for 43 days when the governor was removed from office. An African American, Justice Jonathan Jasper Wright of South Carolina, served on the state supreme court during the Reconstruction. Thus, the election of African Americans to the high offices of government occurred during the Reconstruction, but the elevation of Blacks to political office in the 20th and 21st centuries far surpasses anything done in the 19th century.

Africans on the Ballot

Since 1970, thousands of African Americans have been elected to various posts in legislative, judicial, and executive offices throughout the nation. In fact, there were 1,469 Black elected officials in 1970. By 2001, the number of Black elected officials had reached 9,101 (www.jointcenter.org). This rapid progress toward participation has not escaped the presidency. There have been several Black candidates for president or vice president including Angela Davis, Shirley Chisholm, Lenora Fulani, Jesse Jackson, Carol Mosely-Braun, J. C. Watt, and Al Sharpton. Most of these candidates have entered either the Democratic or Republican primaries, but some have been candidates of third parties. However, each of these candidates had a defined agenda, mainly social, that spoke to the issues of race and discrimination in the American society or, as in the case of Watt, Davis, and Fulani, articulated strong partisan issues of party politics outside of the usual race and cultural discourse. The first serious candidate for the presidency was a woman, Shirley Chisholm, who was the first African American Congresswoman and a powerful representative for New York. Those who followed her believed that a person should be able to run for the presidency regardless of race or gender. They also accepted the fact that there were so many Whites that believed in the inferiority of Blacks that it would be hard for a Black person to be elected to the presidency. This coin of the campaign, nevertheless, was not enough to prevent these very qualified candidates from running in the primaries or general elections. However, their running, in some respects, broke down the barriers about Black capabilities and opened the doors for participation. Whites saw—some for the first time—Blacks on the political platforms with Whites in debate and discussion. None of the Black candidates who ran for president was incompetent; each had the intellectual ability to be president. Thus, they cleared the path for an Obama candidacy in ways that had not happened before. They also opened the country up to the possibility of innovations in the discourse around the presidency.

Structure of the Political Economy

Any U.S president would inherit and would have to deal with the structure of a unipolar capitalist state. There are certain infrastructure elements that will dictate the outcome of any political decision a sitting president would make. Some facts would remain the same for any person elected to the high post of the presidency. Here is what any president faces: (a) a budget that is out of control and a growing national deficit; (b) a military that cannot support the political commitments made by the government; (c) a broken immigration policy; (d) an increasingly criminalized society with prisons being built at an accelerated rate; (e) education standards that are falling behind because the No Child Left Behind program takes good teachers out of the classroom; (f) an inordinate relationship between the military and huge corporations; (g) health care and housing needs of millions of citizens; (h) a loss of American moral leadership in the world because of deception, lies, and corruption in the national administration around the Iraq invasion; and (i) the persistence of income and wealth differentials between Whites and African Americans.

There is nothing that can change these realities before the next president is elected; therefore, should Barack Obama be elected president, he would have to deal with the persistent national issues deeply embedded in the nature of the American nation. In addition, the political economy structured along lines of corporate law and corporate interests will clearly constrain every potential president. Industrial, informational, and economic realities will not change just because an African American is elected to the White House.

Whether the president is Barack Obama or someone else, the president will have to deal with the fact that the United States carries a large budget deficit and has trade imbalances with many nations, including Mexico and China. This problem is at the root of the dollar's weakness against other currencies and will follow the next president throughout the presidential term. Of course, there will also be a problem with the fact that the military of the nation is overstretched to the point that a draft may be an option that will be floated by the Congress. Indeed, it is conceivable that the draft might be resurrected should the Bush administration create another military adventure prior to the election. By 2007, the United States had spent more than a half of a trillion dollars on the Iraq war—money that will have to be repaid to the treasury by the children of today's American citizens. If you add to the list of challenges a broken immigration policy that has created strong tensions in the United States since 2001, it is easy to see that one of the tasks of the next president will be to fix the immigration problem. Otherwise, the split that has emerged between numerous White American groups and Latino citizens along the fault lines of immigration will not heal. There will have to be special leadership on the part of the next president; clearly, the issue of the American borders and the corporate use of undocumented aliens will be at the heart of the debate on immigration.

The problem of the criminalization of the African American community and the construction of prisons as a growth industry will have an increasingly negative impact on the African American community. Race matters in the case of justice and injustice in the American system (Harding, 1981; West, 1993). In addition to the construction of prisons and the criminalization of the African American community, the education issue is one of the major domestic problems. The No Child Left Behind initiative that came out of the Bush White House has essentially left many schools in deeper education trouble than ever. This is an area needing immediate assistance from the executive office.

There are several other critical issues that will confront the next president. Of course, the granting of contracts to large corporations, such as Halliburton, in Iraq drew the nation's attention to the inordinate relationship that often existed between the military and huge corporations. Yet the health care needs and housing possibilities for homeless Americans have gone underresolved by politicians. Finally, the new president will have to deal with other international and domestic issues from the loss of American moral leadership and the gap between White and African American people. How a Barack Obama, or any other president, will deal with these issues will be the defining characteristic of the presidency.

The Role of the Presidency

Executive power in the United States is now derived from the American Constitution; however, there were executives before the Constitution. Both British governors and leaders under the Articles of Confederation, such as John Hanson, were executives. Those early conceivers of the executive and the later conceivers of the Constitution could not have imagined in their day or the future that the United States would have a serious contender for the presidency of African heritage. Neither James Madison, Alexander Hamilton, James Wilson, Gouverneur Morris, or George Washington, men dedicated to the creation of a strong executive, could have anticipated the point in American history where Barack Obama, the son of an African father and a European mother would be contending for the presidency if only at first as candidate for the nomination of a political party.

The Issues

Every contender to the office of president has developed certain ideas about the nature of the future of the country. Most have dealt with either domestic or international issues, and in some instances, presidential candidates have concentrated on simply business or the military. In the case of Obama, the issues have been more visionary, idealistic, more a call to a new agenda than the reiteration of persistent partisan issues from the old agenda. He attracted immense crowds of young people at every political stop and established himself as the front-runner when it came to inspiring young voters. Should Obama be able to bring into the electorate a larger group of young voters and a wider range of people, he will create a new political climate. In some ways, this is a sign that the electorate may have tired sufficiently of poor government at the executive level that it is ready to consider the rhetoric of vision as a possible balm for the stress of dealing with perceived incompetence and deceit. How does Obama confront the issues of the political climate? In the first place, it appears that he quickly understood the gap that existed between what people believed their government should be doing and what the government was actually doing in the case of the Iraq War. There is a need for the American electorate to be brought into the international world in a conscious way so that the decolonization of history becomes a part of the political discourse (Alvares, 1979). There are many Obama supporters who seem to believe that he has the best opportunity to enlarge the American vision of the world. One element in Obama's campaign is to distance himself from all forms of provincialism.

Thus, it was clear that the best strategy for Obama would be to run against the war, although many of his opponents could not run against the war since they had voted for the war. This distinguished Obama and made him the person most admired by those who felt that the war in Iraq was a betrayal of the trust that good people had placed in their political leaders. If the Democratic contenders could not run against the Bush war and the strategy that Bush's Administration had laid out for the struggle between Israel and the Arab powers, then they could not compare with Obama's passionate commitment to a new politics. Once Obama entered the race for the Democratic nomination, he was clearly the front-runner when it came to taking a Democratic position on a Republican war. What struck most people, particularly the young, was that here was a candidate of their generation that had found the tone and the melody of the times and was willing to share it with them. In the eyes of some people, here was a man of international peace, of social vision, of dreams of what could be, and of what must be, to revive the American spirit.

In effect, Obama played the role and the part of being every American who had ever dreamed of American character, goodwill on earth, leadership in peace, and victory over all forms of guile and deceit. This was his call to arms, and it was a radical call based on trying to do good for the benefit of the American nation and for the world.

Of course, this position, although popular with those who support Obama, is not universally approved. Thus, it would be necessary for Obama to ensure the electorate that he would be capable and willing to strengthen the American military if necessary. He could not be a pushover and could not give the impression that he would acquiesce in the face of tough terrorist activities. In other words, he had to show his fundamentally "cowboy" character to convince some of the voters that he would be strong enough on defense to protect the promised land (Luedtke, 1988). How could a liberal senator from Illinois really convince the American public that he would not sell out the military? Somewhere in the American consciousness during the political season is the John Wayne masculine character. It was this character that Ronald Reagan cloaked himself in, and it is the same character that George Bush, the Second, tried on with his "tough guy" image. Because of his African American culture, perhaps Obama will be able to escape the dilemma of the American cowboy image that has followed many White presidents into the White House. One can also see that Hillary Clinton has opted for the "tough girl" image by showing that she will not apologize for her vote to go to war with Iraq.

The Five Initiatives and Their Political Consequences

Every major politician seeks to propagandize his or her policies. This is the strategy that is being employed by all of the candidates. One believes that by doing this, the thinking of the masses would be directed toward the candidate's views. In this vein, on April 23, 2007, this is what Obama laid out as his Five Initiatives:

1. Bring a responsible end to the war in Iraq and refocus on the critical challenges in the broader region.
2. Modernize our overstretched armed forces, building the first truly 21st-century military and show wisdom in how we deploy it.
3. Marshal a global effort to secure, destroy, and stop the spread of weapons of mass destruction.
4. Rebuild and construct the alliances and partnerships necessary to meet common challenges and confront common threats.
5. Invest in our common humanity to ensure that those who live in fear and want today can live with dignity and opportunity tomorrow.

However, this could not be the only list of political concerns and issues. Obama knew this as well, but he also knew that he had to hammer home the point that he was strong on defense. In fact, the first three initiatives all have to do with showing his strength as a commander in chief, another acknowledgement of the cowboy motif. He calls for ending the war in Iraq but also concentrating on the broader issues in that region of the world. One has to read the code of this initiative to understand that Obama is seeking to concentrate the attention of the electorate on the issues confronting Israel, an American ally, and its Arab neighbors.

The war in Iraq is therefore seen as a bad war, a misguided adventure, an unfortunate mistake, but nevertheless a mistake. The second initiative that is mentioned by Obama is the modernization of the military. He indicates that the military is overstretched, something most commentators know and something that troubles the ordinary American and therefore should be deployed with more wisdom. A third initiative is also about the role of the American military or political might in the world in an effort to conduct a global effort to stop the spread of weapons of mass destruction. The final fourth and fifth initiatives, rebuilding partnerships and investing in common humanity, are critical to Obama's view of the future. He sees a world where the American nation takes leadership for fighting against weapons of mass destruction but not engaging in adventurism for the sake of adventure.

The Inevitable Contradictions

What would Obama face, and why would he face it? Clearly, the issues confronting Obama would not be different than those for others who would be president. But there would be some unique contradictions that he would have to deal with as president of the United States that would create enormous pressures on the presidency and the nation. The result of this pressure would be a more definitive character to the nation and a more evolved presidency. Of course, this will depend on how a President Obama would answer the issues confronting him. For example, I take it that President Obama would have to craft a strong reply to racist exploitation in a way that would not necessarily challenge White presidents. More likely, he would have to deal with issues of reparations for the enslavement of Africans without avoidance, the nature of patriarchal and racist exploitation, the sensitivity of the bosses of the military-informational agencies, the control of the immigration issue, the contradiction of the Haiti and Cuban situations, the suffering of the Palestinians for 50 years, and America's own neoimperial moves on the continent of Africa, particularly with the establishing of the AFRICOM to control oil-rich areas of Africa. These and other contradictions will challenge the first African American president in ways that a White president would not be challenged. This is not a judgment about whether Obama could deal with the challenges because I believe, given his intelligence and political savvy, he would establish himself as an innovator in political areas, going possibly where others because of their less committed stances would not even tread. If this is so, then Obama would be a trailblazing president with the potential of leaving a strong and positive legacy. All of this depends, of course, on whether he could become the Democratic nominee and then if he could win the presidency in a general election.

The Prospects and Possibilities

Obama has enough experience in the state legislature and the Senate to know that executives cannot perform their duties without the cooperation of the legislature. This is as true for states as for the United States. Thus, it is important for Obama to re-read the *Federalist Papers*, something I believe few presidents have done in recent years. One thing Alexander Hamilton (1788) wrote in the *Federalist Papers* was that presidents would almost naturally seek the right to declare war and to raise armies but that this had to be objected to. As a well-read politician, a Harvard trained lawyer, and an avid reader of politics, Obama will understand that the prospects for his success and the possibilities of his success, should he be elected president, would depend as much on his character as would the legislature. In effect, he could not govern without the legislature, and if he governed in a cooperative rather than a confrontational manner, in a transparent rather than a secretive style, he would win supporters and convince even his opponents that he was a person of good character. Ultimately, however, the type of person he is will emerge in the heat of debate and discourse.

In Relationship to Success

The prospects for success or failure are about the same as for other candidates. This usually means that Obama must remain true to his base and speak from strength and never from meanness and fear. One must recognize that with all of his personal diversity, Obama is an American citizen and an American politician who is actively campaigning to become the president of the American nation. He will not be the Kenyan or Indonesian president, and he cannot be expected to be the Black president. There are many areas of interest here because Obama's prospects might be tied to the legacy of the Bush appointees Colin Powell and Condoleezza Rice.

In a strange sort of way, the visibility and success of Powell and Rice as public servants advanced the cause of Obama's candidacy because they made it possible for Whites to view Blacks in America as capable of leading policy on the issues that confront the country. If a Black person could serve as secretary of state and lead policy for the nation, then why not serve as president and make policy for the nation? Thus, Obama's possibilities for president might be tied to the visibility, perceived competence, and intelligence of Powell and Rice. Furthermore, unlike either of them, he is a Harvard-trained lawyer and an elected U.S. senator. But such a comparison also suggests the dangers inherent in an African American running for the presidency. It is easy to believe that symbols of change are the equivalent to actual change or that representation is equal to power. Although there is something to be said for the empowering positions held by African Americans in the American government, it is important to remember that a Barack Obama, much like the Black appointees of George Bush and despite the presidency, still serves the interests of American foreign and domestic politics, and these interests have often been against the best interests of African people. How Barack Obama, should he be elected, navigates the treacherous waters between his heritage and White racial domination and globalization strategies will be instructive for future Black politicians.

References

Alvares, C. (1979). *Decolonizing history: Technology and culture in India, China and the West 1492 to the present day*. New York: Apex.

Asante, M. (1998). *The Afrocentric idea*. Philadelphia: Temple University Press.

Hamilton, A. (1788). *Federalist papers* (No. 69). New York: McLean's Edition.

Harding, V. (1981). *There is a river*. New York: Harcourt.

Luedtke, L. S. (1988). *Making America: The society and culture of the United States*. Washington, DC: United States Information Agency.

Mazama, A. (2003). *The Afrocentric paradigm*. Trenton, NJ: Africa World Press.

West, C. (1993). *Race matters*. Boston: Beacon.

13

OBAMA'S WHITENESS

Shawn Michelle Smith

Department of Visual and Critical Studies, School of the Art Institute of Chicago

Barack Obama is not only the first black American President; just as notably, he is the first biracial American President. Almost unique among public figures of mixed racial ancestry in the history of the United States, Obama has maintained his 'white half' in the media framing of his person and life. I would like to examine Obama's racialization, and specifically the racialization of his whiteness, in order to explore the current status of race and racism in the United States. In doing so, I hope to preserve the collective triumph of the nation in electing its first African American President. The fact of Obama's blackness has significantly transfigured a long legacy of American racism. The fact of his whiteness, and the representation of that whiteness, however, holds a more ambiguous grip on the American imagination.

During the presidential campaign, 'Daily Show' comedian Samantha Bee proclaimed that 'Barack Obama is already what all of us wish we were: Half black. Half white. Half Comanche. Half Viking. Half wolf.'[1] In a send-up of America's romance with Obama's racial 'exoticism', Bee also satirized the American obsession with racial quanta. Americans have long been intent on categorizing and quantifying 'color'. Since the infamous one-drop laws of the late 19th century, the precise proportions of one's racial ancestry have been accorded profound meaning and consequences. Historically, blackness has always trumped whiteness; at the turn of the century, having one great great grandparent of African or African American descent legally defined an individual as 'black'. Established to maintain a white supremacist fantasy of racial purity, such laws policed the bounds of whiteness, and deemed any racial mixture a negation of whiteness. Historically, one could never be 'half

Source: Journal of Visual Culture, August 2009; vol. 8, 2: pp. 129-133.

white' – or even 15/16ths white'. If one had any African or African American ancestry at all, one was simply black.

Obama's 'white half' remained eerily salient throughout the campaign. As David Hollinger (2008) has noted:

> Press accounts of Obama's life, as well as Obama's own autobiographical writings, render Obama's whiteness hard to miss . . . Obama's white ancestry is right there in the open, visible in the form of the white woman who, as a single mother, raised Obama. (p. 1034)

As the election approached, I heard people quip: 'Just vote for the white half.' And Obama himself joked about his 'white half'. On the 'Daily Show' the night before the election, when John Stewart asked Obama if he was afraid his 'white half' might try to sabotage him in the voting booth, the Democratic candidate good-humoredly performed a Dr. Strangelove parody in which he tried to prevent his 'white hand' from casting a vote for the white Republican candidate John McCain. Both the comedian and the presidential hopeful played on cultural anxieties that 'racial loyalty' would secretly assert itself in the privacy of the voting booth, leading white Americans to cast their votes for whiteness.

In the long lead-up to the election, Obama's racial 'parts' were visually represented in varied ways. The December 2007 cover of the *Atlantic* presented a creepy amalgam in which a ghostly image of Obama's face emerged through a grid of small images sampling some of America's most fervently divided political leaders.[2] The composite that becomes Obama's face includes such polarizing figures as Newt Gingrich, Dick Cheney, Al Sharpton, Bill Clinton, Hillary Clinton, Keith Olbermann, Jesse Jackson, Mike Morris, Al Gore, Rush Limbaugh, Rudi Giuliani, John Kerry, Howard Dean, Karl Rove, George Bush, Oliver North and Ann Coulter. Obama's apparition appears where those smaller images have been lightened; it is as if the component portraits of America's contentious politicos are fading into the whitened outlines of Obama's face.

Overlaid on top of this complicated image is the title of the cover story by Andrew Sullivan (2007: 46): 'Why Obama Matters'. Sullivan suggests that Obama, born in 1961, at the tail end of the Baby Boomer generation, is not part of the generation that has remained bitterly divided since the Vietnam War over myriad cultural issues, not least among them race and racism. In an otherwise considered and thoughtful essay, Sullivan asks, 'What does he [Obama] offer? First and foremost: His face.' The *Atlantic* cover image seems to highlight the uniting force of Obama's face, dissolving fractious figures in Obama's whitened countenance.

Much media attention has been devoted to Obama's face. Magazine covers of the Democratic candidate, President-elect, and President have often focused closely on his visage. *TIME* magazine made Obama's face the center of its disturbing 20 October 2008 cover, in which it literally whitened half of the candidate's face.[3] Here Obama's head floats disembodied on a stark background that is divided down the middle into black and white halves. His face is similarly divided down the middle – half brown and half chalky white. The right half is presented 'in color' – Obama's naturally brown skin against a white background. The left half is presented in high contrast 'black and white' – his face bright white against a black background. This 'campaign special' issue includes a 'special report' about 'why people vote the way they do' and an article about 'how worried white voters are turning toward Obama'. In bold red letters that cover Obama's whitened forehead, the issue promises to explain 'why the economy is trumping race'. This complicated combination of image and text seeks to express a post-racial dynamic at play in the election. It juxtaposes Obama's 'color' to a stark black and white binary, suggesting that 'color' – Obama's 'blackness' and 'whiteness' – may no longer be a 'black and white' issue. However, the image could just as well be heightening a racial binary as surpassing one, underscoring racial binaries with its starkly contrasting halves.

The 17 November 2008 *TIME* commemorative issue following the election presents on its cover a tightly cropped portrait of the President-elect, framed according to the dictates of monumental respectability.[4] Shot from below, at a two-thirds angle, Obama looks loftily outside the frame, his eyes and forehead shining in the light from above. This is the face of leadership. The small white text on the black background of the cover quotes the President-elect – ' "Change has come to America" ' – and image and text together suggest that Obama's face *is* the change that has materialized.

The back cover of *TIME's* commemorative issue provides an intriguing partner to its front cover. It presents a photograph of Tiger Woods, also shot from the side, but turning to look directly out at viewers. The image is an advertisement for the Swiss watch company TAGHeuer, and its text asks: 'What are you made of?' Woods is a famously 'post-racial figure' (Sullivan, 2007: 54) whose race has nevertheless been the subject of careful delineation. For those who want to know what Tiger Woods 'is made of', Wikipedia carefully outlines the racial heritage of Woods's parents by percentages, and concludes: 'This makes Woods himself one-quarter Chinese, one-quarter Thai, one-quarter African American, one-eighth Native American, and one-eighth Dutch'.[5] The striking pairing of Obama's portrait with Woods's advertisement on opposing covers of the *TIME* commemorative issue underscores the idea that what the President 'is made of' has transformed America.

What Americans are made of was the subject of one of *TIME* magazine's most infamous special issues on multiculturalism and racial mixing in the United States. On the cover of the 18 November 1993 special issue, a tightly framed image of a computer-generated woman's face was presented as 'The New Face of America'.[6] This 'new Eve' was a composite portrait made up of racial parts: '15% Anglo-Saxon, 17.5% Middle Eastern, 17.5% African, 7.5% Asian, 35% Southern European and 7.5% Hispanic' (*Time*, 1993: 2). As I have argued elsewhere (Smith, 1999: 222–5), *TIME's* new Eve was indebted to racial and visual logics established in the 19th century, in the sciences of phrenology, physiognomy, biological racialism and eugenics, and dramatically emblematized in Francis Galton's composite photographs.[7] In accord with those logics, the 'new Eve's' mixed' visual parts were carefully measured and maintained. In other words, the preservation of racial categories and quanta in this mix was the result of eugenicist thinking, which always sought to shore up Anglo-Saxon identity. *TIME* presented the face of its 'new Eve' as an emblem of the future of race in the United States. Fifteen years later, the mass media have similarly strained to frame and tame Obama's face. If, on the one hand, the discourses surrounding Obama's whiteness suggest that one-drop racial logics have finally been overturned, on the other hand those same discourses also re-energize a trenchant eugenicist logic in which racial categories are never dissolved or resolved through racial mixing.

TIME offered its 1993 visual experiment in racial mixing with articles that expressed anxiety about demographic changes in the United States. The editorial (*Time*, 1993: 5) that introduced the special issue discussed 'America's Immigrant Challenge' and declared: 'Sometime during the second half of the 21st century the descendants of white Europeans, the arbiters of the core national culture for most of its existence, are likely to slip into minority status.' Its cover image was the imagined face of a future America in which whites would be a minority. In August of the 2008 election year, census reports proclaimed that 'non-Hispanic' whites would be a minority in the United States by 2042, confirming the predictions espoused by *TIME* magazine in 1993.[8]

Obama's race has also been represented in relation to immigration. As Hollinger (2008) has emphasized: 'Obama's black ancestry is *immigrant* rather than U.S.-born' (p. 1037), and 'in the long run, the fact that Obama is the son of an immigrant may prove to be almost as important as the fact that he is the son of a black man and a white mother.' Obama is a key transitional figure between the racially divided generation of the Baby Boomers and the future generations that will see the decline of a white majority in the United States through immigration. Perhaps this is why his whiteness seems to matter so much. If, as the son of an immigrant Kenyan man, Obama represents a new kind of blackness, perhaps he also represents a new kind of whiteness – a mixed whiteness to be sure, but for now a whiteness that is tentatively maintaining its hold on an anxious American imagination (or at least its 'white half').

Notes

1. I am paraphrasing from memory here. I think Bee's formulation was actually more extensive, and more humorous.
2. http://www.reobama.com/MagazinesUS.htm
3. http://www.reobama.com/MagazinesUS.htm
4. http://www.reobama.com/MagazinesUS.htm
5. http://en.wikipedia.org/wiki/Tiger_Woods
6. http://www.time.com/time/covers/0,16641,19931118,00.html
7. Many other scholars also assessed this famous image (see Berlant, 1997: 200–9; Burgin, 1996: 258–64; Haraway, 1997: 259–65).
8. http://www.census.gov/Press-Release/www/releases/archives/population/012496.html.

References

Berlant, Lauren (1997) *The Queen of America Goes to Washington City: Essays on Sex and Citizenship*. Durham, NC: Duke University Press, 1997.

Burgin, Victor (1996) *In/Different Spaces: Place and Memory in Visual Culture*. Berkeley: University of California Press.

Haraway, Donna (1997) *Modest_Witness@Second_Millennium.FemaleMan_Meets_OncoMouse: Feminism and Technoscience*. New York: Routledge.

Hollinger, David. A. (2008) 'Obama, the Instability of Color Lines, and the Promise of a Postethnic Future', *Callaloo* 31(4): 1033–7.

Smith, Shawn Michelle (1999) *American Archives: Gender, Race, and Class in Visual Culture*. Princeton, NJ: Princeton University Press.

Sullivan, Andrew (2007) 'Why Obama Matters', *The Atlantic*, December: 40–54.

TIME (1993) Special issue, fall, 142(21).

14

PERCEPTIONS OF LEADERSHIP AND THE CHALLENGE OF OBAMA'S BLACKNESS

Charlton D. McIlwain

New York University

Though several African Americans have embarked on the path toward the American presidency, Barack Obama is widely seen as the nation's most equipped Black candidate to date to offer a serious run for the office. Obama has been distinguished from previous Black candidates such as Jesse Jackson, Shirley Chisolm, and others because of his firm support among African Americans, his broad appeal to White Americans, and his message and approach, which, different from the others, is not premised on the pursuit of racial group interests. Despite such characterizations, recent research on the use and effectiveness of White racist appeals demonstrates that racial prejudices, resentments, and fears still persist in the minds and feelings of White voters. When primed by various forms of persuasive appeals, they are effective in influencing White voters' perceptions and political decisions, to the detriment of Black candidates and/or Black interests (Mendelberg, 2001; Valentino, Hutchings, & White, 2002; Valentino, Traugott, & Hutchings, 2002).

Given these circumstances and others, Obama's candidacy has been framed largely around the question, "Is America ready for a Black president?" That is, are White voters willing to vote for a Black candidate? This is the question being asked of millions of Americans by pollsters, press, and pundits prognosticating about Obama's presidential aspirations. Although this is perhaps the most salient underlying question as to Obama's presidential prospects, I argue that this is the wrong question to ask. Much study on race of interviewer effects and other social desirability factors (Finkel, Guterbock, & Borg, 1991; Krysan & Couper, 2003) demonstrate that posing this question to White voters is unreliable.

Source: Journal of Black Studies, September 2007; vol. 38, 1: pp. 105-115, first published on July 18, 2007.

The most realistic barometer of Obama's success lies not in questions about voters' willingness to vote for a Black candidate; it is whether voters, particularly Whites, can view Blacks generally and Obama specifically as a leader. In the following pages, I argue that the question of leadership is, for White voters, a proxy for race. That is, it is the most salient manner in which White evaluations of a Black presidential candidate get expressed. I demonstrate this by first looking at the idea of leadership and its role in shaping public opinion about presidential candidates generally and more specifically during the 1988 presidential primary campaign of Jesse Jackson. Assuming this relationship between race and leadership, I then look at the manner in which the question of leadership was a salient issue of the media agenda during the beginning months of the Obama's candidacy. I also look at the way in which media framing of Obama through the lens of presidential leadership is likely to influence Obama's prospects for emerging successfully atop the field of Democratic party candidates during the primary election, and the whole of the electorate in a general election contest, should he make it that far.

Before continuing, a brief discussion of the role of leadership in presidential politics is in order. Presidential leadership has become an important aspect of shaping the role of presidential politics, as well as shaping public opinion about presidents' effectiveness. According to Tulis (1987), perceptions of presidential leadership and the consequent efforts of presidents to demonstrate certain leadership qualities through their governance are a primary aspect of the rhetorical presidency. The rhetorical presidency is characterized, in part, as an approach to governance in which presidents appeal directly to the people, educating and convincing them about the import and soundness of their public policy initiatives. This direct relationship between the president and the public, Tulis argues, has elevated the importance of being perceived as a strong leader, above all of the criteria by which the public should judge presidential effectiveness. Because public perceptions and evaluations of presidents have the power to define a president's tenure in office (former presidents Jimmy Carter and Ronald Reagan are two opposing examples), it has become paramount that presidential candidates portray an image of being a strong and effective leader (Gelderman, 1997; Hart, 1989). It is within this dynamic relationship between image and perception that the issue of leadership justifies its prominence among the list of likely criteria on which to evaluate presidential candidates.

Jesse Jackson: Perceptions of Leadership in the 1988 Campaign

As with any campaign, one can only speculate about the outcome. What separates some speculations from others is the degree to which assumptions about future decisions and outcomes are based on similar previous cases. Only one such case exists on which to base speculations about how America, particularly White America, is likely to perceive and evaluate an African American presidential candidate. The case is that of Jesse Jackson in the presidential primaries of 1988. From the beginning, Jesse Jackson's presidential prospects were viewed as minimal. This minimization largely accounted for what was later largely seen as Jackson's surprising success. At the end of the primary season, Jackson had received a total of 1,218 delegates, finishing second behind Michael Dukakis. His success was almost singularly because of the new structural circumstances in 1988 that created what was then referred to as "Super Tuesday." In an effort to gain greater influence on the presidential nomination process, a number of states, primarily Southern, moved up their primary election day to early March. At the end of the day, Jackson had carried five states, propelling his candidacy well beyond what many had thought possible (with the addition of later winning the South Carolina and Michigan primaries).

Data and Variables

When we look at election and public opinion data prior to and during the primary election cycle of 1988, what emerges is an outcome decided largely around perceptions of leadership and its effect on evaluations of Jesse Jackson and the differential manner in which Whites and Blacks perceived Jackson's leadership qualities. The data for this inquiry are based on the official election results of the 1988 Super Tuesday primary and the 1988 Super Tuesday National Election Study. Two sets of variables were of primary interest in assessing the factors most influencing voters' opinion of Jesse Jackson. First were a number of variables that indicated voters' perception of Jackson and other leaders in the primary field on a number of presidential candidate characteristics. These included their evaluations of the candidates on matters of intelligence, compassion, morality, inspiration, decency, caring, and leadership. The second variable of import was voters' overall feeling thermometer ratings of the candidates. Later, the percentage of votes for Jackson in each Super Tuesday primary state was added to the data.

Results

To determine the relationship of each of the above candidate characteristics to respondents' overall feeling thermometer ratings and the percentage of votes Jackson received in all states included in the Super Tuesday primary, a simple bivariate correlation was run. These results, presented in Table 1, provide the first indicator of the basis on which voters evaluated Jackson. Although all candidate characteristics, except for leadership, were significantly correlated with respondents' overall evaluation of Jackson, leadership exclusively was significantly correlated with the percentage of votes garnered by Jackson. These results suggest that although respondents' view of Jackson was strongly related to their evaluations of him on each of these characteristics, the only

Table 1   Correlation Between Jackson Candidate Characteristics, Feeling Thermometer Rating, and Vote Percentage in All Primary States

	Feeling Thermometer Ratings	Total Jackson Vote %
Intelligent	.526*	.057
Compassion	.674**	−.048
Moral	.668**	−.251
Inspire	.514*	.069
Leader	−.046	.822**
Decent	.632*	−.026
Cares	.526*	−.083

Note: Results are bivariate Pearson coefficients.
*p < .05. **p < .01.

factor bearing any relationship to the actual voting percentage received by Jackson overall was the degree to which they viewed him as a strong leader.

Bearing out these results is the outcome of a regression analysis, shown in Table 2, in which each candidate characteristic was figured in as a possible predictor of the total percentage of votes received by Jackson. Here again, the predictive models do not significantly predict vote percentage until the last step, when leadership is figured into the model, showing a strong predictive value and accounting for 57% of the total variance, all of which is determined by leadership exclusively.

It is possible that the relationship between leadership and vote choice is indicative of voters' evaluation of candidates irrespective of race. To test this possibility, the same tests were run for the leading White candidates in both the Democratic and Republican party primaries—the eventual nominees Michael Dukakis and George H.W. Bush, respectively. However, this is not the case for either Dukakis or Bush. The correlation between leadership and vote percentage for each candidate is statistically insignificant (.153 and .048, respectively). As expected, leadership is not a significant predictor in the regression models predicting the vote percentage for either candidate. Thus, only when evaluating Jackson, not either of the White candidates, is leadership a significant factor in terms of voting outcomes.

The picture thus far indicates a relationship between candidate race and leadership as the most salient factor influencing vote choice in that this relationship holds only for Jackson, the Black candidate. The racial element here increases focus when we consider the state breakdown of average leadership ratings of Jackson and percentage of votes garnered by Jackson in each state. Those states voting for Jackson in large percentages were the states that evaluated him highest as a stronger leader; the opposite is true for the states where he received fewer votes. Of the three states where Jackson received

Table 2   Selected Regression Models Predicting Jackson's Vote Choice

	Model 1	Model 2	Model 3	Model 4	Model 5	Model 6	Model 7
Intelligent	.105	.241	.420	.302	.259	.239	.313
	(.511)	(.655)	(.668)	(.690)	(.721)	(.752)	(.426)
Compassion		−.255	.138	.056	−.222	−.538	.221
		(.724)	(.800)	(.816)	(.999)	(1.19)	(.695)
Moral			−.701	−.970	−1.2	−1.18	−.105
			(.632)	(.712)	(.855)	(.890)	(.564)
Inspire				.648	.512	.620	.380
				(.754)	(.824)	(.880)	(.501)
Decent					.693	1.50	−.777
					(1.32)	(2.01)	(1.26)
Cares						−.822	−.301
						(1.48)	(.848)
Leader							**1.813
							(.428)
F	.042	.082	.465	.525	.445	.393	3.62
Adjusted R^2	−.073	−.151	−.129	−.157	−.247	−.351	.567
R^2 change		.010	.099	.061	.024	.030	.556

**$p < .01$.

the most votes (Virginia, Mississippi, and Alabama), the average leadership rating given to Jackson was 29%, although the three states where he received the fewest (Oklahoma, Kentucky, and Massachusetts) gave him an average leadership rating of 18%.

Furthermore, when we look at the demographics of these states in relationship to how many people in them voted for Jackson and how they rated him in terms of leadership qualities, the results are clear: Southern states and/ or those with large African American populations accounted for the highest leadership ratings and largest vote totals for Jackson. This point is compounded by the data that show a stark racial divide in the degree to which voters evaluated Jackson as being a strong leader: In a cross-tabulation comparing Black and White respondents' leadership evaluations among all states, 70% of Blacks and only 20% of Whites agreed that Jackson would provide strong leadership ($p < .01$).

Together, these results show that of all other candidate characteristics, leadership is the most salient in terms of the Jackson vote. Thus, the Super Tuesday primary results can be explained in large part by results showing that the states where Jackson was most successful were those with large percentages of African American voters, whose overwhelming leadership evaluations exceeded the overwhelmingly low evaluations of Whites, and were the driving force behind the percentage of votes garnered by Jackson. It reasonably suggests that evaluations of leadership for a Black candidate are a function of race. These results are consistent with previous studies by Terkildsen (1993) and Williams (1990) showing that when compared to White candidates, Black candidates are significantly much less likely to be perceived by White voters as a strong leader.

The findings in this analysis suggest that Obama stands at a disadvantage by virtue of his being African American, given the predilection of White voters to perceive Black candidates less as strong leaders, though the election primary circumstances of the 2008 presidential election suggest he will benefit from the same advantage that Jackson did (in addition to the 1988 Super Tuesday states, a number of states with large Black voting populations have moved up the date of their primary elections, including California and New York).

This notwithstanding, the degree to which this question of leadership will be a significant detriment for Obama depends greatly on the degree to which leadership is a significant item on the public agenda. That is, the salience of leadership for voters in 2008 will largely determine the impact of White voters' evaluations of Obama. As agenda-setting theory has long suggested, salience of political issues and criteria of candidate (especially presidential) evaluation are largely determined by their prominence in the media agenda. The role leadership plays in news reporting during the 2008 presidential campaign cycle will likely be compounded by the likely framing of Obama's candidacy in racial terms (Caliendo & McIlwain, 2006), such that both leadership and race may both be salient factors of the media agenda and thus the public agenda. The following section analyzes the media reporting of Obama since the announcement of his candidacy as a way to determine the degree to which the media will play a role in placing the characteristic of candidate leadership on its agenda and its salience among the public agenda.

Leadership and Race in Newspaper Coverage of Obama

A content analysis of newspaper coverage (both news stories and editorials) of Obama's candidacy was conducted to assess the degree to which various aspects of leadership and race appeared in stories focused on Obama since his February 10th official announcement. A 30% random sample of newspaper stories about Obama between February 10, 2007, and April 27, 2007, were coded on a number of variables.[1] The primary variables for analysis included whether *leadership* was mentioned in the headline and the story as a whole, whether Obama's experience or qualifications were mentioned, whether his experience or qualifications were questioned, and whether race was mentioned in the story. This analysis is meant to be primarily descriptive, though differences between the newspapers and the month in which the story appeared were used to assess any possible differences in terms of the presence of the above variables related to leadership and race.

Table 3 presents the descriptive results of the analysis, showing the degree to which the aforementioned aspects of leadership and race were present in stories. First, though *leadership* is, on average, seldom mentioned in story headlines (the most prominent visible aspect of stories for readers), it figures prominently in the overall reporting on Obama's candidacy. Leadership appears 44% of the time on average, and Obama's experience is mentioned in one third of all stories. Additionally, almost one quarter of stories explicitly question Obama's leadership, experience, or qualifications. Also, race (of the candidate or voters) is mentioned in more than one third of stories on average. It should be noted that when these leadership characteristics are mentioned, they are overwhelmingly mentioned by the reporter rather than the candidate (Obama), other candidates in the presidential race, or other sources quoted in the stories.

Though differences between the newspaper outlets reporting on these issues are ancillary, such differences were, nevertheless, included in the analysis. The only variable on which the news sources differed was in the degree to which Obama's experience or qualifications appeared in the story ($p < .05$). As can be seen again in Table 3, *USA Today* and *Los Angeles Times* accounted for the highest percentage of stories mentioning this aspect of Obama's candidacy, whereas the *Chicago Sun-Times* accounted for the fewest (the percentage for the *London Telegraph* was not included because of the few number of total stories included in the analysis). On all other variables, however, the newspapers were virtually similar in their reporting on such matters.

Figure 1 presents a graphical representation of the presence of these variables across the almost 3 months since Obama has been an official candidate. Statistically significant differences between the months of coverage were present for whether leadership was mentioned in stories ($p < .10$), whether race was mentioned ($p < .05$) and whether Obama's leadership was explicitly

Table 3   Frequency of "Leadership Variables" in News Stories

Newspaper	Leadership in Headline	Leadership in Story	Experience in Story	Leadership Questioned	Race Mentioned	N
Washington Post	0	59%	47%	35%	41%	17
Atlanta Journal Constitution	10%	40%	30%	20%	70%	10
Chicago Sun-Times	5%	24%	17%	17%	46%	41
London Daily Telegraph	25%	25%	0	0	25%	4
Los Angeles Times	38%	63%	50%	38%	25%	8
New York Times	4%	31%	19%	12%	39%	26
USA Today	0	67%	67%	33%	0	3
Average	12%	44%	33%	22%	35%	Total – 109

Figure 1   Mentions of Leadership and Race by Month

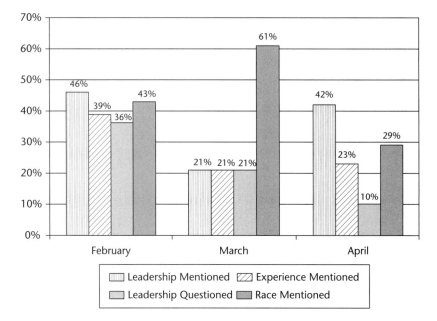

questioned ($p < .05$). Leadership was mentioned in stories most frequently in February, waned in March, and rose again in April to levels close to that in February. Leadership overall was a centerpiece of stories at the beginning, yet the media's apparent interest in that topic steadily declined over the 3-month period. Race figured prominently in stories at the beginning of Obama's candidacy, swelled in March, and fell by almost half in April's coverage.

These data show that these variations on the theme of leadership and race appear rather episodically in news coverage to date. Leadership emerged as perhaps the sole, tangible critique the media could offer at the beginning of Obama's road to the White House, after having spent considerable time in the months prior hyping the candidate's celebrity status. Similarly, race was the most visible theme and characteristic distinguishing Obama from the rest of the candidate field. Along with that novelty about his candidacy, it is perhaps to be expected that it would be a prominent feature of the initial coverage. Continued reporting on race, especially throughout March, seemed mostly because of the supposed competition between Barack Obama and front-runner Hillary Clinton over African American votes, including much coverage of the showdown in Selma, Alabama, where both candidates simultaneously delivered speeches to a broad African American audience a short distance apart from each other.

Conclusion

The conclusion of this article, of course, is that there has yet to be one. Data analysis of public opinion during the 1988 presidential primary campaign of Jesse Jackson demonstrates quite convincingly the relationship between race and leadership in voters' evaluation of Jackson and presumably of other African American presidential candidates. Although this seems to disadvantage Obama's election hopes from the beginning, its influence on today's voters' future choice of candidates is unclear, largely because the degree to which voters will use leadership (and race as a proxy) as a salient criterium for making their evaluations will likely be determined by how much the media make leadership, experience, and race a salient issue in their coverage of the 2008 presidential campaign. The results of the content analysis presented here suggests that though media attention to leadership and race has ebbed over time, even at its lowest point, both leadership (specifically Obama's lack of experience) and race figure prominently into the media's coverage.

However, a close reading of these stories to date also suggests that opinions about Obama's lack of experience largely depend on the person to whom he is being compared. His lack of experience seems less significant when the experience of President George W. Bush is the measure and more significant when he is compared to Hillary Clinton on the Democratic side or to figures such as Rudolph Giuliani or John McCain on the Republican side. Given the media's penchant to talk about issues of race and leadership in the absence of explicit prodding from outside sources, it seems that should any of Obama's competitors in the primary election or the general election (if he becomes the nominee) continue to make an issue of either race or leadership, the media's attention to these issues will also likely increase. In such a scenario, to Obama's detriment, voters are also likely to evaluate the candidates primarily on the basis of leadership.

Note

1. Six national newspapers were used, including *Washington Post, New York Times, Chicago Sun-Times, L.A. Times, Atlanta Journal Constitution*, and *USA Today*. One international newspaper was also included, the *London Daily Telegraph*.

References

Caliendo, S. M., & McIlwain, C. D. (2006). Minority candidates, media framing, and racial cues in the 2004 election. *Harvard International Journal of Press Politics*, 11, 45-69.

Finkel, S. E., Guterbock, T. M., & Borg, M. J. (1991). Race of interviewer effects in a preelection poll: Virginia 1989. *Public Opinion Quarterly*, 55, 313-330.

Gelderman, C. (1997). *All the president's words: The bully pulpit and the creation of the virtual presidency.* New York: Walker & Company.

Hart, R. (1989). *The sound of leadership: Presidential communication in the modern age*. Chicago: University of Chicago Press.

Krysan, M., & Couper, M. P. (2003). Race in the live and the virtual interview: Racial deference, social desirability, and activation effects in attitude surveys. *Social Psychology Quarterly, 66*, 364-383.

Mendelberg, T. (2001). *The race card: Campaign strategy, implicit messages, and the norm of equality*. Princeton, NJ: Princeton University Press.

Terkildsen, N. (1993). When White voters evaluate Black candidates: The processing implications of candidate skin color, prejudice, and self-monitoring. *American Journal of Political Science, 37*, 1032-1053.

Tulis, J. K. (1987). *The rhetorical presidency*. Princeton, NJ: Princeton University Press.

Valentino, N. A., Hutchings, V. L., & White, I. (2002). Cues that matter: How political ads prime racial attitudes during campaigns. *American Political Science Review, 96*, 75-90.

Valentino, N. A., Traugott, M. W., & Hutchings, V. (2002). Group cues and ideological constraint: A replication of political advertising effects studies in the lab and in the field. *Political Communication, 19*, 29-48.

Williams, L. F. (1990). White/Black perceptions of the electability of Black political candidates. *National Political Science Review, 2*, 145-164.

15

BARACK OBAMA AND THE POLITICS OF RACE: THE MYTH OF POSTRACISM IN AMERICA

Martell Teasley and David Ikard

Florida State University

W hite Americans find it as difficult as White people elsewhere do to divest themselves of the notion that they are in possession of some intrinsic value that Black people need, or want. And this assumption—which, for example, makes the solution to the Negro problem depend on the speed with which Negroes accept and adopt White standards—is revealed in all kinds of striking ways, from Bobby Kennedy's assurance that a Negro can become president in 40 years to the unfortunate tone of warm congratulations with which so many liberals address their Negro equals. It is the Negro, of course, who is presumed to have become equal—an achievement that not only proves the comforting fact that perseverance has no color but also overwhelmingly corroborates the White man's sense of his own value (Baldwin, 1962, pp. 94-95).

When Baldwin (1962) takes Robert F. Kennedy to task in *The Fire Next Time* for conflating the election of a Black president in 40 years with African American socioeconomic progress (and Kennedy was clearly not off in his prediction by much), he is not discounting the historical significance of such an event. Given that many of Baldwin's political ideals are in line with Barack Obama's, it is hardly a stretch to say that if Baldwin were alive today he would find much in Obama's election and presidency of which to be enthusiastic and even proud, especially as an African American. Baldwin's chief point is that, however well intended are his motives, Kennedy's postrace declaration is fundamentally flawed because it renders invisible the material realities of "race" as a significant and determining factor in shaping interracial power relations.

Source: Journal of Black Studies, January 2010; vol. 40, 3: pp. 411-425.

Here, Kennedy "races" the African American experience and naturalizes the experiences of the dominant culture, meaning in this instance that the true cause for celebration is not necessarily the election of a Black president but that African Americans would have "excelled" to White norms of success. Not seeing race in this instance only benefits Whites because it allows them to ignore their unearned privilege and hold Africans Americans up to a high social standard for which no group, including Whites, can realistically achieve. That said, it would be a mistake to interpret Baldwin's rejection of Kennedy's postracial declaration as a rejection of the promising possibilities of a postra*cist* society. His chief argument in *The Fire Next Time* is that our end goal as a society, of what he rightly deems cultural and racial hybrids, should be to obliterate racial categorization. His point is that we cannot hope to achieve this end goal if, like Kennedy and uncritical proponents of postracial thinking, we prematurely foreclose the discourse on race and jettison in the process a useful gauge for understanding and correcting problems of social inequality in the United States.

Of course, the racial and political climate in the United States has dramatically changed from the 1960s when Baldwin penned his now iconic essay. For many citizens, including a significant segment of the African American population, Barack Obama's election does mean that the time has come to foreclose the discourse on race. An undeniable reality is that his presidency has engendered a new and indeed intoxicating feeling of optimism across race, class, and gender lines and pressed many of us to reassess, if not overhaul, our basic assumptions about the ways that "race matters" in the 21st century. Even though it is important not to underestimate the symbolic and real significance of Obama's historic presidency and the groundswell of interracial enthusiastic and goodwill that has accompanied it, it is equally as important not to overestimate it either. Using Obama's election as hard evidence that we have transcended race in the United States, many political proponents of postracial thinking are agitating for the end to all race-and-ethnicity-centered social policy mechanisms aimed at reducing social inequities. This argument is indirectly reinforced in academe where an emerging and intensifying perspective is that class should replace race as an analytical marker because it provides a better gauge for understanding the racial and ethnic economic disparities among and between racial and ethnic groups (Curtis, 2009).

In this essay, we demonstrate that despite all the advancements we have made to explode racial inequalities—advancements that have doubtless cleared the way for Barack Obama's historic rise to the presidency of the United States—we have a significant way yet to go and on multiple socioeconomic fronts before we can actualize true racial transcendence. Highlighting the salient disconnect between the Obama-inspired optimism among African Americans that a race-free society is imminent and the realities on the ground that reveal a decidedly bleaker social and economic outlook, we consider, at once, the pitfalls of postracial thinking as it pertains to African American agency and policy formation to end social inequities and the potential for Obama's "rhetoric of hope," to borrow Atwater's (2007) phrasing, to be transformative in material and substantive ways for our most economically vulnerable communities. To lay the groundwork for our engagement with Obama's real and symbolic import, we spend the first segments of the essay contextualizing and historicizing the idea of postracial thinking. What will become clear is that we are fundamentally dealing with old ideas that have found new life in the Obama era. The pressing issue at hand is if Obama can "change" or strategically recalibrate this perceived postracial paradigm to attack social inequities that break starkly along racial lines or become a "bound man," to riff on Shelby Steele's (2008) convenient phrasing, and become a prisoner of his own "color-blind" rhetoric, reifying the status quo instead of challenging it.

The Dynamics of Race and Politics in America

The notion of a postracial society has been with us for some time. It became a convenient tool of the political Right as a form of backlash to affirmative action policies enacted during the 1960s and the 1970s. It is a cause championed by those who benefit from its use as a form of social capital in maintaining the status quo of the American power structure (Marable, 2000) where African Americans and those of Hispanic/Latino decent own less than 5% of the wealth yet constitute at least 25% of the U.S. population; where the median net worth of African American families in the United States is $20,600 and that of Latino families is $18,600, compared to the $140,700 median net worth of Whites. African Americans, then, compose only 14.6% of the median net worth of Whites, and Latino families even less at 13.2% (Muhammad, 2008). Given these economic disparities, we are interested in the tangible analysis of race as a form of social capital, and we seek to assess substantive issues that are affected by postracial thinking and actions.

Race Analysis

An appropriate analysis of race and social outcomes should not only address economic and structural factors that affect the life course of African Americans (Mason, 1997, 2001) but also be attentive to historical mechanisms that have transcended generations of the American republic in the oppression and marginalization of non-Anglo-American ethnic groups. Marable (2000), Mason (1997, 2001), and Myers (2002), to name a few, have introduced formulations that directly engage this type of analysis. Generally speaking, race analysis is the systematic application of the tools of historical and cultural analysis to understand the social and economic circumstances facing Blacks and other non-Anglo racial/ethnic group members. Clarifying the pressing need of such an analysis, Myers writes, "Many of the core problems that occur in the study of race relations can be characterized as problems that pit efficiency against equity" (p. 171). Myers defines *efficiency* as any method that is aimed at the conditions of inequality for historically disadvantaged groups, but not at the expense of the majority. The discourse on efficiency is much more palatable than attempts to enact social policies that focus on *equity*, which, in general, is couched to the public as giving one group an advantage over another (i.e., affirmation actions).

As a substantive issue, there are two *primary categories* in the analysis of race: One is viewing race as a social construct, and the other is viewing it as a biogenetic construct.[1] Any cursory review of scientific literature finds several inherent challenges to race as a social construct: (a) It does not explain human biological and ethnic variations, (b) its meaning has been diluted and subject to various social and cultural interpretations, (c) there is a lack of consensus of its meaning within scientific disciplines, and (d) when used as a causal genetic variable, it perpetuates biological determinism to the exclusion of other causal factors for human behavior and social conditions (Kittles, 2008). The key point here is that the idea of race as a social construct can be appropriated and/or manipulated to conceal a more scientific analysis of race based on biogenetic factors or outcomes. What this means in practical terms is that when "race" as a biological factor is invoked in public discourse, even when someone like Obama uses it to promote racial unity as he does in his famed "Race Speech" (discussed in greater detail below), it can easily be dismissed or misinterpreted as either biological determinism (i.e., social Darwinism) or racial divisiveness based on phenotype. Even though the pitfalls of such thinking are well documented scientifically (Kittles, 2008; Rutledge, 1995), there has yet to be a productive discussion of this phenomenon as it pertains to the national politics on racial discourse.

The Myth of a Postracial Society

We submit that many proponents of postracial thinking give race what logicians (Copi, 1978) refer to as *existential import*—the notion of attributing a tangible property to race that really does not exist—when it is politically convenient to do so or to intentionally obfuscate the realities of clear and present social inequity for oppressed populations in the United States. Those who give race existential import tend to collapse the distinctions between the two primary categories of race as if they are interchangeable. Legislatively speaking, this prevalent mind-set means that even social justice policies designed to combat social inequities based on race tend to be ineffective because they grow out of faulty logic and skewed perceptions of racial realities. As Myers (2002) suggests, "The process of getting the right answer to an incorrectly formulated policy question is characteristic of many race-related policy questions" (p. 175).

Noted conservative provocateur Steele (1990) offers a striking case in point in his book *The Content of Our Character*. Decrying the problems of affirmative action legislation and policies aimed particularly at African American socioeconomic progress, Steele opines, "The great ingenuity of interventions like affirmative action has not been that they give [White] Americans a way to identify with the struggle of Blacks, but that they give them a way to identify with racial virtuousness *quite apart* from Blacks" (p. 93). Clearly operating on the idea of race as existential import, Steele collapses the distinctions between race as a biogenetic reality and race as a social construct. Only Blacks are biologically "raced" and have a history of race. In stark contrast, Whites are unraced (i.e., American and "normal") and have no history and role in racial oppression. Little wonder then that Steele can claim that Blacks receive affirmative action because of radicalized thinking and White guilt. Based on his faulty logic and *ahistorical* race analysis, Blacks are responsible for the problem *and* the solution of racial inequality. Lost too in his formulation is the fact that White women, not Blacks, are arguably the biggest benefactors of affirmative action policies in the United States.

Steele's analysis on race and social policy is just one example of postracial thinking that cleverly shifts the burden of racialized thinking to the victims of racial inequality. Others include William Julius Wilson's (1980) *The Declining Significance of Race?* John McWhorter's (2001) *Losing the Race: Self-Sabotage in Black America*, and, more recently, Thomas Sowell's (2005) *Black Rednecks and White Liberals*.[2] To be clear, we find the uncritical preoccupation with past racial social inequities unproductive and potentially dangerous. Ours is not a desire to create and/or perpetuate a false dichotomy, pitting postracial thinkers against divergent thinkers on race and politics. Rather, our central aim is to call attention to problematic formulations that shift the public discourse from a focus on verifiable racial inequalities to a focus on race exclusively as a property of existential import. However well intended, these postracial formulations operate discursively as *efficient* methods of downplaying historical and contemporary inequities and their linkage. To be precise, they deemphasize race as a substantive narrative toward achieving social equity through policy implications on the one hand and emphasize race as a measure of social efficiency on the other (Myers, 2002). In its current form, then, postracial analysis clouds more than clarifies our understanding and critical assessment of human deprivation for some of our most vulnerable citizens. The greatest tragedy is that their issues are misrepresented and/or misinterpreted one-dimensionally as self-inflicted and, concomitantly, the exclusive responsibility of the individual/group to ameliorate. Given the ways that dominant social perceptions have historically trumped socioeconomic and scientific realities in U.S. policy formation, it becomes imperative that we challenge and reject, if necessary, postracial thinking that romanticizes self-determination or ignores our rocky historical legacy of racial inequities in the United States.

The Symbolic Capital of Hope

Obama's famous rhetorical dexterity has given progressives as well as centrists reasons to believe he shares their values and outlook. (Hayes, 2008, p. 14)

If one were to base one's assessment of Barack Obama's presidency solely on the postracial media hype that largely defined his presidential campaign and that continues to dominate the ways that the United States and the international communities view him, the historical contribution of other Black political figures who transcended the politics of race and that facilitated the ascendency of Barack Obama could easily be disregarded. Suffice it to say, there is a long history of political rhetoric and rhetorical speech making among African American politicians that precedes Obama's rise and political oratory fame. This point is expressed in several recent works on the Obama presidency. For example, in *What Obama Means . . . for Our Culture, Our Politics, Our Future*, Asim (2009) highlights the history of what he refers to as "secular sermonizers"—orators who invoke a sort of American scripture through the best language that the nation has produced via the American Constitution and the Declaration of Independence. Included in this elite, interracial fraternity are Abraham Lincoln, Frederick Douglass, and Barbara Jordan.

Dealing more squarely with Obama's connection to the African American rhetorical tradition in the *Rhetoric of Hope*, Atwater (2007) demonstrates that Obama's success is the outgrowth and culmination of a history of inspirational Black rhetoricians who have galvanized large interracial constituencies around the idea of hope and the possibility for racial reconciliation and equality. She cites the 1984 presidential campaign of Jessie Jackson as a key historical marker in the rise of the charismatic image and ethos of a unifying Black leader in American national politics. She asserts that his campaign simultaneously brought together national and international backing and transcended feeling of White supremacy through a unifying sense of universal possibility. Obama's "audacity of hope" rhetoric is for Atwater a revised and updated version of Jackson's "keep hope alive" slogan. Common rhetorically to both is their

use of symbols to get Americans to care about . . . [and] regain hope and faith in this country, and to believe that we [Blacks and Whites] are more alike than we are different with a common destiny and a core set of values. (p. 123)

However we contextualize Obama's legacy, the fact is his campaign and presidency have ushered in a new feeling of optimism in American, especially for African Americans. An April 2009 *CBS News/New York Times* poll bears this out, showing that the election of Barack Obama as president of the United States indicates that for the first time many Black Americans feel good about the overall state of race relations in the United States: "[59%] of African-Americans say race relations in the U.S. are good, compared with only 29% who thought so less than a year ago, before the election of Barack Obama" ("State of Race Relations," 2009, p. 1). Of Blacks, 61%, and 81% of Whites, agree that there has been real progress in diminishing racial discrimination in the United States since the 1960s. This compares to a December 1996 poll where only 37% of African Americans felt that real progress in race relations has been made since the 1960s. What is more, a December 2008 article in *The Economist* reports that 80% of Black Americans polled say that Obama's victory is "a dream come true," and 96% of them think it will improve race relations ("Search for the Promised Land," 2008).

The crucial issue becomes if this new and growing optimism will result in substitutive structural change. Though this is certainly a many-sided issue with an infinite number of potential outcomes, we focus on what we see as the best- and worst-case scenarios based on what we have witnessed thus far in Obama's presidency. To consider the best-case scenario first, African Americans are much more likely now than ever before in history to feel that they have agency because Barack Obama broke through not only a glass ceiling insofar as ascending to the highest office in the country but also a collective psychological racial barrier. Assuming that this African American optimism is sustainable beyond the euphoria of the historical election, it may result in a renewed energy to fight against social inequities based on race. It seems all but certain that it will encourage more African American participation in politics at the national and state levels. If people feel their perspectives and actions matter, there is a high probability that they will be more inclined to get involved in reshaping their communities for the better. For the youngest generation of African Americans, it may prove the biggest advantage of all because, unlike generations before them that hoped for, preached about, and agitated for these types of changes, they have at their disposal palpable evidence of what is possible. We can also find optimism in the fact that Obama has directly and repeatedly engaged the problem of social inequalities based on race, even if in strategic and lofty rhetoric that emphasizes nation over race, forward thinking over historical reckoning, interracial healing over group accountability. If we take into account the dynamics of racialized thinking that inform and complicate how Obama can talk about race and speak to social inequities based on race, we can view his fence-straddling rhetoric as a necessary, if regrettable, political ploy.

Consider his famed "Race Speech," for example. The racial reality from the standpoint of the dominant culture was, and continues to be, that African Americans cannot be objective when it comes to discussing race, that they tend to embrace victimization and blame Whites rather than accept responsibility for their actions and take charge of their destiny. Caught, as the cultural saying goes, "between a rock and a hard place," between wanting to not appear the victimized Black and alienate his White voters or to ignore the legitimate experiences from which his pastor Jeremiah Wright's racial skepticism derived and potentially upset his Black ones, Obama strategically refocused the debate from the White historical disenfranchisement of Blacks to Wall Street greed and Washington political corruption as the indirect blame for past and existing racial strife. Even though there were undoubtedly many African Americans who were not thrilled with his rhetorical sleight of hand and how it minimized White participation in Black social and economic domination, most, it seems from the rounding support he received from Black communities, appreciated his difficult circumstances even if they ultimately disagreed with the romanticized portrait of Black–White tensions that his speech projected.

An optimist might also see Obama's selection of, say, Eric Holder to the office of attorney general of the United States as a promising sign that he understands the limitations of postracial thinking. Indeed, on February 18, 2009, when Holder stirred up national controversy during his first major national address by stating that "in things racial we have always been and continue to be, in too many ways, essentially a nation of cowards" (Cooper, 2009, p. A26), Obama did not cave to the then mounting pressure from the political Right to denounce Holder. Instead, he remained conspicuously silent on the issue for nearly a month, finally offering what amounted to only a mild rebuke in an interview with the *New York Times*: "If I had been advising my attorney general, we would have used different language" (Cooper, 2009, p. A26). When pressed to clarify whether he agreed with Holder, he responded in a way that both dignified Holder's comments (he never patently stated that he disagreed with Holder) but also, at once, remained in keeping with his rhetoric of hope:

> I'm not somebody who believes that constantly talking about race somehow solves racial tensions. . . . What solves racial tensions is fixing the economy, putting people to work, making sure that people have health care, [and] ensuring that every kid is learning out there. (Cooper, 2009, p. A26)

But, alas, there are significant, and perhaps even dangerous, consequences bound up in the, at times, uncritical optimism that abounds in Barack Obama's presidency and his near-hypnotic rhetoric of hope. Inspiring though it may be to Americans in general and African Americans in particular, Obama's rhetoric of hope has the potential to engender a false sense of hope, masking the realities of gross racial/ethnic disparities and inequality and worsening economic conditions, not only for many Black communities but also for the majority of Americans in general. The fact is that wealth disparities are increasing in the United States, particularly for the majority of African Americans and Hispanics/Latinos (Muhammad, 2008). To illustrate, the top 1% of income earners (the superrich) took home an average of $29.6 million in income in 2006, as compared to only $5.4 million in 1980 for this same group. Compare this to 1980, when "families in the bottom 90 percent averaged $30,446 in income, after adjusting for inflation, $72 more than the $30,374 comparable families earned in 2006" (Thompson, 2009, p. 25). In his essay "Race and Extreme Inequality," Muhammad (2008) explains that the small wealth gains of recent decades for Blacks and Latinos have all but evaporated with the subprime mortgage meltdown. When compared to Whites, Blacks are 3 times more likely to receive a subprime home loan and 4 times more likely to receive a subprime refinancing home loan. It is estimated that African Americans will lose between $71 million and $92 million during the subprime financial meltdown; similarly, Hispanics will lose between $75 million and $92 million in the marketable worth of their homes from subprime loans.

We find it ironic that the media largely ignore the increasing economic and wealth inequality but are fascinated to the point of obsession with the less substantive properties of a postracial national dialogue. Void of critical analysis, and fixated on the possibility of a postracial America, the discourse on many pressing economic issues as they pertain to social inequality, class, and status is romanticized at best and vacuous at worst (Bobo & Charles, 2009). For example, the discourse on the national economic recession is framed as a discussion of how the challenges of American financial institutions will affect international markets and the plight of the middle class, but not the poor. Fiscal policies crafted by the executive branch of government and endorsed by Congress brazenly rewarded negligent investments with a financial bailout for lucrative banks and their executives at the expense of tax payers; this was succeeded by state legislators and municipalities cutting services and benefits to public universities and schools and health care programs for the poor. Banks and corporations cannot fail, but families and communities can. There is no discourse or discussion on the poor, who are disproportionately Black and Hispanic, and how they will fare in this era of economic downturn for the United States (Muhammad, 2008).

It can, at times, be difficult to discern Barack Obama's take on such issues because of his shifty and shifting rhetoric of hope. Indeed, Obama's rhetoric masterfully straddles the line of existential import. It provides little in the form of giving substance to race, but it also does not totally deny the agency of race as a substantive entity and as a battle cry for racially oppressed populations seeking equity and social justice. When asked by a reporter at the press conference on his first 100 days in office what he may do about the disparities in unemployment and underemployment for Black men throughout that nation, President Obama replied, "Keep in mind that every step we're taking is designed to help all people" (Washington Wire, 2009). Although President Obama believes that affirmative action policies are still needed in the United States, he contradictorily maintains that race is an inappropriate discussion for policy analysis.

Yet as masterful as President Obama is at gauging the pulse of the nation's tolerance for racial discourse, when he did "step out of bounds" as determined by the criteria of White America, speaking on race, say in the case of the questionable arrest of a prominent African American Harvard University professor Henry Louis Gates, his comments were partly responsible for his summer 2009 national approval ratings decline.[3] According to a July 2009 Pew Research Center publication, his comments, where he stated that the arresting Cambridge, Massachusetts, police officer, who was White, acted "stupidly," were followed by a national approval ratings drop from 53% to 46% within 48 hours of his comments. Ironically, although more White Americans disapprove (45%) than approve (24%) of his comments on the Gates arrest, the same Pew research poll indicates that "Obama is widely liked by the public on a more personal level, with close to three-quarters (74%) saying they like the kind of person he is and the way he leads his life" (Pew Research Center for the People and the Press, 2009, p. 1).

Generally speaking, the social and economic success that Barack Obama has enjoyed before and after his rise to the presidency is atypical to the experiences of most African Americans. But the country's inherent fixation with race as an a priori in its national discourse and as an accompanying explanation for many of its social ills—mostly to the disadvantage of Black people— is something that even a master rhetorician like Obama may not be able to overcome, as his drop in presidential approval ratings indicates. As Julian Bond notes in an April 2009 forum on affirmative action, wealth, race, and ethnicity, "Changes in our society, not least in the election of our first African-American president, do not signal a shift in our [racial] temperature . . . [or] mean the difficulty of the climb [to socioeconomic prosperity] has been erased for all others" (Curtis, 2009, p. 6). Moreover, a 2008 Pew Research poll shows that nearly half (45%) of African Americans born to middle-income parents during the post–civil rights era have descended into near poverty or poverty as adults (Younge, 2008).

But, the danger here is not just for African Americans: The symbolic capital that facilitates the development of a postracial euphoria, that beguiles America at the beginning of the Obama administration, has created a sort of mystique that somehow quells the clamor of national moral degradation and the impact of near financial implosion on the poor. It is not so much the ascendency of Barack Obama as the symbolic hope that he brings for all of America, renewing the country's "Camelot" experience, invoking the country's stance as a leader in the democratic world, and championing the country's subconscious psychic fixation with race as an inescapable, romantic national saga.

As even Steele (1990) reveals, "Racist societies enforce the idea of race as home by making race an inescapable fate. So, still today, this fundamentally odd—even primitive—idea remains embedded in our democratic national culture, the legacy of our past" (p. 4). Thus, as demonstrated by Barack Obama's fluctuating national approval ratings of which sentiments about race are an intricate component, his rhetoric of hope based on racial discourse is somehow viewed, as unfair as it may seem, as synonymous with any characterization of appropriate remedies for a radicalized and morally and economically ailing nation. In our opinion, even as it has successfully reduced and exacerbated national anxieties and raised our collective spirits, Obama's rhetoric has also detrimentally obscured our national economic decline, the ballooning wealth disparities, and the probable chaos of fighting two foreign wars with no end in sight.

Conclusion

Through our analysis, we have identified three inherent challenges to postracial thinking and discourse and subsequent public policy analysis: (a) It obfuscates the meaning of race, (b) it ignores gross economic disparities between racial and ethnic groups and their historical and contemporary antecedents, and (c) it disregards the enactment of social policy mechanisms that maintain economic disparities. To this end, the dominant culture attempts to hold underprivileged Black Americans and other marginalized non-White groups accountable for their participation in a meritocracy while simultaneously ignoring the reality of past and present racial and ethnic inequality. From our position, many proponents of postracial thinking deny the reality that they claim the election of Barack Obama promotes, that is, the promotion of *agency* and self-determination for Black people. Giving Black Americans agency makes them *subjects* and stewards of their own destiny and not *objects* of the experiences and wishes of others (Asante, 2003).

To be subjects of their own experience and destiny in America, Black people will need many structural changes in American society. These changes should include social policy enactments and monetary investments that reduce educational and health care disparities and outcomes, greater investment and revitalization in the nation's declining urban infrastructure where nearly 70% of African Americans reside, and grants for college and business entrepreneurship within Black communities (Muhammad, 2008). All of these suggested structural changes are similar to what FDR and the U.S. Congress enacted for White Americans at the end of World War II at the exclusion of Black Americans (Muhammad, 2008).

Although we acknowledge the significant milestone and meaning of the Obama presidency, we contend that in a capitalistic economy and society, freedom and self-determination in many ways constitute, at a minimum, economic viability and the accumulation of wealth. To this end, President Obama's rhetoric of hope cannot change the fact that African Americans compose 12% of the U.S. population but possess only approximately 3% of the country's wealth, that they have gained less than 2 percentage points in terms of wealth accumulation since post–Civil War Reconstruction (Davis & Bent-Goodley, 2004).

The truth of the matter is that African Americans would like nothing more than to end racism and racialized thinking in America. Many African Americans not only understand their victimization based on race in the past but also understand the more sophisticated methods of racial inequality that reduce their capacity to engage in self-determination today. The problem for African Americans in terms of racialized thinking is not that they are fixated on race as the central theme in the progression of their humanity and their participation in the American experience. Rather, it is, as W. E. B. Du Bois prophesized nearly a century ago, their "unforgivable [B]lackness" that America will not put to rest.

Notes

1. As a biogenetic construct with sociocultural implications, race does matter because of its long historical significance as a convenient tool in the oppression of people based on phenotype. Dr. Rick Kittles (2008), a biogenetic scientist at the University of Chicago Department of Medicine, reviewed research findings examining household net wealth in relation to disease manifestation and individual genetic ancestry. His review of genetic research included populations in Cleveland, Chicago, Washington, D.C., and Maryland. It included the genetic ancestry of Caribbean islands Jamaica, Barbados, and St. Thomas. Sampling Whites, Blacks, and Hispanics within these areas for their genetic makeup, Kittles determined that, as an aggregate, those individuals with the highest amount of DNA from West African ancestry (where most of the slaves sent to the aforementioned areas came from) were the poorest in terms of wealth and health outcomes.

2. Readers should note that there are other scholarly works by these authors concerning the analysis of race and class in America.

3. According to the Pew Research Center for the People and the Press (2009),

News about the arrest of the prominent African American Harvard professor at his Cambridge home was widely followed by the public and 79% are aware of Obama's comments on the incident. Analysis of the poll data found that the president's approval ratings fell among non-Hispanic whites over the course of the interviewing period as the focus of the Gates story shifted from details about the incident to Obama's remarks about the incident.

References

Asante, M. (2003). *The Afrocentric idea*. Philadelphia: Temple University Press.

Asim, J. (2009). *What Obama means . . . for our cultural, our politics, our future*. New York: HarperCollins.

Atwater, D. F. (2007). Senator Barack Obama: The rhetoric of hope and the American dream. *Journal of Black Studies, 38*, 121-129.

Baldwin, J. (1962). *The fire next time*. New York: Vintage.

Bobo, L. D., & Charles, C. Z. (2009). Race in the American mind: From the Moynihan report to the Obama candidacy. *Annals of the American Academy of Political and Social Science, 621*(1), 243-259.

Cooper, H. (2009, March 8). Attorney general chided for language on race. *New York Times*, p. A26. Retrieved May 1, 2009, from http://www.nytimes.com/2009/03/08/world/americas/08iht-08race.20669415.html?scp=1&sq=Eric%20Holder%20March%208,%202009%20Helene%20Cooper&st=cse

Copi, I. M. (1978). *Introduction to logic* (5th ed.). New York: Macmillan.

Curtis, K. (2009, April 16). Miller center debate: Should inequality be addressed by race-or class-based affirmative action? *UVA Today*. Retrieved May 1, 2009, from http://www.virginia.edu/uvatoday/newsRelease.php?id=8471

Davis, K., & Bent-Goodley, T. B. (Eds.). (2004). *The color of social policy*. Alexandria, VA: Council on Social Work Education.

Hayes, C. (2008, December 29). The pragmatist: It's a label Obama has embraced, but what does it mean? *The Nation*, pp. 13-16.

Kittles, R. (2008, January). *Race, genetics, and health*. Paper presented at the Society for Social Work Research conference, New Orleans, LA.

Marable, M. (2000). *How capitalism underdeveloped Black America: Problems in race, political economy, and society*. Boston: South End.

Mason, P. L. (1997). Race, culture, and skill: Interracial wage differences among African Americans, Latinos and Whites. *Review of Black Political Economy, 25*(3), 5-39.

Mason, P. L. (2001). Annual income and identity formation among persons of Mexican descent. *American Economic Review: Papers and Proceedings, 91*(2), 178-183.

McWhorter, J. (2001). *Losing the race: Self-sabotage in Black America*. New York: Free Press.

Muhammad, D. (2008, June 30). Race and extreme inequality. *The Nation*, p. 26.

Myers, S. L. (2002). Presidential address—Analysis of race and policy analysis. *Journal of Policy Analysis and Management, 21*(2), 169-190.

Pew Research Center for the People and the Press. (2009, July 30). *Obama's ratings slide across to board*. Retrieved September 5, 2009, from http://pewresearch.org/pubs/1298/obama-rating-falls-health-care-proposals-pay-for-changes

Rutledge, M. D. (1995). Social Darwinism, scientific racism, and the metaphysics of race. *Journal of Negro Education, 64*(3), 243-252.

Sowell, T. (2005). *Black rednecks and White liberals*. San Francisco: Encounter Books.

Steele, S. (2008). *A bound man: Why we are excited about Obama and why he can't win*. New York: Free Press.

Steele, S. (1990). *The content of our character: A new vision of race in America*. New York: HarperCollins.

Search for the promised land: What will Barack Obama's presidency mean for race relations? (2008, December 8). *The Economist*. Retrieved March 12, 2009, from http://www.economist.com/world/unitedstates/displayStory.cfm?story_id=12725114.

The state of race relations. (2009, April 27). *CBS News/New York Times*. Retrieved May 7, 2009, from http://www.swamppolitics.com/news/politics/blog/2009/04/27/CBS%20poll%20on%20race%20relations.pdf

Thompson, G. (June 30, 2008). Meet the wealth gap. *The Nation*, pp. 18-27.

Washington Wire. (2009, April 30). Transcript of Obama's 100th day press conference. *Wall Street Journal Blogs*, p. 8. Retrieved May 1, 2009, from http://blogs.wsj.com/washwire/2009/04/30/transcript-of-obamas-100th-day-press-conference/

Wilson, W. J. (1980). *The declining significance of race? Blacks and changing American institutions*. Chicago: University of Chicago Press.

Younge, G. (2008, June 30). Beneath the radar. *The Nation*, p. 10.

16

"THE REALITY OF AMERICAN LIFE HAS STRAYED FROM ITS MYTHS": BARACK OBAMA'S *THE AUDACITY OF HOPE* AND THE DISCOURSE OF THE AMERICAN RECLAMATION JEREMIAD

Willie J. Harrell Jr.

Kent State University

I can't help but view the American experience through the lens of a Black man of mixed heritage, forever mindful of how generations of people who looked like me were subjugated and stigmatized, and the subtle and not so subtle ways that race and class continue to shape our lives.

—Barack Obama, *The Audacity of Hope: Thoughts on Reclaiming the American Dream*

While writing *The Audacity of Hope: Thoughts on Reclaiming the American Dream*, Barack Obama remains responsive to the ideological consensus of what it means to be a Black man in America. Representing the American Dream in his unparalleled way, Obama participates in this consensus by rightfully positioning *The Audacity of Hope* into the American jeremiadic tradition. Like other politicians before him who utilized the jeremiad to address America's need for change,[1] Obama confronts America with a profound discourse that criticizes the nation for straying from its ideological myths, while offering his opinion and potential approaches to reform in order to recover from economic disaster. Grounded in historical analysis, Obama's restoration rhetoric in *The Audacity of Hope*, I argue, functions as the American

Source: Journal of Black Studies, September 2010; vol. 41: pp. 164-183, first published on July 15, 2009.

reclamation jeremiad, in which he employs political discourse to restore a positive vision of America's democratic mission and warns Americans of the dangers of not fulfilling that mission. By combining this ideological warning in his positive vision of America, Obama constructs a message that is unifying while at the same time indicative of a risk in not challenging the destructive path of the American political system. Ultimately, Obama's plaintive cry in *The Audacity of Hope* indicates his belief that something is wrong with America, but he is unsure how to fix it.

As a vehicle for jeremiadic discourse, *The Audacity of Hope*, published in 2006, is unusual because of its structural makeup of narrative combined with autobiography and political assessment. Committed to mapping Obama's thoughts on the challenges that Americans face as a nation, *The Audacity of Hope* serves as a "blueprint for his political career and . . . his belief and stand on major issues" (Atwater, 2007, p. 126). His argument is simple: Americans, regardless of political designation, are "weary of the dead zone that politics has become." How, then, can Americans "begin the process of changing our politics and our civic life?" Obama admits that his intentions in *The Audacity of Hope* are not to offer a "unifying theory of American government, nor . . . provide a manifesto for action" in solving its problems (p. 9). However, he expresses his vision for America clearly and intelligently—where he believes the nation is going and how policy changes can aid in the process.

In the classic jeremiadic fashion, Obama calls America to political repentance, an innovative kind of political system that builds on the communal understandings that will unite all Americans. He calls Americans to trust in the optimism that has sustained the nation's democratic principles, "a tradition that stretched from the days of the country's founding to the glory of the civil rights movement" (p. 2) to the present day. J. Murphy (1990) argues that the American jeremiad functions to transform "dissent and doubt about American society into a rededication to the principles of American culture" (p. 402). Since America's "democracy has gone seriously awry" (p. 22), Obama ultimately utilizes the rhetoric of the jeremiad to call Americans to reform in order to reclaim the ideological American dream. A junior U.S. senator from Illinois at the time *The Audacity of Hope* was published, Obama painstakingly laments America's increasing economic instability, "the racial and religious tensions within the body politic, and the transnational threats—from terrorism to pandemic" (p. 10) that gather beyond America's shores.

The American Reclamation Jeremiad

Scholarship on the American jeremiad has focused on the three primary characteristics that exist within this distinctive discourse: a chastising of society because it has sinned by violating its basic values, a warning that calamity is imminent if society does not reclaim its basic values, and a calling to return to the basic values so that society may prevent such destruction (Bercovitch, 1978; Howard-Pitney, 2005; Johannesen, 1985, 1986; Jones & Rowland, 2005; Moses, 1982; A. Murphy, 2009; J. Murphy, 1990). According to Bercovitch (1978), the American jeremiad "was an ancient formulaic refrain, a ritual form imported to Massachusetts in 1630 from the Old World. . . . The American jeremiad owes its uniqueness to this vision and mode of rhetoric" (p. 6). Bercovitch's analysis suggests that while the jeremiad foretells devastation, it is, at the same time, optimistic concerning future events. Moses (1982) identifies the Black jeremiad as the formulaic "warnings issued by Blacks to Whites, concerning the judgment that was to come for the sin of slavery" (pp. 30-31). Howard-Pitney (2005) concludes that the rhetoric of the American jeremiad ultimately develops into something distinctively Afro-American because of its call for social prophecy and criticism. He suggests that the rhetoric set out to warn White America of the "declension from the promise of a Christian America" (p. 12). Jones and Rowland (2005) suggest that when political leaders choose to employ these characteristics, they do so "because it is consistent with their objectives and worldview" (p. 160). And as Howard-Pitney (2005) argues, when African American intellectuals and "political figures have employed a rhetoric anchored in social consensus, they have had to keep their goals within its non-revolutionary bounds" (p. 186). Obama's reclamation jeremiad replaces the beliefs of Puritan religion, established in the conventional jeremiad, with what can be expressed as the civil religion of the American Dream; as such, it does not carry with it the apocalyptic condemnation and guilt that is customary in American jeremiads. Instead, his jeremiad takes on political doctrines, as illustrated in *The Audacity of Hope*. Unlike previous African American Jeremiahs, such as Frederick Douglass, W. E. B. Du Bois and Martin Luther King Jr., Obama believes in America's imminent reformation.[2] As Obama sees it, America's present sin has been committed because Americans have failed to realize that they all have a "stake in one another and that what binds" them together is "greater than what drives" them apart. If enough Americans believe in the ideological future of the nation and act accordingly, America "might not solve every problem," but it "can get something meaningful done" (p. 2). His restoration rhetoric of traditional values becomes the standard feature of his reclamation jeremiad.

The reclamation jeremiad attempts to set society back on the path of reclaiming its basic values and principles. This recovery must occur in the public sphere. The object is not simply to spark public interest in reclaiming those values and principles but to attempt to create new areas of public concern from topics currently submerged in public consciousness while lamenting the current status of society. The rhetorician interested in restoring public interests must expose uncertainties, doubts, and challenges dormant in peoples' consciousness. Through his employment of the jeremiad, Obama attempts to achieve this when he calls Americans' attention to how their visions of an idyllic life have essentially manifested in public sphere: "A gap exists between our professed ideals as a nation and the reality we witness everyday" (p. 22). A. Murphy (2009) declares that the rhetorical power of the American jeremiad "grows out of its ability to frame political discourse from the early colonial period all the way down to the dawn of the twenty-first century, in this perennial and dynamic tension between perceived decline and enduring national promise" (p. 127).

In *The Audacity of Hope*, Obama spends a great deal of time lamenting that only a total reformation of American society can reverse the nation's backsliding from impending doom: "For it's precisely the pursuit of ideological purity, the rigid orthodoxy and the sheer predictability of our current political debate that keeps us from finding new ways to meet the challenges we face as a country" (p. 40). Obama's lamentation echoes Ronald Reagan's sentiments (1992) in his "To Restore America" speech, delivered March 31, 1976: "The problems facing our country are problems that just don't bear any party label" (p. 146). No one, Obama laments, is "exempt from the call to find common ground" (p. 68) in which to begin the process of reclaiming those basic values that establish the continuity of America's democracy. When he calls all Americans to the task, he suggests that the challenges facing America do not bear any party affiliation, race, sex, or creed. He presents himself as a leader who could aid in this restoration process:

> I thought—having the audacity to believe despite all the evidence to the contrary that we could restore a sense of community to a nation torn by conflict; the gall to believe that despite personal setbacks, the loss of a job or an illness in the family or a childhood mired in poverty, we had some control—and therefore responsibility—over our own fate. (p. 356)

That audacity, he believes, joins "us as one people" (p. 356). Obama's reclamation jeremiad is, above all, engaging because, unlike the Old Testament prophets, the American Puritans, and African American Jeremiahs before him, he blames not only the government for many of America's problems but also those policies that "consistently favor the wealthy and powerful over average Americans" (p. 10). Although he condemns government, he is optimistic that "government has an important role in opening up opportunity to all" (p. 10). Obama believes that if the American government is to truly represent its people, "a different kind of politics" is required:

> That politics will need to reflect our lives as they are actually lived. . . . It will have to be constructed from the best of our traditions and will have to

account for the darker aspect of our past. We will need to understand just how we got to this place, this land of warring factions and tribal hatreds. And we will need to remind ourselves, despite our differences, just how much we share: common hopes, common dreams, a bond that will not break. (p. 25)

In his reclamation jeremiad, Obama charges that Americans have been misguided by leaders who violated this covenant and that the nation is suffering. The Republican Party, he reveals, has constantly been able to win elections "not by expanding its base but by vilifying Democrats, driving wedges into the electorate, energizing its right wing, and disciplining those who stray from the party line." If Democrats are to ever take control again, "they will have to take up the same approach," he reveals (p. 39). Obama's reclamation jeremiad, then, calls attention to an imminent economic disaster because of the loss of jobs to globalization, the need for innovation in American industry, the rising costs of health care, and the need for tax relief as an economic stimulus.

The Emergence of a Political Jeremiah

The potential for the jeremiad found space early in Obama's political career. Delivering the keynote address at the 2004 Democratic National Convention thrust Obama into the national spotlight. Then a U.S. senatorial candidate, Obama's electrifying speech outlines his family's pursuit of the American Dream and his belief in a "genius of America." Speaking about changes in government's economic and social precedence, he laments,

> People don't expect government to solve all their problems. But they sense, deep in their bones, that with just a slight change in priorities, we can make sure that every child in America has a decent shot at life, and that the doors of opportunity remain open to all.[3]

Making known his mythic vision of America, he heavily criticizes partisan views of the electorate and calls Americans to unify. Obama laments, "There is not a liberal America and a conservative America; there's the United States of America." Themes of responsibility and nationhood chime throughout his rhetoric—Obama charges, "We have more work to do." As Clayton (2007) argues, a great deal of Obama's "appeal is his ability to transcend race" (p. 54). For example, in his 2004 speech, Obama laments,

> The pundits like to slice and dice our country into Red States and Blue States; Red States for Republicans, Blue States for Democrats. But I've got news for them too. We worship an awesome God in the Blue States, and we don't like federal agents poking around in our libraries in the Red States.

We coach Little League in the Blue States and yes, we got some gay friends in the Red States. There are patriots who opposed the war in Iraq and patriots who supported the war in Iraq. We are one people, all of us pledging allegiance to the Stars and Stripes, all of us defending the United States of America.

According to Clayton, Obama's "charismatic style" attempts to unite Americans to rise "above racial stereotypes" (p. 54).

As an Illinois state senator, Obama devoted his interests to reforms and policies, making and changing some accordingly. He enthusiastically participated in creating the Earned Income Tax Credit program, meant for helping people in the low-income groups. He goes on to initiate reforms in the fields of health care and child care. In 2005, Obama was sworn in to the U.S. Senate. After that victory, Obama continues to add his voice to issues from raising the threat of avian flu on the Senate floor to speaking out for victims of Hurricane Katrina to pushing for alternative energy development and supporting better veterans' benefits.

His optimistic views shine through his speech as he endorses, "Hope—hope in the face of difficulty. Hope in the face of uncertainty. The audacity of hope!" rightfully earning the nomenclature "clear savior of not only the Democratic party but of the integrity of American politics" (Rogak, 2007, p. i).

Race

In *The Audacity of Hope,* Obama writes that his speech at the 2004 Democratic National Convention "seemed to strike a chord" of jeremiadic rhetoric when he revealed, "There is not a Black America or a White America and Latino America and Asian America—there's the United States of America" (p. 231). Obama demonstrates that his gift of jeremiadic discourse could serve the interests of all Americans: "Those lines in my speech describe the demographic realities of America's future" (p. 232). Even though he believes that some who criticize his speech interpret it as "postracial politics," he offers an imminent warning:

> To say that we are one people is not to suggest that race no longer matters—that the fight for equality has been won, or that the problems that minorities face in this country today are largely self-inflicted. . . . To suggest that our racial attitudes play no part in these disparities is to turn a blind eye to both our history and our experience—and to relieve ourselves of the responsibility to make things right. (pp. 232-233)

Obama assures Americans that prejudice has not vanished: "None of us—Black, White, Latino, or Asian—is immune to the stereotypes that our culture continues to feed us" (p. 235). The problem, as he sees it, is not that race relations have gotten better; on the contrary, he believes the everyday experiences of people of color are decidedly prejudiced due to more creative forms of bigotry. Although Obama laments, "White guilt has largely exhausted itself in America" (p. 233), he admits that some discrimination is not necessarily racial but rather the result of inexperience and lack of knowledge. Therefore, when he criticizes this fundamental stain on American society, he employs a "double consciousness" ideology of seeing, not a race, but a nation through a double lens:

> To think clearly about race, then, requires us to see the world on a split screen—to maintain in our sights the kind of America that we want while looking squarely at America as it is, to acknowledge the sins of our past and the challenges of the present without becoming trapped in cynicism or despair. (p. 233)

This outlook serves a dual purpose. As he employs a double consciousness ideology, Obama again criticizes American's perceived idyllic social life and its actual materialization. The idea of American reformation, he admonishes, need not just be restored but expanded. However, ideas of "equality [and] citizenship under the law" have presently been marred by "racism and nativist sentiments." This continues to occur, Obama laments, because the "powerful and the privileged" have continued to exploit "prejudice to further their own ends" (pp. 231-232).

Although he employs restoration rhetoric, Obama is not calling for a return to how race relations were in the past; instead, he is calling for further progress. Obama believes that to eliminate the persistent gaps in race relations, the nation "might start with completing the unfinished business of the civil rights movement—namely, enforcing nondiscrimination laws in such basic areas as employment, housing, and education." Under the "recent Republican administrations," Obama laments, civil rights laws have been "tepid at best . . . essentially nonexistent" (p. 243). He reveals that all Americans, even those who do not support affirmative action, should be concerned about government's role in enforcing nondiscrimination laws. If affirmative action programs are properly enacted, he prophesizes, they will "open up opportunities otherwise closed to qualified minorities without diminishing opportunities for White students" (p. 241). Obama believes that affluent Blacks should not be treated in any special way when they apply to college and that poor Whites sometimes should. He remains hopeful and optimistic, however: "Still, when I look at what past generations of minorities have had to overcome, I am optimistic about the ability of this next generation to continue their advance into the economic mainstream" (p. 241).

The responsibility for closing this gap on race relations should not lie solely on the steps of government: "Minorities, individually and collectively, have responsibilities as well" (p. 244), he laments. African American leaders "need to appreciate the legitimate fears that many cause some Whites to resist affirmative action" (p. 68). However, any transformation in attitude must "begin in the home, and the neighborhoods, and in places of worship" (p. 245). He admits, however, that the most important instrument to bridge the gap between race relations may have little to do with race. What could help the Black community is the same thing that could help the White community:

> the opportunity to earn a living wage, the education and training that lead to such jobs, labor laws and tax laws that restore some balance to the distribution of the nation's wealth, and health-care, child care and retirement systems that working people can count on. (pp. 245-246)

Obama's ideological America knows no distinctions of class or color. To eliminate the remnants of the disgraceful and dishonorable legacy of racism that continues to plague the country, though, Obama exhorts Americans to react to instances of racism with lucid condemnation. If they do not, he warns, "danger will come" if people of color are not granted basic civil liberties:

> The rights and opportunities that we take for granted, and tolerate the hypocrisy of a servant class in our midst; or more broadly, if we stand idly by as America continues to become increasingly unequal, and inequality that tracks racial lines and therefore feeds racial strife and which, as the country become more Black and brown, neither our democracy nor our economy can long withstand. (p. 268)

Simultaneously, however, he appeals to people of color to relinquish the semblance of victimization that, he suggests, confines their capacity to achieve their full potential. "Few minorities," he laments, "can isolate themselves entirely from White society—certainly not in the way that Whites can successfully avoid contact with members of other races" (p. 236). Government, however, is still the problem, according to Obama's assessment. "Government could kick-start a transformation of circumstance" (p. 258) and dismantle remnants of racism that impede progress. The time for racial preferences, he admonishes, must surely be past. Continuing his optimism concerning race relations, though, Obama laments, "Whatever preconceived notions White Americans may continue to hold, the overwhelming majority of them these days are able—if given time—to look beyond race in making their judgments of people" (p. 235).

Soaring Utopianism: Obama's Mythic Vision of America

Obama's mythic vision of America evolves from his interpretation of America's history. In this respect, *The Audacity of Hope* is also a narrative that interweaves the creation of the Constitution, America's individuality, its fate, and its passage into a nation divined with greatness. Obama cannot "brush aside the magnitude of the injustice done," he reveals, "or erase the ghosts of generations past, or ignore the open wound, the aching spirit, that ails" America today (p. 97). Therefore, his mythic vision of America is rooted in the values that have always made the nation great. "I think America has more often been a force of good," he laments, "than for ill in the world" (pp. 10-11). He later reveals that his love for America goes beyond discussing its negative values: "I love America too much, am too invested in what this country has become, too committed to its institutions, its beauty, and even its ugliness, to focus entirely on the circumstances of its birth" (p. 96). For him, myth underlies values, constructing an optimistic worldview in which America's modern problems will be surmounted by the valiant actions of average Americans instilled with the basic values at the core of the myth:

> The core of the American experience are a set of ideals that continue to stir our collective conscience; a common set of values that bind us together despite our differences; a running thread of hope that makes our improbable experiment in democracy work. (p. 8)

In Obama's words, America's "improbable experiment in democracy" suggests that he believes that America has failed at achieving the goals and aspirations of the Constitution. Americans have shared in the opportunities created by its economy, however; as such, Obama envisions a soaring utopianism where Americans must build a foundation that empowers hardworking families to climb the ladder of success. "Through our own agency," he proclaims, "we can, and must, make of our lives what we will . . . [a belief] that every American understands" (p. 53). This, Obama believes, is at the heart of the American Dream. Forging this kind of future, he reveals, will not be an easy task. It will require the kinds of policies that finally display the values of America. However, in spite of the resilience, sanguinity, and hard work of many Americans, their dreams have been too often thwarted by economic policies. Accordingly, Obama reveals that Americans do not seem to "possess a shared language with which to discuss" those ideas. As a shared community, Americans also do not possess "the tools to arrive at some rough consensus about how . . . to work together to bring those ideas about." Thus, he laments, "the reality of American life has strayed from its myths" (p. 8).

Throughout history, however, America has been able to surmount all barriers because Americans have maintained a commitment to "foundational principles including political and economic freedom, the sanctity of every individual, and a faith in individual initiative" (Jones & Rowland, 2005, p. 162). Despite all these changes, Obama believes that America is still on the road to prosperity. "A constant cross-pollination is occurring . . .[a] peaceful collision among people and cultures," he reveals. "Identities are scrambling, and then cohering in new ways" (p. 51). Accordingly, values are at the core of Obama's mythic vision of America, and they are the foundation to solving any problems that America faces. Values can "inspire [Americans] to pride, duty, and sacrifice" (p. 8). At the nucleus of Obama's values is a vision of America in which no person is excluded. His reclamation jeremiad draws no lines of segregation among citizens but clearly proclaims that all are included in the American family. For example, while Obama understands the "falseness of the choices being presented to the American people" (p. 34), he simultaneously sets out to rescue America from error and return it to the road to recovery. To achieve this, Obama believes that all Americans, regardless of political affiliations, need to "reengage in the project of national renewal" to see their "own self-interest as inextricably linked to the interests of others" (p. 40). No obstacles can fundamentally endanger America's values if the nation continues true to the values at the core of the myth. "Each of us arrives with a bundle to rights that can't be taken away by any person or any state without just cause" (p. 53), he laments.

The Constitution

Throughout *The Audacity of Hope*, Obama draws upon the ideas of the Constitution, intuitively understanding that these ideas allow him to represent his reclamation jeremiad so powerfully to the American public. Like all American jeremiads, *The Audacity of Hope* is unquestionably overflowing with political discourse. As Jendrysik (2002) argues, the "modern jeremiad is a partisan document designed to appeal to supporters, or to convince the unaffiliated to join a cause. It is not designed to convert political opponents" (p. 363). With that being said, Obama is not attempting to build a political following per se. Instead, he argues that if a solution is not found to the present crisis, America will surely self-destruct. Early in the text, Obama reveals,

> The nation's most significant challenges are being ignored. . . . If we don't change course soon, we may be the first generation in a very long time that leaves behind a weaker and more fractured America than the one we inherited. Perhaps more than any other time in our recent history, we need a new kind of politics, one that can excavate and build upon those shared understandings that pull use together as Americans. (p. 9)

This passage provides an ideal expression of the mixture of jeremiad and threat that characterize Obama's reclamation jeremiad. As a constitutionalist, Obama struggles with the implementation of the concepts in the Constitution. He warns the nation about a number of issues, from politics to faith to race, but he coalesces these warnings with a fundamentally positive proclamation in which he seeks to reclaim America's promise to the basic standards and principles that he felt were embedded in the Founding Fathers' documents: "The Declaration of Independence, the Federalist Papers, and the Constitution—present themselves as the product of men," he bemoans. How then should we read these documents? The Constitution is not a "static but rather a living document, and must be read in the context of an ever-changing world" (p. 90). He admits, however, that there is a "fundamental humility to this reading of the Constitution and our democratic process. It seems to champion compromise, modesty, and muddling through" (p. 94). Obama believes that the founders' documents have shaped Americans' attitudes toward rights and common law. "Wherever we lie on the political spectrum," he laments, "we all subscribe to the founders' teachings" (p. 86). The values, ideals, principles, and achievements that the founders laid for the nation now collectively provide the basis for arguments and appeals, although interpretations of these elements are often controversial. By respecting these values and America's "system of self-governance," Obama believes that Americans will "give shape" to the nation's "values and shared commitments" (p. 84).

Obama trusts in the redemptive value of the Constitution. For example, when he calls for rededication to the values set forth by the Founding Fathers' documents, he furthers his belief that the Constitution could "organize the way by which we argue about our future." Thus, the Constitution is the answer to reclaiming America's ideological premise of "deliberative democracy," in which all Americans must unite "in a process of testing their ideas against an external reality, persuading others of their point of view, and building shifting alliances of consent" (p. 92). Arguing that America has dishonored the Constitution's basic pledge, he is optimistic that the ideals behind it present an essentially promising view of the meaning of America: "The Constitution envisions a road map by which we marry passion to reason, the ideal of individual freedom to the demands of community" (p. 95). In doing so, Obama positions himself as an American Jeremiah who believes in the power that the Constitution possessed. As such and unlike conventional jeremiadic discourse, which persistently indicates that continuing calamities are imminent if society does not return to its idyllic stance, Obama maintains that America's continuing commitment to those basic values found in the Constitution will help the nation find the answers to problems faced today.

The Economy

Since the pledge to seek economic stability in America is in large part initiated by political self-determination, the economy is of great concern to Obama. The economy is strongest, he reveals, when all Americans prosper. Since the economy is in a downward spiral that is costing Americans faith in the fundamental promise of prosperity, Obama goes through great pains to lament how America's economy has evolved over the years and has influenced America's social, cultural, and political ideologies. He perceives that America's economic and education system is neglecting the underprivileged, the exploited, and the marginalized. Therefore, Obama wholeheartedly agrees with former president Ronald Reagan when he laments, "Government is not the solution to our problem; government is the problem" (p. 147). "Instead of innovation and bold reform of our schools," Obama argues, government "for close to two decades has been tinkering around the edges and a tolerance for mediocrity" (pp. 160-161). He believes, for example, in the value of the No Child Left Behind Act. He argues, though, that the law has significant flaws. It is unethical for government to require all schools to meet certain requirements without supplying them with the proper funding. "Money does matter to education," he laments. "Many urban and rural schools still suffer from overcrowded classrooms, outdated books, and inadequate equipment" (p. 161). To reform the education system, Obama posits a number of workable resolutions, including merit-based pay for teachers and alternative education arrangements. In exchange for the merit-based pay, however, Obama calls teachers to become "more accountable for their performance" (p. 162). Reforming the educational system must go beyond "an improved elementary and secondary school system" (p. 163). The task at hand is to "identify those reforms that have the highest impact on student achievement, fund them adequately, and eliminate those programs that don't produce results" (p. 161). He maintains, however, that education reform has been demonstrated, either through previous performance or through experiential research, and he believes that Americans have great responsibility by investing in the educational system.

Obama forewarns that the economy is on the threshold of disaster, and he highlights the urgency of the situation. He criticizes the Bush administration's tax cuts for the wealthy, for example, revealing them to be "both fiscally irresponsible and morally troubling" (p. 47). He reminds Americans that "we're going through a fundamental economic transformation" (p. 145). And globalization, he continues, is partly to blame. Obama reveals yet another duality in his jeremiads when he prophesizes that if globalization continues on its present track, Americans will both profit from it and feel its disruptions to the American way of life: "Globalization has brought significant benefits to American consumers . . . [and] has greatly increased economic instability for millions of ordinary Americans." Allowing globalization to continue, however, with all of its promise and pitfalls, he forewarns, will not "result in the imminent collapse of the U.S. economy" (p. 145, 146). However, if nothing is done to correct it, America's economy will transform into a "very different" America "from the one most of us grew up in" (p. 148). To motivate the seeds of reformation, Obama paints a vivid picture of the economic calamity at hand:

> It will mean a nation even more stratified economically and socially than it currently is. . . . It will mean an America in which we continue to mortgage our assets to foreign lenders and expose ourselves to the whims of oil producers. . . . It will mean an America that's more politically polarized and more politically unstable, as economic frustration boils over and leads people to turn on each other. . . . Worst of all, it will mean fewer opportunities for younger Americans, a decline in the upward mobility that's been at the heart of this country's promise since its founding. (pp. 148-149)

Obama bemoans that there is a need to move expeditiously to save America from this disaster. If the nation follows the correct path, it will be able to negotiate change that will surely follow, and America will be better prepared for the 21st century. "If we want an innovation economy," he suggests, "then we have to invest in our future innovators" (p. 166). With optimism found in the moment, Obama believes that America possesses the "talent and the resources to create a better future." However, he then critiques the nation for not possessing "a national commitment" to take the steps necessary to "make America more competitive" (p. 149). He laments that Americans might be on the verge of decline because their values are misplaced: "It sometimes appears that Americans today value nothing so much as being rich, thin, young, famous, safe and entertained" (p. 68). As such, Obama again utilizes the jeremiad to lament the calamitous state of the economy and indicates, as powerfully as possible, the size and significance of the crisis facing the nation:

> We say we value the legacy we leave the next generation and then saddle that generation with mountains of debt. We say we believe in equal opportunity but then stand idle while millions of American children languish in poverty. We insist that we value family, but then structure our economy and organize our lives so as to ensure that our families get less and less of our time. (p. 68)

Obama challenges Americans to make a clear, firm decision concerning the country's economy. "We can afford to do what needs to be done," he urges. "What is missing is not money, but a national sense of urgency" (p. 167).

In keeping with the jeremiad tradition, Obama intertwines his lamentation of economic anguish and denunciation of economic woes with optimism concerning a better future for all Americans. Early in the text, he reveals that "our condition is the natural result of radical conservatism or perverse liberalism" (p. 24). Later, he affirms that solving these differences will not only "require changes in government policy" but also "require changes in hearts and minds" of all Americans (p. 215). In juxtaposing America's hope for a future to the foreseeable failures accompanying a continued lack of commitment to a common creed, Obama laments that America's greatest asset has been its "system of social organization, a system that for generations has encouraged constant innovation, individual initiative, and the efficient allocation of resources" (p. 150). According to Obama, the Republicans are "fighting the last war, the war they waged and won in the eighties"[4] and the Democrats are "forced to fight a rearguard action, defending the New Deal programs of the thirties," (p. 158); as such, he warns that "unless political leaders are open to new ideas," there will not be enough Americans ready "to initiate a serious energy policy or tame the deficit" (p. 40). Obama believes, however, that restoring America's mission can be achieved if Americans heed the past; for him, the past offers corrective ways of dealing with the present. The nation can be guided throughout this process by "Lincoln's simple maxim: that we will do collectively, through our government, only those things that we cannot do as well or at all individually and privately." Obama further laments, "We should be guided by what works" (p. 159).

Religion

The civil religion of the American Dream penetrates Obama's reclamation jeremiad. Obama grounds his critique on religion in the country's religious history: "The Pilgrims came to our shores to escape religious persecution and practice without impediment to their brand of strict Calvinism" (p. 199). As he centers his discussion on the polarization that has come to describe the American political realm in recent years, Obama confronts the issue of religious faith, focusing on the differences between politics and religion: "Politics . . . depends on our ability to persuade each other of common aims based on common reality," he declares. Religion, however, "insists on the impossible. If God has spoken, then followers are expected to live up to God's edicts, regardless of the consequences" (p. 219). According to Obama, as the Republican Party has become more and more connected with evangelical Christianity, Democrats have to some extent have repeatedly assumed the opposite position, and mounting numbers of progressives seem willing to attack all reference to religion in governmental contexts. "The tensions and suspicions on each side of the religious divide will have to be squarely addressed," he laments, "and each side will need to accept some ground rules for collaboration" (p. 216).

Not being raised in "a religious household" (p. 202) Obama relates his own passage from faith, declaring that the organization of religion has strengthened and intensified his moral beliefs. "It was because of these newfound understandings—that religious commitment did not require me to suspend critical thinking, disengage from the battle for economic and social justice, or otherwise retreat from the world that I knew and loved," he writes (p. 208). He forewarns Americans, however, of what will come to pass if religious debates are abandoned. "Scrub the language of religious content," he warns, and Americans "forfeit the imagery and terminology through which millions . . . understand both their personal morality and social justice" (p. 214). He proclaims,

> When we ignore the debate about what it means to be a good Christian or Muslim or Jew; when we discuss religion only in the negative sense of where or how it should not be practiced, rather than in the positive sense of what it tells us about our obligations toward one another . . . others will fill the vacuum. (p. 214)

The "others" whom Obama mentions are likely to be those with the most limited outlooks on issues concerning faith, or they will "cynically use religion to justify partisan ends" (p. 214). Obama does not suggest, though, that progressives promptly "latch on to religious terminology" or that they desert the "fight for institutional change" (p. 215). He calls progressives to rid themselves of some of their prejudices. If this occurs, they will be able to find common ground for future cooperation. He warns that Americans will "recognize the values that both religious and secular people share when it comes to the moral and material direction" of America (p. 216). More important, however, Americans will "recognize that the call to sacrifice on behalf of the next generation, the need to think in terms of 'thou' and not just 'I,'" will resonate in "religious congregations across the country." All Americans of faith need to be involved in "the larger project of American renewal" (p. 216).

The Sin of Politics

A pragmatist, Obama strives to have his common sense guide his principles and politics. Told since he was a child that he was "destined for great things" (p. 107), Obama has a life that is an all-American success story. With a brief biographical sketch early in his political dissertation, Obama sets out to illustrate that he is clearly a product of the American experience through his unique racial heritage: His mother was White American while his father was Kenyan; his grandparents served the country during wartime; and he has relatives of many races over three different continents. A self-proclaimed "pure product" of the sixties, Obama reveals that if the "social upheavals that were then taking place" had not occurred, his life "would have been impossible" and "opportunities entirely foreclosed." Living in Hawaii and Indonesia, however, he was too young to understand "the fall-out on America's psyche" (p. 29). Obama spends time tackling his life in broad strokes throughout *The Audacity of Hope* and his life in relation to his senatorial position. However, he reveals that it is the American way to hold politicians responsible for the nation's problems. The sins of politics help to shape these ideas.

Although Obama agrees that America has been "marred by the original sin of slavery," he does not spend a great of time lamenting those sins. He praises America because its "genius has always been its ability to absorb newcomers, to forge a national identity out of the disparate lot that arrived" on America's shores (p. 231). He takes the time, however, to lament the sins of politics. "Most of the sins of politics are derivative of this larger sin," he reveals, "the need to win, but also the need not to lose" (p. 109). Whatever the motivations, "both sacred and profane," that push politicians to achieve this feat, those who become successful "must exhibit an almost fanatical single-mindedness, often disregarding their health, relationships, mental bal-ance, and dignity" (p. 105). According to his assessment, a progression into the political realm makes it challenging for politicians to sincerely maintain their values. "It's hard to deny that political civility has declined in the past decade" (p. 125). Sworn in as a U.S. senator on January 4, 2005, Obama was the fifth African American senator in U.S. history and the third to have been popularly elected. To become a senator—someone exceptionally experi-enced to speak for one's constituency—requires a "certain megalomania," he reveals. Obama discovers that it is "neither ambition nor single-mindedness" (p. 105) that accounts for a politician's behavior. Politics, he laments, has become so increasingly bitter and biased that politicians cannot deal with the true problems plaguing the economy. Changes need to occur. These changes, however, cannot happen by themselves.

> Each would require a change in attitude among those in power. Each would demand that individual politicians challenge the existing order; loosen their hold on incumbency; fight with their friends as well as their enemies on behalf of abstract ideas in which the public appears to have little interest. (p. 134)

Because the values of America's politicians are regularly tested, Obama exhorts them to loosen their grip on the embellishments of power in order to promote the kind of functional, discursive government that best serves the needs of the American people. He warns them, "Say one thing during the campaign and do another thing once in office, you're a typical, two-faced politician" (p. 117).

Conclusion

In American political and religious rhetoric, the jeremiad has been traditionally used to respond to situations of crisis and threat. Whether purposely or not, Obama appropriately utilized elements of the jeremiad to respond to the many challenges Americans face today. If, as J. Murphy (1990) argues, the jeremiad "limits the scope of reform and the depth of social criticism," (p. 402) how effective is Obama's reclamation jeremiad? The solution is to reclaim America's confidence in government before it is too late. The power of *The Audacity of Hope* as a rhetorical jeremiad stems from its ability to position analysis of Obama's ideology of reclaiming America's mythic mission. In his perspective, Obama challenges Americans to seek a common ground between advocating the preservation of traditional religious, cultural, or nationally defined beliefs and prejudices. America can still be rescued, he believes. As a vehicle for jeremiadic discourse, *The Audacity of Hope* asserts that America is a nation that possesses the innate potential to offer hope to all, despite racial, religious, and economic experiences. For this to occur, however, reform is essential. Instead of relying on the apocalyptic rhetoric associated with the Puritan jeremiad, Obama develops a reclamation rhetoric that fits comfortably within the conventional tradition of America's political jeremiad. *The Audacity of Hope* offers Americans the courage needed to hope again and believe in America's future.

Notes

1. See Johannesen (1985, 1986), Jones and Rowland (2005), A. Murphy (2009), J. Murphy (1990), and Ritter and Henry (1992).
2. See the revised and expanded edition of David Howard-Pitney's *The African American Jeremiad* (2005) for his discussion on African American Jeremiahs, from Frederick Douglass to Alan Keyes.
3. For the text and audio versions of the keynote address at the 2004 Democratic National Convention, see http://www.BarackObama.com.
4. Referring to Ronald Reagan's Reaganomics, Obama argues that Reagan's political formula "worked at the time" (p. 32). He also suggests that Republicans who followed Reagan were probably not "entirely comfortable with the direction politics had taken" (p. 33). Obama admits, however, that Reagan's election as president made clear that the American people "wanted the government to change" (p. 156).

References

Atwater, D. (2007). Senator Barack Obama: The rhetoric of hope and the American Dream. *Journal of Black Studies, 38*(2), 121-129.

Bercovitch, S. (1978). *The American jeremiad*. Madison: University of Wisconsin Press.

Clayton, D. (2007). The audacity of hope. *Journal of Black Studies, 38*(1), 51-63.

Howard-Pitney, D. (2005). *The African American jeremiad: Appeals for justice in America* (rev. and exp. ed.). Philadelphia: Temple University Press.

Jendrysik, M. (2002). The modern jeremiad: Bloom, Bennett, and Bork on American decline. *Journal of Popular Culture, 36*(2), 361-383.

Johannesen, R. (1985). The jeremiad and Jenkin Lloyd Jones. *Communication Monographs, 52*(2), 156-172.

Johannesen, R. (1986). Ronald Reagan's economic jeremiad. *Central States Speech Journal, 37*(2), 79-89.

Jones, J., & Rowland, R. (2005). A covenant-affirming jeremiad: The post-presidential ideological appeals of Ronald Wilson Reagan. *Communication Studies, 56*(2), 157-174.

Moses, W. (1982). *Black messiahs and Uncle Toms: Social and literary manipulations of religious myth*. University Park: Pennsylvania State University Press.

Murphy, A. (2009). Longing, nostalgia, and golden age politics: The American jeremiad and the power of the past. *Perspectives on Politics, 7*(1), 125-141.

Murphy, J. (1990). A time of shame and sorrow: Robert F. Kennedy and the American jeremiad. *Quarterly Journal of Speech, 76*(4), 401-414.

Obama, B. (2004). *Keynote address at the 2004 Democratic National Convention.* Retrieved March 15, 2009, from http://www.barackobama.com/2004/07/27/keynote_address_at_the_ 2004_de.php

Obama, B. (2006). *The audacity of hope: Thoughts on reclaiming the American Dream*. New York: Three Rivers Press.

Reagan, R. (1992). To restore America. In K. Ritter & D. Henry (Eds.), *Ronald Reagan: The great communicator* (pp. 145-154). Greenwood, CT: Greenwood Press.

Ritter, K., & Henry, D. (1992). *Ronald Reagan: The great communicator*. Greenwood, CT: Greenwood Press.

Rogak, L. (2007). Introduction. In *Barack Obama: In his own words* (pp. i-xiii). New York: Carroll & Graf.